'Snobby' Coffee

By

James D. Skaug

Drink and Talk like a 'Coffee Snob...'

But Without the Cost!

Answers to some of the most frequent questions about Coffee;

that 'Coffee Snobs' (or 'would be Coffee Snobs') might have!

Cover and select other photographs, by Joshua James William Skaug.

ISBN: 9781986386135

DISCLAIMER

This book is not intended to provide, and does not constitute and medical, legal, or other, 'professional' advice; and is for 'educational and entertainment' purposes only – and contains 'tips, tricks and techniques' of brewing coffee through various methods.

All 'opinions,' other than 'questions' asked by individuals to the author, are

DEDICATION:

This book must be 'Dedicated' to my late father, George William Skaug; whom, unfortunately, did not live long enough to see the 21st Century or its current, 'Coffee Revolution!' He was not a 'Coffee Snob,' but a Coffee 'Purist,' in his own right; as he would never drink Coffee in any way, shape, or form, other than "*Black and strong,*" as he would say! However, he would have loved to 'learn' more about today's coffee brewing methods and paraphernalia – and I can 'picture' him, 'playing' with different brewers as I, often, do!

He died while on a fishing vacation in 1975, of a massive heart attack; behind the wheel of his RV… with a tall mug of regular, 'Black Coffee' in his hand!

This book is, also, dedicated to my wife Terry and my son Joshua; who put up with all my 'Coffee Nonsense!'

"*Among the numerous luxuries of the table…coffee may be considered as one of the most valuable. It excites cheerfulness without intoxication; and the pleasing flow of spirits which it occasions… is never followed by sadness, languor or debility.*"

~ (Attributed to) Benjamin Franklin

ABOUT JAMES D. SKAUG AND HIS COFFEE

A Recollection of Coffee:

Once called, *"The 'Storyteller' of Coffee,"* due to his lecturing, writing, and 'coffee brewing' skills, James exposure to coffee goes back to two instances; first, as a child, where one of his first remembrances was the smell of 'boiling' coffee in the mornings, and then, later in life – as a middle-aged adult, when he was 're-exposed' to, what some would call, *"Designer Coffee!"*

His father, George, a 'Space Systems' engineer, during the Mercury, Gemini, and Apollo Space Programs (and being an avid coffee drinker), always started his day – rain or shine, Spring, Summer, Fall, or Winter– with a *"Pot of Joe,"* as he called coffee, on a burner in the kitchen. But, during the Summer, while on three-month-long, 'family' trips to British Columbia Canada, the Yukon Territory, Alaska, or (occasionally) 'South' to Mexico, coffee was 'boiled' in a 'Pot' of lake or river water; along with 'coarsely ground' coffee beans, over a campfire! This is where James first learned to brew coffee! It was seldom that James' father would even drive down the road without a homemade, 'non-slip' cup sitting on his 'RV's' metal dashboard; filled with hot, black coffee! In fact, James has very few memories of his father, in which he '<u>did</u> <u>not</u>' have a cup of 'black coffee' with him!

Skipping ahead to more modern times; and although 'exposed' to coffee in various forms throughout his life, James seldom drank any coffee… choosing to enjoy tea or other beverages instead. However, when he reached his 50th birthday, he was exposed, by a friend, to an entirely 'new world' of coffee, brewing methods, and beverages that he never knew existed!

While 'celebrating his birthday,' his friend insisted James try what he called *"Designer Coffee;"* made with freshly roasted coffee beans, espresso, additives of syrups, creams, caramel, powders, foam, and even whipped cream and chocolate sprinkles. His friend, also, introduced him to 'roasting beans' and 'degassing' the grind; as well as 'blooming' the grounds; as well as several 'brewing and grinding' methods James never knew existed!

Dinner that night turned in to a 'many hours long,' <u>Coffee</u> <u>Lesson</u>; which lasted well into the early hours of the following day!

From there, the rest is coffee history!

Perhaps, a more appropriate name for James book might have been: *"Coffee: Elementary School,"* as James, whom considers himself, *"The worlds most experienced Coffee Novice,"* covers the 'constant changes' within the coffee industry in the past century! To this day, there is not a time in which James is not 'still <u>learning</u>' about coffee! He even brought coffee into his Neuropathy, 'Health Care' office; and often, served what he called, 'healthy coffee' to his waiting patients! It soon became a standard, conversation point with many people. It was not long before 'patients' started taking home a cup of 'Office Coffee' after appointments. Soon, however, they were 'stopping by' the office *"Just to say hello"* (and 'pick up' a cup of coffee)! Even 'building security' and nearby office workers started coming into James office for a 'free' cup of what was known as his, *"Healthy, Specialty Coffee!"*

Word of James coffee spread like 'Wildfire' around town – and soon, he had more 'Coffee Customers,' than he had 'Neuropathy Patients!'

Being a 'public speaker' on the topic of Neuropathy for many years, the question of 'Coffee,' often arose during James lectures; as those in attendance seemed to wish to *"Know more"* about the 'beverage served,' than the lectured subject! It was only natural, that 'Coffee Classes' and 'Coffee Tastings,' hosted by James, would soon follow! From there, he started looking for others who shared his interest in the 'methods' of brewing coffee; as well as the 'taste' of the beverage itself! He tried joining several different, local coffee groups – only to find, that they seemed to be filled with, what he felt, were 'intense, snobs…' people with 'pre-conceived' ideas… whom, seemed more interested in the 'cost' and 'impressive rights' of brewing methods and equipment, than they were in the coffee itself! After years of trying several groups, James joined a successful and friendly, local, club in nearby; Chico, California.

Be it Neuropathy, Coffee, or other books or articles, readers enjoy James 'personal manner' of writing; *"As if the reader were right in the room with James during one of his lectures,"* some have stated! In the case of this book, however, not only the readers, but James himself, attempts to determine *"What is a Coffee Snob;"* and, if he and his readers <u>are</u> 'Coffee Snobs' themselves – something, that <u>is</u> <u>not</u> necessarily, a bad thing, these days!

James books are found in various, international bookstores and at Amazon.com; just by searching for 'James Skaug.'

TABLE OF CONTENTS

INTRODUCTION: YOU MIGHT BE A 'COFFEE SNOB,' IF YOU...

What makes a 'Coffee Snob?' Money? Well, there is undoubtedly that; but brewing methods, types of beans, paraphernalia/tools, education, brand names, 'toys,' and more, can dictate the '<u>degree</u>' of 'Coffee Snob' many of us 0even those in the business) tend to become! Sometimes, we can tell right away if someone is a 'Coffee Snob' or not; just by their actions, questions, or 'reactions' to what we say or 'brew!'

For example, recently, at a 'Club' function, at a local, 'Name Brand' Coffee Bar, my wife ordered a *"Large cup of Black Coffee."* The Barista, somewhat arguing with her, replied to her order with many, 'nonsense options;' regarding 'how' she <u>should</u> <u>have</u> ordered her coffee – including the fact, that she apparently 'broke etiquette' by using the 'unknown' term of '<u>large</u>!' Many other patrons, vocally, seemed to agree! After, graciously, declining his offers of assorted sizes, additives, mixtures, and creams, she was forced to respond, *"Look, I just want a large, Black Coffee, please!"* The Barista understood the 'coffee,' part, but, acted as if he did not know or understand what she meant by the term *"<u>Large</u>!"* Frustrated, she replied, *"Just give me the biggest cup of Black Coffee you have got!"* Appearing annoyed, the Barista complied, begrudgingly! There should not have been any 'confusion' on the Barista's part!

Many of us feel it is enough to *"Want!"* what we order; without, having to make a 'dozen decisions' as to the size or 'contents' of our cup – or have to '<u>justify</u>' our decision to others! In some cases, I suppose, it <u>does</u> make us something of a 'Snob!' However, we can say the same of the Barista as well; as the previously mentioned one, serving my wife, was so '<u>pushy</u>!' My wife viewed all the 'options' presented as coming from, what she perceived, a 'Coffee Snob;' especially, when the Barista handed the coffee to her like it was 'something dirty!' Unfortunately, this was not an isolated incident! Since this incident, she has changed her usual order to something like a 'Caramel Mocha Latte' (in whatever '<u>specialized</u> <u>name</u>' cup the store sells), in most coffee bars, to avoid an argument with the Barista!

However, she is correct in the fact that she '<u>should</u> <u>be</u> <u>able</u>' to order 'what she wants' easily; and knows 'how' she wants it! 'Options' are nice; but in the above case, she stated she, *"Just wanted a Large, Black Coffee"*... which should have been easily understood by the Barista! However, for many Baristas, their coffee must 'stand out' in some way; or be <u>extraordinary</u>... in other words, be '**<u>better</u> <u>than</u> <u>some</u> <u>other</u> <u>Baristas</u>**' in some way!

Unfortunately, sometimes, this can merely equate to the coffees 'cost!' *"The more expensive, the better,"* some 'Coffee Snobs' say! In the same sense, one would suppose, that if someone wanted to *"Talk the talk"* when it came to coffee, they would need to be either 'highly educated' in the field... or, would be qualified enough to 'have an opinion' – good or bad! Unfortunately, many Baristas in Coffee Bars – and 'Coffee Snobs' in clubs – are not afraid to share (or even force) their views with people... right or wrong!

I have found this opinion with many of the so-called, 'Coffee Clubs' my family have joined over the years. Surprisingly, we have discovered some 'members' really are not very interested in coffee! In fact, the last group we were members of had several members who did not even drink coffee; the group was more of a 'Singles Club' for tea drinkers, it turned out! But, some of the 'actual coffee drinkers,' did tend to be 'Snobby' about their beverage!

Most of the 'clubs or groups' we have attended have had 'weekly meetings' held in various Coffee establishments; i.e., Coffee Bars, roasting facilities, members' homes, and such. In each club, the activities seemed like a promising idea of 'what would be fun!' They were not... 'fun,' that is! We, soon, found that each group was more concerned with coffee price, prestige, and 'being single,' than they were coffee itself! Nobody understood or even cared about different brewing methods! However, even though being something of 'self-proclaimed, coffee experts,' we joined these groups; in hopes that we could 'learn' more about local coffee methods and establishments, as well as enjoy 'coffee talk,' with other 'coffee lovers.' It was not too long before we decided, between the 'Singles Club' and the 'Coffee Snob' aspects of these clubs, they were not for us! 'Self-education' was going to be the way for us! We did, eventually, find a local Coffee Club we enjoyed, in the nearby town of Chico, CA!

'Aficionados' of any kind, can sometimes, become... well, 'snobbish;' for example, most people have known 'Wine Aficionados' to refuse to drink anything but 'certain' types or brands of Wine. The same is true with coffee. Nonetheless, perhaps, we (and those reading this), are 'Snobs' ourselves! There is one way to, possibly, determine this fact, by 'checking oneself' with the questions on the following pages.

Questions, came from once asking members of a former, local Coffee group: *"What do you think constitutes a 'Coffee Snob'?"* Check for yourself on this 'Snob Test' on the next few pages. Many answers may 'back up or confirm' other questions. One may be surprised by ones answers!

1. Do you have a favorite, or regular, Coffee Shop/Coffee Bar to which you go – and, find that no <u>other</u> shops/bars will do?

2. Do you own an expensive, 'High Fashion' brand of Coffee Maker?

3. Are there particular 'chains' or 'individual Coffee Bars' you will not frequent – other than your 'not liking' the way they prepare your coffee; i.e., for political, social, or 'cost' reasons?

4. Do you feel that 'anyone can prepare your coffee' in a shop – or do you seek out a 'regular' or 'particular' Barista?

5. Will you <u>only</u> go to 'Starbucks™' and no place else?

6. Did you used to love, 'Latte Art;' but now, 'turn your nose' up at it?

7. In the same sense as the above question, are you 'disappointed' if your Latte <u>does</u> <u>not</u> come with 'Art?'

8. Do you travel with your own, personal, coffee, grinder, water, brewers, filters, or creamers?

9. Do you 'Home Roast' and 'Grind' your beans; or <u>only</u> purchase from a 'particular,' Commercial Roaster?

10. Do you lack patience, or are 'annoyed,' with others who profess knowledge of coffee; but do not <u>share</u> your opinions?

11. Do you 'turn your nose up,' at those who admit they drink (and enjoy) 'pre-ground, canned' coffee?

12. Do you feel obligated to 'ask' Coffee Bars/Shops about their Beans?

13. Do you ask your Baristas *"Where"* they received their coffee education; or *"How long"* they have been *"Pulling Shots?"*

14. Do you 'make up lies' to avoid drinking 'Instant, Keurig®, Campfire, or Percolator' coffee?

15. Do you judge people on the cost of their coffee brewing equipment?

16. Do you know and use 'specialized' Coffee Lingo?'

17. Would you be 'appalled' at being served 'Instant Coffee?'

18. Do you view 'Campfire' or 'Percolator' coffee as being "*Boiled*," and thus, 'not worthy' of drinking, 'ruined…' or, consider it 'unhealthy?'

19. Are you among the first to try, so-called, 'fads' like 'Bulletproof Coffee' when they come out?

20. Do you almost 'throw up' at the thought of using a processed, 'flavored creamer' in your coffee?

21. Does the thought of using just 'cream or milk' in your coffee bother you? What about diverse types of milk; i.e., 1%, 2%, or 'whole' milk? What about 'canned or boxed' milk? What about 'other types' of milk – such as 'almond' or 'lactose-free' milk?

22. Are you upset when served coffee in a 'mug' rather than a 'china cup?'

23. Do you refuse to drink out of a 'Cardboard or Styrofoam' cup?'

24. Do you find yourself annoyed when someone does not realize the 'Natural Sweetness' of the brewed coffee… moreover, adds sugar or 'artificial sweetener' to it?

25. Do you take notes regarding 'coffee tasting' in Coffee Shops?

26. Do you get upset when you have returned home from a trip to Europe or Australia; and nobody seems to 'care' that you found the coffee "*Undrinkable*" there?

27. Would you feel 'shock and dismay' to learn that your favorite 'Coffee Guru,' drinks and enjoys coffee from McDonalds™?

28. Do you lose patience with people who say "*Expresso*" (stressing the 'X') rather than "*Espresso?*"

29. Will you only purchase 'Green or Roasted Beans' from a commercial roasting company? Do you insist upon, only, 'Fair Trade Coffee?'

30. Do you have to 'always' have the 'same size' cup of coffee?

31. Do you own a 'Coffee Spoon' for tasting? If so, do take it with you when you go to professional 'Coffee Tastings' or 'Cuppings?'

32. Do you 'post' photographs of your coffee through 'Social Media?'

33. Do you 'taste' coffee as you would fine wine… 'slurping' to 'suck up oxygen;' then choosing to 'spit out' and rinse your mouth with water rather than swallow the coffee during tastings?

34. Are you willing to try different roasts, grinds, water temperatures, filters/strainers, or different brewing methods?

35. Will you drink 'Iced Coffee?' If the answer is "*Yes*," will you <u>only</u> drink the 'Japanese brewed' type?

36. Do you, or would you, drink coffee brewed from 'Canned' grounds?

37. Have your family or friends ever accused you of speaking in "*Too technical*" or "*Nonsensical terms*" about coffee?

38. Will you only drink coffee when brewed by a certain method – claiming, it is the "*Only way to brew coffee?*"

39. Do you have to let your freshly ground, coffee beans 'breath' or 'degas' for 1 - 24 hours before brewing?

40. Do you use a timer or thermometer to brew your coffee?

41. Do you own obscure 'accessories' to make your beverages?

42. Do you judge people on their 'coffee serving' China or equipment, i.e., Silver, Bone China, et cetera?

43. Are you <u>only</u> willing to brew your Espresso or Coffee immediately after grinding; or insist upon 'watching' a Barista 'grind' your coffee?

44. Do you genuinely believe that one can 'taste and see' a significant difference between a $200.00 Coffee Grinder and a $2000.00 one? What about the difference between a $50.00 Grinder and a $500.00 one? What about a $1000.00 Espresso Machine which grinds beans directly into a Portafilter – and does not 'bloom' the grind?

45. Would you ever consider 'cooking' with either 'left-over' coffee, or using a commercial 'pre-bottled' Coffee Concentrate or Instant?

46. Would you 'pass' on being served coffee brewed by some other method than what you use; i.e. 'Pour-Over' rather than 'French Press?'

47. Have you ever attended 'professional classes' to be able to accurately judge aroma, flavor, body, texture, color, fruitiness, and acidity; as well as properly prepare beverages?

48. Must 'brewing water' only be a 'certain type or brand?'

49. Does the thought of using 'un-foamed milk' in your coffee repulse you? Do you feel the same with 'steamed' milk? What about 'canned' milk?

50. Are you a member of a 'Coffee Club or Blog' of some sort?

51. Do you judge your 'Espresso or Cappuccino' by its 'appearance' rather than taste – or, the equipment in which it was created?

52. Are you 'surprised' when served a 'good' cup of coffee by an 'amateur?'

53. Do you <u>only</u> drink your coffee 'Black'… to taste its true essence?

54. Do you own any travel brewers – such as an 'HandPresso®?'

55. Do you subscribe to 'Rare Coffee,' Subscription Services?

56. Do you own any coffee 'Toys?'

57. Do you own any coffee equipment which looks like it may have come directly from NASA or a science experiment?

58. Do you own any 'Custom Corsets' (sleeves, such as Snakeskin or custom printed) for your cardboard, coffee cups in Coffee Bars?

59. Do you have any 'preconceived' ideas about coffee; or, are you 'unwilling' to even discuss any differences?

60. Are you 'horrified,' just by the thought of 'Decaffeinated Coffee?'

Surprisingly, there are no 'right or wrong' answers here; as everyone has different tastes, opinions, 'coffee education,' and upbringings! However, some solutions might 'lean' toward the obvious! For example, if one 'will not' go to 'certain' franchises of coffee houses – due to 'fashionable' or 'political' reasons, or feel that there is no one, "*Who knows how to brew coffee beside themselves*" – one might consider that they <u>are</u> a bit more 'particular' than other coffee drinkers!

The same thing comes into play, if someone spends 'hundreds or thousands of dollars' on 'Coffee Accessories' – such as, fancy grinders, mills, or 'designer' plastic or Bamboo stirring sticks, and collars, for freshly ground coffee; or 'specialty tools,' saying, "*Must be used before the coffee grounds can be 'compacted down' with a Tamper*"… well, that <u>is</u> leaning toward the 'Snobby' side!

The same thing holds if one owns a 'Coffee Leveler,' 'Custom Tamper' or 'Tamper Holder' – which can cost hundreds of dollars! Many people truly feel that these tools are "*Going to work better*" than simple 'hand tampering;" or, it is going to "*Really make a difference,*" in the quality of one's Espresso! Some say, a cheap plastic, cast, or wooden Tamper' (not to mention, ones' thumb) "*Cannot possibly work well*" (regardless of the fact, simple tools or 'fingers' have worked – and worked well – for hundreds of years)! Again, perhaps, someone 'thinking like above' might be something of a 'Snob!'

To start things off, let's look at some 'Minor Coffee History,' on the next pages, and then, see some 'common' questions, often, sent to me about coffee. Remember, one cannot 'be or talk' like a 'Coffee Snob,' without knowing some basic 'history, lingo, and techniques!' When needed, I will go into more detail about certain subjects; then return to questions. Then, I will throw in a few recipes for some of the more 'popular' Coffees, Creamers, Powders, Liqueurs, and Syrups. The main thing I want the reader to remember is, any method or recipe listed can be <u>augmented</u> countless ways; and, be as simple or complicated as desired!

(Nancy Aster speaking with Winston Churchill.)

Nancy: "*If I were your wife, I would put poison in your coffee!*"

Winston: "*Nancy, if I were your husband… I would drink it!*"

'QUICK' AND 'MINOR' HISTORY

First, this needs to be said: 'Coffee Snobs' aside, it does not matter if one likes 'Instant Coffee,' (considered the cheapest and worst coffee), or 'Kopi Luwak Coffee' (considered one of the most expensive and best coffees in the world); the key to enjoying coffee, is to 'drink what you like...' and, I will say this often in this book! However, many experts, connoisseurs, and 'Coffee Snobs' are going to differ with this fact; as "*Why would one not want to drink something rare, exotic or expensive*?" However, the fact remains, whatever way one enjoys their coffee – regardless of how it is brewed, or what they put into it – is the way their coffee should be drunk! Do not let anyone tell you different!

Worldwide, the 'masses' drink (by some estimates) up to 4 billion cups coffee each year; and, have used coffee, in one form or another, since the 10th century – perhaps even earlier! One common legend seems to state, "*Coffee Berries/Cherries were first observed by religious leaders having 'interesting effects' on animals or birds who ate them.*" Since the observed animals did not die after eating them, it was only natural that one day, some human would try the berries themselves! Of course, what they found inside, was a pit/seed/kernel or 'bean' (as it was later known); which was found to be more useful than the fruit!

Another similar legend, from the 10th Century (but from other parts of the world), tell of Sheepherders (one guy in particular) "*Witnessing their sheep and goats eating the berries, then 'dancing about' with robust energy;*" (possibly, part of the root of, the origin of the word 'Robusta'). It was not long before the Sheepherders themselves were eating and cooking with the berries – if nothing else, but to 'help flavor' certain foods and beverages. These people, as with the animals, seemed to feel that they "*Had more 'energy,' after consuming the berries.*"

A third legend (again, believed to be from around the same time), is about a Monk who made what was, probably, the first 'coffee beverage' out of a handful of Coffee Berries. Again, he and other Monks felt that 'more energy and awareness' came from the drink!

The public, soon, started mixing the berries with animal fat and grains to create something of a 'protein-rich snack bar.' Of course, the berries, now known as 'Cherries' (due to their 'cherry-like' appearance) were also allowed to ferment; to make something of a wine! In fact, early Europeans first referred to the drink as "*Arabian Wine!*" Some people make a variation of this

[15]

wine, still, today! But, consuming the cherries as food remained popular for an extended period. It was, approximately, during the next 100 years, that many believe 'Coffee' received its name: coming from several languages; first from the Arabic, "*Qahhwat al-bun*" or "*Wine of the bean.*" The term evolved into the word 'Kahveh' – in Turkish, and then 'Koffie' in Dutch. In English, these terms seemed to translate to 'Coffee;' and we still call it that today!

By the year 950AD, Arabs (like the previously mentioned Monk) started removing the fruit and soaking the Pits (Green Beans) in water to make beverages. This went on until, approximately, the 13th century, when some 'smart sole,' started 'roasting' the beans before making 'his or her' beverages – but, more on that later!

However, as 'facts and history' often change with time, there is a new belief, stemming from a study at the University of New Mexico, in which researchers, and anthropologists' findings, state: "*The 'Native People' of the Southwestern United States, may have been drinking caffeinated beverages made from Coffee, Cocao, or Yaupon Holly, as early as 750AD!*" The interesting part of these findings is, these plants are not native to Southwestern America; so, the people had to, somehow, find them through 'trade.'

I am sure the truth is in there somewhere in these stories, but we will never know, for sure! What we do know 'for a fact,' is that the people of Ethiopia seem to have started 'public' coffee usage; but going back so many centuries, who knows how coffee was discovered or used initially. Perhaps, it was used as a medicine or 'poultice' of some kind! Alternatively, maybe, only 'Kings' could consume the cherries, initially; or perhaps, they 'were not good enough for Kings…' and only the poor could or would eat them! The possibilities are endless; and will always leave us wondering!

In any event, coffee usage spread like wildfire over the centuries – and became very controversial in some areas! History mentions, in the year 1511AD, coffee was declared by the government of Mecca to be "*Illegal;*" for "*Causing radical thinking!*" And by the 16th century, religion got involved again; and wanted coffee 'banned' in Italy for "*Being a Satanic Drink!*" Even Sweden and Prussia took turns banning coffee – as late as the year 1800! Moreover, some religious groups today, even 'ban' coffee, to a certain degree, as it is considered a 'stimulant!'

But not too far into back into the 16th century, many Middle Eastern, Asian, African, and European countries stopped feeding Coffee Cherries to their livestock and were drinking or cooking with them themselves; at least, in one form or another. One can only presume, that somehow, somewhere, someone 'threw' a handful of Cherries into a pot for some 'added flavoring' to something they were cooking; and 'liked it,' when it 'bonded' with animal fat! Presumably, still, someone tried 'drinking' the left-over water – again, finding it 'uplifting' or enjoyable (perhaps, not by our standards, today), but enjoyable still.

In theory, somehow, 'left-over' pits (beans) made it – possibly spilled – into a fire... and 'roasted;' only to be found, once the fire had gone out! Again, as people back then seldom 'wasted anything,' someone tasted the roasted beans and found them interesting; and maybe attempted to 'rehydrate' them by 'boiling them' in some water. The water darkened, and the person felt compelled to taste it – again, liking it! Coffee as a beverage (or at least, a cooking ingredient) was born! Over time, one can only imagine, someone somewhere, ended up with a handful of 'broken beans' – and found that 'boiling them' made an even darker, and more flavorful, liquid. From there, perhaps, people 'purposely' started 'breaking or crushing' the roasted beans into smaller pieces; and they found, the 'smaller' the coffee bean part, the darker and more flavorful the liquid; and, the more 'stimulating' the effects!

It was not too long, before coffee beans, most likely, became a form of 'currency' or 'trade;' such as with spices or products. 'Trade' might explain how the Native Americans came to acquire a 'food source' not grown in their area!

Bypassing the early 'trade issues' and different locales of 'coffee bushes' or 'trees' throughout the world, coffee (as a beverage) was probably, and primarily, first consumed in the 'Islamic World' – and, became part of many religious observances, where it, still, may be used today. The beverage, soon, started 'branching out' from there; with even more traders carrying it everywhere.

Moving ahead through time and history, the first 'Coffee House' was opened in Vienna in the year 1683. 'History' states, a Polish Military Officer opened the 'Coffee House;' and helped popularize the custom of adding sugar and milk to the coffee. To this day, a beverage many call "*Mélange*," is served in Vienna; and considered typical. It is nothing more than coffee served with hot, foamed milk, and a glass of water. Perhaps, this is starting to sound increasingly like the Lattes and Cappuccinos we know of today?

By the mid to late 1700s, 'Coffee as a beverage' (and 'Coffee Houses') had spread across Europe… and even started to appear in America; as tea fell out of fashion (Boston Tea Party) – and was replaced by the consumer by coffee. However, it was not until the 1900's that 'roasting methods, bean blends, grinds, and different brewing methods' all started to take hold. 'Coffee Houses' were experimenting with all kinds of ways to 'roast and brew' their beverages… moreover, the 'public' liked it!

'Jumping ahead,' to the middle of the 20th century, we have the 'Coffee for a dime' thing going; which included, 'Coffee Houses for the Beatniks' and Jazz Clubs. Espresso became big in those days – especially, for its 'caffeine buzz' – as did different blends, flavors, and roasts of beans! It was not until later in the century, that 'Coffee Houses' had changed into establishments like Starbucks™; which included increasing the cost of coffee tenfold, and then tenfold again, and then, tenfold once again! What used to cost a Dime for 'unlimited' cups, now cost multiple dollars to buy just one cup!

Few establishments (except food restaurants) offer 'just a cup' of 'Black Coffee' anymore. They offer "*Lattes, Mochas, Mokas, Mochaccinos, Cappuccinos, Blends, Lattes, Frappe's, Filters, Cold Brews, Iced Coffees, Blended Coffees,*" and more of their own invention and name… not to mention, desserts! In the same sense, what might be called a 'Frappé' in one Coffee Bar, might be called something else altogether in another shop; and yet, be called something still different in the next… moreover, their 'tastes' are all going to vary due to machinery, brewing time, brands of coffee, roasts, cleanliness, and Barista preferences! It is difficult, sometimes, to receive the 'same order' twice – even, within the same shop or with the same Barista! Luckily for the shops and Baristas, many consumers 'do not know' the differences between beverages, 'tastes,' or brews!

"*A cup of coffee – real coffee – home-browned, home ground, homemade, that comes to you dark as a hazel-eye, but changes to a golden bronze as you temper it with cream that never cheated, but was real cream from its birth, thick, tenderly yellow, perfectly sweet, neither lumpy nor frothing on the Java: such a cup of coffee is a match for twenty blue devils and will exorcise them all.*"

~ (Attributed to) Henry Ward Beecher

HEALTH – PRO AND CON

Unless one has an 'allergy' or 'sensitivity' to coffee or caffeine, 'coffee as a whole,' tends to have more 'benefits' than 'detriments' – that is, depending upon which doctor 'talks' to! Fortunately, less than 4% of the population have <u>actual</u>, 'food allergies!' However, a Coffee 'allergy or sensitivity' <u>can</u> cause:

   ~ Accelerated or Weak Pulse
   ~ Breathing Difficulty or Shortness of Breath
   ~ Chronic Cough
   ~ Diarrhea
   ~ Dizziness
   ~ Fainting
   ~ Headache
   ~ Heart Palpitations
   ~ Nausea
   ~ Paleness or 'Blue' Skin
   ~ Rash or Hives
   ~ Stomach Cramping
   ~ Sudden Decreases in Blood Pressure
   ~ Swallowing Issues
   ~ Vomiting
   ~ Wheezing
   ~ and More!

Coffee holds over <u>1000</u> different chemical agents in it; which can cause or contribute (if nothing else) to a multitude of medical issues – at least, by themselves! But, when mixed, researchers have found (at least this, current, year) that coffee can be <u>healthy</u> for the average person – even upwards of six, 8-ounce cups per day! And, other than giving someone 'the Jitters,' or keeping them awake at night, the caffeine in coffee, is no longer thought to have a significant effect on medical conditions… even Blood Pressure! Honestly, I have seen questions regarding 'health and coffee' every year for the past 20 years in many of the medical papers I read! One year, coffee is 'healthy;' while, the following year, coffee is the 'unhealthiest' beverage one can consume! This year (at this writing), it is back on the 'healthy' list… at least, for the most part! In California, however, it is, somewhat, back on the 'unhealthy list' (but more on that later)!

Nonetheless, throughout the centuries, people have always worried about their health and what they consumed; and indeed, *"Worried about the 'health aspects' of coffee,"* as my father often stated! My father, back in the early 1960s, was ordered by doctors to *"Limit his coffee or tea caffeine consumption"* to *"One cup, per week"* (if any), due to his heart and high blood pressure issues. I remember Dad having to 'change over' from 'regular coffee' to Sanka™ brand of coffee – a decaf; but he, first, had tried many other types of coffee 'knockoffs' and brands… like Postum™ (a wheat, bran, and molasses, imitation coffee) or Herbal and 'Chicory' coffees; before settling on, caffeine free, Sanka brand coffee. He saved 'regular' coffee (one or two cups), for 'special occasions' or 'holidays' – when he could put eggnog or whiskey in it!

His 'General Practitioner' (an 'active' Mormon) and his 'Cardiologist' (an 'active' 7 Day Adventist) – both being 'non-coffee' drinkers – agreed that *"Coffee could kill him,"* in their medical opinions; by *"Raising his blood pressure to dangerous levels…"* and, they forbade him drinking it. Today, had my father still been alive, things might have been different – as coffee has been awarded certain 'health benefits.' Not surprisingly, however, some 'benefits' are still being argued by many health care professionals.

Myself, being a health care professional – aside of writer – advise my patients (unless they suffer from 'uncontrolled' blood pressure), to not only *"Enjoy coffee,"* but *"Use coffee for various medical issues;"* such as, to help with constipation… moreover, use it as an 'antioxidant' to help control 'Free Radicals!' However, as I previously mentioned, California is trying to have coffee – both served and processed – come with a 'Health Warning' as cigarettes do; as some studies show that coffee can cause cancer or cause congenital disabilities! However, as of June 3, 2019, California's state regulator of the 'Office of Environmental Health Hazard Assessment,' concluded that there is *"No association between coffee and a significant risk of cancer"* – and coffee is now, *"Exempt,"* from Proposition 65 warnings. However, many restaurants and coffee shops still have their 'warning signs' posted.

'Cancer or Congenital disabilities' aside (as I, personally, do not believe a pregnant woman should be drinking 'caffeinated' coffee, soda pop, alcohol, et cetera, due to their 'unhealthy' nature) there is medical proof that coffee can prevent certain cancers and other diseases, too (but, again, more on that later). Go figure!

However, the truth or facts of the matter is as follows: Coffee is like a game of tennis: in the fact that it is 'batted back and forth,' by the so-called experts when it comes to its health benefits or detriments!

Whereas coffee may not be healthy for 'everyone' for assorted reasons, it has been proven to have certain 'health benefits' for <u>certain</u> disorders. Some studies have stated that: "*Some people achieve Migraine relief by drinking an Espresso or consuming a few cups of coffee;*" while other studies state the opposite! In the same sense, still more studies state: "*People who drink coffee are up to 50 percent less likely to develop rectal, colon, or breast cancers. Moreover, coffee can help prevent the development of Type II Diabetes!*" However, I do think it needs to be pointed out, that if one already has Type II Diabetes, there is not much coffee can do for the Diabetes (according to 'studies' at this point); short of adding 'antioxidants' to the system.

In still more studies, researchers confirm what they have said, "*Some 'natural ingredients,' found in Roasted Coffee, such as 'Chlorogenic Acid,' can not only prevent the formation of Diabetes, but help reduce the risk of heart disease or stroke.*" New information is released every day; for example, I heard on the national news just this morning; researchers have, again, said, "*Four cups of coffee per day, can help to prevent a heart attack;*" but later that same day, on another channel, "*More than four cups of coffee per day can be 'deadly' to the average person!*" I wish researchers could decide on 'one story,' and 'stick with it!'

On a positive note, research, by yet another group of doctors, suggests that "*Where there may not be any risk to drinking 'too much coffee,' the 'risk' of developing Parkinson's disease can be reduced by as little as 2 cups of coffee per day!*" They stated further, "*If one already has Parkinson's disease or MS, the antioxidants in coffee can help reduce symptoms or pain by <u>reducing</u> inflammation.*" I have noticed similar findings through my research; that 'sometimes' (when coupled with a decent diet) Peripheral Neuropathy symptoms may be, somewhat, reduced using coffee along with other 'antioxidants!'

However, as a Health Care professional, I am often asked about "*Drinking too much coffee*" concerning the Liver… such as, when one has Cirrhosis. First, "*Drinking too much coffee*" is different from 'drinking too much alcohol!' The fact is, I have never met anyone who 'drank too much' coffee – although, it is certainly possible; just like it is 'possible' to 'drink too much water;' and causing 'Water Intoxication.' Fortunately, studies have shown, "*Those who drink coffee, regularly, are __80 percent__ less likely to develop Cirrhosis of the Liver!*"

Of course, the question of 'Diet,' also, often arises! My wife, if fact, recently asked me about "*Using coffee for losing weight.*" Certainly, it is going to depend upon what one 'puts in' ones' coffee. Drinking it 'black' is going to be the best way for dieting; especially, if one is 'substituting' a cup of coffee for a snack or dessert! However, filling it with sugar or sweet, flavored creamers is undoubtedly <u>not</u> going to help one to lose weight! However, coffee <u>can</u> help to get some people 'up and going' first thing in the morning! By doing so, one is more likely to '<u>want to</u>' exercise more to burn off calories and boost metabolism. Moreover, as coffee is a natural diuretic, it can help to help with 'excess water weight' as well; not to mention, help those who suffer from edema!

Also, as the coffee passes through the stomach, it 'cleans' as it goes! Remember, for many people, two cups of coffee in the morning is the beginning of their 'morning abolitions;' meaning, it 'sends them to the bathroom' for a bowel movement – and, <u>naturally</u>, aids with constipation. Some of my patients will, purposely, 'over-drink' coffee; if they haven't had a 'good bowel movement' in a few days. The 'end result,' a 'useful and healthy' (but rather 'explosive'), situation in the bathroom! It is nothing to worry about; or, as my maternal grandmother used to say… *"Everyone needs a good 'cleaning out' from time to time!"*

It goes to say, that coffee alone is not going to reduce ones' weight (other than, perhaps, in 'excess' fecal matter); as 'exercise and diet' are going to need to be added to <u>permanently</u> lose weight. This is where the caffeine comes in handy again; as it 'increases' energy! Just look at some of the so-called 'Energy Drinks' on the market. Basically, 'Energy Drinks' are just high amounts of herbs, B-vitamins, and caffeine! Some people even 'brew' with Energy Drinks; in fact, right down the road from me is a small, 'drive-thru' 'Coffee Shack;' whose 'claim to fame' is their 'Red Bull™' Infused Coffee – or vice versa!

Coffee seems to have <u>many</u> 'health' uses! One of my patients, even claims her coffee, *"Aids with her Asthma and Arthritis symptoms."* I researched it, and she is correct! Coffee does help to reduce Asthma symptoms – but it is the caffeine in the coffee which is the so-called, 'magic' ingredient; a caffeinated tea or soda pop would, probably, do the same thing for her! In the same sense, Gallstones, Kidney Stones, and even Bladder Stones are, often, found to be reduced in occurrence by drinking coffee too; as it lowers the levels of cholesterol in bile. For 'Arthritis?' Well, we are back to 'antioxidants,' again; to help reduce pain caused by excess inflammation!

However, to play 'Devil's Advocate' here, new studies, also, show that *"Unfiltered coffee (coffee not run through a paper filter – not metal or nylon) can increase LDL cholesterol and triglycerides in the blood."* So, technically, the 'healthiest way' to drink coffee – to achieve the most health benefits – is to drink it 'paper-filtered' in some way… generally, this will be with a 'Pour-Over' type brewer. However, I use a 'Paper Filter' in my Automatic Drip Coffee Maker as well! When 'liquid coffee' passes through a paper filter, the paper 'captures' the majority of 'Cafestol' (a diterpenoid molecule); which is what raises LDL cholesterol and triglycerides.

Getting back to the 'Health Warning' (Proposition 65) regarding Coffee and Cancer/Birth Defects' here in California, even with its 'cancer-preventing' agents, coffee still has other ingredients, besides caffeine, which can be of concern; namely, 'Acrylamide' – which is presumed to be a potential 'carcinogen'… at least, in 'lab rats;' who drink an over-abundance of coffee! What happens is, the body converts the Acrylamide to 'Glycidamide' – which can damage DNA, and cause cancer or congenital disabilities (frankly, pregnant women should be only drinking 'decaffeinated' coffee anyway). Studies are inconclusive, in my opinion; especially, as lab rats assimilate chemicals differently than humans – not to mention, most humans do not drink as 'high in volume' of coffee as the 'lab rats!' Luckily, as mentioned a few paragraphs back, the amount of 'Acrylamide/Glycidamide' is, now, considered "*Insignificant*" in the state of California… at least, this week!

However, even if the 'warning' were 'significant,' we do not have to worry about Acrylamide or other chemicals; as there is one thing to help remedy it – use of the aforementioned, 'small weave, Paper Filter; ' which will help to remove (filter out) most or all the adverse substances. For most 'Drip' drinkers/preparers, this is not much of an issue; as most people, already, use a 'paper filter' in their brewer! If they use a 'mesh' filter, they can add a paper filter as well – which is precisely what I do!

It is easy to visually see the 'oils' left in my 'paper filters!' However, I find ways to use the paper filters when using my Percolator or other, typically, non-filtered coffees; usually, by 'pouring' the coffee through a standard cone with a paper filter, when serving. Not only do I have a 'cleaner and sweeter' brew, but filtering helps to eliminate the 'objectionable' substances!

However, it is even easier with a 'Drip' brewer! In the photographs on the next page, I show the steps I use; starting with a 'pre-wet' filter! 'Blooming,' can now be performed as well – should I have the time and interest! For my particular purpose, I use the two filters more out of habit, than of need; however, as I 'save' my coffee grounds for one of my patients garden plant, I find it easier to 'dump' the metal filter than a 'slippery' paper one!

[23]

First, I place my 'Paper Filter' in the Drip ground basket. On top of the Paper Filter, I put my 'Wire Mesh' Filter Basket – technically, it is not needed, but I use it out of habit! If I were only to use the 'Mesh Filter,' one would be able to see the 'coffee oils' floating on top of the finished coffee; and feel them on the walls of the brewer 'holding tank.' The oils will, 'visibly,' not show up in the Mesh Filter itself; but if I were only to use a Paper Filter (or use both a Mesh and Paper Filter) they can, easily, be seen as 'shiny' on top

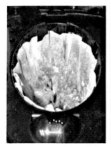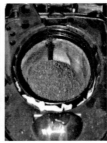

of the paper filter – as can be seen in the fourth photograph above. Also, 'Fines' (overly small, coffee grounds) can be easily seen. These 'fines' are coffee particles which can pass through the Mesh Filter – and, 'muddy' a cup!

Most 'Drip type' paper coffee 'filters/strainers' are round and have a flat bottom; so, they fit into a Drip Brewer basket better. However, if using a 'Pour-Over' Cone – which is 'V' shaped – it has been my experience, that it can 'fold over' when the hot water is applied to the basket – thus, interfering with the brewing process. Many manufacturers, however, have thought of this; and have created 'V-shaped' paper filters – a #2 filter is being used in the cone to the right; directly under the 'Mesh' filter. Again, as I 'save' grounds for one of my patients' garden, I find the Mesh filter easier to dump!

Most of these commercial, 'paper' filters come with an 'imprinted/pressed' seam along one side and the bottom. These 'seams' should be folded over before being placed into the device ground holder; to aid with 'keeping its shape' when brewing. 'Both' a Mesh and Paper Filter can be used in most cones; with the appropriate changes in 'cone shape;' as in this photograph or the one at the top of the page!

To reiterate what I stated earlier in this book, a 'Paper Filter,' regardless of the brewing method used, can <u>reduce</u> or <u>eliminate</u> most potential (suspected) carcinogens and LDL cholesterol-raising agents – as well as, potentially, create a 'cleaner, sweeter and fruitier' brew! However, a

'Wire/Mesh Filter' will only stop the 'large particles' of coffee grounds; it will not prevent the 'ultra-fine' coffee particles, suspended colloidal chemicals, or oils from entering the cup.

Does this mean we should all (or, at least, the people still worried about Prop 65) stop drinking 'unfiltered' coffee? No; but it does mean, that if someone already has high cholesterol and triglycerides – or, are worried about cancer or birth defects – perhaps, should save coffee which is 'unfiltered' for something like 'French Press' brewing, 'Turkish Coffee,' or for 'special occasions;' rather than drinking it all day!

Not surprisingly, some French Press manufacturers have already thought of 'paper filters' in regard to 'Prop 65,' 'coffee oils' and sediment; and their presses offer the 'choice' of adding a small, paper filter to the bottom of the metal filter – similar to the way an 'AeroPress' uses filters! This process was considered 'so good an idea' by the industry, that even 'K-Cup/Pod' brewers, now, offer additional 'Paper Filters' for the coffee brewers; and they not only provide added 'protection' from oils and chemicals, but greatly cut down on small particles as well! What the Brewing Manufacturers do not mention, is that the added 'Paper Filter,' can, also, 'slow down' the brewing process – thus, 'improving' the extraction and taste of the brew!

Getting back to other health benefits, yet another health issue – Dementia – is thought by some doctors to be "*Improved*" by two or more cups of coffee per day; at least, the patient is more alert as the coffee stimulates their systems and brains! The same claim might be considered for some Alzheimer's patients; however, at present, there have not been many studies about the 'effects of coffee' on Alzheimer patients. I have seen some Alzheimer patients appear 'better' after a few cups of coffee – at least, more alert; but if the patient tends to be a bit 'violent' (as is found often in 'advanced' cases) 'more alert' is not necessarily a good thing! This would be like giving a 'drunk' large amounts of coffee to 'sober them up' (and ending up with a 'wide awake' drunk)! One would not want to give someone 'aggressive,' something to provide them with more energy or 'stimulate' them, unnecessarily. The patient with Alzheimer's may become more aggressive with caffeinated coffee!

What are some other negative aspects of coffee? Primarily, there are reportedly higher incidents of GERD (Gastroesophageal Reflux Disease) or 'Heartburn;' as the acids in coffee can increase symptoms – but, this is where something like 'low acid, Cold Brewed' coffee can help! In addition, 'caffeine'

[25]

can cause agitation, anxiety, headache, increased breathing rates, increased heart rates, insomnia, nausea, nervousness, restlessness, stomach upset, tinnitus, vomiting, allergic reactions, and more – such as, the afore mentioned, 'increased' LDL cholesterol – so, perhaps a 'Decaf' coffee would be in order as well! Of course, 'research' states, that a *"Lower acid coffee"* may be used to combat these issues too!

In the same sense, I tend to become 'dehydrated' easily; so, I like to use coffee to help keep myself 'hydrated' (even though, technically, it is a diuretic)! Plus, coffee helps remove my 'excess blood sugar;' when coupled with my diabetic medication – providing I do not fill the coffee full of 'sugary' additives. **Special Note:** Everyone with a 'medical condition' of some kind, should check with their doctor, dietitian, or nutritionist, to learn of any 'risks' coffee may have on their health!

I should mention, again, the newly retracted, 2019 'Death Warning' regarding coffee; other than California's, 'Cancer' warning. This warning from 'medical experts,' pertains to *"Drinking too much coffee;"* which equates, to 6 or more cups per day. According to 'The American Journal of Clinical Nutrition,' *"Drinking six or more cups of coffee per day, can result in a 22% increase in the risk of developing heart disease and other issues."* Of course, 'overindulgence' in anything is never a good thing! I think researchers would find, most coffee drinkers only consume between two and four cups per day; which, keeps coffee on the 'healthy side' of the debate! In any event, I would think the above statement might be a little vague, as everyone is different and has different 'tolerances' for different substances!

I should think that, as with medication, coffee and caffeine would affect people of different size, age, and health, 'differently;' which is 'why' I may take a 'larger dose' of blood pressure medication (as a large man weighing over 200 pounds) than one of my elderly, female patients, taking the same medication; who weighs less than 100 pounds.

To reiterate, a young, large, and active person, who is physically fit and 'active,' is going to 'tolerate' coffee (with all its chemicals and caffeine) much better than someone who leads a sedentary lifestyle; and whom is diminutive, elderly, and frail!

There is one last 'negative' aspect to coffee when it comes to health – in this case, 'oral health;' and that is the effects of 'Tannins' on the drinker's teeth!'

'Tannins' are organic substances found in plants; and as coffee is a plant, it has more than it is fair share! Stains occur on teeth when 'Tannins' build up on the tooth enamel. As they build up on the teeth, so does bacteria; eventually, leaving a 'beautiful' gray/brown 'plaque' for the dentist to 'grind' or 'blast off' with an ultrasonic device. The 'Coffee Tannins' are, also, responsible for most drinkers needing a more intensive, 'deep cleaning' (below the gumline) of their teeth! Left untreated, the bacteria can cause halitosis (bad breath), and even lead to other, severe, mouth and body issues!

However, 'Coffee Plaque' can be prevented by brushing one's teeth regularly, using 'Baking Soda;' which can help to cut through the plaque; and allow it to be 'brushed' away! **Special Note:** from experience, I can safely state, it takes 'actual' Baking Soda – rather than 'Toothpaste' with Baking Soda in it – to clean 'Coffee Stains' from teeth! After receiving a 'deep cleaning,' recently, I immediately picked up using both on my teeth; at the recommendation of my 'Oral Hygienist!'

It is time to start looking at some questions people have, recently, sent me:

"I never drink coffee at lunch. I find it keeps me awake for the afternoon."

~ (Attributed to) Ronald Reagan

MISCELLANEOUS QUESTIONS & FAQ'S

Over the past few years since my first Coffee Book, "*Coffee for the Average Joe*" came out, I have received countless questions; many of which are 'scattered' throughout this book – for instance:

Question: "*What is Fair Trade Coffee?*"

Answer: 'Fair Trade Coffee,' are coffee beans which have been 'certified' as having been produced to 'Fair Trade Standards;' meaning, 'Fair Trade' organizations – such as the <u>Fairtrade Labeling Organizations International</u>, the <u>World Fair Trade Organization</u>, the <u>Network of European World Shops</u> and/or the <u>European Fair-Trade Association</u> – whom have all agreed to 'transparency of business practices;' and 'greater equity' in international trade, as well as prohibiting 'ultra-low' wages, child labor, or 'forced' labor.

Often, but not always, 'Fair Trade' coffees are considered 'Organic' in nature, as well.

Question: "*What is 'Organic' Coffee?*"

Answer: "*Organic Coffee*" is grown and produced without the use of pesticides, herbicides, or other 'artificial' chemicals – although, a 'natural' (animal) fertilizer, could be used. Often, 'Organic Coffees' are grown on smaller farms and plantations; as they can receive more 'attention' to growth and development.

Question: "*Are there diverse types of Coffee Beans?*"

Answer: There are over 100 different species of coffee plants grown. However, other than a few obscure, natural, or experimental, 'sub-species' (which are more often sold as 'specialty' brands or types – such as Typica, Caturra, Bourbon, Blue Mountain or other types/brands), there are only 'four' main types of coffee beans available for commercial sale:

- Coffea Arabica (a.k.a. Arabica) – A 'high altitude,' and 'more expensive,' plant or bean to grow; which makes up 63% of the coffee market. 'High End' coffee bars, generally, serve this type of coffee.

Arabica contains almost twice the 'natural sugar' of Robusta – the second most favorite coffee. The plants tend to grow 'smaller' than Robusta or other types of coffee; and their 'coffee beans' tend to be more 'oval' in shape, as opposed to other bean types.

- Coffea Canephora (a.k.a. Robusta) – A 'lower altitude,' but 'wilder' and 'cheaper,' grade; which is 'easier/cheaper' to farm! 'Robusta' coffee; makes up 27% of the coffee market. Beans tend to be more 'circular' than Arabica beans; and unless an 'ultra-high grade' version of Robusta, the taste is found to be a *"Bit rubbery;"* according to experts. Therefore Robusta tends to be 'mixed' with other types of beans. Many 'canned coffees' uses a 'blend' of Arabica and Robusta beans for a better taste, than just cheaper Robusta, alone. However, some 'ultra-cheap' coffee brands tend to use only Robusta beans – which is 'why' many of those coffees do not taste too good when compared to other brands or 'upper end' Coffee Bars!

- Coffea Liberica Bull ex Hiern (a.k.a. Liberian Coffee) – A 'species' of its own – which grown in Malaysia, Liberia, and the Ivory Coast; and makes up about 3% of the 'World Coffee Bean Market.' At only 3% of the world market, it is seldom used or sold; except in 'Specialty' coffee bars, or Gourmet stores. However, 'Liberian,' sometimes, is mixed with other beans! 'Liberian Coffee Beans' are more 'teardrop' shaped than round or oval!

- Excelsa – (a.k.a. Liberian, now, as well) Excelsa was recently 're-classified' as a variety of Liberica – but, some brands still carry it as a separate species. It accounts for an estimated 7% of world coffee production, but not the market. It grows on large trees at medium altitudes – so, it should become popular with growers. Beans tend to be larger than other types and have an 'asymmetrical/teardrop' (or Almond) shape, which makes them resemble Liberica; but average bean size is considerably smaller than regular Liberica.

Excelsa grows mainly in Southeast Asia; where it is used as a 'blending' coffee, especially for 'in-house' blends, to add complexity and depth. Excelsa has a distinctively bold, tart, fruity, dark, mystifying taste.

Brewed on its own, Excelsa is a 'unique coffee experience' for some people. Some people may compare it to a good 'Scotch Whiskey.' However, like Scotch Whiskey, a cup of 'pure Excelsa' is not everyone's favorite drink. And most people don't find the aroma of Excelsa beans themselves to be attractive; although, as everyone is different… some people love it! I do not enjoy the taste or the smell of Excelsa Coffee by itself. None the less, when mixed with a good Arabica brand (or even with a good 'Robusta') it is not too bad.

Question: *"What is the difference between Arabica and Robusta beans?"*

Answer: Other than the 'altitude' issues as listed previously, 'Robusta' beans are a 'hardier' coffee bean than Arabica – meaning, it can grow in a warmer/harsher environment. Originally, Robusta was developed in Africa; and existed in the same 'Coffea genus' as Arabica Beans. However, Robusta Beans are not nearly as 'flavorful' as Arabicas – thus, producing a bitter, more 'pungent' taste to coffee, regardless of the brewing method.

'Pure Robusta' roasts are enjoyed by many in European, Middle East, and Southeast Asian countries – and, are beginning to find quite a following here in America. Surprisingly, Brazil and Indonesia – which are famous for some of the highest quality Arabica Beans – grow <u>more</u> 'Robusta' beans than they do 'Arabica.' But the real difference lies in the part of the world where the coffee grows! For example, one 'high altitude' Arabica bean, grown in, say… Columbia, may taste different than a similar Arabica from Kenya; and different still, from another similar Arabica from Jamaica or Hawaii. This is due to many factors; such as, weather, air temperature, soil acidity; or perhaps, 'volcanic ash' in the soil – as in Hawaiian, Kona Coffee. Even actual altitude can be a factor – as well as the amount of rainfall per year (climate), forest cover, drainage of the soil, and even processing. Robusta does not grow well at the higher altitudes!

Different varietals of both beans can have 'descriptive' names; such as 'Bourbon,' with Arabica beans!

Question: *"Can I grow Coffee Bushes in my backyard for my beans?"*

Answer: The answer would be, <u>technically</u>, *"No…"* at least, not commercially; or with achieving any significant or worthwhile yield of Cherries. However, I have heard of at least 18 new 'Specialty' growers in California; whom, opened for business in 2018. Their 'unique tasting' beans are sold in many 'high end' Bay Area coffee shops; and should be showing up in grocery stores, soon!

Question: *"Are 'Flavored' (like chocolate) Coffees grown?"*

Answer: 'Flavored coffees,' such as 'Chocolate Macadamia Nut,' or 'Cinnamon Vanilla Swirl,' are not grown; they are 'created;' usually, after the roasting process is complete – although, there are some coffee 'sub-species' and processing methods (such as Kopi Luwak) which might have a slight 'chocolate' or another natural flavoring; if processed and roasted a particular way!

Before a bean can be 'flavored,' it must be decided 'how dark' a roast one wants in the first place! After the roasting process, and while the beans are still warm, 'oily' flavor extracts are applied to the beans – either by spraying, soaking, or dipping them. Since roasted coffee beans are so hard, very little flavoring is absorbed into the bean fibers. In other words, the flavor is more on the 'outside' of the beans than 'in' them! Therefore, one can create their own, 'custom,' flavors at home, if they wish! For example, one man I know 'pours' chocolate extract over his freshly roasted beans; then 'stirs them around' until dry; while another man I know, 'mists/sprays' cinnamon flavoring onto his freshly, ground beans with an atomizer.

Having tried both 'flavored' coffees, I have to say, *"Both men's coffee is just as good (if not better) than professionally flavored coffees."* I have found, however, that 'natural extracts' leave a nice 'after taste' to the coffee; while, 'artificial' ones, usually, taste 'nasty…' at least, in <u>my</u> opinion!

Question: *"Why should I buy expensive 'Specialty' coffee beans over 'store-bought,' canned coffee?"*

Answer: Throughout this book, I speak a lot about the 'freshness' of the beans; and why one does not want to 'freeze or grind' too much to use right away; as the 'grind' starts to lose its aroma and flavor immediately after grinding. So, it makes sense that 'pre-ground' beans in a can are going to lose their flavor after grinding as well! The only difference is, 'Canned Coffee' is Vacuum-Sealed! Therefore, the can tends to 'hiss' when first punctured by a can opener or vaper seal broken! This 'Vacuum' does not stop the grind from aging, but only <u>slows</u> it down. The canned coffee tends to lose even more flavor when opened – even if it has been 'Nitrogen Flushed' (which extends shelf life) before canning or bagging! Therefore, if using a 'canned' product, one might only wish to purchase small cans of coffee – as, hopefully, it can be 'used up' before becoming too 'stale.' The same can be said about 'fresh' beans! Roasted beans, if properly stored, can last a substantial amount time;

[31]

however, once ground, they deteriorate quickly. Therefore, one should not 'grind' more than just a few days' worth's of beans before using, to achieve the <u>best</u> flavor!

Until Starbucks showed up on the scene, most people were willing to accept the taste of various brands of 'Canned Coffee' as being *"Tasty and enjoyable;"* even if 'the can' had been open for a month or longer! It was not until Starbucks, and other coffee bars, convinced coffee drinkers that there is *"Something more to coffee than just opening up a can,"* and today, I am afraid that I have yet to meet a 'Coffee Snob' who will admit that they enjoy drinking 'Canned' coffee over fresh! The only thing 'Canned Drinkers' can count on, is that they will always find the coffee to be 'roasted and ground' consistently – meaning, every can, other than substantial canning age – is going to look, smell, and brew, relatively, the same, from can to can!

Depending upon the drinkers preferred brewing method, this might work out quite well for many people; or, at least, make an acceptable cup of coffee! Nevertheless, I tell my various 'coffee friends,' if they are *"Going to buy a 'Canned Brand,' do not buy it at a 'Discount' or 'Big Box' store!"* Some stores, like 'Costco®,' will buy 'trainload pallets' of canned coffee; so, they can offer a 'low price,' and 'varied selection,' to their consumers. Smaller stores, on the other hand, might only get their cans by the single pallet or 'case' load… moreover, they must charge <u>more</u> for them; as their 'wholesale cost' is higher! But, considering the store 'Buyers' (the people who decide which products to sell, to begin with, not to mention the coffee sellers, the processing plants, and a multitude of other people or issues), one might just get a '<u>fresher</u>/<u>newer</u>' can of coffee at the local grocery store than a 'Big Box Store!' The reason… because, 'large amounts' of the same roast are not just 'sitting around,' waiting to make it onto the store's shelves – or, pushed to the back of the rack when the additional stock comes in!

In reality, unless one was 'extremely trained' in the different tastes of 'canned' coffee, the average person, probably, is not going to be able to taste much difference between one can of coffee (same brand) to another! It just stands to reason, *"The younger the Roast… the 'fresher' the beans!"* However, even a 'coffee novice' can tell the difference between 'brands' of coffee. Again, roasts, processing, and more come into play to make up differences!

Besides the roast and age of the 'canned grind,' one can, also, take bean quality into effect as well! Often, major brands of canned coffee will '<u>mix</u>' both Robusta and Arabica beans to make a good tasting, 'average' grind – available at a lower cost to the consumer. However, this action is also, often, used to mask the cheaper (and lower quality) Robusta Beans, 'inferior' flavor! However, the companies who <u>do</u> <u>not</u> mix 'lower quality' beans (choosing to mix only 'fine quality' Robusta with Arabica), are truly making a '<u>superior</u>' mix!

'Superior' mixing can, usually, be 'tasted' in some of the 'higher end' brands of coffee – like some types of Folgers®, Farmer Brothers®, or Yuban® brands! Lastly, as previously mentioned, 'atmosphere' can undoubtedly add to the enjoyment of <u>any</u> coffee as well; as sometimes, even a 'lower end' coffees taste may not be noticed as much if the surrounding atmosphere is pleasant! Frankly, the average coffee drinker/brewer, at home is not going to notice too much difference between a fresh and canned coffee first thing in the morning; when they are waking up and hurrying to get dressed for work.

Many people are going to pour in a 'Flavored Coffee Creamer,' anyway! I guess what I am saying is, *"As long as one enjoys their coffee… it does not matter if the grounds are 'canned' or not; as long as one 'enjoys' the coffee!"*

Question: *"How are 'raw' Coffee Cherries 'processed' before roasting? Do different procedures make a difference before the beans are roasted?"*

Answer: 'Proper procedure' is a subjective thing; and various farms/companies may claim their 'processing' *"Creates the best taste!"*

'Processing,' starts with the 'Coffee Cherries' being picked either by hand or by machine – usually, depending upon the growers 'wealth and size' of the farm. The 'ripe' cherries are moved to the processing plant; where they are 'processed' by either 'wet or dry' methods.

With the 'Wet' method, the Cherry pulp is separated from the bean by a 'Pulping' machine. Beans are then moved to where the 'sticky mucilage' (parchment coatings) are removed. This action is performed by the beans being placed into buckets or tanks of water; and allowed to 'soak or ferment' the mucilage away.

The dry method, also, allows the 'Cherry Pulp/Seeds' to sit in tanks or buckets – but dry; then, nature can take its course. The Mucilage is removed by hand; without the aid of water. Sometimes, depending upon the farm, another form of 'Dry Processing' allows the coffee cherries to dry on the tree – beyond their natural ripening. These cherries are considered *"Coffee Raisins;"* and are then harvested, stored, or transported for pulping to a mill… where the 'ripened beans' are separated from 'un-ripened' ones; and the tree stems and leaves are removed by hand. 'Dry processing' on the tree is considered 'too risky' by most large growers today; as the cherries can easily 'over-ripen' and fall to the ground to rot. There is, however, a newer mechanical method for dry processing; which uses a machine to 'buff' the Mucilage/Parchment from the seeds; but smaller farms do not tend to use, or can afford, this method as of this writing.

After the Parchment is removed, the seeds/beans are rinsed and dried by various methods. They can be 'laid out' on the ground to dry for up to two weeks; and 'raked' several times a day help the process. Alternatively, they may be transported to 'covered,' concrete 'patios;' where sophisticated drying racks can help protect them from the weather. Again, the seeds are often 'stirred' or 'raked' to help them to dry. 'Richer/larger' farms might even have 'forced air' machines to help drain/dry the beans. Once the seeds are dry, they are then considered "*Stable, Green Beans,*" by the growers and moved on to other processing; such as added cleaning and bagging!

I would doubt that the 'average' person could taste any difference between 'Wet or Dry' processing methods once the beans are roasted!

Question: *"Do some kinds or brands of coffee have more caffeine than others?"*

Answer: Yes. The Arabica Bean has <u>half</u> the naturally occurring caffeine found in Robusta beans; and genetically 'designed' sub-species can have more, or less, caffeine. However, there are some companies which add additional caffeine to their beans. However, some coffee brands, such as 'Death Wish®, 'credit' the beans, and their roasting process, for their coffees 'high caffeine' content. They specialize in both great taste and 728 Milligrams of caffeine! The Death Wish brand caffeine content is so high; it even comes with a 'Danger' warning – for those who must watch their caffeine intake!

Other brands may even have higher caffeine content! These brands include names like: 'Atomic Coffee®, Banned Coffee®, Biohazard®, Black Insomnia®, Bomb Coffee®, Bone's Coffee High Voltage®, Double Tap Coffee®, Killer Coffee®, Perk Up Coffee®, Red Goat Coffee'®, Shock Coffee®, and more – all of which give 'Death Wish' a run for its money! Personally, one of my favorites, 'High Caffeine' coffees, comes from a local gas station – and, I get it when I am going to travel long distances, at night, to help 'keep awake.' Its caffeine content is like having a 'Double Shot' of Espresso – so it is not too dangerous! Plus, additional caffeine may be added if I need or want it; in a bottled, 'additive' form!

Question: *"Why are there 'different size grind settings' for coffee on grinders?"*

Answer: There are as many 'different grinds or degrees' of beans, as there are various brewing methods and 'tastes.' Plus, different brewing methods call for 'various degrees' of grind – so, assorted flavors, oils, and aromas may be, properly, extracted by 'that' particular method!

Whereas the first coffee ever made, most likely, used 'whole beans,' 10th to the 13th-century man discovered that 'more flavor' could be released from the roasted beans if they were 'broken up' into smaller pieces. Through 'trial and error' over the years, people found that control over 'some' brewing methods 'tasted even better,' when the coffee was 'broken' into similar-sized pieces.

We still follow that procedure today. For example, a 'coarse' grind is preferred for 'French Presses' with large filters; while, 'fine or extra-fine' grinds work best with 'Espresso Machines' or when brewing Turkish coffee. But then, this is where personal (or 'Snobby') taste can come into play too! The general rule of Baristas today, say: *"Whatever brewing method one uses, a 'fine enough,' filter must be used to catch any grounds which would, otherwise, pass through to the brewed coffee in the cup."* Another option, however, would be to use a 'coarser' grind! For example, a 'fine' grind, if used in a French Press, will leave bitter 'mud' (grounds) in the bottom of the cup, unless additionally filtered! Plus, different grinds are going to 'brew and taste' differently, according to the brewing method.

Question: *"I would like to roast coffee beans as a hobby. Where do I find Green Coffee Beans? They do not seem to be in the Supermarket with the other coffees!"*

Answer: Most grocery stores or supermarkets do not carry 'Green' Coffee Beans – unless, they are a 'Specialty or Gourmet Store' of some kind. However, there are several ways to buy 'Green Beans.'

First, as Green Coffee Beans (if properly stored) have a long shelf life, it is safe enough to find a source 'Online;' and buy them directly from the growers or roasting companies. However, by buying 'online,' who knows what one is getting unless buying from a 'substantial dealer;' who has an excellent reputation to uphold. Secondly, many Coffee Houses/Bars sell both green and roasted beans to their customers. This may be an effective way to buy a 'good mixture' of tasty beans. A third way, is to look for a 'local

Roastery;' who roasts the beans to sell to many, smaller, Coffee Houses –
these, sometimes, are the Coffee Houses which 'sell' some of the
'bagged/roasted' beans as their 'own brand.'

I prefer to buy directly from a 'local' Roaster. Beans are 'fresher,' and less
expensive; as the 'middleman' and 'shipping and handling' have been
removed! This is, also, a 'clever 'way to get to know ones 'Roaster;' as he/she
can recommend 'different beans' or mix 'custom blends' of beans for you.
This can even apply to 'high and low' altitude beans as well as types; for one
to 'custom blend' one own, 'home roast.'

My local 'Roaster,' sells to both individuals and 'Restaurant/Beverage
Supply' companies (as well as selling their own 'brand' of bean; and, they have
become the biggest 'Coffee Roaster/Supplier' in town! The most popular
'Coffee Bar' in town (whom, also, 'franchises' brewed coffee in many stores
and bookstores, and sells their own 'brand' of bagged, roasted beans)
purchase their beans from this same, local Roaster... whom is more than
happy to put the Coffee Bar's label and logo on the bags! Technically, I could
say that I brew this 'famous brand coffee' myself – even though, the bag my
coffee beans come in does not carry the franchise name or logo!

'Relabeling' is a widespread practice among many brands of the most
products! For example, I remember taking a tour of the, now defunct,
'Olympia Brewing Company' in Tumwater, Washington. They had a wall
covered in both cans and bottles of different beer brands (and of different
prices) – which, they admitted were all "*Oly*!"

"*We love you to purchase our Olympia Beer*," the tour guide told us, "*But if you
want to purchase by 'price...' any of these other brands will work for you... as they are all
the same beer!*"

I did it myself with Vitamins once! I carried my 'own brand' of 'Chico
Holistic Healthcare Vitamins;' with my company name, logo, and label. They
were the same as what one could find in any Drug Store, under the store's
name! However, I could sell them cheaper to my patients!

It is, often, the same way with many Coffee Wholesalers and Roasters!
These 'Wholesalers' may sell to some of the larger Grocery Stores in town as
well. Everyone has seen them in stores; large, overhead or upright 'bins,'
which dispense 'loose' beans for the consumer to 'bag' themselves. However,
I have, yet, seen any grocery store or chain sell 'Green Coffee Beans'... not

to say there are none! Surprisingly, many 'Wholesalers' will also sell 'Retail' Green Beans to private individuals like me! But the easiest way to purchase is through the Internet!

Question: *"Do I need to purchase special, 'Dark Roasted Coffee' for my Espresso maker? Alternatively, can I use any roast… light or dark?"*

Answer: Technically, <u>any</u> <u>roast</u> may be used to make Espresso – even 'flavored' beans – although, traditionally, it is a 'Medium Dark' (or Espresso) Roast which is used in most Coffee Bars! Technically, this is because of many 'smaller' Coffee Bars (wanting to use a 'cheaper bean' to make their Espresso) think that a 'Dark Roast' will 'hide' the cheapness of the coffee. However, as previously mentioned, it is the 'grind' (extra fine) which is the most crucial factor in Espresso; otherwise, the 'flavor' of the Espresso, is a 'matter of taste!'

Question: *"I bought some roasted coffee beans which turned out to be a 'lighter roast' than what I prefer. Unfortunately, for me, I bought a 5-pound bag – to save money. My question is, can I 're-roast' the beans to make a 'darker' roast?"*

Answer: *"Re-roasting' coffee beans…"* good question; I wish I had a 'good' answer for you. 'Re-roasting' can cause beans to lose some of their 'delicate' qualities – as once the beans have 'cooled,' they cannot be 'recooked' once again with the same, typical results. However, I have heard some people do 're-roast' their coffee beans to obtain a 'unique' flavor; which I would have to presume, would be an 'acquired' taste!

Unless experienced with 'Roasting' Coffee Beans, I would try one or more of a few different things first – before, attempting 're-roasting:'

1: Never purchase any beans of which you may be 'unsure' of! However, this should go without saying!

2: 'Mix' your 'undesirable' beans with some 'really delicious' beans (or roast) that you do enjoy. Most likely, you will not like this coffee mixture as well as what you, usually, enjoy; but it could give you a 'unique' new flavor.

3: My personal choice before anything else, try grinding the beans to a 'finer or coarser' grind. This, alone, could make a difference!

4: Try brewing the grind by a different method. For example, I have had some 'Drip' coffee made with what I would call an 'inferior' bean; however, when brewed in a 'French Press,' I have found I have enjoyed it a lot more!

5: Use a lot of 'flavored' Creamers or Syrups' in your coffee!

"I like coffee exceedingly..."

~ (Attributed to) H.P. Lovecraft

ROASTING COFFEE BEANS

First, a question before getting into details:

Question: *"What is a 'Roast' Name?"*

Answer: 'Roast names' can be varied – according to what is accepted by 'Roasters' as standard; or, by the Roasters own 'branding.' Many beans are available in 'Light, Medium, or Dark' roasts – but, can have similar characteristics; for example, 'Cinnamon and Light Cinnamon roasts.' Many people would be 'hard-pressed' to tell the difference between some roasted beans! However, the following list shows examples of the most common 'Roast Names' which any coffee drinker should know:

- **American** – 'Medium-brown' in roast color; which can come from assorted varieties and tastes 'lighter' than other roasts.

- **Cinnamon** – Similar to 'American,' a 'medium-brown' color; and may come from 'mixed' beans.

- **Dark French** – A quite 'dark' and 'oily looking' roast – often confused with Italian Roast, but with 'sweetness' and 'low' body.

- **Death Wish** – Is a high caffeine content, 'dark roast;' but which is, really, a brand – and not a Roasters term. It is not a roast type – but I have included it here; as there are a lot of 'Coffee Snobs' whom, mistakenly, 'think' it is a 'particular' roast!

- **Espresso** – A 'medium, deep brown' (or darker) roast with just a hint of 'oil' on its surface. It tends to be full-bodied; with sweetness and a caramel flavor, due to it 'carbonized' sugars.

- **French** – A 'deep brown' roast; which appears slightly 'oily.' It has low acidity; and may taste and smell slightly 'burnt.'

- **Full City** – A 'medium-brown' roast; which, like Viennese, is evenly balanced in flavor, body, and aroma.

- **Green Beans** – Coffee Beans which have not, yet, been Roasted.

- **Italian** – A very 'dark and burnt' tasting roast, with a lot of surface oil; but with very little acidity and body.

- **Liberian** – Not only a Roast but a bean type. Generally, a 'dark and oily' roast. Sometimes, depending upon the roaster, tasting 'burnt.'

- **Light Cinnamon** – (not to be confused with Cinnamon), Is 'light-tan' in color; and slightly 'sour…' with little body.

- **New England: a.k.a. Light Brown** – Which, is, also, its color. It tends to be one of the more 'inexpensive' coffees.

- **Spanish** – A 'Dark brown,' and very 'oily,' coffee; considered a 'burnt' coffee with a charcoal taste.

- **Viennese** – A 'medium-brown' roast; quite mild and balanced.

- **White** – Coffee beans which have been roasted at a lower temperature, and for a shorter time. Roasted beans are still, somewhat, 'greenish' in color, rather than actual 'white;' and have a, slight, 'nutty' flavor and lack body. Beans are very hard; and can damage some grinders.

- **Zebra** – A rare mixture of both light and dark roasts; which, generally, are only produced locally in some coffee markets.

More about Roasting – as in 'Home.'

First, an essential word about 'Home Roasting…' "*Don't…*" that is, unless one is a real, 'do-it-yourselfer;' then, it can be a great and rewarding hobby – just like, 'Home Brewing' of Craft Beer!

Personally, I receive great satisfaction from choosing my mixture of 'green beans;' then, roasting them to perfection!

There are countless ways to roast beans; such as, in a 'handheld' device - held over a burner or fire (such as the 'Whirley Pop' shown here), a Wok on a stove, a BBQ, an 'Air' Popcorn Popper, 'Countertop Roasters,' Big Drum Roasters, Electric Coffee Roasting 'Pots,' ovens and many more! It is, however, effortless to '<u>burn</u>' beans; not to mention, challenging to achieve consistent results every time – unless, one has something of a 'mechanized' Roaster with an adjustable temperature setting, automatic 'stirrer,' and timer! Therefore, most people who choose their green beans, have also 'made a deal' with the seller to 'roast the beans' for them, to a chosen darkness. This is one way to ensure <u>consistency</u> from 'batch to batch' of beans! Remember, however, each year, every farm and crop of beans are going to be different, due to 'growing conditions;' and every Roasting Company employee, may have their '<u>own</u>' way of 'mixing' beans or running the machines! So, roasted coffees may vary from batch to batch of the same beans!

However, if one is going to roast beans themselves, and looking for a suitable method, a 'Stovetop Popcorn Popper' (with a crank, such as the 'Whirley Pop' shown on the previous page) works quite well; as it has a 'stirrer' built into it. Many 'roasting (or popcorn) devices,' like the 'Whirley Pop,' can be found in stores for less than $30.00. Some models can even have a 'thermometer' added to the top of them if desired. Growing up, this was how we used to roast coffee beans on a camp stove or over a campfire while on vacation; and, we (as kids) loved using it; even though we did not drink the coffee afterward – and nobody ever worried about 'bean temperature' back in those days!

Plan on 'roasting' a small batch, for five or more minutes – depending upon 'how hot' ones' fire is – then, add time if necessary! I do this over my barbeque; as I can control the heat more accurately. I, generally, roast over 'medium' heat for, 8 to 10 minutes – with, continued stirring. If roasting often, one should keep accurate records regarding 'bean type,' volume, temperatures, how many minutes of roasting, and so forth! If one wants '<u>consistent</u>' results, however (and should you have 'tugged' on your left ear the first time roasting), you had damn well better, 'tug on the ear' once again to duplicate any results! Seldom, I have found, can I, fully, 'duplicate' results!

Many people wonder about the 'Chaff' (the little flakes of 'dried husk' which come off the bean while roasting) at this point. I use a can of 'Compress Air' (or better yet, my breath) to 'blow Chaff off' while the beans are roasting! Regardless of roasting methods, Chaffe can easily be 'blown off' after roasting too. Just do not let it build up within a  roaster – such as an electric, Air Popcorn Popper; as it can become a fire hazard. Luckily, with most 'Air Poppers,' the Chaffe will 'blow out' the device front as it is created! Even a 'hot air' hair dryer can be used to remove Chaffe! I do this, sometimes, when roasting in an open Wok; and, it helps to control the temperature as well!

[41]

What does one do if they do not own a Wok or Popcorn Popper? Any kettle may be used; even it does not have a lid. Lids or covers, however, will promote faster roasting – but, do not be surprised in the bottom of the kettle 'scorches' a bit – as it is difficult to 'stir' the beans when a top is added. Personally, if not using my 'pre-heated' Wok; I will use a 'Dutch Oven/Kettle;' as, I can stir the beans easily, every minute or so, with a long-handled, wooden or plastic spoon… without spilling any beans! Moreover, I can start it off with the lid on to 'pre-heat' to the initial temperature. The Chaff is easily 'blown off' as well; as 'Compressed Air' will not 'blow out' the beans due to the 'tall sides' of the Dutch Oven!

Whereas we have always been strong advocates of 'do it yourself' in our household, experience tells us that roasting one's 'green beans' may not be the most practical thing to do – at least, not at first! Moreover, it is not like, simply, 'roasting something in the oven!' The main issue to worry about (besides 'over or under' roasting) is the 'smell' of the roasting beans; as it can be intense! In my former home – before the devastating 'Camp Fire' (in which almost my entire town of Paradise, California was devastated) – my next-door neighbor would often complain when I roasted beans outside (or even barbequed Chicken for that matter)! We, now, live on 3.5 acres, surrounded by orchards, so the smell of 'roasting coffee' is no longer an issue!

Another easy way to roast is to use an (previously mentioned) electric, 'Hot Air Popcorn Popper.' Just throw in a handful or two of beans into a pre-heated 'Popper' and wait for 6 to 8 minutes – the hot air stirs the beans for you; and they evenly, roast. Of course, sometimes it is nice to modify the popper with temperature gauges or more! Temperature can be controlled by simply turning on and off the appliance for several seconds; or, again, 'blowing in' some canned, compressed air. Modification plans for Poppers can be found all over the internet for different brands of Poppers! In any event, as with the previous methods, roasting beans is something that one should do outside – as it is going to both 'smoke and stink up' a house! Just remember to use a bowl, sink or box to catch any 'Chaff' which 'blows off' the roasting beans; unless one does not mind a small amount 'blowing' into their yard. Of 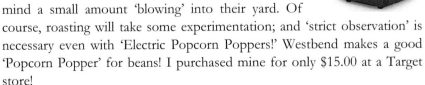 course, roasting will take some experimentation; and 'strict observation' is necessary even with 'Electric Popcorn Poppers!' Westbend makes a good 'Popcorn Popper' for beans! I purchased mine for only $15.00 at a Target store!

Again, most 'Coffee Snobs' would be reluctant to use this method – preferring to buy an actual 'Home Coffee Roaster' with a built-in 'catalytic converter' to arrest (stop) most of the smoke and smell. Also, the beauty of those units is that they can be used 'indoors' for the most part – and have enormous 'bragging rights!' Unfortunately, 'Popcorn Poppers, Woks, or Kettles' do not have much in the way of 'bragging rights!' Nevertheless, I do know some 'Roasting' enthusiasts ('Coffee Snobs'), who enjoy this method; as it is fun for the whole family – if easily entertained, that is!

However, there is one more way to roast; of which I have heard a few people in various Groups brag about… that is very much like "*Roughing it;*" and, I have done so myself while camping and at home – as the photograph below shows!

Taking an old pan of some sort (I use the same 'double' tray/pan that I use for 'smoldering wood' on my grill when 'smoking meat) I line it with Aluminum Foil and set it on my 'pre-heated' grill. Then, I fill it with 'Green' coffee beans. I happen to like to either use a long-handled spoon, or a pair of BBQ tongs – as shown here, to keep the beans 'stirred' while roasting. Shown, are the equivalent of 'two' pots of coffee, once ground and brewed. Moreover, with this type of pan, I can 'roast' two different coffees at the same time.

Closing the lid of the Grill, I will allow the beans to roast for one minute; before opening the grill and stirring the beans. I do this repeatedly, for four minutes; but not forgetting to 'blow-off' any Chaff which appears. After 4 minutes, I will open the lid of the Grill, and watch the beans roast for the remaining time – still, stirring them as they 'roast.' One does not want to use compressed air to blow off Chaff with this method; as it will be 'too strong;' and will 'blow' the beans out of the pan or tray! Although, it cannot be seen in the above photograph, the beans on the left for Espresso, and the beans on the right are for French Press. The burner on the right side of the grill is turned off a minute or two (approximately at the six-minute mark) before the left-side – and the tray turned so that only one side is over the heat.

The beans on the left continue to roast, and the beans on the right begin to cool – especially, when stirring. Of course, this is only possible through 'time and experience;' to keep from either 'over-roasting' or 'under-roasting' the beans on either side.

[43]

When finished roasting (8 to 10 minutes – and through observation of 'roast color'), remove the tray/pan from the heat and allow the beans to cool for several minutes; then, place the beans in a mill and 'grind' to the desired degree. The grind is, then, ready for a coffee maker of some sort – unless 'Blooming' is needed – and one will have the 'freshest' cup of coffee imaginable! However, even without 'Blooming,' one might want to allow the 'freshly roasted' beans to 'degas' for an hour or more – especially, after grinding (I prefer, 'after' grinding); however, this can depend upon ones,' personal, taste.

Does the 'home roasting' taste good? Perhaps, if not 'burnt' or 'under-roasted;' but that might be debatable by some 'Snobs.' However, there is something to be said for the 'rewarding feeling' one feels, from starting with 'Green Beans,' and ending up with a cup of 'time-consuming' coffee – which could rival the 'big name' Coffee Houses! Frankly, I enjoy my beans more – and do not know any other 'self-roaster' who does not – besides, people whom 'home roast' are more 'forgiving' of their coffee taste!

'Coffee Bean Roasting,' works with the most <u>consistent</u> results, when using an actual commercial brand, coffee 'Roasting' device; which can be expensive! Good Roasters start around $175.00 – and can 'reach up' to the thousands of dollars! However, again, it does make for an enjoyable hobby or family project when using cheaper methods! Nonetheless, 'hobby' or 'family bonding' time aside, as it is so easy to either 'scorch or under-roast' the beans, it is generally best to leave the roasting to those who are <u>experienced</u> with such a process; or purchase a quality 'Home Roaster' – which comes with a thermometer, has adjustable heat, automatically 'stirs' or 'tumbles' the beans, and has a built-in 'Catalytic Converter,' to keep from 'smoking and smelling up' ones' home or neighbors!

I know that I just said the coffee roasting "*Can be expensive*;" but there are several excellent, and reasonably priced brands of 'Countertop Roasters' available in both stores and online. For example, the 'Breville, French Roast,' and 'Nesco' brands are good machines; and are sold, generally, for under $200.00. Often, one can find 'used' Roasters for sale for under $100.00 – and they have only been used once or twice. Why? Because people will try roasting once and hate it; due to the results (usually bad, the first few times), and smell! Surprisingly, I have found it is, usually, the 'Coffee Snobs' who give up the Roasters after only a few tries!

Most 'Coffee Snobs' leave the roasting to the 'gourmet' Coffee Houses; and, consumers can purchase 'fresh' roasts there! However, there are some of us whom genuinely enjoy 'cooking or baking' from scratch; and once learned, 'Coffee Bean Roasting' can be a great hobby; not to mention, the best way to get the freshest and delicious 'Cup of Joe' possible! Moreover, the smell that comes from roasting beans... well, what can I say! Just the smell of freshly roasted and ground beans is enough to encourage some people to have a cup – unless, 'burning' the beans; and they end up smelling 'skunky!'

Contrary to popular belief, 'Roasting' is not that difficult to learn; and is something akin to 'wine or beer' making! The best results come with time, patience, and practice! Over time, the real 'Coffee Connoisseur,' will find that they are saving up to 50% of the overall cost of their coffee!

My advice for 'Home Roasting,' is to start with some simple roasting methods – such as a Wok on a grill, or a simple, Electric Hot Air Popcorn Popper! If you enjoy the effort and results, move on to a $200.00, Countertop Roaster!

Back to questions:

"Morning sex, or morning coffee... decisions, decisions!"

~ (Attributed to) Unknown

Question: *"I drink a lot of coffee; and I purchase 'Roasted Beans' at the grocery store… but, prefer to 'grind' them at home in my own device, rather than at the store. This way, I can have the 'freshest' ground coffee each time I brew! I grind my beans in my Food Processor – but, I could swear that my coffee tastes a bit different every time I make it; even though, I am using the same beans! A friend tells me, I am 'grinding' my beans wrong. Is there a 'right or wrong' way to grind coffee beans?"*

Answer: It sounds like you have a good 'taster!' Remember, 'ground coffee' started just being beans 'crushed by a rock,' over a thousand years ago. From that, came hammers, rolling pins, or anything else heavy enough to 'break' the hard, roasted bean! Few cared 'how coarse or fine' the bean grind was; as 'coffee grind and brewing knowledge' was not conceived yet! People just learned, through experience, that 'smaller chunks' seemed to make better coffee! So, today, 'size-grinding beans' and 'brewing/enjoying coffee,' is a 'subjective' thing; as it seems 'everyone' has an opinion, and everyone has <u>different</u> taste! Different sized 'grinds' are going to give <u>different</u> 'tastes;' as more or less of the beans 'ground surface' is exposed to the brewing water!

A true connoisseur or 'Coffee Snob,' may say, *"There is only one way to grind beans… with a Burr Grinder;"* but, this is far from the truth! There is no 'right or wrong' way to grind beans – providing, one enjoys the results… moreover, that would include '<u>pounding</u> them <u>with</u> a <u>rock</u>' or using a 'Spice' grinder as in the 17th century!

However, <u>there</u> <u>are</u> some ways, 'better' than others, to grind coffee beans; and a variety of methods may be needed, as 'different brewers' require 'different sized' grinds! It is surprising how 'different' even just a subtle change can be, between grinds! Just yesterday (at this writing), for example, my son and I took a 'Coffee Tasting' class given by a nearby Roaster (yes, we still pursue education, because everything changes… often)! Along with tasting a difference between water temperatures, we tasted the difference between just 'one notch' on a commercial coffee grinder – going with what the coffee grounds 'should have been' for the brewer we were using, then comparing them to a 'slightly coarser' grind…. all, of course, with the same batch of roasted beans! We, then, did the same thing with 'one grind finer' than suggested too. It was difficult to 'see' much difference in grinds! However, we quickly found a difference in taste, body, acidity, and aroma! It was amazing! Just the slight 'variation' in the grind, amounted to whether the coffee tasted 'fruity, sour, bold;' or, even 'how oily' the coffee was in the cup!

In general, 'grinding' should match the 'brewing process' first; then, be 'augmented' through 'trial and error' for 'ground size;' for proper extraction and flavor. For example, one would not want to put a 'Coarse' Grind into an Espresso Machine – as it needs an 'Ultra-Fine' grind to extract the best flavor. However, the 'individual,' might prefer the taste a slightly coarser, 'Medium-Fine' grind over the recommended, 'Ultra-Fine!' Again, taste is a 'subjective' thing!

A 'Food Processor' can be acceptable to use; providing it 'grinds' the way one likes… however, it works like a blender – 'crashing' the blade into the beans. The beans are 'pulverized;' meaning, 'cut and pounded' into little, odd-shaped pieces. Think of it this way: if one were to take a coffee bean, and set it on a solid surface, then using a hammer, hit it as hard as they could… the bean would 'fly apart' in different sized pieces. Close observation would show, some pieces would be 'fine dust;' while others might be 'large chunks!' If a 'micro-cup' of coffee could, somehow, be brewed from that one, 'crushed' bean, it would taste (and perhaps, even look and smell) quite different than if all its crushed pieces were the same, uniform size! When 'enough' coffee is used for actual brewing, it is easy to see and taste this same thing. Depending upon the brewing method, the difference in 'ground size' can make the difference between a 'bitter' tasting coffee, or a 'mild' one! Unfortunately, using a 'Food Processor,' is not going to, always, give a 'uniform' size to a grind!

Therefore, I recommend 'experimentation' with 'Grind Sizes' to all my Coffee Students; and keep good 'records;' even when using the same water, brewer, temperature; as 'close looking' grinds, can taste quite different from cup to cup!

As previously mentioned, my grandmother's method was something like using a 'food processor' in the late 1800's; as using her 'Marble Rolling Pin' on a hard, Marble surface, 'pulverized' the beans! Nonetheless, it worked great for making 'boiled,' Cowboy-type Coffee; as there was no 'specifically chosen' grind size (nor 'canned' coffee) for her to purchase in those days, at a grocery store!

It may sound strange, but it is a fact; 'grind size' can release different amounts of flavor, oils, essences, acids, et cetera; depending upon brewing methods. If it did not matter, we would all place a handful of 'Whole Beans' into our coffee makers!

'Whole Beans' <u>can</u> work – at least, under certain circumstances and to a certain degree; but they are not going to give the person brewing, the best tasting (or strongest) cup of coffee!

A good experiment is to grind both a 'medium-fine' and 'coarse' grind out of the same coffee beans – then, using the same brewer (preferably, a 'Drip' coffee maker) make a cup or pot of coffee out of each. Taste the difference! There <u>will</u> be one! One may even 'see or smell' a difference! 'Experimenting' is how one is going to 'learn' what they like best! Again, just be sure to keep accurate notes! One might even try using 'whole beans;' to see what coffee was like, back in the early 1700's! Not surprisingly, brewing an equal amount of 'whole beans,' as opposed to 'ground beans,' will make a much 'weaker' brew (as seen in the third photograph below) – again, this is because there is less 'surface area' to the 'Whole Beans;' as opposed to the surface area of the 'ground' beans! The coffee looks like very 'weak tea!'

If one were to try to create 'similar' grinds with a 'food processor, blender, or blade grinder,' they might find they have a different tasting coffee once again – and, it would be difficult to duplicate! Only through testing, timing, examination, record-keeping, experience, and trial and error, can one always create the proper-sized 'grind' with a 'blade grinder, blender, or food processor,' for the type of brewing they enjoy!

Regardless of how one grinds, refer to any <u>notes</u> taken; and attempt to 'grind' the same way once again. In other words, the same kind of beans, the same roast, the same amount (weight) of beans, the same setting and amount of time grinding, the same brewer, the same temperature of the water, et cetera! We call this 'Standardizing' on ones' coffee, grind, and brewer!

Using Burr Grinders, however, can cut a lot of trial and error steps; as the 'Burrs' (gear-like grinders) 'grind' beans into uniform size every time! As a general fact, it is presumed by many people, that the *"More expensive the grinder, the more 'uniform' the grind is going to be*;" and, there are actually 'Coffee Snobs' whom claim they can *"Taste a difference between coffee ground in a $50.00 Burr Grinder and a $200.00 Burr Grinder."* Some 'Snobs,' even claim they can *"Taste the difference between a $200.00 grinder and a $2000.00 one*!" Frankly, I cannot tell much difference between the 'cheapest' of grinders (when done by someone who knows what they are doing) and a $2000.00 Grinder!

The thought by experts is, *"Burrs are going to give you, all degrees of grinds, in all sizes chosen… individually, all the time."* This uniformity is how Coffee Houses, and even brewers at home, can make the 'same tasting' coffee every time; and, 'standardization' does make sense when trying to, consistently, create the same brew and taste, repeatedly! Of course, different plantation 'batches' can make a difference in taste too; but we are presuming here, that one has a pound or more of the same beans at home to 'grind' over time.

Old style, Burr Grinders, however – notably, the antique 'Hand Burr Mills' (like what my family used) – tended to 'grind beans,' only, into a 'Medium/Coarse' grind – which most coffee brewers (pots or percolators) required at the time. Generally, even though these machines had a 'long life,' when they 'wore out,' they were just 'thrown out!'

Some modern devices, however, may have 'Replaceable Burrs' as an option; so that they may be replaced, due to wear! However, with most recent, 'Electric Burr Grinders,' there are settings from 'Ultra-fine' to 'Ultra-Coarse' – so that, not only 'different brewer' requirements be met, but the drinkers 'specific tastes' be considered as well! However, some 'Coffee Snobs' may not find even this is enough; and will own different 'Burrs' or 'Professional Grinders' for the standardization of 'different grinds, brands, types, or flavors' of beans!

Alternatively, as one 'Coffee Snob' in a group once told me, *"Beans are irreverent! It is money, that determines 'how good' my coffee tastes*!" You know… he could be right!

Now, let us look at the different types of Coffee Grinders, their options, and their Burrs:

GRINDING, GRINDERS, AND MILLS

Starting back when 'Mills' were first started being purchased by families – around the middle of 17th century (and up through the Great Depression) – grinding roasted coffee beans was something of an event – especially, for families… moreover, frankly, it smelled great! 'Grinders were called 'Mills' (more of a forgotten term, today) in those days; similar devices, which are still used today by  'hobbyists,' and are used to 'grind' grains into flour. Perhaps, the term 'Grinder' became popular, as the 'Burrs' (gears) of the device, tended to 'grind' the beans into powder! The 'Mill' shown above is a miniature model of what my grandparents and parents used.

In my parents' family, back on the farm in Minnesota, the chore of 'grinding coffee beans) fell upon the 'family kids!' – they would be given the chore of 'grinding' the beans; just as they would be assigned 'churning' the butter, or 'cranking' the ice cream maker! The kids thought it was 'fun;' and the parents did not have to do the work! My father 'passed down' the same activity when my sister and I reached an age, old enough, to be trusted to properly; 'turn ice cream,' 'popping' popcorn, or 'grind beans!' Fortunately for we 'kids,' we had a small, electric grinder, by that time, for coffee!

My families 'large,' farm grinders 'hopper' would be filled with roasted coffee beans (purchased or traded for with a local merchant), and its crank would be turned. The internal cutting burrs, along with gravity, pulled the beans down through them – where they were (hopefully) all cut to a standard size! Seldom, however, was there ever a choice of grinds – at least, at home; but then, there was not much of a selection of 'roasts,' types of coffee, or brewing methods in those days either.

Coffee was purchased (or traded for) by my Grandfather, in 'burlap bags' at a 'neighborhood' market or hardware store; and 'ground' – either by the store owner/employee or taken home to grind. A small portion of the beans, then, was either 'boiled' or 'perked' in a Coffee Pot or Percolator at home on a stove. In fact, my father once told me, he could not remember a time in which there was not a pot of coffee sitting on the stove… day or night! Oddly enough, our family 'type' of the old grinder, was used for both coffee and nuts! Surprisingly, its 'type' is still used by many people today!

'True Coffee Snobs,' may use an 'Antique Grinder – even though it might have only one setting – as there still is a certain degree of 'Bragging Rights' which go along with antiques. Not surprisingly, <u>most</u> coffee 'connoisseurs,' probably, would not use an antique grinder any more than they would a blender or food processor to grind their beans!

'Hand Grinders' are still made today; although, unless purposely made to look 'antique,' they have evolved into 'slim and streamlined' tools; which may be 'set' for many different grinds. The photograph shown to the left is the 'manual,' Hand Grinder I own and use. It has <u>18</u> <u>levels</u> (more, technically) of 'grind settings' to choose from; and I find that it is much <u>consistent</u> than an electric machine! When it comes to grinding 'ultra-fine' grounds for Espresso or Turkish coffee, it is even 'more accurate' than the $200.00 model my local store has! However, when it comes to a 'medium' or 'coarse' grind, I find that there will be 'smaller particles' mixed into the grind as well… what we call *"Fines."* These 'fine particles' ('Mud') are what one will find in the 'bottom of their cup,' after drinking.

Today, unless we roast the beans ourselves, many stores – even Costco and Sam's Club – have at least one, 'commercial grinder' which is available for the customer to use. Most look like the device shown below – only cleaner; and would cost between $200.00 - $2000.00 to purchase.

Usage is easy; as the knob on the front allows the customer to choose which 'degree of grind,' for 'which type' of the brewer use. If there is any confusion regarding 'degrees of a grind' for one's coffee maker, there are simple 'illustrations' on the machine for each 'grind listing;' to show 'which grinds' works best with 'which coffee brewer!' Grinding at the store, is an excellent way for the 'Coffee Novice' to start – as they can 'tailor' the grind to suit their own, personal taste. For example, while I make more 'Electric Drip' type coffee than anything else, I started with the 'middle, Electric Drip' setting on the machine – some machines, one might note, will have two to three settings for each brewer. However, through experimentation, I found that I preferred the next, 'finer,' grind when using 'flavored' coffee; such as Chocolate Macadamia Nut beans.

[51]

'Trial and error' are how one is going to find 'just the right grind' for themselves! However, I recently had someone tell me, "*I cannot buy a pound of every grind to try, and then throw away, if I do not like it! It costs too much!*" Well, this can be true for many people. But, who says, one "*Has to,*" buy a <u>whole</u> <u>pound</u> of ground coffee? For example, later in this book, I include photographs of grinds done with a machine like the one shown on the previous page – as I wanted to show 'real,' commercial machine grinds. So, knowing that the

'commercial device' I use has 'two' settings for most grinds – except 'Turkish' or 'Pulverized' – before leaving home for the store, I took a Magic Marker and wrote separately on 11 small, plastic bags the words, "*Turkish, Fine #1, Fine #2, Medium, Medium #1,*" and so on, up the scale to "*Pulverized!*" This method was especially handy for 'learning' the difference in 'size' or 'coarseness' of the grounds!

Each small bag used (found for sale in most grocery stores), can hold up to 1 cup of dry material; and is marked in ¼ cup increments. Once at the store – and after making my bean selection – I placed a large 'handful' of coffee beans in the machine's hopper. I then turned on the grinder, set it for the first setting (Turkish), and filled the first bag to the '¼ cup mark' with the ground coffee – and marked it 'Turkish' with my marking pen!

Before placing a new bag on the machine, I change to the next level of grinding – while the machine was still running. I, then, marked the next bag 'Fine #1," and once again, filled it to the '¼ cup...' just as I had done with the 'Turkish' grind. I did this again for the following two grind settings; giving me <u>four</u> different grinds to try in my Espresso maker. I did not grind any more beans, knowing, that I would not use any 'coarser' grind than a 'Fine #3,' in my Espresso Machine.

From that point, I continued '<u>up</u>' the 'grinder scale;' filling 'marked bags' for my 'Drip' coffee maker – but now, I filled each bag to the '½ cup' level to match what I use in my 10 cup, 'Drip' machine. Remember, purchasing a whole pound of grind is not necessary for testing; regardless of the device or method! Just keep, proper, notes as to 'how much' of each bean/grind you might use! 'Notes' are necessary when using different brewing methods, or beans and roasts; as it is difficult for most people to remember the differences between all the different brewers and 'chosen' roasts!

Each plastic bag filled, went into one of the 'Paper, Coffee Bags' supplied by the store for ground coffee. Yes, one is 're-paying in weight' for the already purchased plastic bags; but we are only talking pennies here!

Special Note: If one is going 'standardize,' they might wish to go to their grocery store early in the morning or late in the evening; to keep from monopolizing the coffee grinder for too long. Now, just by buying one (plus or minus) pound of beans, one can have enough coffee grounds to make 'entire pots' of each 'grind size' for themselves to try and compare.

Does one have to do this with all the settings on the grinder? No. I just did it with eleven of the most popular grind sizes that I might use, with the 'limited choice' grinder at my local store; but many grinders have eighteen or more selections for 'fine-tuning' coffee. I knew I would not like 'Coarse Grind,' Drip Coffee… however, I tried it anyway! The 'average' coffee drinker should try two or three of the 'recommended' grinds for their brewer. The difference between 'Medium #1, Medium #2 and Medium #3,' is amazing! If one 'owns' a coffee grinder, this is very easy (and fun) to test!

Through trying different grinds (yes, this can be a waste of a pot of coffee if not drunk), one can decide exactly *"Which grind"* they prefer for flavor, strength, body, aroma, fruitiness, color, and more. I found that with my 'Drip' Brewer, I preferred a 'Medium/Coarse' grind; rather, than the recommended 'Medium/Medium' grind. However, I tend to prefer a 'Medium #1' in my French Press – which should require a 'Coarse' grind! However, a 'Coarse/Coarse' grind for my 'Clever Dripper' brewer seems to taste best to me… all, from the same beans!

One might notice I mention 'notes' on several pages; I keep detailed notes dealing with the roast/bean types, different brewers, and modest changes in grinds… not to mention filters! Often, my notes look like the photograph I have here.

Again, one does not have to do this with every setting! If they are reasonably 'sure' that they would not use a 'Turkish' grind in their 'Drip' or other coffee makers… do not grind it! Only purchase enough of any grind to make enough coffee to sample –

2019 Grinds For Brewers

Drip Brewer
Breakfast Roast Beans: Medium/Fine Grind – Double Filter, Mesh and Paper
Dark Roast/Black Silk Beans: Medium Coarse Grind – Double Filter, Mesh and Paper

Keurig
Breakfast Roast Beans: Medium/Coarse Grind – Paper in Pod
Dark Roast/Black Silk Beans: Medium Grind– Paper in Pod

French Press
Breakfast Roast Beans: Medium/Coarse Grind – Pour through Filter
Dark Roast/Black Silk Beans: Coarse Grind – Pour through Filter

Clever Dripper
Breakfast Roast Beans: Coarse Grind – Single Filter
Dark Roast/Black Silk Beans: Coarse Grind – Single Filter

Primula
Breakfast Roast Beans: Coarse Grind – Cone Paper Filter in Metal Cone
Dark Roast/Black Silk Beans: Coarse/Medium Grind – Paper Filter in Metal Cone

Moka Pot
Breakfast Roast Beans: Fine #1 Grind – No Filter or Pour Over if Requested
Dark Roast/Black Silk Beans: Fine #3 Grind – No Filter or Pour Over if Requested

Espresso Machine
Dark Roast/Black Silk Beans: Fine #3 Coarse Grind – No Filter

preferably, with family or friends! However, for teaching classes, I will often grind all degrees of coffee; to allow students to 'taste' the subtle differences – even, with 'Turkish' grounds – in a 'Pour-Over' brewer! I would suggest, one start with the 'recommend grind' for the brewer; then, go one setting above and one setting below the recommendation for comparison. This 'standardization,' will determine all future 'grinds' for ones, particular, brewer – at least, with 'this years' crop of beans. Ideally, next year's batch (or another brand/type of beans) will require a similar test. Different roasts/types of beans are exactly 'why' I wish to own a grinder! I can change my grounds to suit not only the beans, but the brewer and water temperature as well! I only need to keep 'notes' as to 'what' I enjoyed best; so, I can 'duplicate' results the next time – and, this is especially, important for my students!

Grinders come in many forms and styles – but, in only <u>three</u>, basic, types – being either electric, battery-powered, or manual! Sometimes, they are 'built-in' to the brewer, itself! Most 'Blade Mills' are electric; and are not available in too many models. However, Burr grinders come in, not only, several models and styles, but in both 'manual and electric' models – and the 'Burrs' can be made of Stainless Steel, Cast Aluminum, Ceramic, or other materials. They can be Block, Flat, Conical/Disc, or 'Masticating' in style.

Unfortunately, there is more to 'grinding' these days than just putting beans into a grinder and 'switching on!' As with 'brewing Espresso,' over the past few hundred years, apparently, we have been 'grinding beans' wrong all this time; regardless of our 'grinding methods' – according, to the 'Coffee Snobs,' that is! However, 'things' <u>are</u> different, now, than they were a few hundred years ago!

For Example, there is something called, the 'RDT' (Ross Droplet Technique) method of grinding beans; which 'boils down' to 'wetting' the beans with a drop or two water (or other liquid) before grinding. It is supposed to reduce static in the grinder, thus, eliminate dust; and give an 'accurate weight' of the ground beans! Some of my students and patients use Colloidal Silver as their wetting agent; however, others do not use any 'wetting' agent at all! They use an 'anti-static' gun or photographic 'Static-Master' to 'zap' both the beans and the grinder, to eliminate 'static!' Just do not overdo the wetting process!

Let us look some more at 'Mills;' starting with the 'Bladed' type:

Electric Blade Grinders (Mills) – Although inexpensive, 'Blade' type grinders use a sharp, spinning 'blade;' like a blender or food processor. They tend to 'hack' the beans apart inconsistently – and inconsistent grinds do not necessarily make for the best cup of coffee! However, it is my preferred 'grinding method' when making Cold Brewed, Percolator, or 'Cowboy' coffees; as I prefer the taste of the 'irregular' shaped grounds with these methods of brewing. Other people may not prefer this taste or preference!

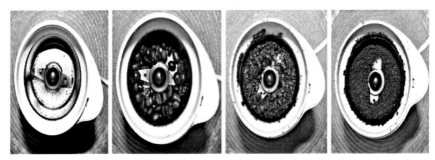

As previously mentioned, if the 'wrong grind' of coffee is used, the 'best of all' <u>flavor</u> <u>essences</u> cannot be released; thus, one might find their brew weak, bitter, or have excess acid! Unfortunately, with few exceptions, 'Blade Grinders' are not very consistent in their 'grinding/chopping' of beans – as the third photograph above indicates. To achieve a more 'consistent' grind of beans, the Grinder must be run for several seconds more. I am not saying one cannot achieve a 'tasty grind' using a Blade Grinder; however, this is where 'taking notes' comes in again – as well as the use of a 'Scale' and 'Stopwatch' for consistency, every time grinding!

Again, I use a Blade Grinder for 'specific' purposes (and for camping); as I have 'worked out' the 'consistency' I enjoy most, in brewing certain coffees. Moreover, I am not about to tell people '<u>not</u>' to purchase one! Blade Grinders are the 'cheapest' form of grinder available... and with a little effort, can 'grind a <u>good</u> bean! I have the brand shown on above; a 'Cuisinart...' and have used it for more than 35 years... and not just for grinding coffee beans!

Blade Grinders/Mills are available in many brands, sizes, kinds, styles, and colors; but they <u>all</u> work the same way! Popular brands include Krups®, Mr. Coffee®, Cuisinart®, Sears®, Black and Decker® – any brand one can imagine; and if the company makes a 'brewer' of some sort as well, expect them to promote their '<u>own</u> <u>brand</u>' of 'Blade Coffee Grinder!' Just remember, Blade Grinders (although, there is nothing wrong with them) are not very precise in their grinding! However, one <u>can</u> 'standardize' on it – and make a very acceptable brew for most devices! However, it is easy to 'over or under-grind' ones' beans! Plus, older models (which many people find in Thrift Stores) tend to 'run hot;' so if one is grinding many beans, there is a chance of 'scorching' the grind – especially, if grinding for Espresso!

This photograph is an example of exactly how 'inconsistent' using a Blade Grinder can be!

After several seconds of 'grinding' (the recommended time for the grinder used), notice how the coffee is in various sized 'chunks' – ranging from 'ultra-fine,' dust-sized particles, to whole beans! The reason for 'smaller sizes on top' is, they were on the 'bottom of the grinder,' when 'grinding' first began – meaning, they were the 'first' to be ground; and continued to 'grind' for the entire time the grinder was switched on. When the grinder was stopped (again, according to the recommended time), all degrees of the 'grind' was found – as one can easily see, not all beans had been 'pulled' down through the blade. There is no way to extract just the right 'amount of anything' to fit with any brewer; except, that is, something like 'Japanese Cold Brew, Cowboy Coffee,' or some 'Pour-Over brewers!'

Had this same coffee been run through a 'Burr' grinder for the same amount of 'recommended' time, perhaps, not all of the beans would have been 'ground' either; but what 'had been' ground, would have been of a consistent size (of course, depending upon the quality of the Burr Grinder)!

Would a 'Coffee Snob' own a 'Blade Grinder?' Probably, not that they would admit… at least, the ones which I know; not for the 'poor grinding quality,' but for the price – often, found for sale under $20.00!

Let's look at more Grinding and Grinders:

Unfortunately, I have had several people differ with me overusing a Blade Grinder, Blender, or Burr Grinder – of which I will go into in a few paragraphs. Moreover, I can understand that! For example, some people spend hundreds of dollars to buy brands of 'Blenders/Food Processors' called 'VitaMix™,' BlendTec™, or Cuisinart™; and, they are all <u>top</u> <u>model</u> devices! I have owned a VitaMix blender and a Cuisinart Food Processor for over 40 years, but I <u>do</u> <u>not</u> grind coffee beans in them!

However, I have seen various 'Blender Dealers' at the California State Fair 'hawking' that their blender was *"Perfect for grinding coffee beans to just the correct coarseness;"* and they served, small cups of 'very good coffee' to prove it! Do not believe it! Yes, Blenders may be used; but remember what I previously said about 'Blade Grinders;' *"Blades 'crash' into beans – and the product result, is a grind of 'assorted/splintered' size! 'Blade' grinders will work very much like a Blender;"* but, frankly, will do a better job than a blender – as the blade is smaller and fits the 'bean chamber/hopper' better.

I <u>do</u> know people (besides State or County Fair 'carnies') who 'grind beans' in a VitaMix; and <u>do</u> achieve pleasing results for themselves. Remember, the way to 'Roast, Grind and Brew' your beans, is 'how' <u>you</u> enjoy it best! There is no 'one, right way – and people can get used to almost anything!'

However, the 'VitaMix' (or any other blender) <u>can</u> be used providing 'standardization' (once again) is considered in the grinding. A close watch of 'time and pulsations' need to be performed (just as one would do with a 'Blade Grinder); to keep from 'over-grinding' the beans. Plus, one is going to have to 'experiment' with blender speeds for best results. For myself, I can say, that even 'blender coffee' can be acceptable while camping – and frankly, this is where some of the 'alternative' brewing methods I talk about, later in this book, might come in handy; as some brewing methods use more of a 'mismatch' of grounds than others!

One thing to be especially careful of, however, is if using a blender – such as a VitaMix – they are designed to 'cook' as well as blend… especially the old ones like mine! Running the blender at high speeds (or reversing the direction of the blades) can make heat (and thus, why the VitaMix manufacturer advertises *"Make ready to eat, hot soup in your VitaMix!"* The blender works great for soup – but, if it is going to make 'steaming hot' soup, what are the odds that it might 'scorch' a delicate, Coffee Bean? Oddly enough, I <u>have</u> tried first 'grinding beans' in my VitaMix, then adding water and 'reversing' the blades, to make 'heated coffee…' grounds, intact. After pouring the coffee through a filter, the brew was acceptable… although, something in taste to 'Campfire' coffee!

I will not even bother discussing 'Food Processors;' other than to say, if 'Roasted Coffee Beans' are going to be 'ground' in them, 'higher end' machines tend to do a better job than cheaper brands – as their blades may be 'lower' to the bottom of the bowl; and may 'fit' the better. What does 'lower to the bottom of the bowl' mean? It means that the coffee (or other foods) is going to be 'ground more effectively;' leaving less 'chunks' which can evade the blades, simply by being 'too small,' at the bottom of the bowl, to be hit by the blade! This is often found to be the case when using a 'Food Processor' to grind vegetables or meat – such as, when making Salsa or a 'Pâté.' Not all the 'chunks' may be 'chopped' fine enough!

Burr Grinders – Burr grinders are explicitly designed for those seeking 'specific coarseness' and uniformity of their grounds; and should be used only for 'specific' purposes... such as coffee! Many people use this grinder, however, to grind many things; i.e., spices, nuts, and other things. One of my favorites is a simple 'handheld' model – as seen here. It is not as easy to use as an 'electric' model, but it is more precise. I find it 'more precise' than other grinders when it  comes to grinding 'Extra Fine' grounds for my Espresso Maker!

There are a lot of 'technical' terms, explanations, and questions when it comes to Burr Grinders – such as *"Which type' is best for 'Chocolate Flavored or Nutty Beans,"* or, *"What type of Burr' is better for 'exotic or common' beans?"* However, all that aside, most 'Burrs' are created from, 'Cast Metal, Stainless Steel,' or a 'Ceramic' substance – and, they will all grind coffee beans to various degrees, for multiple brewers! The Burrs (cutters), look and act like 'gears' for the most part; and have changed very little since their invention!

'Cast' Burrs can become dull quickly; while 'Stainless Steel' Burrs stay sharper; and tend to be the less expensive alternative... however, they do not have as 'long a life span' as the 'Ceramic Burrs' – which, unfortunately, can 'chip.' Therefore, it is sometimes worth purchasing 'Replacement Burrs' at the same time as the grinder purchase. The Ceramic Burr may be more expensive and last longer; but, as previously mentioned, they are subject to easier damage – such as, if one were to run into small rocks or staples leftover from bagging. Baristas, however, prefer the 'Ceramic Burr;' as they produce a 'finer' grind; 'Coffee Snobs' prefer them too!

As with a 'Blade Grinder,' Ceramic Burrs start their lives 'sharp;' but rather than 'indiscriminately chopping the beans (like a Blade Grinder);' beans are 'drawn through' the Burrs; where the beans are 'ground' into predeterminant sizes – according to 'how' the user sets the device. Most modern, 'Electric Burr Grinders,' grind from an 'ultra-fine' grind to an 'ultra-coarse' grind; while antique 'Hand Grinders,' usually, only had one 'setting!' The most current, 'Burr Grinders' (manual or electric) have multiple grind settings!

Some 'hand-operated,' antique, Burr Grinders are real 'works of art;' and look beautiful just sitting on a decorative shelf. Unfortunately, 'antique' grinders do not always work well; as the wood is dry and the Burrs have become dull over the years! However, several companies manufacture 'new,' 'antique-looking,' grinders. They work; but if one is a 'collector' they must be observant in their purchase – as 'replicas' are sometimes 'passed off' as 'genuine antiques' by some disreputable people!

Block Burr Grinders – Block Grinders are, usually, the 'cheaper' brands (manual or electric) that one might see for sale. The electric ones tend to have small, electric motors; and are not designed for any more than 'light duty' use. Because of the design of the 'Block Burr' – which has varied and larger angled Burrs – they tend to 'crack,' rather than grind, the beans; meaning, more 'fines' (small, dust-like particles which can clog up a grinder); which are, also, known to 'muddy' a cup!

Electric, Flat Disk Grinders – (considered 'Espresso' Mills) These grinders use two 'spinning' disks, sitting horizontally, to 'smash and cut' the coffee beans into precise, uniform grinds. Their precision is suitable for home use; and one can even achieve a truly 'Extra-Fine' Espresso grind. Unfortunately, they can also run hot; and if one is not careful, can 'scorch' the beans or grind.

'Coffee Snobs,' (if they know anything about grinders) love these models for their high price and 'classy' appearance!

Masticating Grinders – Aka: 'MG's,' tend to 'chew' the beans, rather than cut them into various, standard sizes. This type of machine is what most people are familiar with in grocery stores! However, despite their soaring prices, 'Masticating Grinders' tend to have <u>less</u> consistency in grind sizes!

[59]

This can be easily seen in one of the upcoming photographs of 'Turkish' grind; where the 'store machine' <u>did</u> <u>not</u> 'grind' as precisely as my small, 'handheld' device.

Few 'Coffee Snobs' would consider using or owning this grinder – at least, not that they would admit! However, I do know a few 'Snobs' who 'own' these; as they want the versatility of the different 'mid-grinds' (and they, also, enjoy paying a 'high price' for them)!

The store type, 'Masticating Grinders,' tend to be in the $900.00+ range; but, as expensive as these are, a 'truly professional' grinder can cost thousand dollars <u>more</u> than these!

Conical Grinders – Being the most common of 'home grinders,' this type uses two 'Conical Burrs;' one, inside another. Coffee 'feeds' more efficiently through these machines; as beans are 'pulled through' the grinder, rather than just 'gravity' fed. These machines can be either 'more or less' expensive than others – depending upon the brand and where one shops – but, they are the natural choice of <u>both</u> 'coffee professionals' and 'enthusiasts' alike. Conical Grinders are the 'workhorses' for the home or office; and, they can produce 'Precision Grinds' for even 'Turkish' coffee… with their slow, cool-running motors.

Most 'Coffee Snobs' will own an 'amateur' version of type of grinder – as they can be both practical and 'pricey (up to several hundred dollars);' although, in my opinion, the 'cheaper' brands (approximately $50.00 to $100.00) do just as good a job! However, many, so-called, 'experts' claim they can "*Taste a difference*," between the cheaper or more expensive brands of this type of grinder; but frankly, after trying many brands, of all prices, I find that I cannot taste any difference; but, not to say that someone could not!

For a 'bad analogy,' think of 'Grinder' models, like brands like cars – a Rolls Royce and a Volkswagen will both get someone where they need to go; but one is a lot less expensive than the other! As far as "*Tasting a difference*," this is where one may wish to try a 'half-step' between grinds, to brew and taste any differences.

Disc Grinders – Many Baristas consider 'Disc Grinders' as 'different… (which is not always good)' but, they <u>are</u> still Burr Grinders; and give the most <u>precise</u> grinding – due to all the serrations/grooves cut into the Discs. The coffee beans 'fall' in between the two Discs and are <u>accurately</u> 'crushed or ground' between them to a chosen size! They are 'nice for the price;' if one can find a 'good deal' on them. The best deals are usually located on the internet on some 'over-stock' type stores.

'Snobs' love them; but for we 'average' coffee drinkers, 'cheaper' Burr Grinders seem to work just as well! Which grinder would I recommend? When it comes to Espresso, all 'Grinders and Mills' work about the same – as there is very little difference in brewing Espresso. If anything, the 'higher end' Burr Grinders do tend to last longer; and stay 'sharper,' for an extended period. They, also, tend to have a few more features, functions, and are built 'sturdier.' Other than that, unless one is opening a 'coffee shop' of some kind, a $50.00 - $200.00 grinder will serve most people! Frankly, I would doubt that anyone, except a 'top-notch' Barista or 'professional Coffee Bean Cupper/Buyer,' would ever be able to taste any difference between 'Home' coffee grinders!

Low-Speed versus High-Speed Burr Grinders – When it comes to 'consumer grinding,' anything will work... at least, from one degree to another! Of course, most 'Low Speed' ('slower RPM') grinders are, usually, the 'inexpensive' brands – costing $200.00 or less. Most of the Burrs are not only 'Conical,' but 'smaller' in size as well! Unfortunately, many 'Coffee Snobs,' may like them for their 'cooler running' speeds; but may dislike them more, due to their low price; rather than their 'inconsistent' grinding! Frankly, I think most 'Coffee Snobs' would love 'Low-Speed' grinders if they just tried them... I know, I do!

Overall, I would have to say; there is nothing wrong with 'Low-Speed' grinders; again providing, one 'standardizes' on their grinding/brewing methods! They seem to be especially useful for grinds which need 'pressurized' brewing – like Espressos or K-Pods.

'High-Speed,' grinders, however, tend to be the 'high end' of Burr grinders... at least, in price! They tend to cost between $200.00 and $1000.00, on the average. This is because, they have larger, stronger, and 'hotter, running' motors; which turn two 'Flat-Plate Burrs.' Some brands are 'Direct Drive' models – which do not need as many 'gears' to turn the Burrs! 'High-Speed Grinders' have a longer 'lifespan' than the 'slower' models; and, are 'more worthy' of purchasing 'Replacement Burrs' at the time of the grinder purchase. Sometimes, they can be found at 'discount' prices, again, at 'over-stock' type stores!

[61]

The 'Coffee Snobs' I have met, usually, go for as 'fast a speed' as possible; even though, it might <u>not</u> be the best grinder to do the job; and, might run 'too hot!'

Dosing Grinders – A 'Dosing Grinder,' simply put, allows the coffee beans to be 'ground' to a specific size, then 'dosed' into a portafilter basket directly.

Some Coffee and Espresso machines have them 'built-in;' but, may allow 'Distribution Rings' to be used with them.

Non-Dosing Grinders – 'Non-Dosing' Grinders are designed to 'grind the bean' into a container under the grinder delivery spout. Any 'transfer of grounds' into a Portafilter or Ground Basket must be performed by hand.

As with a 'Dosing Grinder,' some of these machines will accept 'Distribution Rings' too; which can be left on the Portafilter during 'filling' as well; so no, valuable, 'grains of coffee' will be spilled.

There are many 'pluses and minuses' on both types of grinders – such as more or less static, or use for 'group (multiple) servings;' but they each are designed to achieve the same purpose; to accurately grind the coffee beans (and enough of them) to meet the needs of the individual brewer!

Let us look at some more 'questionable' grinding details, including the 'Seasoning' of Coffee Grinder Burrs, on the following pages:

"I would rather suffer with coffee than be senseless!"

~ (Attributed to) Napoleon Bonaparte

'SEASONING' OF BURRS

Most electric grinders do not 'adjust well' when in a 'stopped' condition – especially, 'store' models. Therefore, it is best to 'change one's grind size' with the grinder motor running – this helps to 'push out' old, smaller, particles as well. However, over time, as the grinders are used, the Burrs will become dull. Nevertheless, some people say, "*If one were to 'Season the Burrs' when they first purchase a grinder – just as they would do with a Cast Iron frying pan – they would not only last longer but stay sharp longer as well.*"

Outwardly, the idea of 'Seasoning' would seem to make a little sense; but it is a falsehood – most likely, created by some 'Coffee Snobs' or 'bean sellers!'

Perhaps, 'Seasoning' should be mentioned under 'Troubleshooting;' but the word 'Seasoning' itself, is something of a misnomer. Most of the instruction books, which come with the machines, do not mention 'Seasoning;' and with good reason... it is not needed! Some people still say, "*Burr Grinders need to be 'broken in' or 'conditioned' before using!*" So, some bright person – probably playing on 'Snobby Seasoning' idea – came up with the idea that "*10-50 pounds of 'hard' beans need to be run through (and thrown away, rather than brewed) a grinder before any brewing can commence!*"

My first thought upon hearing this was, "*What a waste of Beans!*" However, some 'Snobs' claim, they "*Always 'season' their new grinders – and can 'see and taste' a difference if they do not!*" Frankly, I have difficulty believing that anyone would purposely waste "*10-50 pounds of coffee beans!*" However, I could, probably, be talked into "*Grind and brew a few times, of a single grind, to 'break in' the machine...*" maybe; with the 'promise' of "*Each cup is simply going to become better and better;*" however, this is not the case, or even necessary! I did check it out with some 'experts' when it came to 'Seasoning;' just to make sure!

For example, recently I visited a local 'Kitchen Store;' and I mentioned 'Seasoning' to the store's owner... a man whom, not only, 'specializes' in selling Kitchen Equipment to homes and restaurants, but has a 'Coffee Bar' and sells his 'own brand' of coffee beans and 'coffee equipment' within his store. My question seemed to start a 'mini-debate' among other store patrons and clerks! The owner and I were walking over to his display of grinders when I mentioned 'Seasoning' to him. He stopped walking, looked at me like the RCA Victor Dog (with his head 'tilted' to the side, and mouth slightly open), and said, "*Huh,*" (he had never heard of such a thing)!

[63]

Another customer, nearby, overheard our conversation and 'chimed in,' "*I always 'Season or Re-season' my Burrs to get them to last longer, but I only use beans of a coffee I do not like to drink! I am not going to waste 50 pounds of <u>good</u> beans!*"

To that, a store clerk, stocking shelves, added: "*Oh no, you must <u>only</u> use the same beans that you are going to drink; or you will not get the Burrs to 'Season' or grind properly! Moreover, you need to 're-season' your Burrs for every type of bean you use! Therefore, I own 'multiple Burrs' for 'multiple beans' to save money – one set of Burrs for Espresso beans, another for Clever Dripper and French Press coffees, and the third set for my Drip Coffee Maker… moreover, do not get me started on 'flavor' contamination or 'decaf' beans!*"

The store owner and I stopped and looked at each other for a moment, then continued to the grinders. I could not help but think, "*Here was a man in the business of not only selling grinders but 'selling and serving' coffee beans and brewed coffee – and yet, he had never heard of such a thing… not even from his employees; that is, not until now!*"

In the same sense, my son and I recently took a 'Barista' class from a 'major' Coffee Roaster in our state capitol. The instructors were grinding 'multiple types of coffee beans' with the same grinder for tasting. I asked the head instructor about 'Seasoning.' He seemed a bit surprised by such a question; but stated, "*Well, whenever we get a new grinder* (and theirs were $2000.00+ models) *we do run a cup or two of beans through it…to 'test and adjust' for 'normal grinding;' at least, for what we like to serve! We do not worry about the types of beans! Again, we <u>do</u> 'test brew' to see if the new Burrs or machine will 'grind' the way we are accustomed to; if not, we then 'augment/adjust' grinding if needed for consistency!*"

So… 'Seasoning' is ridiculous; but I think it is equally absurd to believe that Burrs need to be 're-seasoned' with every 'change of type' of coffee bean – meaning, 'more wastage' of coffee! If the need for 'Seasoning' were factual, then I could, indeed, understand owning multiple sets of Burrs or machines for use! However, this is simply nonsense! 'Seasoning' is <u>strictly</u> a 'Coffee Snob' (or Coffee Bean Sellers) idea to 'impress;' or to "*Sell more beans!*"

I do not even believe in owning 'different Burrs' for 'different grinds' or flavors (out of fear of contamination of flavors) of coffee; but then, there is something to be said for '<u>contamination</u> of flavors.' I learned this one a few years ago during the Christmas season! I had made some fresh coffee and was very surprised by its flavor – as it had a slight 'Peppermint' taste and smell to it. I had cleaned my Drip Coffee maker, ground some beans, and made my coffee; but, unbeknownst to me, hours before, my son had made some too. As I had cleaned the coffee maker, I knew it could not have contaminated my brew. I checked with my son; and he <u>had</u> brewed some holiday, 'Peppermint Coffee' in the coffee maker. I thought for a moment – as I had cleaned the coffee maker, I determined that my son must have ground 'Peppermint Coffee Beans' in the grinder – and, I did not check it to see if the grinder was 'clean' or not. It was the grinder itself which had contaminated the brew! The coffee was not bad tasting, but I did not receive the brew I wanted!

My wife had something similar happen, one other time, at the grocery store; she did not investigate the store grinder to see if anything was in the hopper first. She poured in her beans and started the machine; but what came out, was a mixture of someone else's choice of beans and her own; which was obvious, when I poured it into my storage container. The coffee on top of the bag was what I expected to see – a deep, dark brown; while the coffee in the bottom 1/3 of the bag was a light brown – obviously, the person using the machine before her, had not 'ground' <u>all</u> the 'Light Roast' beans they had before stopping the grinder. Nevertheless, 'our' coffee did not taste as it should have!

We, now, always check, not our home grinders, but 'Public Grinders' before adding our beans – and, always turn them on for several seconds before adding our selection; to remove any lingering 'contaminating' grounds or chunks! In fact, not only will I perform a 'quick clean' on the store's machine, I will run a small handful of beans through the grinder after setting my choice of grind; to remove any beans or oils which might be 'stuck' in the grinder! **Special Note**: Stores hate when customers do this!

However, getting back to 'Seasoning,' once again, running different beans or grinds through ones' grinders are not going to change the Burrs in any way; except 'clean between grinds and flavors!' To reiterate what I stated before, and what I tell my students, think of it this way: 'Seasoning,' or 'changing Burrs' on ones grinder between bean types, is like *"Living in a hot, dry, desert… and putting 'snow tires' on your car, just because it is Winter!"* It is totally, un-needed!

There <u>are</u> times and places to change Burrs; and that is when they wear out! As previously stated, with 'average' grinders, being as inexpensive as they are, unless one purchases 'Replacement Burrs' at the same time as the grinder, it is just as cheap to purchase a 'new' grinder when the 'old Burrs' wear out!

[65]

Unlike products with 'planned obsolescence,' (like computers which are 'out of date' before one can get them home from the store), Burrs (such as the 'Flat' one shown here), come from the factory, 'pre-sharpened,' mounted, and ready to use in each grinder! The consumer does not have to do anything other than 'plug in' the grinder, 'fill it' with beans, and turn it on! The Burrs are not going to get 'any better' through 'Seasoning;' as they do not need additional sharpening or conditioning, from running '50 pounds of beans' through them! All grinders should always be 'standardized' on, however; to ensure one receives the 'exact grind' for the 'coffee taste' of which they are seeking!

I would suppose, it would be possible for one to take a 'tiny file,' and 'hand sharpen' each cutting edge on the Burrs; but how practical is that?

One of the most difficult things to visually judge, is the 'coarseness' of a ground, coffee bean! The cause of this is because, every grinder manufacturer has their 'own' version of 'Coarse, Medium, Fine' grinds – even though, there are standards which manufacturers must follow! Some devices, such as my hand-operated model, will make 18 different (unmarked) sizes of grind; but the most commonly used commercial brand grinder – found in most grocery stores – will only have 9 to 11 settings – taking in, only the most common choices! Many machines even have illustrations to show the most common brewing types; as the photograph above shows.

Let us look at some Coffee Grounds; and examples of 'grinds' on the next pages:

"The best Maxim I know in this life is, to drink your coffee when you can, and when you cannot, to be easy without it."

~ (Attributed to) Jonathan Swift, Writer, and Satirist

EXAMPLES OF 'GRINDS'

The previous image is an example of a typical store grinder 'setting knob' – which allows for multiple grinds. However, the choices on the dial are only 'generic settings;' as one's ' personal taste' must be taken into consideration. Some other store machines (which I prefer) even have '1/2 or 1/3' settings for 'fine-tuning' a grind.

Even more machines might have <u>both</u> a 'Turkish' and 'Ultra-Fine' setting on them; so, depending upon ones' Espresso maker (or their 'Turkish' brewing), one may wish to experiment a bit with grinds. With the previous machine photo, look at the Espresso setting on the right of the dial; it not only shows two different settings for Espresso – but a third setting for Turkish – which should be the 'ultra-fine' setting. Other machines, similar in design, might not have a 'Turkish' setting at all – but merely a third, 'Espresso' setting. My advice: Try them all separately in your Espresso maker or Turkish Cezve (pronounced "jezz-va") or Briki pots; then purchase your favorite grind the next time, accordingly.

I wish I could include samples from several different grinders, to show the difference between grinds and machines. However, the closest thing I can come to is with the photograph below of 'Turkish' from my, little, 'Hand

Operated,' Burr Grinder, and from what the grocery stores Coffee Grinder says, "*Should be the same thing!*" If one takes a close look at the 'Turkish' and 'Actual Turkish' grounds from my Hand Grinder, and compares it to the $900.00+ Commercial, Store Coffee Grinder, it is easy to see a difference! Surprisingly, the Hand Grinder, 'grinds' a much 'finer' coffee ground.

As one can see in the previous photograph, even 'Professional Mills' can have inconsistencies. The so-called, 'Turkish' grind was not anywhere near the 'fine flour' texture that it should have been; so, I could not use it for <u>my</u> brewing purposes – and achieve the desired results.

Some people would find that the 'Turkish' grind shown, ground by the same machine that did the other grinds would be 'good enough;' and, it is… for some people. Other people might not share the same observations – myself included – as the grind is 'coarser' than what most Baristas would allow. However, even with the 'small hand grinder' that I used to get more of a 'Bakers Flour' consistency to the grind, the grounds would, probably, still be turned down by most Baristas; as <u>still</u> being 'too coarse' a grind!

However, I have found, that with most Espresso Machines, this grind 'works fine' to make ones Espresso; and, brew a 'taste' like what one would receive in a 'high end' Coffee Bar! Surprisingly, to truly achieve an exact grind, many people will own <u>two</u> coffee grinders; in both electric and manual types – so that one mill is used for grinding Espresso, and another one for grinding everything else!

Let us take a closer look at grinds:

Ultra-Fine Grind – Considered a 'Turkish' Grind, 'Ultra-Fine' grounds look and feel something like 'brown, Bakers Flour' or 'Confectioners' Sugar;' as no individual grains of coffee can be felt between the fingertips. It is, primarily, used by Baristas for their 'Custom Pulls' of Espressos; as well as for making 'Turkish' or 'Greek' (Briki) Coffee. Although difficult to see in the previous photographs, actual 'Turkish' grind is going to appear 'lighter in color' than a 'Fine' grind, due to its 'ultra-fine' state… even, from the same beans. The supposedly, 'Turkish' grind shown, is <u>not</u> lighter in color; and has <u>coarser</u> <u>grains</u>, almost like table salt. It can, however, be still used to, adequately, make either Turkish coffee or Espresso.

Fine Grind – Having two settings of 'Fine' for Espresso, a 'Fine Grind' coffee will have a consistency of 'All-Purpose Flour' for one setting, then as 'coarser Table Salt' for the other – and individual grains of coffee <u>can</u>, somewhat, be felt between the fingertips. It is used, primarily, in Espresso Makers, Stovetop Moka Pots, or AeroPress (I find it works well in my Moka Pot). However, it is often used in some, 'straight through,' Pour-Over brewers as well; with only a 'one-minute' brewing/extracting time. 'Fine-Grind' could be an 'acquired' taste – but be prepared for 'Mud' in one's cup!

Medium-Fine Grind – An 'Auto Drip' setting, 'Medium-Fine' grounds tend to appear 'finer' than 'Beach Sand.' This grind is best (and more often) used in some 'Immersion' coffee makers; like Clever Drippers or Bonavita coffee makers. 'Medium-Fine' grounds, are also, for use in Pour-Over Cones like Hario or Kalita Wave; as well as Vacuum Brewers, Technivorm, and once again, an AeroPress. Brewing/Extracting time, depending upon the Baristas personal taste, is generally between two to three minutes.

Medium Grind – Another 'Auto-Drip' setting, according to the grinder dial, 'Medium Grind' is what one would find in most households; in either fresh or canned grounds. It looks and feels like coarse 'Yard Sand,' or 'Ground Pepper.' It is mostly used in most 'Automatic Drip' coffee makers; but also recommended for Percolators, some 'faster brewing' Pour-Over Brewers, Siphon Brewers, Flat Bottom 'Drip' Machines, and, once again, with AeroPress. Brewing/Extraction time is three minutes; but, usually longer if a machine is being used.

Some might wonder "*Why*" I have mentioned the 'AeroPress' under three different grinds – it is because the AeroPress has different 'brewing times' for varying degrees of coffee grounds! All 'Auto-Drips' have their own 'set time' for brewing 'full' pots – generally, several minutes. For other methods, like Percolators, temperature, taste or color dictates brewing time; and with 'Pour-Over' or other methods, <u>three</u> <u>minutes</u> is about average. With an AeroPress, almost anything goes! It all depends upon what the 'drinker' prefers!

Medium-Coarse Grind – Considered an 'Electric Percolator' or yet another 'Drip Machine' grind, 'Medium-Coarse' grind is more 'Gritty;' similar to coarse, Cement sand. It is considered 'best used' in Chemex, Incred-a-Brew, Bonavita, or Clever Dripper brewers (like an 'AeroPress,' Chemex, Incred-a-Brew, Bonavita, and Clever Drippers can utilize 'different' degrees of grinds; depending upon one's taste). Of course, 'Medium-coarse' grind is very good for 'steeping,' or 'specialized' Drip coffee makers. It is, also, recommended for use in other 'Immersion type' brewers – such as Sowden Soft Brew, or Eva Solo Brewers. I enjoy this grind, best, in my French Press!

Brewing/Extraction times are, again, three or more minutes – or, depending upon 'taste and color' for an 'Electric' Percolator.

Coarse Grind – Considered a 'Syphon' grind, 'Course Grind' is often the size of 'Kosher Salt' or 'Raw Sugar' size granules. Besides Syphon Brewing, this grind works best in certain 'Pour-Over' brewers, French Presses without filters, or Percolators. It is also used for 'Steeping' or 'Cold Brewing.' For some reason, some 'Experts' prefer to use this grind for 'Coffee Cupping/Tasting;' although, 'actual brewing' would be with more of a 'Medium' grind.

Brewing times are, usually, three to five minutes, for extraction (except for 'Cold Brewing) – depending upon one's taste. I do know people who use it in their 'Drip' machines; as they enjoy the 'harsher' taste! It, also, works well for brewing different 'Egg' coffees; or when brewing, 'standardized,' 'Cowboy' Coffee!

Extra-Coarse Grind – This is considered a 'specialized,' French Press grind. 'Extra-Coarse' is comprised of mostly large particles; about the size of 'Ground Peppercorns.' Many 'experts' consider the grind to be 'too large' in particle size to fully extract flavors and oils from most brewing methods. As with a 'Pulverized Grind,' an 'Extra-Coarse' grind works best with Cowboy Coffee or in Percolators – which can 'boil out' the flavors and oils. Some 'Coffee Snobs,' prefer this brew for 'Clever Drippers' as well – so they can 'steep' the grinds longer. This grind requires one to three minutes for extraction time, on the average; or several minutes – depending upon the brewing method, taste, or color desired. Some people, also, prefer this grind for 24 to 72-hour, 'Cold Brew!'

Pulverized Grind – 'Pulverized Grind,' can have particles from 'Fine' to 'large chunk' or even 'whole beans' in size. This grind is what 'pioneers' would have used; as they may not have owned a mechanized, 'Hand Grinder!' Coffee would have been 'pulverized' with a rock, a hammer, a rolling pin, meat tenderizer mallet, or something 'heavy;' then, brewed when the granules reached smaller sizes.

Native Americans used a 'Mortar and Pestle' to grind with; or pounded it with a rock, initially. This grind is, generally, used for 'Boiled Coffee' and 'Cowboy' Coffee Pots – 'boiled' for several minutes or longer for color or taste; and 'kept hot' all day! I suggest everyone try a 'Pulverized Grind' least once; and, compare it to the flavor of an 'extra-coarse' grind... alternatively, any other grind for that matter!

As stated before, all the above grinds – and everything in between – can still be used (or adapted) in <u>any type</u> Brewer; according to one's' own, personal taste; and 'with or without' a filter! Unless using an 'old bean' (or by personal taste), all 'fresh' grinds should 'Off-Gas' for at least an hour after grinding. If not 'off-gassing,' then, indeed, 'Blooming,' is in order before brewing! Many Baristas, however, go directly from 'Bean to Grind, to Brewer, to Cup,' without any 'off-gassing;' but then, many Espresso Machines, have a built-in 'pre-wetting' (or Blooming) function before extraction!

Here are a couple of 'quick questions' regarding 'Grinders:'

Question: *"Does it matter if a Burr Grinder is a 'Manual' or 'Electric'?"*

Answer: Not really. In the past, 'Manual' grinders, unless grinding for an extended period, produced less heat; so, more 'flavor and aromas' (in theory) were preserved; but they did take a little effort to crank!

Modern, 'non-electric,' devices are still difficult to use. I 'hand-ground' some beans, yesterday, with modern equipment; and my arms became tired! However, after a few minutes, I could start feeling heat 'building' from 'grinding and friction' – just as with an, older, 'Electric' model! For example, my 40-year-old, 'Electric' grinder, feels hot after only a few pulsations! Regardless of the grinder, we have to accept the fact that 'friction' is going to 'make heat;' and an 'electric' grinder is, probably, going to make even more heat with its motor, the longer it runs! However, most, modern, electric devices do not produce near as much heat as they used to – so there is negligible risk of 'burning the grind;' especially, when grinding 'small amounts' of beans. In any event, I would be surprised if anyone, other than a 'Seasoned Barista,' could taste the difference between modern 'electric or manual' grinders – although, many so-called 'Coffee Snobs' claim, *"They can!"*

[71]

Question: *"How does one clean their Coffee Grinder? I have heard of many ways – or, should I leave it alone, as a 'coffee expert' friend tells me? Howe ever, one friend even recommends putting my manual grinder in the dishwasher!"*

Answer: Many grinder brands come with 'small brushes' to clean the grinder; as 'coffee dust' can build up under the Blades or Burrs from gravity or 'static electricity.' Generally, with smaller (and cheaper), 'hand or electric' grinders, they can just be opened and 'shaken or blown out;' and then be 'wiped down' with a damp cloth! With my Mills/Grinders, I tend to do what one 'should not;' and that is, to 'tap' the bottom of the Mill on the counter or edge of the sink; to 'dislodge' any dust or grind. It works, but can, possibly, damage the device. My machines are so old and 'beat up' anyway, there is little 'damage' I can do to them!

A *"Dishwasher?"* I have never heard of such a thing; although, I would suppose it would be possible… but not practical! My 'Hand Mill' comes apart into several pieces; leaving the anodized aluminum, grinding cylinder and cup. The Burrs themselves, not to mention the handle, are metal. I would suppose I could take the Mill apart and put it into a dishwasher… by why? It would have to be carefully, and thoroughly 'dried' to prevent rusting of some parts! Simple dusting, wiping out with a damp cloth, or 'shaking out' is, generally, all that is needed to 'clean' a Coffee Grinder… 'Manual or Electric!'

Let us look at some more 'involved' ways to clean ones' grinder on the following pages:

"The most dangerous 'drinking game' anyone can play is seeing 'how long I can go without a cup of coffee!' Coffee helps me maintain my 'never killed anyone' streak!"

~ (Attributed to) Anonymous

CLEANING ONES' COFFEE GRINDER

Eventually, every 'Coffee Grinder,' regardless of the brand, type, or cost, is going to need to be cleaned for one reason or another! One good reason, besides 'blades or burrs,' becoming encrusted with oily, coffee dust, is a 'flavored' coffee – like peppermint, for example – being ground in the same device as what a 'regular' coffee would; which will contaminate the next beans with 'left-over' dust or oil.

Do 'flavored beans' really matter to cleanliness? Try it yourself; grind some 'Peppermint Beans;' then grind anything else… and <u>brew</u> with it. Ones' coffee will have a slight 'peppermint' taste or smell to it – from left-over, from oils and dust in the grinder! Bad tasting? Not if one enjoys peppermint; but if they are looking for a soothing, 'special grind' of coffee for an evening 'Cappuccino' to 'relax,' why would they want to drink something that is 'invigorating,' such as peppermint? I often see this with store grinders, as I have previously, mentioned.

When using a 'public,' grinder, I will often use the brush provided with most machines (usually, chained) to 'slightly' clean it (sometimes, the brush is not very clean, however). Then, I will turn on the device before setting my grind; this, also, makes sure <u>every</u> earlier bean has been 'ground' out of it. Depending upon the machine, I might lift off, or open, it's front 'door,' exposing the Burrs; of which, I merely 'dust off,' again, with the supplied brush. Closing the door, I, put a small 'handful' of beans into it; and quickly run the grind through. I mentioned this earlier. Yes, this does waste a few beans (and stores hate it); but it helps 'clean-out' whatever might have been 'forgotten' in the device – where I could not reach to clean – including some 'stuck' beans, oils, and dust. So, cleaning helps to remove any 'lingering' flavors, which may, also, remain in the machine.

If using a 'Blade Coffee Grinder,' however, there is not too much to do when it comes to cleaning. Frankly, my 'Blade Grinder' is over 40 years old; and I cannot ever remember cleaning it – other than, just wiping it down inside and out! When it comes to 'Burr Grinders,' however, cleaning is a bit more complex; one cannot 'shake or blow out' the grinder, as one could with a blade grinder. Coffee 'dust' gets into every little 'nook and cranny!' Plus, as there are oils involved (as well as static electricity), 'Coffee Dust' is going to want to 'stick' to the sides of the grinding chamber, the 'Burrs,' the outside of the grinder, the hopper… anything, which might have a touch of coffee oil on it! Moreover, remember, avoid 'rancidly smelling or tasting' coffee, by cleaning the hopper at least once per week – even when using the same beans.

So, the first thing which needs to be done is to remove any dust and debris from the hopper with a moist cloth or paper towel; as well as the storage container and the inside of the machine; sometimes, I might use an 'alcohol wipe' from my work supplies, if I have one handy.

A can of 'compressed air' would work quite well too! Remove any 'removable' part and wipe it down once again. Remember, the 'oily dust' is going to want to <u>stick</u> to both the inside and outside of the grinder. If the Burrs are easily removable for cleaning or replacement, carefully remove them (remembering 'how' they came out, so they may be put back the same way). If ones' mill did not come  with a cleaning brush, an old toothbrush or small, artists paintbrush could be used to wipe off/out any dust. There is no need to wash the Burrs, but one might wipe them down. Before replacing, blow or wipe out the Burr chamber a final time for any 'settled' dust.

Special Note: If the Burrs have any 'compacted' grind in the 'grooves,' and a small brush will not remove them, use a toothpick to 'break loose' the grounds. Typically, they will <u>not</u> be 'compacted,' however, unless old.

There is one other way to do some 'cleaning' without removing the Burrs; and that is to run some 'uncooked' rice through the grinder – but, I do not recommend it; as eventually, the rice can 'clog' the Burrs too. However, there are 'Grinder Cleaning Pellets or Tablets' which can be purchased in some stores or on the internet! Like the rice, they can be 'run through' the grinder to clean the Burrs – and, hopefully, they will not do any 'clogging'… at least too soon. Unfortunately, they may create more dust in the long term.

 However, they are ideal for emergencies; such as, when one has 'accidentally' ground some 'French Vanilla Mint Mocha' beans through their grinder; and may not have the time for a full cleaning regime before grinding another 'flavored bean!' The 'Urnex' company makes one excellent brand of 'Cleaning Tablets;' and it is a 'high grade' product for most types of coffee and espresso makers. I used the product once per month. Remember,

when it comes to 'flavored beans,' even 'Cleaning Pellets' may not be perfect; as all devices still need to be 'wiped out, blown out, or disassembled; to fully clean!

Back to more related 'Questions:'

Question: *"How long should any Burrs or Grinders last with 'moderate' use? Do they ever need replacing?"*

Answer: On a 'Home Machine' – and with 'moderate' use – one is looking at a minimum of three to five years before the 'Grinder Burrs' need to be replaced with new ones. The machines themselves – for a 'good brand and model' – run somewhere in the $200.00 to $300.00 range; but, Replacement Burrs, generally, do not cost more than $20.00 to $30.00. Unfortunately, most modern grinders have the <u>same</u> lifespan as the Burrs – three to five years – so, 'replacement' Burrs may not be worth it!

Cheaper, but still good, brands of grinders start in price around $30.00; and go up from there – again, with the average price, hovering in the $80 to $150.00 range. Like their 'expensive' brothers, they are only designed to have a three to five-year 'lifespan' too. Replacement Burrs are, also, available for these machines – and, cost around the same as the expensive brands – somewhere in the $20.00 to $30.00 range.

Sometimes, buying 'Replacement Burrs' at the time as the machine purchase is a bright idea – especially, with Ceramic Burrs; which may dull or chip! However, if Burrs are, typically, only going to last 'three to five years' anyway – and machines do not last much longer – then why bother with replacement at all? I may sound like a 'Snob' for saying this, but *"Just purchase a new machine;"* especially, if buying a 'cheaper model' in the first place! In three to five years, grinders, most likely, are going to be of a different 'style;' making it difficult to find replacement Burrs for the older machines. Moreover, if one is only going to spend only $50.00 on a grinder in the first place, why spend $30.00 to replace the Burrs on an old, 'cheap' machine which is already worn out? Just buy a new grinder and keep it clean!

Question: *"Does 'Clean' coffee refer to the cleanliness of the brewing equipment?"*

Answer: I would suppose it could; as 'cleanliness of machines and tools' is very important to brewing coffee – I would not want to brew coffee in a dirty pot! However, the term 'Clean' is, generally, referring to 'brewed coffee;'

free of roasting, processing, water, or brewing defects... resulting in coffee, which is very 'clean tasting!' However, coffee will taste 'cleaner' if brewed with 'clean' equipment too!

Question: *"What is meant by 'Complex' coffee?"*

Answer: Complex or 'Complexity in coffee,' refers to <u>all</u> the elements of the coffee; such as color, texture, taste, and aroma. Moreover, it also applies to a 'perfect' cup of coffee. 'Poor tasting' coffee, a Barista might say, "*Lacks complexity!*"

Question: *"What is 'Sweet' Coffee? Is it just using a sweetener, like sugar?"*

Answer: *"Sweet,"* is considered a 'roasting term' for a 'Full City' roast of coffee; which is, generally, 'caramel' flavor – and considered soft, mild, or even 'mellow.' In other words, the flavor appears 'balanced' with other characteristics. 'Sweet,' will be pleasant to drink; and, an example of 'good roasting' of the 'type' of the bean. Some coffees, taste 'naturally sweet;' but, yes, of course, 'added sweetness,' in the form of sugar or other additives, may be added as well!

Unfortunately, most of the 'Coffee Snobs' I know, do not consider the 'roasting' aspect of the beans; and think 'Sweet' only pertains to an 'additive!'

Question: *"What is Acidity in my coffee?"*

Answer: There are several different 'acids' found in coffee; but 'Chlorogenic acids' are, mostly, responsible for the brewed coffees, considered 'acidity.' Generally, it means the 'sensation' that the coffee creates on the tongue and roof of the mouth – but, not the taste; and, acidity can be increased or decreased by the beans roasting. Experts or 'Snobs' describe it as: *"How much 'moisture the coffee brew' can take away from ones' mouth."* 'High Acid Coffee' might bother people with GERD or other digestion problems!

Question: *"Does 'Aroma' mean the coffee's smell when ground?"*

Answer: Aroma can relate to the roasting process, the type of roast, the 'aroma' while brewing, the 'smell' in the cup, the variety of the coffee beans, the 'storage' of the 'raw' coffee bean, or even the beans grind – and is, especially, watched for by professional 'Coffee Buyers;' both with roasted beans and 'brewed' coffee while 'Cupping!'

'Aroma' is created during the roasting process – and, it is easy to identify 'burned' coffee by both its smell and taste. When coffee beans are roasted, the more 'caramelized' they become – and thus, more aromatic. A tasty 'brew' should 'smell good' while brewing (due to the beans aromatics)… alternatively, in the cup too! Even just opening a 'can or bag' of coffee, can 'smell great!' Not surprisingly, some 'experts' judge 'Roasted Beans' by its aroma alone!

Question: *"My Barista asked me if I like my coffee beans 'Baked or Bready'? What does this mean?"*

Answer: I am presuming, that your Barista, also, 'Roasts' the beans; as 'Baked or Bready,' refers to coffee roasting! Roasting over 'too low' a temperature, or for too long, can create more of a 'bready' taste – which some people prefer.

"Baked" coffee beans, however, can mean the exact opposite; 'cooked' (not burnt) over 'too hot' a flame – but, for an average amount of time.

Question: *"What does 'Balanced Coffee' mean?"*

Answer: *"Balanced,"* can refer to both 'variety and roasting;' but the flavor is not limited to just one type or kind of bean, or its roast. In other words, the finished product is 'Balanced.'

Question: *"What is Coffee Body?"*

Answer: 'Coffee Body,' can relate to the roast, once again; but mainly refers to the 'heaviness' or 'texture' of the coffee once brewed. It is considered by some, to refer to *"How strong or thick"* the brewed coffee appears while drinking, or in 'after-taste!' Some people confuse this term with 'strong tasting' or 'watery' coffee.

Question: *"My coffee shop talks about 'strong' coffee. What is 'Strong' coffee?"*

Answer: *"Strong Coffee"* refers to 'Dark, Roasted Beans;' in which 'more grounds/less water) is used in its brewing. However, many people are either referring to the coffees taste or caffeine content. If one wants 'strong' coffee, they need to adjust their 'Water/Coffee Ground' ratio.

Question: *"What is 'Bitter' Coffee?"*

Answer: *"Bitter Coffee"* is just as it says… the brew 'tastes a bit bitter!' Bitterness is about the 'roast or the preparation' of the coffee – such as using the wrong-sized grind in a French Press – or, sometimes, excess Carbon Dioxide (CO_2) in the beans! A 'Bitter' taste can be 'pervasive' when grinding, or 'immediately' brewing; in other words, not giving the beans/grind time to 'degas.'

It can, also, be caused by 'too low' a water brewing temperature. The most common reason for 'bitterness,' however, is 'over-extraction' of the beans during brewing.

Question: *"Is Bittersweet Coffee the same thing as Bitter Coffee? My Barista says, is it not?"*

Answer: Your Barista is correct! As with many 'coffee terms,' *"Bittersweet"* is mostly a 'roasting term.' Some people might, also, describe it as *"Coffee, being overly strong;"* but, it is a result of the beans being 'over-roasted' or 'burnt' – in other words, 'burning the beans' sugars;' and giving the beans something of a charcoal taste.

Question: *"Is 'Burnt Coffee' the same as Bittersweet?"*

Answer: It can be; however, 'boiling' a brew 'too long' can result in something of a 'burned' aroma or taste, also. Often, around coffee houses who roast their beans, there is a 'burnt' aroma in the air; however, the same can be said of anyone 'spilling' coffee or 'boiling over' their coffee – such as when using a Percolator – onto a burner! Also, some people feel that 'Smoky Roasts' are known as *"Bittersweet!"*

Question: *"What is 'Spicy' Coffee? Just adding Spice like Cinnamon to it?"*

Answer: *"Spicy"* coffee can refer to the aroma or flavor. Often, this is found with Guatemalan or Ethiopian coffees – but, more so, relates to a coffee's 'acidity' – or lack of it, that is. However, any 'spice' (such as Cinnamon or even Chili) can be added to coffee, if desired, to make it taste 'spicy!' Just remember, there is a difference between, 'spiced' coffee, and 'spicy' coffee!

Question: *"What is 'Wild, Earthy, or Natural' Coffee? My Barista says I should not worry about it – but then, why did he mention it if it is 'nothing' to worry about?"*

Answer: Not to be confused with 'Winey,' (where the coffee develops a 'wine-like,' sour flavor), these terms refer to when the 'fruit of the coffee cherry' can dry before its bean is removed. 'Earthiness' – or a 'dirt' taste – can, also, be detected. Often, too, this is the case where the beans 'dry' upon the soil, rather than a concrete slab – or, stay 'wet' too long. Unfortunately, beans can pick up 'flavor' from the ground or even mold. I agree with your Barista; and, would not worry too much... as most 'store buyers' will not buy this type of bean to sell – as it is considered 'sub-standard; and could, quickly, ruin a reputation! Some people (and even 'Snobs') do enjoy, and sometimes even 'seek out' the flavor, however!

Question: *"What is Flat Coffee?"*

Answer: 'Lattes' aside ('Flat Lattes' – Espresso with Micro-foam), 'Flat' refers to coffee 'lacking in acidity' – resulting in a lack of taste or aroma. This sensation is comparable to the 'feel' of 'flat' soda pop.

Often, water 'lacking in minerals will create a 'flat' tasting brew. Usually, when one of my students asked me about their 'flat' coffee, we determine it is a direct result of using 'Distilled' or 'Reverse Osmosis' water.

Question: *"What does 'Sour' coffee mean?"*

Answer: This question could go under processing; but 'Sour Coffee,' is an unpleasant aroma or flavor, which occurs when 'natural vinegar' has contaminated the beans. This happens when the coffee beans are not properly washed. It can, also, come from brewing coffee with water which is 'not hot enough' to release all the grinds flavors.

Yet another reason, is when beans 'too freshly roasted' are used – and which have not been allowed to 'degas' through time or by 'Blooming.' The excess CO_2, being released into the coffee, has a 'sour' taste to it. There is one more, 'rare' way to create *"Sour Coffee;"* and that is brewing coffee in a coffee maker which has been recently 'cleaned' with Vinegar – but not 'rinsed' well enough before brewing!

Question: *"What is Fruity Coffee?"*

Answer: *"Fruity,"* is yet another 'High Acidity' term in 'darker roasted' beans. It refers to 'fruity or wine-like' flavor characteristics, found in some 'high altitude,' Arabica coffees. It has <u>nothing</u> to do with pH. Often, it is a 'tasting' term for different coffees.

Question: *"What is 'Rioy' Coffee? My Barista often uses this term during tasting parties – and I have been too embarrassed to ask him!"*

Answer: "Rioy" (pronounced ree-o-ee... after Rio de Janeiro) is a Barista or 'Coffee Buyer' term for harshness. It can also be known as '<u>rough, musty</u>, or <u>dirty</u>.' Usually, this comes from beans which were poorly processed; or stored under 'less than perfect' conditions – like, 'open-air' or 'uncovered' cement slabs... alternatively, beans laying directly on the ground. They could, also, be 'low quality' or 'older' beans, which have not aged well.

Question: *"What is Cold, Brewed Coffee?"*

Answer: It could depend upon the 'comma' in your question; but most likely, it means *"Cold Brew"* – or 'Iced-Brewed Coffee' – which is a 'brewing method,' much the way some 'Tea' is brewed. Coffee is created by 'steeping' a medium, coarse, or extra-course, dark grind (although, any roast or grind may be used) in room temperature or refrigerated water for four or more hours. Generally, 'loose' grounds are used; but 'Steeping Balls,' or 'bagged' grounds can be used as well. If brewing 'loose,' the grounds should be 'filtered out' before pouring/drinking. I, personally, allow my Cold Brew 24 to 36 (or more) 'steeping' hours before filtering and drinking. *"Cold, Brewed Coffee,"* usually means just that: coffee, which is 'brewed and served,' cold!

Question: *"My coffee brand advertises it uses a 'Nitrogen Flush' to help keep their grounds fresh. What is it; and how does that help me?"*

(But first, another very similar question)

Question: *"Can I buy 'Organic Coffee', which has been 'Nitrogen Flushed'?"*

The Answer to both questions: Many larger or 'International Coffee Companies (such as 'illycaffè')' use what is called a 'Nitrogen Flush' to extend the shelf-life for their roasted beans and grinds. This system stems from other food items – such as potato chips – which have been very successful in extending storage; but only recently, has it been used with Coffee Beans.

Once a coffee bean is processed and roasted, it begins to degrade with exposure to oxygen; as oils and other substances start to 'break down' and become rancid! Of course, once a roast is 'ground,' it continues to degrade further… in fact, even faster!

Someone, somewhere, had the bright idea to try a 'Nitrogen Flush' with roasted coffee (as with foodstuffs) – when the beans were bagged. It was a good idea! The package or can is 'Flushed' with Nitrogen – which forces the oxygen out of the container before sealing. 'Flushing' works even better than simple vacuum-sealing alone; as it, also, provides some 'packaging protection' as well. Once the beans are exposed to the Nitrogen, and the bag sealed (often Vacuum sealed), the beans will 'off-gas' faster and more effectively within the container – which expels the gas (if in a 'coffee bag') through a 'one-way' valve. The coffee is not exposed to any oxygen this way. Most roasters claim that their beans will *"Still be fresh, up to a month or longer,"* after being bagged!

However, once the consumer opens the bag (or if the bag seems to have loose grounds in it) the coffee grounds will 'age' and deteriorate just as fast as 'non-flushed' grinds; again, due to being exposed to oxygen. Therefore, 'Vacuum Sealing' is, often, an excellent storage method, after opening the factory bags – or, for 'checking' to see if the bags are still sealed or not. 'Nitrogen Flushed' does not mean a thing if the bag, container, or K-Pod does not have a good seal!

There are no 'Certified, Organic Roastery's/Baggers' at this writing; as a 'Nitrogen Flush' is not considered to be an 'organically-friendly' practice. To keep all 'organic' or 'regular' beans fresh, again, use a Vacuum Sealer to help remove oxygen from the container! The less oxygen exposure, the longer the beans or grind will stay fresh! An excellent way to extend freshness, is to 're-vacuum' and 'seal' the bag, if possible; or transfer the coffee beans or grind to a 'sealable' bag or container.

Question: *"How should I store coffee? Someone told me I should keep it in a zip-lock bag in the Freezer!"*

Answer: 'Nitrogen Flushes' aside, this is both a 'good' and a 'bad' question! If the coffee were the <u>only</u> thing in a standard freezer (non-frost free) and both the coffee container and the freezer were well sealed, it would not be too bad – at least, for a while!

Seldom, would anyone have a 'standard freezer' just for Coffee – however, I do know a 'Coffee Snob' in one of our groups, who owns a small, 3.5 cubic foot one just for his coffee! I saw the freezer once; however, it smelled 'stale' when he opened it – all 'built-up' with ice, which will affect his 'open' coffee bags or containers! His coffee beans/grounds smelled equally 'stale' when opened! So, unless a freezer is not only 'Standard' (meaning it is <u>not</u> 'Frost-Free') and kept 'free of ice' (not to mention, kept free of food items), the coffee can 'pick up' smells and tastes! This is because the 'roasted coffee beans or grinds' are 'hygroscopic;' meaning, they can absorb moisture, odors, and flavors from the surrounding air.

As a rule of thumb, if one must 'freeze'… make it whole beans; and only do so in a 'Standard' (not Frost-Free) freezer, in <u>airtight</u> containers; as a 'Frost-Free' freezer will 'Freeze Dry' the coffee, and something like a 'zip-lock' bag might 'leak' air!

<u>STORAGE</u> <u>AND</u> <u>VACUUM</u> <u>SEALERS</u>

Many bags – vented or not – of 'Beans or Grind' are sold 'Vacuum Sealed' by the Roaster or the Wholesaler. 'Vented,' as previously mentioned, means there is a small, 'one-way' valve on the bag, which allows CO_2 and other gases to escape. Unfortunately, smaller bags – such as this one shown – <u>do</u> <u>not</u> have 'valves' on them; so fortunately, this type of bag does not allow air to pass back into the bag, either! These bags are designed to be 'used quickly' before the grounds can become stale.

One other thing to consider when one 'freezes' coffee beans or grinds – not to mention other foods – is the coffees 'cellular structure' changes; and this can prohibit the release of 'natural coffee oils' and aromas! Of course, this 'loss' affects the way the brewed coffee looks and tastes. Alternatively, according to one of my friends, *"Freezing makes my brewed coffee look and taste Murky!"* Some 'Snobs' feel (and, they might be right) that 'Blooming' the frozen coffee will help 'repair' the grounds before proper extraction. I have never tried it, so I cannot be sure!

Coffee Beans store best in 'cool and dark' places; rather than a 'deep freeze!' So, one is better off finding a suitable, sealable container; to keep the coffee in, then, simply 'storing it away' in a dark cupboard. Unfortunately, not all cabinets are 'cool;' especially, in 'warm' climates like mine!

The method I prefer – which, 'Coffee Snobs' would enjoy as well – is to use 'Vacuum Storage Containers;' in which to keep both beans and grounds. A sealable bottle or bag is good, but actually 'removing the oxygen' from the container helps to keep the beans or grounds from 'oxidizing' too fast!

However, if one is 'hell-bent' to keep their beans or grounds in a freezer or refrigerator, then a 'Vacuum Container' of some sort is <u>still</u> best! One does need to remember, however, 'freshly roasted' beans and 'fresh grinds,' need to 'degas' a bit – and can <u>crack</u> or <u>burst</u> a sealed container. 'Degassing,' therefore, the reason "*Why*," most commercial coffee bags have a 'one-way' valve in them! The gas can escape; but air cannot enter the bag!

Over the years, inventors have thought of countless ways to allow food to be stored without spoilage. Dry storing, then 'Dehydrating,' first came about; then, 'Freeze Drying' was thought to be the answer; but today, it is 'Vacuum Sealing' or, simply, 'air removal!'

'Vacuum Sealing' can be done in several diverse ways; and even when done 'crudely,' can still be somewhat useful! I know I, always, when using a zip-lock bag, 'squeezed out' as much air as possible… even before I ever heard of Vacuum Sealing! I still know some people, who not only do that, but have a 'Vacuum' of their own sort… using a 'standard zip-lock bag.' Seal all but, perhaps, the last ¼ inch of the 'zip lock;' pressing out as much air as one can… then, slipping a 'drinking straw' into the bag and quickly 'sucking out' any remaining air before sealing the bag. This procedure may be crude, but it is effective! 'Coffee Snob' approved? No!

A 'Vacuum Sealing' machine works, somewhat, the same way. After 'anything' (clothing, dry goods, wet foods or even coffee beans) are placed into a plastic bag, the machine creates a 'semi-seal' around the bags opening; then 'sucks out' the oxygen from it… pulling the 'plastic material' tight and, effectively, compressing the plastic bag. It, then, 'heat seals' the bag. This bag can be stored (or even stacked) anywhere – mostly safe, from oxidation, pests, or weather.

Even brewed coffee can be 'Vacuum Sealed' and stored. In the summertime, I will make copious amounts of 'extra strong,' Cold Brew Coffee for serving at 'Tastings;' but, rather than have several storage containers or carafes taking up space, I can easily make 'custom size bags' with my Vacuum Sealer, pour in the 'Cold Brew,' then seal the end of the bag. The bags can, easily, be stored in the refrigerator until use. I got the idea years ago when traveling in Mexico; and finding brands of Pasteurized Milk, sealed in plastic bags, being sold in stores.

To use, I can just take out single bags as I need them, 'snip off' the corner of the bag, and pour it directly into glasses or a carafe; or, if frozen for a few hours, place the 'frozen coffee' into a 'wide mouth' decanter; and allow it to 'de-frost' as it is being served! Alternatively, as I am fond of doing, 'break up' pieces of 'frozen coffee,' place it into a glass, and 'swizzle' chocolate and caramel syrup down the inside of a glass. I, then, 'half-fill' the glass with liquid Cold Brew; and add flavored foam, top with whipped cream, and add chocolate sprinkles on top! It is a sweet, cold, and refreshing treat, or dessert! As the 'frozen coffee' melts, it 'refills' the glass!

Another advantage to using 'Vacuum Plastic Bags' is, when they are opened, the beans can be 'poured out,' easily, as much as needed. The bag can, then, be 'Vacuum Sealed,' once again, to remove oxygen and place back into storage. The main thing to remember is, <u>do</u> <u>not</u> try to store too much – only store as much as can be 'ground and used' within a short period; such as only a few days' worth for ground beans, or a months' worth for whole, roasted beans. 'Green' beans may be stored for several months in a Vacuum Bag! The principal, problem with 'Plastic Vacuum or Storage Bags,' is (like coffee pods) they 'last forever' in our landfills! Luckily, there are some other options – such as biodegradable bags made from Hemp!

Some people do not want to 'mess' with making or filling plastic bags; or, trying to 'stack' anything of odd shape or size – nor, do others wish to contribute to 'plastic waste' in our landfills! So, for those people, 'Vacuum Canisters' are available – and, I use them myself for convenience; especially, on items which are used daily!

Frankly, when I get up at 4:00 or 5:00 AM (especially, after a late-night) I'm in no mood to work with a 'Vacuum Storage' machine or deal with opening and resealing plastic bags; and I certainly do not enjoy 'spilling' the loose beans or grind all over the floor, after I cut open a bag! So, I will use a 'Stainless Steel, Vacuum Storage Canister' – which I can keep on my kitchen shelf, just to the side of my 'Pure Water Dispenser' and  'Drip' coffee maker.' It is a simple matter to fill the coffee maker with water and open the Vacuum Canister for my ground coffee. I even keep a metal 'Tablespoon Scoop' in it; so I do not have to search for one through my early morning, 'Mental Fog!' The canister "*Hisses*" as air is pulled into to it when opened; and after spooning out the proper amount of grind, I push the top back down on the Canister and press the 'built-in pump' several times; to remove most the oxygen, once again!

I used to have canisters which had a 'valve' on their lids, which my Vacuum Sealer attached to; but again, at four or five o'clock in the morning, I did not like messing with the Vacuum Sealer or its noise, any more than I enjoyed handling, an awkward plastic bag filled with beans or grounds!

These Vacuum Canisters, with the built-in pumps, are not very expensive, considering – under $20.00, online, for a medium-sized one. I do not need an enormous container for grind; as I do not want to grind more than just a few days' worth of beans at a time. In fact, just yesterday (at this writing), I purchased a 'Three Bottle, Vacuum Canister Set' at my local supermarket! It came with a small pump, which would sit over a 'one-way' valve. All that is required is to 'push down' on the pump to hold it in place, while 'lifting' on its suction section. One or two 'lifts,' and the canister 'seals.' I only paid $7.99 for the small set (which came in three different size jars). I use the 'smallest' canister (shown above) for only a 'few days' worth of grounds – whereas, the larger ones for 'several days or weeks' worth of coffee!

Overall, Vacuum Canisters are more 'cost-effective' and easier to use than Vacuum Bags! Moreover, a proper 'Coffee Snob,' is more likely to 'store' coffee grounds in a 'Vacuum Container,' as it is 'trendy;' and has a certain amount of 'bragging' rights. However, they might be just as likely, use bags to store more significant amounts of their 'Freshly Roasted Coffee Beans' in a closet or cupboard. Also, they might even place a 'Dehumidifier' in the closet with the coffee. This helps keep the coffee from absorbing moisture and flavors (if there is an oxygen leakage) – another 'trendy' thing to do (like having a custom or 'walk-in' Humidor for cigars).

More Questions:

Question: *"Is it possible to have Coffee Grounds that are 'too fresh'?"*

(Let us look at a related question before I answer)

[85]

Question: *"Are 'Degassing and Off gassing' the same thing?"*

Answer: I have already, somewhat, answered this; but this question can be rather difficult to explain unless one 'roasts' their own beans. But yes, they are the same!

I do know a few 'Snobs' whom 'home roast,' as they only want the 'freshest' coffee; and feel, that *"Nobody but them"* is capable of properly 'roasting, grinding, and degassing!' Also, it is not uncommon to go into a coffee shop to see a 'combination' Coffee Grinder/Coffee Brewer – which will grind the beans, drop them into the brewer basket, then immediately pour hot water over them! I own an Espresso Machine like that, in fact! However, I do tend to be a 'bit selective' when it comes to the beans, I put into it! I try only to use beans which were roasted at least a few days to a week earlier! Then, I use the 'pre-wetting' selection on my machine. 'Pre-wetting' in this case, is the same as 'Blooming or Infusion' of the grounds.

I tend to believe that grounds 'fresh from the roaster' are definitely 'too 'fresh;' however, this can be a matter of opinion! Moreover, I have to agree with, not only my local Barista, but the 'recommendations' of my Espresso machine manufacturer, that even using 'Fresh Roasted Beans,' still make a *"Damn good cup of Espresso*!" I personally believe that using 'week old' roasts makes a better Espresso – and even then, I still like to 'Bloom' the grind!

However, with many people this is all 'moot;' as they are going to be adding creamers and more to their coffees!

Let's take a closer look at 'Degassing.'

"Good Coffee… Cheaper than Prozac!"

~ (Attributed to) Unknown

DEGASSING:

Although difficult to see in this small photograph, look at these 'freshly roasted' beans in the glasses. The beans have cooled for an hour; and they have only been in the glasses for, approximately five minutes. Yet, the insides of the glass appear to have 'steam' (or fog) building up on the inside. If the beans were immediately ground  and brewed, the result could be a rather, 'sour' cup of Black Coffee; however, additives will undoubtedly make a difference in 'how' sour the coffee tastes. I do know some Baristas who have 'standardized' on using such beans; not to mention some 'Coffee Snobs,' whom feel *"Freshly roasted and brewed is the only way to go!"*

 If one were to pour out the beans, the 'CO_2 film' would still be 'clinging' to the glass – making the glass appear 'used.' I recently spoke to a man who compared the process to the 'film/fog' which builds up on the inside of car windshields – when one has a slight leak in their air conditioner. So, can one 'see' the beans 'degas? Not generally; however, I repeated this experiment the following day, to see if I would achieve the same results twice; and found the same an hour after the beans were cool. Once again, the glasses 'fogged up,' as can be seen above – especially, in the smaller cup!

Recently, I was at a local (and <u>huge</u>), '24-hour Super Market' early (5:00 AM) one morning; where I like to buy 'Roasted Beans.' As it takes me longer to sort, mix, and grind, the beans than other people, I like to 'shop for coffee beans' before the store 'fills up' with other people… wanting to use the two store grinders.

The store has close to 40 different, 'over-head' bean dispensers; with at least 5 liters of beans in each of them. I have often wondered, *"There are so many distinct types of beans, and such large containers, how long ago were the beans roasted; and how long ago were these dispensers filled?"* The store staff had no idea when asked. As it happened that morning, the stores 'Coffee Supplier' was making a delivery; and, had just finished 'filling' the dispensers – and was, now, putting products like filters and syrups onto the shelves. I approached him and asked if I could *"Bother him for a minute or two;"* of which, he was happy to oblige.

"How often do you fill the beans dispensers," I asked?

"Every week…" was the reply. *"I 'top off' each dispenser."*

"And, how long ago, were the beans roasted?" I queried. Whereas nobody else in the store knew, this man had the answer right on the tip of his tongue:

"Oh, they are fresh! They were roasted, maybe… sometime yesterday afternoon!"

I asked him a few more questions; and, without telling me exactly 'who or where' the 'Roastery' was, he let slip that the beans were *"From a Professional Roastery, out by the Airport."* That was all I needed to know. Unless someone in a nearby house or an 'unmarked warehouse' was doing the roasting, I knew <u>exactly</u> who the roaster was – as there is only '<u>one</u>' near the airport… the very one of whom I, also, deal! However, it would have been a 'pretty good guess' anyway; as on his delivery cart was the major 'Name Brand' coffee, in 32-ounce bags, which is both sold in stores and supplied to one main 'Coffee Bar' in town. As it happened, this was the same coffee 'brand' that I purchase directly from the roaster myself – the supplier, just had a few 'commercial flavors and beans' which were not, generally, available to the general public from the Roaster!

Looking at the freshly filled, clear dispensers – and knowing that the beans were no longer hot – I could see all the dispensers were so 'steamed up' (so to speak) with CO_2 gas, the beans themselves could not be seen. I mentioned it to the delivery man, and asked, *"Is that steam in the dispensers?"* – knowing, already, that it was not – and he indicated, *"No,' the beans are cool; they are just degassing!"* A few days later, I returned to the store; and rechecked the dispensers for CO_2 gas… they were clear! The 'delivery man' was not lying to me that the beans were 'Fresh;' and were, indeed, 'degassing!'

'Degassed' grind tastes quite different than freshly ground! People who do not roast beans themselves may notice something of the same if they buy 'freshly roasted' beans. Fortunately, or unfortunately, by the time the consumer has purchased their beans or grind (not fresh ground), they have already 'degassed' about as much as they are going to – therefore one can, usually, go directly from 'Grinder to Brewer!' It is always a sign of 'old beans,' when one 'Blooms' their coffee and finds little or no 'bubbles' or 'foam' on top of the wet grounds.

Stepping back for a moment, when coffee beans are roasted, various 'gases' form inside. When roasting is completed, the gases (mostly carbon dioxide) start to 'seep out' of the hard beans. Many 'Professional Roasters' know, that if their customers brew 'too early' with the fresh roasts, they may get a 'flat' cup of coffee – and thus, giving them the 'reputation' of having 'bad' beans. Therefore, some of them do not start selling their 'Roasted Coffee Beans' until a week or longer after the roasting process – to give the beans time to get rid of the excess, carbon dioxide (CO_2), which can 'disfavor' the coffee. Other roasters, however, package at once; feeling that the beans will have 'degassed' within their bags by the time they reach the consumer – and, often they are correct! When it comes to some 'discount' stores, bags of beans are so old, that the coffee has not only thoroughly 'degassed,' but has begun to go 'rancid!'

Age aside, 'grinding the beans,' can 'speed up' the 'degassing' process. As a rule, if the coffee has been 'freshly' roasted (depending upon the beans, roast, and grinding), one should allow anywhere from 1 hour to 12 days to fully 'off-gas.' Most roasted coffee will lose, approximately, 40% of their gases with the first 24 hours of the roast – with darker roasts, usually, degassing faster than lighter roasts. This fact, is why the 'Coffee Supplier' (at the store I previously mentioned) merely, "*Topped off*," the coffee bins; as none were totally empty, and it would take at least 24 hours before the 'new beans' would 'work their way' out of the bin to be purchased!

As most other 'roasted beans' are two or more weeks old before they reach the consumer, grinding and using them at once does not necessarily make too much difference. Nonetheless, in the best of all worlds, we would all want to drink coffee, 'brewed from beans,' which were roasted for no more than 'two weeks' before use.

Often, during many of my 'out and about' lectures, this question comes up; "*What about my Barista? I watch him or her take 'fresh beans' and place them into a Mill – which is mounted above a brewer! His Coffee/Espresso tastes good!*" The best I can answer is, "*Yep... go figure!* Perhaps, you should ask yourself: "*How long ago were the beans roasted?*" Perhaps, the beans are a week or two old after roast! Also, "*Is the coffee being drunk 'Black,' or does it have any creamers, sugars, or other additives added to it; or, is it part of a drink like a Mocha, Latte, Cappuccino, or Iced Coffee?*"

Not surprisingly, people tell me that their coffee is "*Good!*"

[89]

Of course, I always ask people at my lectures as well, *"How long have you been drinking this, particular type of coffee?* Often the answer is, *"For years!"* I would suppose, the definitive answers would be: *"People can get used to just about anything, and enjoy it;"* and, *"This is why, we all need to 'educate' ourselves regarding the differences in brewing methods, beans, grinds, roasts, waters, and more!"* However, maybe a better question is, *"How 'good' is your 'good'?"*

Here is another question, for more detail on 'Degassing:'

Question: *"Someone told me that 'Bloom' is 'deadly' gas which must be released from the coffee before it can be consumed! That is why it is called 'Degassing.' I like coffee, but I don't want to risk Hypercapnia!"*

Answer: To reiterate much of what has been stated before, *"Bloom,"* (or 'pre-wetting/pre-infusion') refers to the 'foam' that appears on the top of coffee grounds when 'pre-wet' with hot water; and the 'Carbon dioxide' (CO_2) trapped in the grounds is released. Even without 'Blooming,' 'Roasted Coffee Beans' are going to 'degas' over time.

There is nothing 'deadly' about any of the 'gases' which may be in the 'Raw,' or 'Roasted' Beans; as the amounts are so minuscule! However, yes… the CO_2 gas is deadly; breathed in high enough concentrations. This condition is called 'Hypercapnia;' a condition where there is 'too much CO_2 in the blood.

To reiterate it is impossible to have Hypercapnia (or CO_2 poisoning) from 'Blooming' coffee!

Let us take a closer look at 'Blooming' on the next page.

"Decaffeinated coffee is the devil's blend."

~ (Attributed to) Unknown Author

BLOOMING (or, Pre-Infusion)

As mentioned several times in this book, 'Bloom,' is the term for 'what happens after placing 'ground coffee' into a French Press, Ground Holder, Portafilter, or Cone Filter of some sort; and a small bit of hot water – only 1 or 2 ounces – is introduced. In other words, just enough water to cover the grounds is used. This process 'prepares' the grounds for coffee 'extraction;' by 'expanding' the grounds; and releasing CO_2 and other gasses, which can make coffee taste 'flat' or 'sour!'

'Blooming' is considered a 'pre-infusion' (some may call it pre-wetting) process – even if the coffee is <u>not</u> being prepared in an 'Infusion' brewer. The 'Blooming' process takes between 30 to 45 seconds; however, some people like to allow their grind to 'expand' for a minute or longer; and some 'brewer manufacturers' even recommend it with their brewing devices; or, as with some 'Drip' or 'Espresso' brewers, have a 'Blooming function built-in!

Some people like to 'Bloom' with cold water – especially when brewing a 'Cold Brew' coffee. 'Cold Blooming,' will still work to a certain degree; but the grind does not expand as much, dissolve, or release as much CO_2! How does this work when making 'Cold Brew,' when, usually, coffee is 'just added' to the water? If brewing for 1, 2, or more days, 'Blooming' does not matter too much. However, some professionals (and 'Snobs') feel that instead of merely 'pouring' loose grounds into a 'Cold Brewer,' if they are placed into a 'Steeping Ball' first... it can be 'dipped' into a cup or pan of 'hot' water for several seconds, to 'pre-wet and expand' the grind. The 'Steeping Ball' is then dropped into the container of cold water. It does make sense; when one considers that the 'expanded coffee grounds' will 'extract' more flavor, essence, and oils, when immersed in the cold water for an extended period.

However, the most straightforward answer to 'Why' we want to 'Bloom' our coffee in the first place, is because it allows the 'coffee bed' (the grounds in the holder or filter of whatever brewer chosen) to have more 'even' extraction during the brewing process; and thus, 'extract' more flavor. Moreover, if I have not, already, been clear enough, the simple answer is: "*To make the coffee better!*"

Is coffee 'bad' if 'Blooming' is not performed? No; but it may taste a bit different (sourer) without 'Blooming' – and that can be "*Okay*" with some drinkers! Again, remember, most people can get used to anything!

In the photographs below, an unbleached paper filter is placed into a 'Pour-Over' brewer. The filter was, purposely, left dry; rather than 'pre-wet' – not only for photographic purposes, but so the bottom of the filter could be 'pre-wet' at the same rate as the grounds. As there are no grounds in the

'top part' of the filter, it can be 'wet' during the Blooming/brewing process; and have less deterioration – or chance of tearing if the grounds are 'stirred' to break up any 'Bloom Crust' (Crust...what forms on top of the grounds from loose grounds and CO_2). Then, one to two ounces of hot water (or just enough to cover the grounds) is poured over them (the water is poured, 'circularly,' to wet the beans thoroughly). As previously stated, the 'Bloom' (bubbles and foam) is formed when the hot water releases the remaining CO_2, or other gases, in the grind – most are released into the air... moreover, this process can <u>improve</u> the taste of the coffee! However, many people feel it necessary to 'drain' any water which has not been absorbed into the grounds – and thus, any left-over CO_2 in the water is disposed of!

I am rather indifferent about it – depending upon my brewer. If using a 'Clever Dripper' – where I can depress the bottom to let out the 'Blooming Water,' I will. If using a 'Drip' device, Percolator, or 'French Press,' I don't bother with it!

The grounds can sit in their 'Ground Holder' from anywhere from 10-30 seconds – traditionally; but, usually, 'time' is set by preference or convenience. I, personally, tend to bloom for upwards of one minute; because it takes me that long to get everything I need together! However, other people might 'Bloom' for up to two or three minutes (according to one's taste); this is why some 'Home Baristas' use a 'plate heater' to keep their pot or cup 'warm' before brewing. If brewing in a 'Pour-Over' Cone – and wishing to 'get rid of' any leftover 'Blooming' water – I recommend 'holding the Cone' over a sink – so, the 'Bloomed' water 'passes through' the grind and drains into the sink. Of course, one needs to either keep their cup warm during this process or 'pre-warm' their cup just before the brewing process.

Depending upon the size, brand, or type of brewer, I might 'stir' the brew, somewhat, after I have poured <u>all</u> the water through; to avoid 'layering' of the extracted coffee, temperature, and any 'Bloom' water. However, 'stirring during the extraction,' can be appropriate as well – but, not always practical!

The finished coffee does not 'layer' quite so much in the carafe or cup when using a 'Clever Dripper' – as it tends to 'mix' as it 'steeps' and drains. This is another reason why some people will pour their hot water into their brewer in 'stages,' when using a 'straight-through' brewer! The coffee will 'mix' better in the cup or carafe – and, it is an effective way to keep <u>both</u> the brewing water, and grind, 'hot!

Some 'Coffee Snobs' claim, *"If the coffee is not 'stirred/mixed' after brewing, any extra CO_2 will 'float' to the top of the pot or cup; and thus, make your first impression of the coffee unfavorable! CO_2 must be either eliminated, or thoroughly 'mixed,' for a 'clean' cup of coffee!"*

As I often put milk or flavored creamer in my coffee (which always needs stirring), 'layers of brew' or 'leftover CO_2' is never an issue!

As previously stated, some Baristas 'Bloom' their grounds with cold water; whereas others, 'swear' by *"210°F or higher temperature water;"* but then, brew with the 'proper temperature' for their brewer. Others might 'Bloom' with water between 165°F-180°F – then, brew with, <u>only</u>, 205°F water! Still more people, like myself, choose to both their 'Bloom and Brew' with the same temperature… mostly because it is 'easier' and we cannot taste the difference!

As I, often, use an 'adjustable and heated, Gooseneck Kettle' to pour with, it is easy to keep the same temperature through both Blooming and Brewing. The kettle goes back on its 'heated' stand, while the grounds are 'Blooming;' and while I am getting my mug and 'additives' ready. Within a minute, my water is back to the 'proper brewing temperature,' which I enjoy most; and I can start brewing!

Frankly, all of this 'Special Temperature for Blooming,' is rather 'Anal Retentive!' Use pure water, of any 'hot' temperature, to 'Bloom;' but remember, 'hotter water works better and faster than cold;' to 'expand' the grounds, and to release the CO_2 and flavor essences!

More questions:

Question: *"What ratio of 'Coffee Grounds to Water' to should I use? Should I use a scale – and how 'exact' <u>are</u> measurements? What about Decaf? Does it make any difference in anything?"*

Answer: This is very difficult to answer; as, again, everyone has their own 'tastes,' as to what they prefer… not to mention, cup/mug sizes for 'how' they enjoy their coffee. The average coffee cup is 5.6 ounces in size; but the 'mugs' I use, are each 12-ounces! I even have some 14 and 16-ounce mugs. The size of the cups is one of the main reasons for everyone's different 'tastes!' A larger cup or mug is going to require a more significant amount of grounds in which to brew – by the cup, that is!

For example, I enjoy my coffee 'rich and dark;' so I use a bit more grounds (about 57 - 60 grams/4 heaping tablespoons) in my 'Drip' coffee maker, than others might – but, not with all beans! As a rule, a '1 to 15' ratio is common, for most people. The directions, which came with my brewer, however, recommend "*1 to 12 ratios*;" but, my 'Roaster' recommends (again, depending upon the beans and roast), "*1 to 14 or 1 to 16 ratios*" for a 'Drip' brewer. Go figure! However, both my 'cans' of Folgers (Decaf and Regular, 'Black Silk') state, "*1 tablespoon per 8 ounces of water – or a ½ cup of grounds – for a standard, '10 cup Drip Coffee Maker'.*" So, 'taste' is going to take some experimentation!

However, when it comes to 'Commercial Pods,' for a Keurig or other 'pod' device, there is very little one can do to change the ratio – short of, adding more (or less) water! Nonetheless, the manufacturers have thought of that; and have added a 'special' feature (Regular or Bold) to many devices. Mine, for example, has not only the choice of 'how much' water to use but 'how long' it takes to be 'injected' through the Pod. The 'amount' of coffee does not change per Pod (unless I use a 'refillable' Pod, 'overfill' it and, perhaps, 'tamper' it down) – but, 'how long' it takes for the water to travel through the Pod does change due to volume – especially, if I use the 'Bold' setting and 'tamper' my grounds, slightly!

Remember, with most brewing devices; it should take three or more minutes to fully 'extract' the flavors, oils, essences, and aromas! Unfortunately, the 'K-Pod' brewer, uses, approximately one-third of that time! The brewer works something like an Espresso Machine; and <u>forces</u> water under pressure, through small 'needles' which 'puncture' the Pod. This is why so many people are 'thrilled' with 'Pod Brewers…' as they 'brew' in a minute or less – not counting 'water heating' time, that is! Under the 'Bold' setting of my brewer, water is forced through the Pod at a 'slower' rate; and thus, the grounds in the Pod are subjected to 'hot water' for a more extended period… making, 'darker' (and 'bolder') coffee! It is easy to see that there are not any (or at least few) 'ratios' to consider when using K-Pods.

My 'overall' advice for 'Coffee Ratios' is, start with one, level tablespoon of grounds (depending upon the roast) for every, standard, '5.6 ounces' cup or mug of water; and add more coffee grounds, if desired, next brewing time to 'fine-tune' the pot. Start slow and try using a 'heaping' tablespoon the next time to 'augment,' if necessary. Moreover, if you ever buy an actual Coffee Scale, 'standardize' on it; so, you always know how much grind to use. Just remember, not all brewing methods use the same 'weight' of grounds! With a scale, one can even determine the exact 'ratio' of coffee to water by measuring both on the scale! It is through this kind of 'standardization,' one can achieve identical results and taste,' over and over – that is, from the same kind/roast of beans! Just remember, different beans, different roasts, different grinds, and different brewing methods may require <u>different temperatures</u> of water; to extract the best flavors!

Question: *"What water temperature should I use to brew coffee? My favorite Barista says he uses 'Fish Eye' (not 'Fisheye') Water – but has never gone into any detail? What is that?"*

Answer: 'Brewing Temperature,' is a subjective thing; as I will show in the following pages. *"Fish Eye,"* however, is known as a 'Chinese term;' and refers not just to the temperature of the water, but 'bubble size…' as a 'visual' way of brewing <u>without</u> a thermometer.

Technically speaking, the ideal temperature for brewing coffee is between 190°F and 205°F (91C to 96C); as grounds do not dissolve or extract well at lower temperatures. However, different brews, beans, and grinds, waters, and altitudes, can <u>all</u> require different temperatures – higher or lower!

'Fish Eye' – Or, as it is sometimes called **'Small Pearls'** water, relates to Tea more than it does coffee; being considered as the 'highest temperature' (usually, in the 180°F-190°F range) one should use for tea. Its 'bubble size' (as seen here) determines 'when to brew' for the Barista! A nice idea… should everyone be able to determine the correct bubble size and if every pot 'boiled' the same way!

Unfortunately, not everyone can be a good judge of 'bubble' size; and, bubbles are, often, found to be different in size, depending upon the pot and heat source being used. Right off hand, I would have to ask, "*What kind of fish has 'eyes' the size the Barista is looking for*," as 'Fish Eye' could be misleading!

Surprisingly many Baristas are, now, considering 'Fish Eye' water, at least, for their 'Blooming!' However, many more are considering many other types of 'Fish (or other creature)s Eyes' for various brewing; as they don't want to bother with thermometers. Frankly, as everything seems to be so 'automated' these days, I do not know why thermometers would even be an issue! However, 'Eye' water is an interesting concept – please compare the photographs on this and the next pages.

This type of 'brewing' needs a 'keen eye,' rather than a thermometer; to distinguish between "*Eyes*" of water bubbles and brewing temperatures! However, in the photographs below, I show several different versions of the water in similar temperature (boiling – 210°-211°); in as much, as different heaters, burners, pots, pans, lids, et cetera, will cause water to 'boil' water differently – especially, at different altitudes!

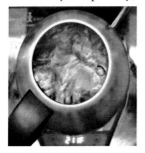

In actuality, 'Fish Eye' refers to the 'pre-boiling stage' of water – and the size of the bubbles ('Eyes') which form in the bottom of the pot or pan; in this case, quite small! 'Fish Eye' temperature is, approximately, 175°F – 190°F (although, there is some discussion on temperature); and, again, the bubbles are considered a 'visual aid' for 'seasoned Baristas.' The unfortunate thing is when it comes to 'bubble size,' there is very little difference optically; unless one 'standardizes' on one, 'accurate,' boiling method! Surprisingly, each water 'boiling' method is going to give different results – as is seen above.

Left 'uncovered,' and in three different containers, I found three different results at, roughly, the same temperatures; and, this did not even take into account 'altitude!' However, when using a thermometer to check the water on the 'Induction Cooktop,' it, also, read out at 211°F. I will not go into 'different containers' when used on an 'Induction Cooktop!' Just trust me, different materials react differently with Induction; and must only be made of cast iron, stainless steel, or carbon steel. A good test is, to place a magnet on the bottom of the kettle; if it 'sticks,' the kettle/pot can be used on the Induction heat source.

When starting with 'Fish Eye' water, 190°F, the 'bubbles' can be seen better than at the starting point of 180°F. 'Baristas' (tea or coffee) call the bubbles "*Fish Eye*," because that is the approximate size of them… at least, in China. They are the size of small, 'fish's eyes.' What kind or type of fish? Well, that information was never disclosed to me! Again, although lower in temperature than what is recommended for most brewed coffee, many people use this temperature to brew; especially, when 'drinking' immediately. One 'former' Roaster I knew, even preferred this temperature for 'Cupping!'

To the untrained eye, the differences of water temperature are very subtle; except for 'Raging Torrent' or 'Rolling Boil.' It should be noted, however, 'uncovered pans' tend to have smaller bubbles – so one must 'learn' to carefully judge their bubbles… 'uncovered' (not to mention, 'know' their brewing altitude, and adapt accordingly). Perhaps, a 'clear' pot works best for this purpose – with the water brought to a boil! Removing it from the heat, for several seconds, generally, lowers the water temperature to the brewing temperature I enjoy most. However, as it is easy to control heat in my Bonavita, adjustable kettle, I can keep the water at 211°F; and not worry about 'bubbles!'

So, invariably, someone will ask me, "*Why should I be concerned with 'Chinese' water? Why would I even care to know about it?*"

The answer is, you do not need to know about it; unless you are a Barista, a 'brewing' fanatic, camping or without a thermometer, or are a 'Coffee Snob!'

Although difficult to judge, here are some other 'Chinese Eye' water temperatures on the next page.

"*I judge a restaurant by the bread and by the coffee.*"

~ (Attributed to) Burt Lancaster

WATER TEMPERATURE – VIA 'FISH EYES'

'Shrimp Eye' – or **'Small Pinhead'** as it is also known, is the 'coolest' of the 'Eye' waters;' ranging in temperature from 155°F – 165°F. 'Fish Eye,' one might remember, is 180°F – 190°F to 205°F. 'Shrimp Eye' is, overall, viewed by Baristas as, *"Too cold"* for proper brewing; but it <u>is</u> the proper temperature for delicate, 'Green Teas' or 'Instant Coffee.' Surprisingly, there are some Baristas who <u>do</u> enjoy this temperature for 'Blooming' or 'Cold Brews.'

It is sometimes called 'Small Pinhead' water; as it has 'bubbles' what are 'pinhead' in size. 'Bubbles,' however, are only beginning to form on the bottom of the pot or pan, and not on the sides; and there is very little steam which can be seen.

'Crab Eye' – Or, **'Large Pinhead'** water, is a bit hotter than 'Small Pinhead' – around 165°F – 180°F; and 'tops off' only 10°F below 'Fish Eye' photograph in temperature; but, there is a huge difference in bubble size. The 'pre-boiling' water has small bubbles forming on the sides of the pan; as well as larger, 'Crab Eye' bubbles forming on the bottom of the pan. 'Crab Eye' temperature is considered by some, to, be a *"More proper"*

temperature for 'Blooming' ones' coffee. Visual steam is starting to develop toward the 180°F range.

This temperature is, more often, used while brewing 'White,' and other forms, of Tea; but, but more commonly, with 'Instant' Coffees! Again, there seem to be more and more Baristas' who are choosing this temperature for not only 'Blooming,' but individual 'Pour-Over' brewers, and for <u>starting</u> 'Cold Brew.' The water is considered 'hot enough' to extract the most flavor from the beans; while not being 'too hot' to be considered a 'Hot Brew.' Coffee grounds are placed into a large container (I use a one gallon, 'Sun Tea' jar with a 'spout'), the 'Crab Eye' water is added, then I place the jar into the refrigerator for 24 hours. It is not 'cold' to start, but it is not 'hot' either!

'Fish Eye' – Or **'Small Pearl.'** The previously mentioned, 'Fish Eye' water follows the 'Crab Eye' (in order of temperature); with still more significant, bubbles, and at 175°F – 190°F. With this photograph, as compared to the 'Crab Eye' on the previous page, there is only 10°F difference between the two pans shown; yet, there is an <u>enormous</u> difference between the bubble and steam size!

Many 'Snobs,' will <u>only</u> use this temperature when brewing with an AeroPress; but it can be used with anything – in fact, I see it more and more with 'individual,' or 'custom,' Baristas!

'String of Pearls' – Or, **'Rope or Small Eye'** as it is, also, known, is closer to what most Baristas (or coffee Snobs) use for actual brewing temperatures… 185°F – 205°F. If sticking, strictly, to 'Coffee Code,' one might note, that this water must be poured <u>immediately</u>; or else it will cool down too much for proper brewing. Perhaps, before pouring, the water should be brought up to 207°F; to allow for 'pouring' at 205°F

(as the temperature is going to 'start to drop off' immediately upon removing from the heat); perhaps, even more, when considering ones 'home altitude!'

Once again, 'brewing altitude' (easily checked on the internet) should be checked for accuracy, and the heat source, 'heating temperature' adjusted. Remember, due to air pressure, the 'boiling point' of water drops one degree for every 500 feet of altitude above sea level!

'Snobs,' and some Baristas, claim 'String of Pearls' is best used for 'Dark Teas' as well as coffees; and say, "*Water any hotter, will 'scorch or burn' the grounds!*" As it happens, many 'hot water pots, or dispensers,' use this temperature – as it works so well with 'Pour-Over' or 'French Press' brewers!

'Raging Torrent' – Or, **'Dragon Eyes,'** is what the average stove, hot plate, or electric tea kettle will create when boiling water – between, 200°F–220°F (remember, 212°F is the actual boiling temperature of water at sea level). This photograph happens to show a 'middle' temperature; of 210°F – just under 'boiling' (I only chose this temperature, as the Induction Cooktop only 'sets' in standard increments). Luckily, when I photographed

these different water types, I was at an altitude was only 50 feet above sea level – so, temperatures are relatively accurate! 'Raging Torrent' is the temperature I tend to use most when brewing – that is, at my 'home' altitude.

If using my Gooseneck Kettle (and out of habit), I allow my water to boil at a slightly higher temperature (220°F); then, by removing the kettle from the heat source, and turning to my coffee brewer, by the time I begin to pour, the water has dropped in temperature to, approximately, the 210°F temperature I was looking for. I don't worry about any 'reduction' of oxygen!

The temperatures ranges are considered 'plus or minus;' generally because many devices (such as my Induction 'hot plate' shown on above) are not adjustable in 'single degree' amounts. They only have 'preset' temperatures for the most popular coffees, teas, soups, or general cooking – and, that is why I am always stressing 'altitudes'… for 'fine-tuning' my temperatures!

Perhaps 'Dragon Eyes,' is a poor choice of words; as there are few 'Dragons' around to compare… even historically! Frankly, I would think Dragons would have to be 'rather small,' if we had to judge them by 'bubble size!' However, 'Raging Torrent' is the temperature many Baristas use for 'Blooming' their coffee. Many of them are like me; and feel that by the time they remove the water from the heat source and 'bloom' the coffee, the water in their kettles have 'dropped' to the correct brewing temperature.

Again, I do not worry about the water 'de-oxygenating,' or 'concentrating minerals' by bringing the water to a boil for less than a minute – and, as my 'Induction Plate' heats fast – I do not have to 'watch it' for an extended time! If I am brewing with a method which requires 'absolute' accuracy in temperature, then I will use my adjustable, Bonavita, Gooseneck Kettle – because it is adjusted able in 1-degree increments. However, I do know some 'non-snobs;' who do not worry about 'boiled' water, lack of oxygen, or 'too high' a temperature, when brewing coffee. They turn their stovetop burner up to 'high,' then (when they remember to return to their boiling water) 'brew' with whatever 'boiling' temperature they might find! There is an 'Eye' water for this too... however, it is 'not' a 'Fish Eye;' it is known as:

'Dog Eye' – Or, **'Severe Rolling Boil.'** Again, no 'Fish' here... 'Dog Eye' is, in theory, when the water is 'fiercely,' boiling; but one cannot, adequately, see the bottom of the pot or pan; as the bubbles are 'boiling so fast and large,' and the steam is thick, it obscures the view – at least, sometimes, depending upon both the pan and heat source. In the pan and heat source shown in the photograph, one can still see the bottom

of the pan reasonably well, however, with a 490°F temperature! Plus, it did not have much of a 'rolling' boil! Had I placed a 'lid' on the kettle or had the pan over a 'gas' burner, it may have had 'larger' bubbles and more steam!

Bubble size? Well, Baristas 'in the know,' call it 'Dog Eye' when the 'bubbles' look more like the ones in this photograph; but at this temperature, it is difficult to judge any bubble size – let alone, 'Dog' – as it is such a 'rolling' boil! Moreover, 'steam' is usually 'fierce!' I had to have someone 'blowing' the steam away while I took the picture; as I could not even 'see' the water in the Bonavita Kettle due to the thick steam!

'Raging Torrent' comes in at 'Roiling Boil' of 212°F; but <u>above</u> that temperature (of which one would not think there would be much difference), there is very little difference in bubble size! Even at 490°F, 'Severe Raging Torrent' has very little difference in bubble size than the 215°F shown above. When the water is 'boiled' at high temperatures, such as 490°F, it will, perhaps, 'de-oxygenate' a bit more, and faster; making the coffee taste a bit 'flatter' than it will at 215°F or lower. If one were to 'Cover the pan' while boiling, it might taste very different still!

[101]

I wish there were enough room in this book to include different heating methods, pots, and pans with lids, to demonstrate the difference in 'bubble size,' about the different heat sources; as well as the differences which come with 'change of altitude!' However, the reader can test these for themselves!

WATER, OVERALL:

'Hard Water… Soft Water… Purified Water… Heavy' Water…?' Just as 'Coffee Snobs' will 'turn their noses up' at, countless, insignificant 'coffee issues,' even the 'type of water' to be used has become a <u>major</u> 'arguing' point with some people. 'Hard or soft' water aside, there are different 'types' of coffee water to consider – and, everyone has an opinion on them!

For example, at one 'former' Coffee Club meeting, I overheard a group of people, at various tables surrounding me, having a 'heated' discussion about water; with none of them 'happy' with the '<u>unknown</u>' type of water and temperature the Coffee Bar used to brew with.

"Never use 'city tap water' to make coffee! It is full of Fluoride, Drugs, Fungus, Bacteria – and, is laced with Sewage!" One man screamed at the others while pounding his hand on the table! He was, obviously, angry!

"I will only use 'Reverse Osmosis' water, that I <u>make myself</u>, for my coffee maker," exclaimed another man, *"From my own, trusted, device,"* he demanded! I wondered why he was even there!

"You are both wrong," one woman joined in from across the room… *"Distilled, Spring water is the <u>only</u> way to brew Coffee or Espresso; and I have it delivered in 5-gallon bottles!"* Again, I wondered, 'why' this person was there when it was common knowledge that the Coffee Shop did not use bottled, *"Distilled Spring Water!"* Why was she drinking this coffee?

"Steam-distilled or mechanically distilled?" One man shouted from another table, *"Steam Distilled water is unacceptable!"* I would have to agree with him, at least somewhat; but I kept drinking my coffee and reading a newspaper!

"I say, 'Alkaline and Ionized' Water is the only way to go," another man, still one more table away, chimed in! Again, I had to wonder, *"Why"* <u>any</u> of these were there.

Finally, one more group member, sitting near me, turned to look at me and said, *"Let's ask the 'so-called, expert,' who wrote the coffee book…"* and they all turned to look at me!

I nearly spit out my coffee. *"Just use the 'pure water' that you think tastes best,"* is how I replied. The group looked at me like 'stunned sheep' for a moment; until one woman stated, *"He, obviously, does not know anything about water and coffee,"* then got up to go ask the Barista *"What water he was using,"* to brew their beverages; and to *"Educate him,"* she said!

I do not attend this club any longer; as they were, often, turning to me to 'take sides,' or decide if someone was 'right or wrong!' Happily, my last group of which I was a member, in Chico, never did that sort of thing!

However, there are some 'factual' reasons 'to and not to' use certain types of water; and, it does not have anything to do with being a 'Snob!' The man stating, *"Never use tap water"* was somewhat correct – not everywhere; but at least, in my town. Most 'City Tap Water' is not fit to drink anymore; and, in places like Flint, Michigan, or Puerto Rico, as of this writing, it is not even fit to cook with or even bath in!

However, with some remote locations – small, family farms and such – I am sure it is still possible to get good, fresh 'Well' water! This too, of course, is dying out; as pesticides from the owners own, or neighboring, farms and ranches can leach pesticides, chemical fertilizers, and animal waste into their 'Drinking Water' wells… so many local governments (at least, in California) are insisting upon *"Everyone having 'City' water and sewer,"* due to the 'poor' groundwater. In the same sense, 'seasonal flooding' can contaminate even remote wells (as well as City Water), with all kinds of 'crud!' For example, one flood or forest fire, and nobody has fit, drinkable water for an extended period – which, is what happened to family and me lately! After a devastating fire, back in November of 2018, in which thousands of us lost our homes and almost our entire town of 'Paradise' burned down, some ten months later (at this writing), both the ground and city water are, still, contaminated and 'unfit' to use! What few businesses are left standing and working, are forced to have to 'truck in' any water to use; as 'Utility and City' authorities claim, *"It may be up to 3 to 5 years before water can be 'restored' to a 'fit,' drinking condition."*

Surprisingly, two of the local Coffee Houses, which did not burn down, were able to 'return to business' after a few months; but, at this writing, have installed Water Storage Tanks, for use. It is not Alkaline and Ionized water, Reverse Osmosis water, Steam Distilled Water, Spring Water, or any other kind of 'specialized' water! They simply 'truck in' Purified Water to use!

[103]

For ourselves, now (living in a new community, on 3.5 acres and next to the Sacramento River) we have 'Well Water!' Unfortunately, we found that our 'Well Water' was 'somewhat unfit' to drink; as not only pesticides from neighboring orchards have contaminated the water, but 'flooding' of the river has 'dirtied/contaminated' the water as well – not to mention, the plumbing in our old 'Farm House' (and pipes underground from the 'Well Tank' to the house) is old and, apparently, rusted and made from lead! Water comes out of the tap (or even the garden hose, for that matter) 'brown' for several seconds; and, has a somewhat 'Sulfur' smell about it! We have attempted to put it through a 'Water Filter' to remove 'Lead' and other substances, but even it cannot 'filter out' all of the 'brown/grey' color. So, we purchase 5-gallon 'Pure' water bottles to use in two dispensers; one 'manual' one for use in 'tastings and classes,' and one 'electric' model – which will dispense both 'hot and refrigerated' water!

When I was a kid, I thought nothing about drinking 'Well' water – or even drinking 'City' water, for that matter… right out of a green, garden hose! Moreover, while camping, prospecting, or fishing, it was not uncommon to 'cup my hands' into the stream, river, or lake, and take a drink when thirsty – providing, it looked clear! We even filled our RV water tank with lake or stream water – and never owned a white, 'Potable Water Hose' to use when filling from a 'random' gas station! We did, sometimes, put in a few 'Purifying Pills' into the tank, however!

Once, we even 'chipped off' <u>clean</u> (inner) pieces of an Alaskan Glacier; to, not only, put into our sodas and mixed drinks, but to 'melt' to make coffee! Today, however, we do not dare; because (global warming 'shrinking Glaciers and aside), there are too many pollutants, contaminants, chemicals, garbage, sewage, industrial waste, heavy metals, ancient pathogens, and parasites in and on the Glaciers and their melting water! This is 'so sad,' as when I was a kid, the Glaciers we would visit were a pristine 'white' on top; with a 'turquoise blue' hue, underneath. The last time I visited a Glacier if we wanted to see any 'white,' we had to take something to 'scrape off' the black dirt, pollution, and contaminants from its surface!

So, what kind of water should be used to make coffee? The technical answer from any Barista, and what a stated a few paragraphs back, is: "*Only Pure Water*;" but, the non-technical answer is, "*Anything you want; and feel comfortable with!*" Try 'taste testing' <u>different</u> pure waters! When purchasing 'less' than 5-gallons of water at a time, I buy a, well-respected, genuine, 'Spring Water' from my local store – having had it proven to me that the bottles were not 'just filled' in the stores 'Restroom,' and labeled 'Purified Spring Water!' It is, supposedly, free of dirt, pollutants, fungi, bacteria, and lead; and, still contains the natural minerals in it which 'bring out' the great taste in coffee!

I can, already, hear people wondering about the last paragraph – so, let us go back to it: *"Restroom Water?"* Yes, *"Restroom Water,"* can happen – in which, the local news, occasionally (and recently in my area) – mentions! Recently, a name brand, 'Natural Spring Water' was found to be nothing more than 'Tap Water' bottled from a 'janitorial/bathroom' area of a factory.

For another example, my family and some friends were once on a trip to Mexico. As I have been to Mexico many times, I knew enough not to drink the local water; and did not have any problems during the two weeks we were vacationing. However, having a delay at the airport before flying home, our group found we had three choices for beverages:

Choice #1: Water directly out of a drinking fountain (even many years ago, it was known 'not to drink' the city water in a distant place).

Choice #2: Bottled, 'Purified Water' from a 5-gallon dispenser.

Choice #3: A can of soda pop out of a machine.

I chose the can of soda pop; as I grew up taking trips out of the country with my family for months at a time; and I knew better than to trust even 'bottled' water in an 'unknown' place! The only 'bottled' water I will drink in a foreign country, is a 'name brand, glass/plastic bottled and sealed,' commercial water – like Alhambra, Shasta, Perrier, or another brand 'sparkling' water. However, if visiting a 'major' resort or restaurant (who caters to Americans), I have always found the water to be safe to drink (but, I still check on it first)!

On, this particular trip to Mexico – and having a 'layover' at the Airport for several hours – my family and friends did not 'heed' my advice; and drank the 'Purified water' out of the 'label-less,' 5-gallon dispenser… which, incidentally, happened to be found outside of the Airport, 'Men's, Restroom!' One can 'guess' where everyone in our group (except me) spent their flight home, and next three days! The big 'tip off' for me, that the water was not safe to drink, was that I found stack of 'empty' 5-gallon water bottles being 'stored' in the 'Men's Restroom,' right next to a laundry sink! An empty bottle, sat in the sink, directly under the spigot! There was no doubt in my mind, that the bottles were 'filled in the restroom;' and installed, as needed, on the water dispenser! Everyone on our plane, who drank the water, became ill! However, had 'purifying tablets' been used, or the water boiled, the water may have become fit to drink – I, probably, still would not have wanted to use it for my coffee!

I guess what I am trying to say here is, part of choosing ones' water for coffee brewing, is 'being observant' as well as making an appropriate choice of water! How is that done? Firstly, watch the news or check with your local water utility company; and take note of any 'warnings' regarding local water quality. Also, some local water 'utility companies' will send 'text' messages or emails to their customers; admitting that they are "*Treating their water!*" My former towns local utility used to warn us, "*When not to drink*" the Tap water for several days, whenever it tested poorly. Not long before our move, however, we no longer received any 'warnings;' but, could often tell from both 'smell and the taste' when the water was being treated – as it would smell like my 'chlorinated,' hot tub!

Another thing to watch for, if buying from 'Self-Serve' water dispensers (located inside or in front of many grocery stores), is to check the posted 'Maintenance or Service Record;' for the last time the machine was 'cleaned,' and its filters changed. If 'nothing' is displayed (or if it has been 'months' since someone last serviced the machine), walk away!

Recently, I checked a machine located within our local 'high end' grocery store; and found that the machine had not been 'maintenance checked, or filters changed' for over six months. If that was not bad enough, there was someone's 'chewing gum' stuck on the machines 'downspout.' Any dispensed water would pass over this, old chewing gum! I am afraid; it is difficult to 'trust' anyone selling water these days! I informed the store about it, but the next day, the gum was still there!

Getting back to the water for the coffee maker, 'Tap Water' is appropriate to use if one knows 'what' is in it – and, it can be one of the best waters for brewing coffee, as it has 'natural minerals' in it! Those minerals can help make the coffee delicious! Unfortunately, some minerals (such as sulfur), which do not taste very good, are found in City Water! For example, I tested my 'office' (in a nearby town) water, for example; and found it not only had 'Calcium Hardness and Sulfur' in the water, but even had 'trace elements' of 'city sewer contamination, as well as many legal and illegal drugs – such as the drug 'Prozac' (Fluoxetine), and Cocaine. I cannot even begin to mention 'how many' other <u>minerals</u>, usually, not found in City Water, were found in my office water – however, regardless of content, it is still, considered *"Good drinking water,"* by our city officials!

Whereas *"Prozac for the masses"* might not be too bad an idea these days, it does not help to make a 'decent tasting' brew! Plus, high doses of coffee and caffeine – when taken with 'Fluoxetine' – may bring on the disorder of 'Serotonin syndrome'… with <u>many</u> negative symptoms. So, overall, I would have to say, *"Forget the Tap Water,"* if for no other reason than if it is too 'Hard' – meaning more or too many minerals – and it may leave 'scale' in one's Espresso or Coffee makers – thus, 'clogging' them! However, it might just bring out 'more taste' in the coffee – as will, a touch of sodium!

On the other hand, if the water is too 'Soft' – or, if one owns a 'Water Softener' – it may add 'too much' sodium (salt) to the brew; and will result in a 'less bitter,' but more '<u>flat</u>' taste… moreover, if the person brewing already adds salt to their coffee, well, the brew is going to be considered *"Undrinkable"* by most – as they do not realize that their 'Water Softener' is already adding salt!

At this point, many people ask me, *"What is 'soft water? How can I tell 'what' I have at home?'* The best way to tell if one has 'Hard or Soft Water,' is to use the following example; if you can wash your hands with soap and water, and the soap washes off quickly, you have 'hard' water – which is full of <u>natural minerals</u> (not to mention, possible contaminants), and can make coffee taste good – at least, to a certain degree ('contaminants, never make for a 'better tasting' cup of coffee)! If the water is 'too hard,' it may have a lot of Calcium in it; which can end up 'clogging' a coffee maker.

'Soft water,' may have 'some' minerals left in it; but is high in 'Sodium;' and that is not, necessarily, the best for drinking or coffee – even though, some people 'add' salt to their coffee! An excellent way to tell if one has 'Soft Water' or not, is when (once again) 'washing one's hands.' If one finds that they are forced to 'rinse and rinse and rinse' their hands, to get the feeling of 'slick soap' off their hands, most likely, they have 'Soft Water!'

Unless separately filtered in some way, most 'Softened Water,' has not had <u>any</u> contaminants, chemicals, chlorine, or lead removed – so, that is another 'adverse taste' and 'health hazard' which may come with Soft, Tap Water; but more on Tap Water later.

The 'kicker,' I suppose, is that many 'Coffee Snobs' say (regardless of the water), *"Water must only be heated – but not boiled – in a Gooseneck Kettle!"* For myself, as I previously stated, I have an 'Instant Hot Water Dispenser;' or, I might use a standard Tea Kettle on the stove, a Pyrex Measuring Cup in the Microwave, or just run Hot

Water through my Coffee or Keurig Pod Makers! However, I do own and use <u>both</u> 'manual and electric' the 'Gooseneck' kettles, as shown here, for Demonstrations, 'Pour-Overs,' or while camping. Realistically, only 'certain types' of 'Kettles' are nonsense! A 'Gooseneck,' <u>does</u> make for an 'easy-pour;' especially, when 'Blooming;' but any kettle or water heating method <u>will</u> work!

At my 'Coffee Tastings/Demonstrations,' I will, always, have all my 'heating options' and kettles available; but my 'Electric Gooseneck' one is what I like to use best; as it allows me to set my brewing temperatures in 1°F increments in just a few minutes. With the smaller, 'manual' kettle, one has to 'watch' the temperature gauge on top of the kettle lid. When the indicator shows the desired temperature, the pot is ready for pouring. However, this kettle is an excellent way to see 'how fast' the temperature of the water can 'drop' between the heat source and the pouring!

Looking at some more 'Tap' and other waters:

Tap Water:

Oddly enough, even with all its contaminants, there are those people who still prefer their brewing water *"Right out of the 'City Tap or Well';"* as many have told me, in essence, *"My taxes pay for this water, and I pay 'rates' to use it…so, by God, I am going to use it!"* Sometimes, that is okay! However, 'taxes' or 'rates' aside, 'City Tap Water,' as mentioned before, is not always <u>good</u> to use!

Sometimes, 'Coffee Snobs' differ with me (and, even with each other) – which makes me wonder *"Why,"* they are considered 'Snobs' at all! I have some 'coffee friends,' who say, they could *"Dip water out of the toilet and still make a good pot of coffee;"* which is, probably, true… for them! *"Water is water; and it does not matter,"* they, also, claim; plus… *"It passes through a Paper Filter; and 'heating the water' to almost boiling, purifies it…"* right, like I <u>believe</u> this!

'Boiling' water is useful to help purify... as are paper filters; but it is not going to rid the water of impurities or minerals... and, can, even, 'intensify/concentrate' them! The reason being, some of the water is going to 'turn to vaper (evaporate); leaving the minerals, suspended, in less volume. However, boiling will kill any 'antigens or parasites' in the water! Plus, boiling will remove substances such as ammonia, chlorine, (at least, somewhat) and chloramine – which is used to treat 'poor quality' water – but it is going to take at least 15-20 minutes of 'boiling' to do so. Again, so much for 'Coffee Snobs' saying, "*Never boil your water!*" Perhaps, one should have their 'Tap' water tested to see 'what' is in it; before deciding, which water to brew with!

Other 'Coffee Snobs' may add-in, "*This is what something like a 'Brita Filter' is for... to filter ones' water before or after boiling!*" Again, this can help; but when it comes to chlorine, the filter may only remove upwards of 30% of it. Most consumers 'presume' their purifier will remove contaminants; but, just read the information which comes with many, 'pitcher type,' water filters: "*This product will reduce chlorine taste and odor, zinc, and health contaminants; such as copper, cadmium, and mercury!*" The 'Key Word' here, is 'reduce;' it does not say: 'eliminate!'

So, getting back to the people who insist, "*Water is water,*" when they come to visit, I will, jokingly, hand them an old 'Pyrex' Percolator and ask them to "*Go fetch me a pot of water out of the bathroom toilet!*" Their reluctance (plus the horror on their faces,) usually, starts our 'Introductory Coffee and Water Lessons!' It has been my experience, that many of the friends visiting, or students in classes, 'usually,' end up purchasing commercial, 'Purified Water' of some sort in which to brew.

The purified and bottled, 'Coffee Water Snobs' – I have found to be, somewhat, 'untrusting' – are just as likely to have their 'particular brand' of bottled or machine water, 'professionally tested' before they brew; just as they would do with Tap Water. They test it, not only, for purity, but many other issues as well!

The following chart, on the next page, are the 'testing guidelines' of 'SCAA Water Standards' (Specialty Coffee Association of America). Some Baristas feel it is necessary to 'test' their water before using it; and, it is not a bad idea! However, even this test will not show how 'fit' the water is to drink. For example, as mentioned previously, after the Paradise 'Camp Fire,' the

[109]

water is 'dangerous' to drink – and will be 'unfit' for a few years to come! Unfortunately, the 'SCAA Water Standards Test' (as shown below) may not show the dangers of those waters.

Nonetheless, providing the water is 'reasonably' acceptable, the majority of 'Water Testing' companies, like to test for the following:

Characteristics	Target Goal	Acceptable Ranges
Any Odor	Clean/fresh, odor-free	
Color	Clear color	
Chlorine Amount	0 mg/l	
TDS (Total Dissolved Solids)	150 mg/l	75-250 mg/l
Calcium Hardness	4 grains (68 mg/l)	1-5 grains (17-85 mg/l)
Alkalinity	40 mg/l	At or near 40 mg/l
pH	7.0	6.5-7.5
Sodium	10 mg/l	At or near 10 mg/l

The test results, generally, dictate not just what 'Coffee Snobs' purchase, but what they <u>do</u> with their purified water as well – when it comes to both 'brewing and impressing others!'

More, Popular, Waters:

City Tap/Well Water: As previously mentioned, until recent years, 'Tap Water' was considered, by experts, to be the "*Best*" water to use for brewing – because of its, moderate, minerals. However, today, 'Tap Water' (including 'Well Water'), are often found, "*Not fit to drink;*" by many Baristas, due to contaminants. Moreover, even if ones local water district 'treats' the water to 'purify' it, often many contaminants and parasites are still left in the water; and, the 'purifying chemicals,' often become a 'contaminant' themselves – causing an 'unfavorable' flavor to 'drinking' water or coffee. In many cases, this water can be considered 'Ground Water' as well; coming from aquafers, underground water storage units, or, as in my case, water taken from a local reservoir or river (surface water). When it comes to 'Well Water,' however, the problem could come from 'old pipes,' a 'faulty' Well, or a bad/old, 'Bladder/Pressure Tank;' as well has 'high mineral' concentrations. Many times, one first starts seeing this when filling a pot or glass of water – and rust, sand, or sediment, is found in the container… not to mention, 'water spots' left on glassware; not to mention, 'brewers' which need 'descaling' more often!

Bottled, Purified Water: Bottled waters, mostly, come in two types – 'alkaline' ones – with almost 'brackish' mineral levels (so, there is certainly no reason ever to add salt to this water) – and 'acidic' ones (with higher mineral levels). Very few 'bottled' waters have the intermediate 'hardness levels' found in most municipal waters. Most 'Coffee Snobs' (at least the ones I know) seem to use bottled, 'Purified Water' for their coffee – I use it myself – even for classes, or while traveling – as every store carries it!

Pure, Spring Water: Like plain, 'Purified' water, most 'Spring' Water' is considered "*Safe to drink*" by the EPA; and is often considered "*Top of the range*," by 'Coffee Snobs' to use – at least, in 'bottled' form. However, 'natural' Springwater, outdoors, is only as 'safe and clean' as its surrounding area; when it comes to sewage, pesticides, or any animal which might have 'visited' the spring! Therefore, most Coffee Shops and even 'Beer Breweries,' still 'filter' their water – even though they advertise, that they may "*Use pure, Rocky Mountain Spring Water*" in their beers!

When drinking from a Spring, always try to drink only from its source, if possible – as 'who knows' what has been 'deposited' into the water farther up! For example, as a boy, I used to swim in a 'farming canal,' which came from a 'Natural Spring' (all we 'neighborhood kids' in that area, swam in in during the summertime). We never thought there was anything wrong with the water; and, often drank from it as it appeared so 'clean and clear.' That is, until one day when several dead sheep (that a rancher, upstream, had thrown in) floated past us! We never swam in the canal again! Moreover, I would doubt anyone would want to 'drink or brew' with such water!

In the same sense, years ago, in San Blas, Mexico (in what is now called the La Tovara National Park, where there is still a lot of 'jungle'… or, at least used to be), the river water, at the time, was a dark 'rust red' from all the clay and minerals, it picked up, along the way through the jungle!

Surprisingly, many of the area natives still wash their 'white' clothing in it – and I do not know how it always came out white! However, while taking a small boat upstream to the 'source' of the river (a large Spring), I found the river water became 'more transparent,' the closer I got to the head of the Spring. The 'Spring Head,' itself, was a large pool of water, approximately 20 or more feet deep – complete with fish and crocodiles in it! Even though the water was clean and pure (and other people were drinking from it, and a small café was making coffee from the water), I still was not about to drink or swim from it! 'Naturally pure' as the water was supposed to be, I could not help but think about the 'Crocodile Dung' in it!

Artesian Water: Like Spring Water, 'Artesian Water' is from an underground source, known as a 'Flowing, Artesian Well;' which uses 'natural pressure' to bring the water to the surface.

It is considered 'purer' than 'Springwater;' as it comes from a deeper source/Aquifer and is 'filtered' through many layers of earth. Many 'Artesian' wells contain, natural, fluoride, calcium, sodium bicarbonate, and an overabundance of electrolytes.

Distilled Water: 'Distilled,' is very much like 'Purified' water; as it is purified through, either, 'reverse osmosis, steam distillation, or deionization' methods. Most 'Coffee Snobs,' surprisingly, prefer 'Steam Distilled' water; which is made through 'distillation' by 'boiling' the water! Most people understand this method; as it has been around forever! Water is 'boiled' until steam forms; which is, then, 'captured in coils' and cooled. The now, cooled clean, 'condensed' steam, turns back into a liquid; and 'drips down' into waiting containers. The problem with 'Distilled' water, however, is 'boiling' removes the oxygen and minerals as well; and, as I have said before, "*It is the minerals which help to give coffee its, excellent, taste!*" Have I ever used it? Yes, many times – and, realistically, it is not too bad; especially, when adding creamers or other additives to it! It just would not be my first choice of water! 'Exactly when' would I use it? When I have 'run out' of Pure Water!

Is there really a difference between 'Mechanically Distilled' water and 'Steam Distilled?' Well, as Neuropathist – who makes Colloidal Silver for his patients and self – I know that when I use my 'Electrolysis, Colloidal device' with 'Steam Distilled Water,' the product comes out clear – especially, when 'filtering' with a 'bleached' coffee filter; but if I use 'Mechanically' Distilled Water, the Colloidal Silver turns out 'milky' in clarity. This is because there are 'trace elements of minerals' still in the 'mechanically' produced water! Use of 'Mechanically Distilled Water' is terrible for 'clear,' Colloidal Silver; but, not necessarily, for coffee!

Like others, some, 'Coffee Snobs,' "*Swear by Steam Distilled*" water; as being, "*The only way to brew coffee;*" as it is so clean and pure! Unfortunately, it brews a rather 'flat' tasting coffee. Even so, Distilled water, although safe to drink, is considered 'sub-standard;' and thus, "*Unacceptable*," by most Baristas, due to its lack of minerals! If 'Distilled' water must be used, then 'Steam Distilled,' as a type, should be avoided! Just remember the old saying: "*Steam Distillation… good for Moonshine, bad for Coffee!*"

Reverse Osmosis Water (a.k.a. 'Demineralized' water): 'Reverse Osmosis,' is a purification process; which will remove close to 100% of contaminants (as well as minerals, such as calcium and magnesium) from Tap water, through the use of a 'semi-permeable' membrane.

'RO' water (as some call it), is another form of 'Mechanically Distilled' water, (which, like 'Steam Distilled') produces coffee which tastes rather 'flat;' due to its lack of minerals. However, it will create 'drinking water,' which is very 'pure!' Some 'higher end' homes have 'RO Purifiers' installed to filter their water – often, however, it is only the drinking water which is filtered; not the laundry, bathroom, yard, or pool water. There are 'additives' one can put into the coffee brewing water, to replace the missing minerals; and make better-tasting coffee… however, more on that later!

Uninformed 'Coffee Snobs,' often, will choose this method of filtration for its 'cost;' rather than what it can do for 'drinking or brewing.' The only reasons they think they are brewing a 'superior' coffee, is that they become 'used to' tasting the lack of minerals; and can have great 'Bragging Rights,' when it comes to the overall cost of the process! Not all consumers feel this way, but 'yes…' a lot of 'Snobs' that I have met, do!

Mineral Water: Is so named, as it contains… minerals! As with 'Spring' water, 'Mineral' water comes from an <u>underground</u> source; and contains calcium, magnesium, manganese, salt, and other local minerals. There, usually, is not any type of filtration or treatment when bottled; and no further minerals need to be added to the water. Many 'Coffee Snobs' will use 'Bottled Mineral Water' when brewing with 'smaller' brewers – such as a French Press, 'Pour-Over' brewers. 'Snobs' love it Mineral Water its <u>cost</u> as well as taste! And in my area, there is a 'Pure, Spring Mineral Water' distribution company; whom will deliver 5-gallon bottles directly to one's home or office – so it is easy to purchase. If one does not mind the price, it makes very good coffee!

Sparkling Water (a.k.a. Carbonated, Seltzer, Club Soda, Sparkling Mineral Water): 'Sparkling' water is one of the most wasted, but often used, waters to make coffee with; although again, I do know some 'Coffee Snobs' whom will brew with nothing less! The choice of 'Sparkling Water' is simply a 'preference;' and 'acquired' taste! One thing to think about is, if one is 'degassing' or 'blooming' their grind to remove excess CO_2 (as it can 'sour' the coffee), why would people wish to use water which has natural, CO_2 in it… moreover, a lot of it?

'Sparkling Water' is, also, somewhat acidic – which can add a 'tart' flavor to the 'flatness' of the coffee. Again, I would not use it; but I would suppose, it does have a certain amount of 'Snob' appeal, as well as 'acquired' taste!

Tonic Water: Is like 'Sparkling' water; as it is full of 'sour-tasting,' CO_2. However, it also has ingredients such as 'Quinine' added to it – which is going to add a, somewhat, 'nasty' flavor to the coffee. A glass of it has, approximately, 83 calories and 21.5 grams of sugar; but, if used in coffee, it will add bitterness. Save the Tonic Water for alcoholic drinks and leg cramps!

Electrolyte Water: 'Electrolyte Water' is like 'Artesian Water…' <u>Forget</u> it! Some may say, *"Sparkling Electrolyte bubbles in the water will help to remove excess caffeine from the grounds while the coffee brews."* Others think that it helps to *"Extract more caffeine!"* Neither is true; and the coffee will, most likely, taste bad!

Vitamin Water: 'Vitamin Water' is yet another brewing water to forget; although, it is popular with younger people and 'health nuts!' I do know a few people ('Snobs') at our health club who brew with it; and I have to admit, I have never tasted coffee brewed with it. However, the 'grimaces' many people make when drinking it, leads me to believe it is not very good! Knowing what I do about water and vitamins, I am sure it simply is <u>not</u> going to give one the 'best' tasting coffee… 'healthier,' or not! If wanting both 'good coffee and vitamins,' my recommendation is to brew a good cup; then swallow a handful of vitamins with it!

Hydrogen Water: (Sometimes called Alkaline Water). A new water for coffee is called Hydrogen Water! It gets its name, from exactly what it is: Water… chich is 'rich' in Hydrogen! It is made, a number of different ways; but the current 'fad' is to use what one manufacturer calls a 'Hydrogen Ionizer Water Bottle – and claims their water is, "*Proven to provide the drinker with more energy, slow the body's aging process, boost ones metabolism, improve skin health.*" They, also, claim, "*Hydrogen water has been proven, 100%, to help improve the immune system!*" I cannot vouch for those claims, but I can say this: water ionizers can be very expensive… moreover, it is going to be 'healthy' to drink – and, it should not 'hurt' coffee too much! Small 'hand' units, however, can be found for sale on the internet, for under $40.00 - $150.00! As the devices uses 'Tap Water,' and 'Electrolysis' to 'Hydrogenate' (if that is a word) the water, 'minerals' are left in the water to help 'flavor' the coffee. On the negative side, however, some of the smaller, 'hand-held' devices, will create Chlorine and Ozone gas – which, are two of the things we, so-called, 'Coffee Snobs,' are trying to eliminate from our coffee! This, generally, stems from 'Tap Water' which is high in 'salts!' More on 'Alkaline' water, later!

My advice is, if one is going to own one of these devices, they purchase a water, 'test kit;' which should have both 'drops and strips' in it, for testing water for Chlorine and Ozone.

Heavy Water (a.k.a. D_2O): Yes, I know I mentioned it earlier – but, I was facetious. Nevertheless, being that many students have asked me about it, 'Heavy Water' is used with 'radioactive' agents; although, not radioactive itself. One 'could' drink it, or, even brew coffee with it. Although it is not very healthy to drink, it would take a lot of it to hurt the average person.

Now, for something different to do with brewing water:

"Coffee… Now!"

~ (Attributed to) Marlene Dietrich

There are always 'Coffee Snobs' who must have the 'ultimate in everything'... including water – in this case, several relatively <u>new</u> products! Current, popular products, (which include 'Third Wave, Serka, or Global Customized' water) are products invented to <u>enhance</u> 'mineral' flavors in coffee – especially when using 'Steam Distilled' or 'Reverse Osmosis' water!

Different brands contain varying amounts of minerals – such as magnesium sulfate, calcium citrate, sodium chloride, potassium bicarbonate, sodium bicarbonate, and calcium chloride; and, all companies feel they have *"Just the right amount of 'minerals' to 'balance' coffee extraction."*

Of course, 'Mineral Scale' is more likely to occur with any of these products; so, cleaning one's brewing devices may need to be performed more often.

Sometimes, however, use of 'this kind' of product is considered a *"Why bother"* issue, by some people; if only making one, 'fast,' cup! 'Krups and Keurig' do not seem to think it is necessary; or they would include a 'water additive' with their devices!

On the other hand, if one wants '<u>only</u> the <u>best</u>' cup of coffee, I would suggest they purchase a 'mineral additive' as an experiment; and brew some coffee with their regular water, adding the minerals to it! 'Tasting is believing;' so if one enjoys the coffee with added mineral better than just 'regular' water, perhaps one of these products is for them! In the same sense, one might try 'Distilled' water as well; but add the mineral product to it. I have tried it in my office, and there is no question that the added minerals certainly improve the taste of 'Distilled Water Coffee!'

On the 'odd side,' I know <u>two</u> 'Coffee Snob' couples; whom, <u>both</u>, make their own 'mineral' product! One couple merely grinds and dissolves magnesium and coral calcium pills (from their local health food store) into their 'Steam Distilled,' brewing water. Then, when they brew, they add a 'pinch' of table salt to their coffee makers 'ground' basket. Lately, they have started doing the same in with 'Keurig' coffee makers, reusable 'Pods.' I do not think I would do this, but everyone has their own 'likes!' Frankly, I think the 'ground pills' would be an effective way to, eventually, 'clog up' the Keurig – as one cannot be too sure 'how dissolved' they, indeed, were! I know, the 'needle' on my 'Pod Brewer' clogs easily – and that is just with fine, coffee grounds!

The other couple I know goes a different route; and has 5-gallon bottles of 'Distilled' water delivered each month. Using their 'Digital Coffee Scale,' they carefully measure out 3.75 grams of Epsom salt and 1.3 grams of baking soda, to add, and stirred, to each water bottle. One bottle is installed onto their dispenser; which is found directly next to their 'Drip' coffee maker. Frankly, if I were to go to all this trouble, I would use a 'Clever Dripper' or a 'French Press' to <u>really</u> make the 'best-tasting' coffee as well!

Either couples' method is going to produce a 'bit of scale' to watch for – especially if 'mixed' with 'hard' water; so, one needs to keep their brewers 'extra clean' if adding minerals! Moreover, remember – Epsom salt make an excellent laxative; so, one should not use too much!

There is not any need, at this point, to go into 'TDS Meters,' to check for minerals, go into 'Hardness Scales,' or consider the 'importance of GH or KH' when it comes to coffee water – as one's 'coffee maker' is <u>not</u> an aquarium! Although I have to admit, I do, sometimes, check my TDS Meter with 'Distilled' water; if my Colloidal Silver comes out 'milky!' However, then, when it comes to coffee, a few different minerals are useful! This device, shown here, is the inexpensive model I use.

The meter does not tell me 'what' minerals or contaminants are in my water; but it will measure the 'total dissolved solids,' in relation to 'parts per million.' This means that the 'higher' the meter reading, the <u>more</u> impurities – such as heavy metals, pharmaceuticals, chloride, sewage, pesticide, and other contaminants – are in the water besides minerals.

If testing coffee, it should also be noted that 'fines,' as well as dissolved sugar, and salt in water, will <u>increase</u> its 'reading' – but then, that 'reading' becomes 'nonsense!' It, technically, will not mean anything! Remember, these devices will only tell the tester that there is *"Something" in the water;"* not what is 'good' or 'bad' in it. And, if adding something like certain types of Colloidal Silver – such as what my machine makes – its 'Silver Particles' are so small, they won't fully show up on the meter; which would, actually, be handy in determining if the mixture was 50ppm (parts per million), 100ppm or even 500ppm! So, I would suppose, that a meter might be handy to determine if a 'Third Wave' product was being used – but, the water would have to be compared to something one 'knew' was mineral-free to begin with – such as

'Steam Distilled' water – and, with enough experience, one might be able to use the meter to distinguish 'how much' of a 'Third Wave' product has been created. Frankly, it is easier to 'pour in' a packet into a cup or brewing device!

'Third Wave' additives, prices are very reasonable (depending upon where one shops… approximately, $.10 to $1.00 per cup, at this writing); but, if money is a concern, it does <u>add</u> a bit to the cost of ones' coffee. Some 'Coffee Snobs' that I know (some, but not all) seem to love 'making their coffee cost more;' but as some professional coffee 'roasters' recently told me, *"Coffee Water Additives are just taking 'Coffee Snobbery' too far! Just use good water and reasonably good coffee grounds, to begin with!"* I am compelled to agree!

More on Water Temperatures:

More important than 'Water Additives,' can be 'Water Temperature.' I know I have touched upon this before with 'Fish Eye' water; but here is all (or most) of the 'general, water temperature information,' all in one place.

Some experts say to use, *"205°F water when using Tap water,"* or *"Only allow ones brewing water to cool 'one degree' below boiling* (211°F depending upon altitude) *for a 'Purified' Water"* (this is my personal choice – and what 'real experts' claim *"Should be used"*)! While still others claim, *"208°F for Reverse Osmosis Water!"* Even more, so-called, 'experts' claim, *"No warmer than 201°F for French Presses or other Immersion devices – especially, if using Spring Water,"* while, my Coffee Roaster claims, *"180°F works best for most roasts with any water!"* Again, there are <u>still</u> others (and, again, I almost fall into this category) who claim, *"Only brew with cold, pure water; 'temperature' is not important!"* So… who is correct? They all are; but remember, the 'proper' temperature for brewing coffee is what <u>you</u> enjoy most! In the end, good coffee 'boils down' to personal tastes!

In my household, we recently ran a 'test of temperatures,' for fun; using three identical, 'pre-heated and kept warm,' single mugs, 'Pour-Over' cones, filters, and equal/measured amounts of the same grind/batch of coffee. The only difference was, we used 'three <u>different</u> temperatures' of the same batch of 'Purified' water!

We even 'pre-wet/heated' each filter; and each set of grounds were 'Bloomed' for precisely 30 seconds before the brewing water was poured over the grounds, in the same 'counter-clockwise' motion, until <u>each</u> <u>brewer</u> was full. Twenty seconds into the soaking, a 'heated' spoon was used to make three, clockwise rotations in each 'cone filter;' to help 'break up' any forming 'crust.' Everything was kept as 'equal' (and anal-retentive) as possible between brews. It is only when all aspects of brewing with different methods, that one can make an 'adequate judgement' between the 'chosen' aspect to be compared.

The 'differences' between mugs were, 180°F (Fish Eye) water was used in the first mug, 205°F (String of Pearls – and the recommended brewing temperature by most Baristas) water was used in the second mug, and 211°F (Raging Torrent – but one degree below 'boiling') water used in the third mug… none taking into account, our 1778-foot, 'home altitude.' In a 'Blind Test' (to all but myself), by all appearances, the mugs looked and smelled similar. The taste, however, was yet another matter!

The 180°F brew tasted somewhat 'flat, thin, acidic, but 'fruity,' to me – I did not care for it; but my son loved it! My son and I both tasted the 205°F mug; and both had the same reaction, "*Meh*!" It was 'just coffee;' and lacked most 'redeeming' qualities. On the other hand, the 211°F tasted smoother, not 'fruity or too acid,' and had 'full body.' This temperature, was my choice; however, my son thought it was "*Too harsh!*"

My wife was, then, brought in to taste the three mugs; and, seemed to 'like' all three; but chose the '205°F mug;' saying, "*It was the smoothest of all… not too bold, thin, fruity, or acidic!*" Three mugs, three people, three opinions – go figure! We all agreed, that all of the mugs would have been acceptable to most people; if served in a restaurant. Now… how can anyone say, "*Only use a particular temperature of the water when brewing*" – especially, when not considering altitude; and when everyone's 'personal taste' is going to be different? Getting rather technical, ideal temperature – 211°F – in reality, was not just 'one degree below boiling!' It was a 'full boil' due to 'lower' air pressure… however, I liked it anyway!

I have since tried this test again with students in my new home – which is only, approximately, 300 feet above sea level – and some people found they enjoyed the 180°F coffee best; while still more enjoyed the 205°F, best… while I, and the remaining students, enjoyed the '211°F' coffee best! This time, however, the actual water temperature was closer to 211.5°F – but, still, below actual 'boiling' temperature!

Again, my advice is "*Experiment! Then, continue to brew with the temperature you enjoy best!*" Use the Brewing device or roasters 'recommendations' as a starting point; then, augment the temperature 'up or down…' for, not only, your home altitude, but for what you think makes your coffee 'taste best!'

[119]

On a side note, we tested the 'oxygen' issue of the water/coffee as well – or 'lack of,' that is. As previously stated, 'boiling' will remove oxygen from the water. How much? I would suppose, only a scientist could accurately say! Some people state that *"When 'boiled' water is used to brew with, the 'lack of oxygen' will adversely 'flavor' the coffee – much in the same way, using 'Distilled' water will... due to its 'lack' of minerals."* We decided to test this theory – as well as compare a higher temperature, of 'boiled' water!

As our, previous, 'taste testing' was finished, I made a new mug of coffee... with my favorite temperature of 211°F – once again, taking in the same controls. Placing the mug on a 'warmer,' I made a second mug; the only difference being, I thoroughly 'boiled' my brewing water before using – 220°F (Dragon Eye Water) – for several minutes, to (supposedly) remove oxygen. Upon tasting, the three of us could not taste any difference between the 'boiled' water coffee and the mug which used the so-called, '211°F water;' (remember, at my homes altitude, '211°F' was 'boiled' water too). The 'temperature' test was over... our conclusion was, *"Boiled was 'boiled'... regardless of 'how high' a temperature;"* at least, when boiled for several minutes, that is! Had I left the water 'boiling' for an hour or longer, perhaps, there might have been enough oxygen lost for the three of us to tell the difference... perhaps, I will perform that test sometime!

I 'reperformed' the test, with 220°F and 211°F water, one more time – still making two mugs. However, this time, I added five drops of 'Liquid/Dissolved Oxygen' to the 220°F mug and none to the other mug; without telling anyone! All three of us tasted both mugs and chose the one with the 'Dissolved Oxygen' as being the 'better-tasting coffee' of the two! More on Liquid Oxygen later.

These findings forced us to 're-perform' the first test again – and make three mugs of coffee, using three different temperatures. After placing five drops of 'Dissolved Oxygen' in the 211°F coffee, we, once again, found it tasted better! When using drops in the 205°F mug, I thought the coffee was, perhaps, slightly improved; but my wife and son, could not taste any difference. Upon placing drops in the 180°F mug, we found the drops tended to 'degrade' the taste, somewhat. Surprisingly, 180°F coffee was no longer my sons favorite; and he stated that the coffee no longer tasted *"Fruity!"* The reason for the differences, we determined, was 'less' extraction (due to the low temperature of the water); but adding more oxygen to the mug, did not help!

So, what were our 'official' findings? Apparently, 'boiling' water <u>will</u> remove a slight amount of oxygen; and, perhaps, the longer boiled, the more oxygen lost. Did the coffee using the higher temperatures 'taste terrible?' Certainly not; and it took adding a touch of Dissolved Oxygen to one mug, and comparing it to another, for any of us to even consider a difference!

More advice? Remember, different beans or roasts may need <u>different</u> temperatures to extract the most flavor from the beans! 'Taste test' the different water temperatures, beans, grinds, and methods, to see what <u>you</u> enjoy most (this is a good excuse for a 'coffee tasting' party); one might, not only, be surprised by the difference between 180°F and 212°F... but from differences between 'bean to bean,' and 'roast to roast.' However, one must remember, the water temperature in one type of brewer, might not extract the coffee the same way in another; (this is where yet another 'taste test' comes in handy, as well as 'standardization')! Also, different filters can affect the taste as well! I know, I was just as surprised comparing the difference between metal and paper filters, as I was comparing the difference between 'Drip' and 'French Press' coffee makers!

In any event, whatever brewing method one choses, consider 'pre-warming' both the cup and brewer; not to mention, 'pre-wetting/warming' the paper, metal, or mesh filter; and 'Blooming' the grounds – again, with the 'proper temperature' of 'Blooming' water... if there is such a thing!

As a rule, I tell 'coffee students' to: "*Just use the same water temperature to 'Bloom' with that you are using to brew – at least, to start!*" However, keeping one's water from 'boiling' can be very difficult – especially if trying to only come within only 'one degree' from boiling! This is where "*Watching bubble size* (Fish Eyes)," probably, came about. Unless one 'stands over' the heating water, holding a thermometer, and knows ones' location altitude, just 'being distracted' for a moment can allow one's water to boil!

Luckily, with some heating devices, one can 'pre-set' the temperature – according to their location altitude. Unfortunately, it seems, most devices only come with only <u>one</u> heat level – boiling – or have 'pre-set' settings for use with most 'popular' temperatures. Mine, (as shown here) through 'altitude' and 'trial and error,' I have determined the 'true boiling temperature'  for my home and where I teach Coffee Classes! Luckily, my 'Bonavita' Gooseneck, Electric Kettle, will set in '1-degree increments;' so, my water never 'boils;' unless I want it to! Unless performing tests, or some other purpose, I always set this kettle to 210°F – which, will be just 'on the edge' of the water boiling for my altitude!

Looking back at 'Boiled Water,' and as mentioned previously, it is thought, by many experts, to "*Rapidly lose its dissolved oxygen*,"– and thus, make the coffee 'taste flat.' The tests I wrote about a few paragraphs back proved it! Unfortunately, some people (even some Baristas) think that "*Turning down the temperature' can 'bring back' oxygen to the water, once boiled*." This is untrue! Nothing short of an 'oxygenator' (a medical device, or something which adds air/bubbles to liquid – as with my Colloidal Silver generator) can return oxygen to water, once lost! Actually, 'quick agitation' of the surface water, with a spoon, can cause oxygen to be 'dissolved' into the liquid – just as, pouring the water into a jar (with a lid) and 'shaking' will!

I once knew a man who used an aquarium 'Aeration Pump' with his tea kettle. He would hold a plastic hose, connected to the 'running' pump, in the kettle while the water rose in temperature to boiling. I would suppose this would work; but seemed like a lot of trouble and effort to go through... just to keep some oxygen in his water! He, also, believed, "*Boiled water*," supposedly, "*Has other 'hazards' to worry about, besides the lack of oxygen...*" such as concentrated minerals and pollutants! However, an 'air pump' would not do anything to prevent <u>evaporation</u> – yet, another 'presumed' cause of 'concentrated minerals and pollutants!'

To elaborate further, 'Boiled Water,' according to some 'Experts and Snobs,' is supposed to "*Concentrate <u>undesirable</u> <u>chemicals</u>; which are left in the water or kettle*"– again, making the boiled water 'unhealthy.' In what, are the so-called 'experts' talking? Merely 'bringing water to a boil?' 'Boiling' for a minute? What about a half-hour or more? A pot of water is going to have to 'boil,' for some time before it evaporates enough liquid to have any, left-over, 'concentrated' minerals, chemicals, or pollutants! As a general rule, do not worry if <u>your</u> water comes to boil for a moment or two before removing it from the heat; do not even worry about it if it boils for a minute or two!

There are even more 'myths' regarding water. Some, so-called, 'Nonsense Research' says, "*Boiled water is bad enough... notwithstanding; but <u>never</u> 're-boil' water, as it will cause <u>Cancer</u>!*" What is the basis for this? Apparently, 'excessive nitrates,' which can build up in the 're-boiled' water, can cause several types of cancer... as thought by 'some' people! However, the danger does not stop there! "*Arsenic toxicity*," I have heard some 'Coffee Snobs' state, is yet another worry... as, it too can cause different cancers! If this is not bad enough, 're-boiled' water (or coffee) is thought by some so-called 'experts,' to cause both 'bladder and kidney stones in some people;' not to mention, lead to digestion problems, gallstones, arthritis, fluoride poisoning, heart disease and hardening of the arteries! Then, there is 'hypothyroidism,' headache, weight issues, skin issues, and depression.

Then, there is the belief which surfaced in my last 'Coffee Class;' that "*Boiled water – especially, 'double boiled water or coffee' – is hazardous to pregnant women and their babies… even if it is decaffeinated!*" However, my favorite 'warning' is: "*Never drink boiled water or coffee, which is more than one hour old… as it can be lethal to some people! This is why restaurants pour out hour old coffee!*" Honestly, I have never seen a restaurant, 'pour out,' relatively, 'fresh' coffee!

"*What people,*" I often wonder (as a 'health care' professional), whenever, I hear of "*Some people say!*" Also, what is 'magic' about coffee being "*One or more hours old,*" that turns it "*Lethal?*" It is all nonsense! My parents had a coffee pot heating all day – and my 'Drip' brewer, even has a setting to keep coffee 'hot' for up to four hours! Its manufacturer, 'Hamilton Beach,' apparently is not worried about 'one-hour old' coffee 'killing' its customers!

If coffee were to become "*Lethal*" after an hour, more than half the population would be dead by now! I, also, wonder and ask myself, sometimes "*What brings people to even find 'bogus' research results like this?*" These are just 'myths!' For all that, I also ask myself, "*Why would anyone believe such nonsense?*"

Actual scientific research indicates what I have found with my tests: "*Slight boiling does not remove any noticeable oxygen, or any other gases, from water; and, is safe to drink!*" 'Heavy' or 'double' boiling of water can help to purify it, and it is still safe! However, other 'nonsense research' states, "*Even slight boiling of water, concentrate 'heavy metals' and removes all of its oxygen – rendering it 'unsafe' to drink!*" My thought on that is, "*Why would someone drink water which has 'heavy metals' in it in the first place?*" Yes, it is true, that if one 'boils' polluted 'swamp water,' it will leave some chemicals in the water or on the bottom of the pot or kettle!

Moreover, 'heat' can 'change' some minerals and chemicals to be somewhat 'unhealthy!' My question, again, is: "*Why would someone knowingly drink or brew with 'bad' water to begin with?*" Most of we coffee drinkers are going to use a 'good' and 'pure' water to begin with!

On the other end of the spectrum, there is still one more study (of which I do support), which says; "*There are certain benefits to drinking 'boiled' (or merely hot) water; such as, reduced stress, better digestion, improving sinus health, and more!*"

[123]

The only 'risk' I know of when it comes to 'boiling' water (or coffee for that matter), is the possibility of spilling it on one's lap or fingers; or burning' ones' lips, mouth, or throat if consumed, 'Too hot!' My advice is, if one is 'worried' about consuming 'boiled' water or coffee… stay away from it!

The truth is in there somewhere (I lean toward my latter statement); but it has been my experience that severely 'boiled water' does taste better if 'oxygen' has been returned. Also, 'boiling' will alter the 'flavor' of the water; but, not significantly… at least, not enough to notice – especially, when mixing other beverages or ingredients with it. Perhaps, adding a 'Liquid Oxygen' to it 'returns the flavor' of the water to what one would find 'before' boiling! As boiling will, technically, 'remove' a lot of CO_2, chlorine, and some minerals, there may be some, slight, 'flavor' changes when compared to 'non-boiled' water. Often, one can taste something similar when comparing 'Distilled Water' to 'Spring Water!' Is not 'removing CO_2' what we are trying to do with 'Degassing' and 'Blooming?' If someone is that concerned with the 'taste' of their water, then perhaps, they should be looking at the 'alkalinity' of the water itself. However, then, we have already decided that 'testing for pH' is not worth all the time and effort, just for a cup of coffee!

Here is the 'easy cure' I mentioned during the 'temperature taste test;' for those 'worried' about 'boiling their water,' and 'losing' their 'oxygen!' There are various products found in 'Health Food' stores, called 'Dissolved Oxygen.' What I show in the photograph here, is, a product which contains both 'Dissolved Oxygen' and other 'Cell' nutrients! 'Coffee Snobs' might not be willing to use it; but I do – as it  has minimal flavor – and, I cannot taste it once 'additives' are put in… not that it has any 'flavor' to begin with!

After purchase, one can 'add a few drops' to their cup or brewer; if they want more 'oxygen' in their coffee! Shown above, is the product I used to carry in my 'Alternative Health Care' office. It not only has 'Dissolved Oxygen,' but other ingredients to 'feed' the cells! My 'Cancer Patients' loved this product! Moreover, I still use it, occasionally, myself; such as right now, while I type this! Just a few drops in my coffee and I am set! A small bottle like this one shown, will 'last forever;' or, so it would seem! If one is worried about a few drops 'disfavoring' their coffee, then a bottle of only 'Dissolved Oxygen' (which has no flavor) can be used.

Getting back to temperature, however, I do not think that water temperature – of a degree or two – is all that critical; at least not so much that one 'has to' replace any oxygen!

Before typing this next paragraph, I had the opportunity to teach a coffee class; in which, we dealt with what I have been talking about here; 'temperature, oxygen, and altitude!' One of my students mentioned what I had heard so many times from the various coffee groups I have been in; "*Temperature is temperature… so if the Coffee Company/Roaster says that 205°F degree water is going to extract the most flavor from the beans, I am going to believe them!*"

I always respond with another question: "*Where is your 'Coffee Company' or 'Roaster' located?*" Often, the answer is "*Brazil, Columbia, Peru, or Jamaica;*" many places, of which, are located 2000 or more feet in altitude.

I know I have stated the following, elsewhere in this book; but to simplify, and to reiterate what I have stated earlier (and as my students often indicate slight difficulty understanding temperature), water (when at sea level) boils at 212°F. The 'higher' in altitude one goes, the lower the 'boiling' temperature of the water! Let's say that again: **Water boils at lower temperatures, the 'higher' in altitude one goes**! This is due to 'lower' atmospheric (air) pressure; and why someone saying, "*Brewing temperature' should always be…*" (something or the other), may only be correct for his or her particular altitude! In other words, "*One degree below boiling,*" may be 'easy to say' in Newport Beach, California (which is only 5 feet above sea level) – but it is going to be quite different in Colorado Springs, Colorado (which is 6035 feet in altitude). Water is going to 'boil' there, at only 201.06°F! It is easy to understand, how someone may be confused by not allowing their water to boil (at 212°F) but finding their water does boil, at only 201.06°F!

I cannot seem to repeat 'altitude facts' enough in this book (since I seem to need to repeat it, often, in my classes); but, basically, for every **500-foot** 'increase' in elevation, the 'boiling point' of the water is '**decreased**' by, approximately, **1°F**. This is due to Atmospheric Pressure – or lack of it, that is!

Let's look at it like a 'math' problem. The elevation of my former home, for example (when I started writing this book) was 1778 feet above sea level; meaning, the 'boiling point of water,' due to lower air pressure, was 1°F, per each **500-foot rise** in elevation. That works out to 500-feet, plus 500-feet, plus 500-feet, plus 278 feet; which equals 1778 feet above sea level! The actual 'boiling point' of water, is going to **decrease** in temperature by close to 3.5°F – making the <u>actual</u> 'boiling point' of water (at my home), close to, only, <u>208.5°F</u>! Remember, some people (such as myself) enjoy their coffee at 1°F under boiling! The 'big question' is, would that be 1°F under 208°F or 1°F under 212°F? In my case, I enjoy the coffee more at 1°F under 208… that is, at 1778 feet above sea level!

Do you want to know 'for sure' what 'altitude' is going to do for coffee? Do a 'taste test; and 'fine tune' your coffee according to the temperature that you might use!'

Perhaps, the above 'equation' is an excellent reason to learn 'Fish Eye Waters!' 205°F may be 205°F – be it at the top of Mount Everest (29,029 feet <u>above</u> sea level), or the <u>lowest</u> point in Death Valley (Badwater Basin, 289 feet <u>below</u> sea level); but if one 'heats' their water to certain 'bubble size,' in theory, their coffee should always taste the same regardless of altitude! Just remember this 'rule of thumb;' "*The hotter the water, the faster the coffee extraction; but at higher altitudes (and, if the coffee comes out a touch bitter), try dropping the brewing temperature by one or two degrees the next time… alternatively, try going with a smaller 'Eye' water!*"

'Altitude' is not going to make much difference for many of us; but if we wish to be 'Truly Snobby,' then we need to be aware of our 'brewing elevation' as well as all the other factors required to brew a great cup of coffee!

It is time to start looking at some different ways to brew coffee on the next page!

"*I never drink water because fish fornicate in it*!"

~ (Attributed to) W.C. Fields

BREWING METHODS

Question: *"Are there diverse types of coffee beans for brewing methods? How many ways to brew coffee are there?"*

Answer: Just as a 'Coffee Snob,' might proclaim, *"There is only one, 'true way' to brew coffee,"* there are some people who claim, *"There is only 'one type' of bean or roast that can be used to brew decent coffee – especially, Espresso!"* I know many people in various 'coffee clubs' who claim just that, but with their consensus being *"Only"* 'Jamaican or Kona' coffee beans!

In reality, there is no way to say that *"One brewing method, or one bean, is any 'better or worse' than another,"* because <u>everyone</u> has different preferences about taste! For example, my family enjoys a dark roasted, 'chocolate bean' for our Espresso – as opposed to an actual, 'Espresso Roast!' However, as far as 'how many' different 'ways' are there to 'brew a cup…' there are countless ways – and one way, no 'better or worse,' than any others!

Various beans can be of the same or 'joint' varieties, roasts, grinds or even flavorings! Plus, different farms or growers can even grow the same kind of beans as their neighbors; but have very different tastes, due to water content, shade, personal care, picking, weather, drying/processing methods or even storage and packaging! I cannot begin to state how many 'different brands' or 'types of beans/species' (or sub-species) that are available for purchase; but there are only <u>four</u> main types of Coffee Beans which are used for brewing coffee. I went over, earlier, in this book!

What 'Coffee Merchants' may do to those varieties, is something else again! There are new 'mixtures' and 'brands' of beans created every day – and, I cannot say *"One brand or type is any better than another – providing, one enjoys it!"*

The same can be said for 'Brewing Methods;' as there are not only countless 'flavors' of beans available, there are many 'diverse types of brewing methods' being used by individuals and coffee shops every day… not to mention, more methods being invented (or perfected) every day as well! This can be seen within any of my 'coffee groups' or 'classes;' as often, I will serve the same 'beans and temperature' coffee to students… however, brewed by different methods!

The first 'brewed' coffee was, probably, just a handful of coffee beans thrown into a pot of boiling water. As coffee was experimented with (when it came to roasts, grinds, et cetera) by Sheepherders, Monks, or Native

Americans, various 'brewing methods' arose. So many techniques and methods are so close to the ones listed below – such as with 'Immersion' or 'Cone' brewing – that going into 'individual detail' on every method or brand brewer, is not necessary... alternatively, even possible – due to 'space constraints!' However, some of the most popular methods and brands as follows:

Cold Brew Your Coffee – This is more of a recipe, but it is still a brewing method too – and, was probably, one of the first! However, other methods may be applied; with the result being 'Cold Brewed Coffee!' Apparently, (when it comes to brands) any 'brewed coffee' can be called 'Cold Brewed;' even when it is not brewed that way. Authentic 'Cold Brewed Coffee,' however, is where only cold water is mixed with grounds; and they steep for 24, or more, hours. Ancient man, probably, did this with river water, a pot, and some coffee beans. They put water and coffee beans together in a pan or bowl and drank what liquid they found the following day!

'Methods' in which 'Cold Brew' is made, can be anything. I have seen expensive 'electrical' devices, simple 'Pour-Over' type devices, 'Drip' brewers which have 'Cold Brew' buttons on them, and methods – such as the ones following – which are as 'simple' and 'manual' as they can get!

Japanese Cold Brew – Not quite a 'Cold Brew,' the 'Japanese method' is the most 'fashionable' way to brew – but, it is not, honestly, a '<u>Cold</u>' brew! A jar is filled with hot water; and at least a 'cup' of medium to coarse ground coffee is added to it. A lid is placed onto the bottle, and the mixture is shaken! It is, then, cooled quickly with some ice cubes. In Japan, there are even machines to 'hot  brew' copious amounts of coffee; but 'other devices' are used to <u>instantly</u> 'cool it down' for, immediately, serving over ice.

Again, this is not really 'brewing with cold water;' but the Japanese feeling is, that it takes *"Hot water to properly extract flavors from the grounds;"* and, I would have to agree with that! I, also, tell my 'Coffee Students,' that *"Brewing this way is the most effective way to preserve the 'delicate flavors' of the coffee; brew hot, then, make cold;"* and have done just that in the photograph above; and those on the next page.

The 'American' way of 'Cold Brewed' coffee is straightforward: first, pour some medium-grind coffee grounds – usually, more than what one would use in a standard coffee maker – into a 'canning' type jar or carafe. 'Blooming the grind' is considered optional here, and one has the choice of 'pouring off' any 'Bloom' before brewing! Therefore, some people may 'wet' the grind with  'hot' water to allow it to 'Bloom (pre-infuse)' and the grounds to 'expand.' Then, they fill the jar with cold water. However, some feel, "*If pouring grounds into the water and leaving them there for an extended period, 'pre-wetting' is a waste of time!*" Personally, I feel, that if the coffee is not being brewed with hot water, then 'Blooming' the grounds with hot water is the next best thing. The ground will 'expand;' and thus, extract more flavor once water is added!

Next, the jar 'lid' is 'screwed' on; then, the jar given a 'quick shake,' to disperse the grind throughout the water. The jar is, then, placed into a refrigerator overnight or longer; I prefer longer – usually, 24 or more hours. Moreover, if possible, I 'lightly shake' the jar once or twice during its brewing time.

After 24 or more hours have passed, use another jar or carafe with a 'Pour-Over' type filter, to remove any grounds from the brew. Any 'Filter' will do, however! Using a quart 'Canning Jar,' one will get, approximately, three or four servings of coffee – depending, upon the size of the mug or glass used. Add some ice to your glass; or, any milk, sugar, or flavored creamers that you would like, and enjoy! I enjoy pouring my 'Cold Brew' over vanilla ice cream – to make something of a 'Coffee Float!'

Of course, there are many 'Cold Brewers' available on the market (the one shown here, is one of the many brands/styles I own); but 'Cold Brews' can be made in the refrigerator using any bowl, pitcher, or canister.

Alternatively, it can be made with just about any type of brewing device which does not produce 'hot water:' such as 'Pour-Over' or 'French Press!' Cold Brewed coffee is enjoyed by 'Coffee Snobs,' because, it is a rather 'expensive way' to brew coffee without expensive equipment – at least, in fact that it uses a 'lot' of coffee grounds in relation to water!

Moreover, many people end up purchasing a 'specialty device' to brew in (again, such as, the one I own, shown on the previous page)! Brewers are available in sizes from 'tiny,' to 'very large!'

Special Note: when adding a 'flavored powder' to ones' Cold Brewed coffee, do not be surprised if it does not mix well – as many flavorings, like Hot Chocolate Mix, need a 'hot liquid' in which to 'dissolve' and 'mix' the powder properly. Liquid creamers are, most often, recommended; or, mix a slight amount of hot water with the powdered creamer, to liquify. Then, add it to one's 'Cold' coffee.

From a 'health' point of view, if one suffers from 'Acid Reflux,' Cold Brew is an effective way to reduce excess coffee acid; which, might irritate the stomach or throat.

Another popular type of 'Cold Brew' – which can be served 'hot' as well – is 'Double Brewed' Coffee. When it comes to 'Cold/Hot Brew,' however, it can be made several diverse ways. One popular way is to 'freeze' left-over coffee into ice cubes. After brewing more coffee – in one form or another and cooling it in the refrigerator – it is poured into a glass or mug, along with the 'frozen' coffee cubes. 'Double Brewed?' Well, not really; but, as the 'coffee cubes' melt, they do add more coffee flavor and caffeine.

Actual Double Brewed Coffee – The most popular way to 'Double Brew' coffee, is to 'brew coffee, with coffee!' This can be done by several methods – Percolators, Cones, Drip Machines, Espresso Machines, French Presses... anything. Once the coffee is brewed the usual way, with the usual amount of grounds, it is brewed once again; only this time, instead of using fresh water to brew with, the 'new' coffee is made by brewing with the earlier coffee. Of course, this is an effective way to 'double' the caffeine in ones' brew (and 'clog' one's coffee maker, faster)!

Another 'stylish' way to make 'Double Brew,' is to add a 'shot' of Espresso, to a cup of coffee – I do this myself for the flavor and caffeine; however, most people do not consider this method, a 'Double Brew!' Of course, another way can be to 'double' the amounts of grinds during the initial brewing process. So, it is not surprising that most people are inclined to consider this method, "*Just 'extra strong' brew!*" I would suppose, it depends upon ones 'point of view!'

In any event, the 'Double Brewed' Coffee can be drunk hot or cold – regardless of the brewing method! My family enjoys it as a refreshing, Summer drink – and a quick, 'pick me up... especially, in 'latte' form!'

Coffee Cubes – (not ice cubes) There is one new way make Cold Brewed, Iced,' or even 'Hot' coffee; and that is with a product called, "*Coffee Cubes*." Not to be confused with 'Chewable' (yes, I did say 'chewable' coffee), Coffee Cubes, these act like an 'Alka-Seltzer' or 'Bouillon Cube' when added to water or milk – especially, hot! The 'Cubes' dissolve in the water and the make coffee. 'Cubes' (more of a rectangle, actually), are available in many different flavors/brews.

Being something of an 'Instant' coffee, I must admit, that I have never tried a Coffee Cube – or, a chewable one, for that matter – and I am not sure I really would like to! If one wants a 'good cup of coffee,' then brew one! I might sound like a 'Snob' saying this, but if one is concerned with the 'cost of grinders' affecting the flavor of coffee – as well as the grind size, the age of the grind, water temperature, altitude, 'proper water,' other tools, and more – it would be reasonable to believe, that the 'best tasting' cup of coffee, is not going to come from a 'Cube!' I suppose I would be willing to give it the 'benefit of the doubt' and try it! Besides, I would not expect it to be too different from purchasing a bottle of 'concentrated' coffee from the grocery store! Just add hot water to either... and one has coffee!

If one does not wish to 'brew their own' coffee, however, there are other products besides 'Cubes' or Concentrated bottles. Some products come 'pre-diluted' and ready to drink; such as the product shown here. I seldom will drink this type of coffee; however, if it comes in Frappuccino or Latte form (such as one of 'Starbucks,' many, canned or bottled products), I will purchase one for a 'quick' pick-me-up!

Nevertheless, some people are <u>still</u> determined to 'brew' their own – especially when it comes to 'Cold Brew.' So, there are products in the form of 'pouches,' containing 'grounds,' one can purchase; which are 'pre-measured' to use in any brewer... hot or cold! Often, products like these can be found in hotels; which supply, small, 'Drip' coffee makers for their patrons to use. Of course, 'Coffee Pods' fall into the same category... premeasured, and ready to use!

One popular brand, as shown here, is designed after the 'Coffee Pouches' most hotels use. Coffee grounds are 'pre-measured' to be 'doubly strong;' and being placed into a pouch, of sorts, they work something like a filter too! This product may say it is for 'Cold Brew,' but it works for 'hot' as well! I could be wrong, but it seems that it is only the 'packaging' which is different from other 'pre-ground' coffee products. I have brewed 'hot' with it, and it was delicious!

The beauty of 'instants, pods, packets, satchels, or concentrates,' is most are 'pre-measured!' If not wishing to buy a 'bottled' Cold Brew or a box of 'pre-measured' or 'loose' grounds – and attempting to 'adjust,' if ones' initial coffee is 'too bitter' of a grind – these 'packs' simplify brewing. If the coffee is too weak, try adding an 'extra scoop' of 'canned or ground' coffee to the jar or brewer. It may take a couple of times of 'trial and error' brewing, to discover if the coffee has a 'grind coarseness' problem (if using loose grounds), or a 'too light' (not enough) grounds used in the jar or brewer! Remember, if too strong, add more water!

Unfortunately, as I can't own 'every type' of 'cold or hot' brewer – or method available – the reader needs to use the internet to 'look up' each product, brewer, or method – and then 'research' each product to discover if they would like to use it or not. If it does not sound too 'promising,' 'reject it' and search for something else!

Notwithstanding, there is one more way to drink 'Cold Brewed Coffee' that needs to be mentioned – and that is a current fad. I will only touch upon here, and that is 'Nitro-Pressed' Coffee. I first found the term confusing! In my health care profession, a 'Nitropress' is a vasodilator – that relaxes the muscles in and around the blood vessels, to help them dilate. This results in lower blood pressure and better blood to flow. When I first heard of it with 'brewing,' I was sure this could not have anything to do with coffee; and I was right!

The idea of 'Nitro-Pressed' coffee, came from 'adding Nitrogen' to draft beer; only, in this case, the process uses 'Cold Brewed' coffee as a 'base' for several different beverages. Cold coffee is 'poured' into the device and sealed. Then, a 'Nitrogen' cartage is attached to the container. A 'trigger' is pulled, and 'Nitrogen Bubbles' are added to the coffee; which results in giving the coffee light and creamy head when dispensed into a cup or glass. The coffee is then drunk 'as is' – like an Espresso – or used to make other coffee beverages. I am sure, 'Coffee Snobs' would love it; but, would doubt that many average coffee drinkers would want the cost, time, or the trouble of using it (nonetheless, it would be fun for parties)!

Brewers:

Many 'Automatic' brewing devices fail to make a decent cup of coffee because of two, main, reasons; 'time and temperature!' Still, most coffee drinkers are inclined to 'look for' an 'automatic' brewer of some sort when it comes to coffee! However, there so many 'alternatives' to 'Automatic Brewers' available today; in which one can 'control,' not only, the 'time and temperature,' but other aspects of the brewing as well... such as roasts, grinds, filtering, storage, serving, and more!

Frankly, it is amazing, by 'how many ways' there are to brew a cup of coffee; especially, when it comes to some 'very similar' brewers! I will mention the most popular brewers on the pages which follow:

Chemex™

'Chemex,' was invented in the 1940's; and is considered *"The 'first' of the 'Pour-Over' brewing methods;"* with both a 'Cone' and Carafe, coupled with a highly polished piece of hardwood; and decorated with an 'attractive' leather lace. The wood does provide a function; as it allows the user to pick up the unit and pour it without being 'scalded' by the hot coffee in the carafe. Frankly,  there is little difference between this method and using a standard 'Cone' with an attractive carafe. There are many 'knock-off' models which 'look and brew' precisely like a Chemex; so be careful with your purchase if wanting the 'true' brand!

'Processing' can become as simple or complicated as one wishes; by bringing in different 'filters' for brewing times, and digital scales... for weighing <u>both</u> ones' grounds and water, when calculating the correct brewing ratio required or desired. Moreover, one can 'experiment' with different waters and grinds to 'fine-tune' the brew to suit one's taste. In any event, the Chemex should brew a fine cup of coffee!

[133]

The manufacturer (or at least a promotional website) claims, *"After 'pre-warming' the pot by 'pouring in,' then 'swirling,' a bit of hot water* (some people keep carafes like this on a warming tray afterward)*, a thick Paper or Metal Filter is placed in the 'Upper Cone' to filter out grounds, fatty oils, and to give the coffee a 'smooth,' flavor and texture."* The Cone and Filter should both be 'pre-warmed' and wet (if using paper) – which can be done while 'Blooming.' Serving cups or mugs should be 'pre-warmed' as well; to help keep the brew 'hot.'

The proper amount of ground coffee (according to how many cups are being brewed) are placed within the Paper Filter, and a small 'well' is made in the middle of the grounds. Just enough hot water to wet all the grounds is, then, poured over them to allow 'Bloom.' This action works best with a 'Gooseneck' kettle for 'easy' and 'directional' pouring over the grounds… however, any 'pouring' device will do!

As with other brewing methods, 'pre-warming' everything helps to extract flavor from the coffee. After allowing the coffee to 'Bloom,' half of the hot water is poured into the filter and over the grind. After 30 or more seconds, the remaining brewing water (210°F – 'sea level') – or, one's own choice of temperature – should be added; or, wait another 30 seconds for the water to drain, before completing the brew with any remaining water. Again, an electric kettle works best at keeping a persistent temperature. 'Pausing,' somewhat while adding water, is so that it does not 'pour through' and brew 'too quickly.' Remember, in the 'best of all worlds,' the water should take <u>three minutes</u> to 'pour through' – and, extract the most flavor. However, as the water drains, the filter will begin to 'clog;' and the remaining water will drain more slowly; 'pulling' even more flavor from the grounds, by staying in contact with them longer. Experiment with <u>your</u> 'pours' to reach a three-minute brewing time; then 'swirl' or stir the carafe to 'mix' temperature layers!

Available in multiple sizes and styles, Chemex can stand alone on a table or countertop (some restaurants, even place them on their customer's table for 'self-serving'); or, they can be used with its own 'holder,' of sorts; to have it become more like a 'coffee machine.' However, actual 'machines,' which hold and heat water, are also available to work with the Chemex!

Prices range anywhere from a few dollars for a used model, to hundreds of dollars for 'automatic' brewers. $35.00 seems to be a fair price for a new, basic, stand-alone unit over the internet. 'Extra holders or accessories' are not necessary; but <u>are</u> available!

How does the Chemex rate on the 'Snobby' scale? Snobs <u>love</u> this unit due to its appearance, and I must admit, it is attractive! If one *"Has to make their own coffee,* (a member of our current coffee club, once, told me) *Chemex is the best way to do it!"* Just remember, the Chemex is nothing more than a 'Fancy, Pour-Over Cone;' but its 'Presentation' is what makes it popular!

Automatic <u>Drip</u> <u>Coffee</u> <u>Makers</u>

Today (in the 21st Century) Drip Coffee Makers are as popular as what 'Percolators' were back in the middle of the 20th Century – although, like the Percolator, they are quickly becoming obsolete… in favor of the 'K-Pod' Brewer!

They can come with glass, metal, or plastic Carafes; or be like mine, shown here, which is 'Carafe-less.' Water is placed into the 'water holding chamber' on the right side, grounds are placed into a 'brewing basket' in the middle, and coffee goes into a 'coffee holding chamber' directly under it. Coffee is served by placing a cup, mug, or tall 'travel mug' under a spout; and a large button (as seen in the middle) is depressed. I use this type of 'Drip' brewer, as since my carafes are handled so much, they often get broken! With this brewer, there is no carafe to break!

Back when I was a kid, the only place one saw a 'Drip' Coffee maker (of sorts), was in a restaurant or coffee house. Usually, they looked like a big, clumsy, 'double cone' or 'Syphon/Pour-Over' containers; made from aluminum and glass – and, they pretty much were! Most were found to be more of a form of 'Percolator;' or what we call today, a *"Technivorm"* – which is, still, something of a 'Pour-Over!' These old devices could make 'copious volumes' of coffee in record time – while, previously, restaurants could not make coffee any faster than anyone else! Private individuals were limited to glass, tin, stainless steel, 'pot metal,' pottery, or CorningWare® pots/kettles to place on their stoves. Soon, however, electric, home, 'Drip pots' came about – as well as large, aluminum percolators – for groups, churches, or parties!

'Automatic,' Drip Coffee Makers changed every coffee drinker's life! The only problem with the large, 'Automatic Drip Coffee Makers,' is that most coffees should be brewed at temperatures of 195°F and 205°F; and seldom do brewers meet this requirement; and the 'K-Pod' brewers, today, are even worse, when it comes to 'brewing' temperatures! My 'K-Pod,' for example, makes a water temperature of only 182°F; so, I seldom use it for brewing 'straight' coffee,' unless it is a 'Decaffeinated Grind!' I will, generally, brew something like a 'Latte' or Cappuccino Mix, to make a Mocha Macchiato.

To make matters 'still worse' for the 'antique' Automatic Drip Brewers(from the 1940's – 1960's), most people filled their devices with water straight from the tap. 'Bad water' aside, once turned on, the brewer, immediately, started 'dripping' the cold water over the grounds; while warming the water to what the 'device' thought, was the 'correct' brewing temperature. By the time the water had reached the proper temperature, the grounds had 'Bloomed;' and a fair amount of 'poor' coffee had filled the carafe. We still see this today, with some 'Drip' brewers; mine, for example (if I take my water from my refrigerated dispenser) will only be 'lukewarm' by the time it fills the machine. I have, since, started using 'room temperature' water; from another device.

Unfortunately, with some machines, the water, usually, continued to heat; thus, making the brewing temperature 'too hot' for the remaining brewing! Once mixed with the 'too cold' brew, one had a 'bad' cup of coffee! Therefore, many 'other alternatives' had been invented for brewing coffee – even, when using a 'Drip' device – most, included a 'heater' of some sort to keep the coffee warm for hours; and with the 'old type,' restaurant machines, little control was exercised over the heater… so, the coffee 'cooked' for an extended time! Coffee was still enjoyed by most people, however!

Fortunately, or unfortunately, after a few more years of nothing much changing except styles, sizes, and colors, along came 'Mr. Coffee® in 1972…' with a 'new way' of making coffee at home! It was a 'miniature' Drip machine for home use. Coffee grounds went into a filter, water went into a container, and a carafe was placed directly under it. Once turned on, and in several minutes, one had a 'whole pot' of brewed coffee! Everybody was happy; that is, except for the 'Coffee Snobs' (who were still few in numbers in those days) and 'experts' who <u>knew</u> what they were drinking – namely, Baristas! However, these 'new-fangled' machines were like the old models; in which they started with 'too low' a temperature and finished with 'too hot;' and that is still a fact today, with some 'cheaper' devices!

'Snobs' still went in for 'Beatnik' forms of brewing – such as 'French Press;' but, technically, the 'Mr. Coffee' people were correct! One could make a 'whole pot' of coffee with this new brewing method; and it was easy, entertaining, and did not have the 'boiled or burnt' taste that everyone was familiar with... let alone, the 'smell' of 'boil overs!' Plus, the coffee was ready in less than half the time! It did lack some of the <u>essences</u> of 'Beatnik' methods... nevertheless, it was 'fast;' and, people 'got used to it' quickly. It was not long, before 'Canned Coffee' companies all directed most of their brands to 'brew best' in these types of brewers!

In the same sense, it did not take too long before stores started putting 'fresh' beans into their 'commercial stock' for customers to use with their 'Automatic' Drip Coffee Makers too – and, it improved the taste of coffee for many people – namely, myself!

Next, we were adding extracts, flavorings, and whipped creams to the coffee cup! So faster than one could scream, *"Maynard G. Krebs..."* we were making 'coffee concoctions' as the old, 'Beatnik Coffee Houses' did – but with our 'Drip' devices! Was it good? Well... yes; at least, that is what the coffee machine manufactures, and the coffee bean sellers, told us! Soon, there were many brands of 'Drip' Coffee Makers available – and, in many styles. Some even came with built-in 'Espresso Makers' as well – to be even more like a 'Coffee House;' and, almost every store started selling 'pre-bagged, roasted and ground' coffee beans along with their 'canned' brands!

Today, if a home has a coffee consumer in it, they will also, probably, have an 'Automatic, Drip Coffee Maker' of some sort – but, the 'Coffee Snobs' still use <u>other</u> methods to brew their coffee – as 'Drip' machines are thought by them to *"Be the <u>worst</u>!"* Right? Wrong? Good? Bad? If one enjoys the 'Drip' brewing method, then there is nothing wrong with it! I own <u>two</u> 'Drip' brewers myself; and make coffee with one or the other, almost, daily... however, I also own just every other form of brewer as well!

Moreover, I would not necessarily call 'Drip,' *"The worst!"* If nothing else, it should be called, *"The <u>best</u> of the worst!"* Honestly, there are a <u>lot</u> of brewing methods and devices which are a <u>lot</u> <u>worse</u> than a 'Drip' brewer! Moreover, if one will 'take the time' to 'finetune' their 'Drip' brewer and methods, there is no reason 'why' it could not make one of the <u>best</u> cups of coffee around!

Frankly, I know some 'Coffee Snobs' whom, (although most will not admit it) use their 'Automatic Drip Coffee Makers' most mornings – saving the 'Fancy Brewed Coffee' for weekends or guests! I would guess I, somewhat, fit within this category; as I get up in the morning, make myself a 'K-Pod' cup of Macchiato (to use as a 'creamer' once the drip coffee is brewed), start my 'Drip' brewer, and add coffee, as it brews, to my mug a little at a time – thus, 'diluting' the Macchiato and turning it into merely and 'additive!' After drinking half of the mug down, I will fill the mug, once again, with coffee from the 'Drip' brewer; and add milk, or a 'sugar-free' creamer!

Other brewing methods (such as 'French Press) are, usually, reserved for the weekends (when I have more 'brewing' time) or guests! There <u>is</u> a 'faster' way to get coffee in the morning – in the form of another 'technique' I use; and that would be, to 'fill' both my K-Pod and Drip brewers with water just before going to bed, place a mug under the K-Pod, 'grind' some fresh beans, fill the 'reusable' K-Pod and the Drip brewing basket, and allow the grounds to 'degas' overnight! In the morning, I get up, walk to my 'Brewing Station,' press the 'Start' buttons, and then 'open' the house for the day! By the time I have opened windows or turn 'on or off' lights, and taken the dog out, the 'K-Cup' mug is filled and there are at least four (strong) cups in the 'Drip' brewer! After taking a few swallows from the 'K-Pod' mug, I am ready to top it off with coffee; or pour cups of coffee for my family!

What are the prices on 'Drip' brewers? New, 'Drip Coffee Makers' run from $30.00 to $300.00 – depending upon its 'impressive range' of 'Snobby' features! Some brewers may even 'grind' the beans for you – like some Espresso machines! How does 'Automatic Drip' rank on the 'Coffee Snob' scale? Again, no 'Snob' I know, seems to like them (although, <u>everyone</u> I know owns one)! 'True Snobs,' however, seem to be changing over to the more expensive, 'Technivorm' or 'Fancy K-Pod' coffee makers now!

Do Drip Coffee Makers have 'any' saving grace... Yes; as one can put 'custom,' freshly ground beans of any type, roast, or brand in them, 'finetune' water, or use some 'tricks' to improve the taste; and depending upon one's preferences, brew a 'very adequate' cup of coffee!

<u>Keurig</u>® (or Pod/K-Pod/K-Cup)

Specially designed for people who 'cannot' function (first thing in the morning) enough to brew a pot of coffee... without first '<u>having</u> a cup of coffee,' the almost instant 'K-Pod' or 'Keurig' brand/style brewers are available in multiple sizes (water holding tank sizes, that is). However, some brewers can brew from small cups to tall travel mugs! Some brewers are even 'built into' electric water dispensers and refrigerators!

The idea of 'Pod (or K-Cup) Brewing' is very attractive (except when the used, plastic Pods fill up our landfills); especially, to a 'Coffee Snob;' as it is capable of making quite a number of different drinks like cappuccinos, teas, hot chocolates, or even soups, by the cup… and in a 'concise' period of time! Plus, it is very 'clean;' in the fact that the coffee is in 'Pod' form – no 'spooning' loose grounds into filters or machines (unless, using 'filters,' or 'refillable' Pods, as I do); and in some cases, no additives are necessary; as some brands have 'powdered and flavored' additives included within the Pod with the coffee! Some devices, however, are prone to building up <u>bacteria</u> and <u>scale</u> inside them; especially, when using 'generic' tap water. Plus, the device 'injection needle' can clog, easily, with use!

It would seem, that every 'Coffee Company' has gotten on board with 'Pod Brewing;' and, one would expect it with companies like Folgers or Maxwell House – who specialize in 'Canned' coffees. However, major coffee houses, like Starbucks, also, now sell 'Pods' of their coffee; both in their Coffee Bars and in commercial, supermarkets. Blue Mountain, Dunkin' Donuts, Campbells Soup, even Friskies 'Cat Foods' have 'jumped' into the 'K-Pod' market! Although, some companies, like Campbells Soup, 'jumped' back out after a short time; citing, *"The soup did not perform to our expectations."*

Each Pod of beverage is a small 'plastic cup' of grounds; which goes into a holder on the device. Water, for 'one to several' doses of beverage, is poured into the machine and stored (at least, sometimes); and once the Pod has been inserted, and the device 'lid' closed (which punctures both the top and bottom of the Pod), the machine is activated – heating the water. When the water has reached the, so-called, 'proper temperature' (the machines 'proper' temperature, not mine or the grounds), 'forced pressure' injects/pushes the it through the Pod, where it 'extracts' the coffees flavors and oils; which then, 'drains' into a waiting cup or mug! This all sounds well and good; except, for a few issues that the manufacturers do not, necessarily, divulge. Other than design and features, I do not see that this is much different from using 'canned' coffee – as the 'Commercial Pods' contain 'pre-ground' coffee beans of uncertain age!

The manufacturer's claims are valid; 'Pod Brewers,' <u>do</u>… *"Brew a cup of coffee in record time!"* However, other than 'Coffee Snobs,' anyone who genuinely enjoy the values of 'freshly brewed' coffee, will tell you that, *"Pod Coffee is not necessarily, the 'best tasting' of coffees."* Yes, major/expensive brands can be bought; but (in my opinion), it is, still, '<u>canned</u> (plastic pod or not), pre-ground coffee!' In many cases, this coffee has, already, been 'degassed' by time. Even though, as with canned coffee, many 'K-Pods' are 'Nitrogen Flushed' to hold freshness, the grounds can become 'old and stale' by the time the consumer 'brews' with them!

Special Note: if possible, try a 'taste test' of 'K-Pod' (Keurig) coffee with some other method – such as a French Press, Clever Dripper, or other 'Pour-Over' cone. Compare both time and taste! You might be surprised by your findings – even, when comparing to 'Drip!'

After having some 'Coffee Snobs' lecture me on the 'advantages' of using a 'Keurig' type brewer over any other method, my son, Joshua, and I, decided to put both a 'French Press' and my Hamilton Beach, 'Pod Brewer' to a 'speed' and 'taste' test. "*You will never beat the Pod Brewers speed,*" the 'Coffee Snobs' told us; nonetheless, we wanted to see 'how different' times were for ourselves! To keep things as fair as possible, we both started with 'water' already brought to brewing temperature in our Gooseneck Kettle – but knowing that the Pod Brewer would, probably, still 'heat' the water somewhat!

Having all other items where they, typically, would be at our brewing station, my son found the 'Commercial Brand, Coffee Pod' in which he wished to brew, inserted it into the device, 'poured' in his water (already hot from the kettle), closed everything up, and switched 'ON' the 'Bold' setting to start the machine. While his water was preparing, he 'pre-warmed' his cup with a bit of hot water, poured it out, and placed it under the brewer downspout. We, very soon, could hear the water 'boiling' within the device.

Concurrent with his actions, I prepared my French Press. I opened it up, 'pre-heated' it with some hot water, poured in my ground coffee, then poured in an ounce or so of the kettles 210°F' water – to start the 'Blooming' process. While the grounds 'Bloomed,' I 'pre-heated' the mug I was going to use. By the time I poured the cups water into the sink, the Blooming process was complete; and the French Press ready to fill.

After approximately three minutes of the grounds soaking in hot water (and stirring once to break up any, forming, 'crust'), I placed the Press 'top' on, and 'depressed' its plunger. The coffee was, then, poured into my warm mug. My total preparation and brewing time (until my cup was filled with ready to drink coffee): 4 minutes on the dot! Of course, this did not consider any time for adding creamer or anything else to the coffee.

Joshua, on the other hand, had already finished brewing; and tasted his brew. Time from start to finish… 2 minutes and 42 seconds. As 'per advertised' and expected, the K-Pod Brewer <u>was</u> faster! However, the 'real test' was, yet, to come – when we 'tasted' and compared <u>both</u> coffees. His coffee tasted… "*Well, like Coffee,*" he said, "*Acceptable!*" I had to agree; "*Nothing to write home about, but 'okay;' first thing in the morning,*" was my opinion!

I tasted my cup, "*Delicious! Rich, bold, and with a slight 'Espresso' taste about it!*" Josh tasted it and had to agree… "*Yours is much better! I would rather drink yours than mine,*" he stated!

"*Would it be worth 1 minute and 8 seconds more to you, first thing in the morning, to make it with a French Press?*" I asked. He had to agree, "*It would!*" He, then, interjected, "*I guess, had I used the 'Re-usable Pod,' and put in a filter, and used 'fresh' grounds, the coffee would have taken about the same time as yours, and it would have tasted better!*" That was a true statement! So, we tried it with the changes. The coffee was differently better; but, "*Still not as good as the French Press,*" in both our opinions!

Had he 'tampered the grounds' slightly, and 'pre-warmed' the device, it <u>would have</u> taken even longer than my French Press; and, most certainly, would have tasted better; but still, not as good as the French Press! Had he taken the time to 'standardize' on the 'Pod, Coffee, and 'ground size,' he might have created a '<u>still</u>' better brew!

We performed this experiment twice more – but, this time, with a 'Clever Dripper' brewer instead of the French Press, and with our 'Drip' coffee brewer. The procedure time added, approximately 28 seconds to the overall production time with the 'Clever Dripper,' and 1.5 minutes with the 'Drip' brewer. Again, 'was it worth it?' The answer was "*Yes,*" from both of us, in both cases! Even though we could create a 'great brew' with a reusable filter, good/fresh beans, and a few brewing 'tricks,' 'Pod Coffee' could not begin to compare to the 'Clever Dripper' brewed coffee; nor, was it quite as good as the 'Drip!'

What is my 'main complaint' with 'Pod Brewers?' Other than the, previously mentioned, 'landfill' issue, I would have to say 'freshness' of the grounds. As I stated elsewhere in this book, "*Coffee is only 'fresh,' for a short time, after being ground;*" meaning, 'Roasted Beans' may hold their flavor and freshness for an extended period of time; but 'ground beans' start to lose their flavor, and go stale, immediately upon grinding… so generally, they are only 'fit' to brew, for a maximum of two weeks afterwards – although, many people would disagree with me over that! After two weeks, the flavor starts to go 'downhill!' So, if a 'Pod' is weeks to months old… the coffee grounds in it are going to be 'stale;' even if the Pod was 'vacuum sealed.'

Personally, if purchasing 'Pre-filled Pods,' I would use them as quickly as possible. I still own some pods, which were given to me two years before I purchased my first Keurig – they were supposed to be 'the best of the best!' I would doubt they would be 'outstanding' now! At least, there will be no 'off-gassing' in which to worry!

Another issue with these kinds of devices is the 'brewing temperature' of the water. As previously stated, when brewing coffee, we are 'ideally' looking for a temperature somewhere between 195°F and 205°F – depending upon the bean type, roast, and other issues; and, some of us prefer even hotter temperatures! So, why do people like 'K-Pod' machines? According to the Keurig information I have seen, the manufacturer states that *"The machine creates water approximately around 192°F;"* although, other machines may 'do better' when it comes to 'heating' the water! I tested mine, but it only created 182°F water. Yes, coffee still 'brews,' but it is not extracting what I feel to be the 'best features' of the coffee – so compensations must be made. In other words: the lower the temperature, the 'weaker or flatter' the flavor essence extraction; so, to 'make up the difference; (or achieve a decent cup of coffee) one must change the type of bean, the roast, the grind, or the filtering method – all things that the 'average' Pod user didn't realize they could do! Plus, there are still other 'tricks' one can use!

Remember still, the machine is not 'pre-warmed;' nor, are the grounds 'pre-wet' or 'Bloomed!' After all, that, remember 'altitude' for boiling temperature – and that 195°F to 205°F is considered the 'optimum' 'temperature' for brewing most coffee! A 'K-Pod Brewer' is not going to create that (or its equivalent), unless at a high elevation; so, in other words, a 'Keurig' might brew better in Denver, than in Death Valley!

Couple all these factors with the 'lack of brewing time' – remember, one of the selling points of 'Pod Coffee,' is its 'speed' (around one minute) – and one might not have the best-tasting coffee when compared to other brewing methods. Remember again, 'Pour-Over or French Press' brewing needs at least 3 to 5 minutes to fully extract; and 'Drip Brewers require more like 7 minutes – but, that is for a whole pot! 'Pod Brewers' dramatically reduce this time! Anything less than 3 minutes to extract (short of a pressurized, Espresso Machine), is going to make a 'weak' cup of coffee.

Pod Brewer companies seem to think their devices are *"Something of an Espresso Machine;"* being that they are using 'pressure' (somewhat) to extract – so temperature is not important. I even spoke to one manufacturer representative; and he told me, *"If the coffee is 'hot' when one drinks it, it is 'hot enough' to brew with!"* I tell my students, *"Trust me… it is not quite the same! Drinking temperature is not the same as 'brewing' temperature – or else, we would all 'reheat' Cold Brew Coffee!"* Some of the 'newer' machines, however, do have minor, adjustable water temperatures and brewing times; as well as cup size – but still, some 'technique <u>adjustment</u>' is going to have to be made for a truly, acceptable cup of 'Snobby,' K-Pod Coffee! Moreover, as of this writing, 'new' Pods are being made – which hold, approximately, twice the amount of coffee (as the coffee companies recently discovered), some people use larger 'mugs' rather than small, cups!

"Technique adjustment' can be used to make the coffee better," some might ask – *"Especially, with a 'cheaper' machine, other than a larger Pod?"* Surprisingly, *"Yes,"* is my answer! First, changing the brewing time on the device is often possible; if it <u>can</u> <u>be</u> adjusted, <u>do</u> <u>it</u> (mine, has a 'Bold' setting on it… so, it is, roughly, the same type of thing)! Remember, the 'slower' the brewing time, the better… that is, up to a point! Perhaps, one needs to 'lie' to the machine; and let it think one has a 'larger or smaller' cup than what is genuinely being used; and let the device adjust for that – thus, extending brewing time. For example, I tell one of my Keurig's, that I am using a 'bigger cup' – and, 'more' water is pushed through the grounds. When my cup is full, I place a second cup under the spout; to allow the weaker brew to fill it. I <u>pour</u> <u>out</u> that cup!

Secondly, one does not have to buy 'pre-packed' Pods or 'K-Cups of different brands or types of coffee. As mentioned before, one can purchase 'reusable' Pods; and fill with their own, 'fresh or favorite,' type of grounds! Ground size can even be chosen by the consumer, for a better-tasting cup! Sometimes, as previously mentioned, a combination of 'Reusable Pod' – lined with an added 'Paper Filter'  – will <u>slow</u> the brewing time down enough to extract the best coffee flavors. Even, slight 'tampering,' with a small Tamper (or, ones' thumb), can be performed; to slow down the brewing process even more. However, care should be taken, not 'jam' the brewer; as 'slowed too much,' might cause the machine to 'overflow.' Results can be easily tasted, when comparing something like 'Folgers, Black Silk' coffee grounds from a can – and used in

[143]

a 'Drip' brewer, as compared to the same thing in 'Commercial Pod' form. It is the same type of coffee, but brewing methods will taste different. When using a 'Refillable' Pod, the exact same grounds can be used… but tampered. The taste will still be different, but the K-Pod coffee will be 'closer' in taste to that of the 'Drip' maker.

If using freshly ground beans, (and depending upon one's taste), one may wish to use the Pods immediately upon grinding; or allow them to 'off-gas' for an hour to a few days. Of course, 'pre-wetting' the grind with a teaspoon/tablespoon of hot water might help create a 'tastier brew' as well! Also, adding a pinch of salt to the Pod can help to remove any bitterness. Some people might even try a 'different' type of water or add a 'Third Wave' product for more minerals!

One final thing to try is to 'run' one cycle of water through the machine before brewing the coffee; in other words, run the device without, or with an empty, a Coffee Pod. This action will 'pre-warm' the device; and may increase the brewing water temperature by a degree or two. Also, this is a good way too 'pre-warm' ones' cup or mug! Just pour the water from the cup 'back' into the brewer and start again – only this time, insert the Coffee Pod!

When brewing, do not be afraid to 'remove the cup' (or 'turn off' the device) a few seconds before the coffee has finished filling the cup. With most machines, they will immediately stop dispensing coffee; or the final amount out of coffee – the weakest part of the brew – will drain into the machines 'over-flow.' However, I find that it might be handy to have another empty cup nearby to help keep the machine cleaner! Of course, to reiterate, one may wish to experiment with different filters, grinds, roasts, and tampering as well; to achieve the 'flavor and body' one is looking to achieve!

Some machines, as with my Hamilton Beach 'Flex-Brew', even take 'loose' grounds – and place in a small, 'ground holder' to use instead of a 'K-Pod.' This option, gives the person brewing even more 'leeway' when it comes to 'troubleshooting.' I find this device handy for making only two cups of coffee quickly! Plus, I can us 'fresh' grounds! Realistically, it takes me just about as long to 'custom load' my K-Pod brewer, as it does with my 'Drip' coffee maker. If I 'load' the brewers before I go to bed at night (and especially, if I am using freshly ground beans) the grounds have time to 'degas' overnight before use!

I have to admit, having 'many different choices' of coffee in Pods <u>is</u> enjoyable! I prefer a 'Breakfast Blend' in the morning (if forced to drink K-Pod' coffee); whereas my son enjoys 'Donut Shop' coffee. My wife prefers, 'plain, old Folgers, Black Silk;' like we, often, make in our 'Drip' brewer. Moreover, at night (as previously mentioned), it is enjoyable to make a single cup of 'Decaf' – as caffeinated coffee keeps me awake! Some, 'Coffee Snobs' might enjoy brewing 'Specialty Blends;' as in some states, even 'Marijuana-Infused Coffee Pods' now exist. Other people may also brew with 'energy products' like 'Red Bull™;' so, not only can the drinker get a 'Caffeine Buzz,' they can get a 'Pot or triple Caffeine Buzz' at the same time! It might be noted, however, that some 'Specialty Blends' may clog a K-Pod Brewer faster than others, so more 'cleaning' may be required!

'K-Pod Brewers,' are 'handy' for camping; but only perhaps, if electricity is handy too. For groups? 'No!' I am often asked, *"Are Pod Brewers expensive for what one gets?"* Definitely; especially, when the purchaser adds all the 'accessories' which go along with the coffee maker – even the 'mini' ones! For example, 'descaling solution, reusable filters, reusable pods, miniature tampers, filter holders, storage drawers, cup carousels, 'faceted' travel mugs, water filters/purifiers, rinsing pods, brewer care kits, thermal carafes, side reservoir water filter starter kits, variety packs, optional cocoa bundles, brand name coffee bundles, drip trays, club memberships, latte mixes, cappuccino mixes, tea pods, soups, cocktail mixes, flavored coffee creamers in both powdered and liquid form, beverage and dessert recipe books, and much more can be added to most machines! The 'Coffee Snob' can spend hundreds of dollars to make their first single cup of coffee while camping or at home – but again… just look at all the 'Snobby' bragging rights!

To take us back to the 'health' issues of coffee, if one is worried about 'cancer-causing, coffee oils' – again, at least in California – then the coffee can be poured through a 'Paper Filter' (as I mentioned a few paragraphs back) in a 'Pour-Over' Cone – defeating the aspect of aspect of 'speed' when it comes to a 'K-Pod' brewer! Alternatively, as I mentioned a for use as a 'brewing tool' (to 'slow  down' brewing times), a small, 'paper filter' can be used in 'fill it yourself,' Reusable Pods. These filters will work the same way as the full-sized 'paper filters' do in 'Drip' or 'Pour-Over' brewers; when it comes to 'stopping' any 'cancer-causing' agents or oils from entering one's coffee cup! These filters are easily found in most grocery stores, which also carry 'Reusable Pods!' My local store seems to carry two different types of filters, and six different brands of Pods. Both Filters are the same 'weave' (meaning coffee will be filtered the same) and the Pods only seem to vary in 'price,' not quality or function!

Back to other Brewers:

Sowden 'Oskar' SoftBrew™

Invented by George Sowden, this (often imitated) brewer is available in similar shapes and assorted sizes. 'Sowden SoftBrew' (named, from the coffee having a 'silky, smooth' taste and feel to it) is porcelain pot; which is both a 'brand name' as well as a 'brewing method' (of sorts) – however, it uses 'very specific' brewing steps.

Technically, the 'SoftBrew' is related to an 'Immersion Coffee Brewer;' meaning, the coffee grounds are 'immersed' underwater for brewing; very much like a 'French Press' would do – but, it can be used to make a 'Cold Brew' as well!

The truth of the matter is, 'SoftBrew' is little more than a 'Fancy, Pour-Over or Steeping,' Infusion brewer!

My 'Snobby' Canadian, English, and German friends love these brewers – and so do I! Looking something like a teapot or *"English, Electric Coffee Pot,"* as one woman told me – the standard, 'SoftBrew' is not electric! It is something of a <u>cross</u> between multiple methods – but, brewed coffee tastes closest to that of a 'French Press' or 'Pour-Over.'

'Coffee Snobs' may like 'Softbrew' because it looks 'high-tech;' but 'experts' like it because it works both 'cleanly,' and 'quickly' (in about four minutes)! I own several brewing methods like a SoftBrew… however, I like this method best! Do not be surprised if you see your 'Roaster' using one! In fact, the Sowden's 'Infusion Brewer' is used by many professional 'tasters' to evaluate 'fine coffees' – a fact, that many 'Coffee Snobs' love!

At the center of the pot is <u>another</u> pot or 'ground holding' chamber, of sorts; with an oversized, 'Stainless Steel,' filter/chamber. 'Coarse' ground coffee is placed inside the chamber (one tablespoon for each 6-ounces of water), and an ounce or so of '200°- 210°F water is poured over them – to *"Create a 'Bloom' and release the coffees fragrance,"* the manufacturer states (but, only if desired). After 30 seconds to a minute, any remaining water is either poured out, or the brewer filled with 200+°F hot water. The grounds 'steep' for up to four minutes (or again, according to one's preference), and the coffee served. Some people remove the inner chamber before 'pouring;' however, the manufacturer recommends, keeping the ground chamber in the 'Pot' 'the duration!' In my opinion, this is a 'bad move;' as the coffee will 'continue to brew' in the pot – and thus, ruin the coffees delicate features. Moreover, again in my opinion, 'Blooming' is not required; as water is supposed to be 'slowly poured' over the grounds (in a clockwise fashion). By the time the chamber is full of water, more than 30 seconds have passed; so, the coffee has 'Bloomed' while filling the pot!

When it comes to temperature, I prefer (as with many other methods), to use water 'just off the boil;' but professional 'tasters,' seem to enjoy using 200°F. One of the 'Roasters' I use, even prefers 180°F; feeling that using that particular temperature, exclusively, is going to help him determine 'which' group of beans will give him the best brewing – with the belief that: *"If the coffee is good at 180°F, then it will be great at 205°F!"* Perhaps, he is correct!

Of course, the metal filter is not able to remove any 'dangerous oils' (again, here in California) like other brewing methods. So, many 'Health/Coffee Snobs' recommend, *"Pour the brew through a Paper Filter, to retard the oils, before drinking"* – in my opinion, this action defeats the purpose of the brewing technique – and, again, will 'alter' the coffees delicate flavors.

Standard, 'Coffee Snobs' are somewhat split on this device. Some say the 'SoftBrew method' *"Lacks flavor, body, and fruitiness;"* but will admit, it is *"Long on aroma!"* Others say, *"It makes the best coffee they ever had!"* Frankly, with its ground choice, size, and water temperature options, I think it would be challenging not to make a 'good' pot of coffee – however, my first experience with it was not very good! My Canadian friend, doing the 'brewing,' in my opinion, used much too 'coarse' a grind; choosing, almost, a 'pulverized' grind – of which he had 'ground' in his blender! As he 'spooned out' the grounds, I could see that they would have been better suited to an Espresso Machine – as the grind was so 'fine!' I drank a cup of the coffee once brewed; but did not enjoy it. However, my cup still did not have any 'mud' as expected; as the Sowden filter holes were so small!

[147]

Nonetheless, most 'Snobs,' do not mind the $50.00 to $150.00 price for what the brewer does; and tend to buy the 'Sowden' for its 'name' and reputation.

Moreover, when it comes to 'cleaning,' the 'Snobs' say, "*It is much easier than a 'French Press!*'" This could be only, somewhat, true; as 'yes,' grounds are 'compacted' in the bottom of the French Press – and one needs to 'spoon them out' in most cases. However, unless 'freshly brewed,' and still very wet, the Sowden Filter is difficult to dump too! The one advantage, however, is that the Sowden filter is metal, rather than 'glass' like the Press – so, it can be 'tapped' on a garbage pail to dump the grounds!

Café Solo (a.k.a. Eva Solo) Coffee Brewer®

Like the 'Sowden SoftBrew,' the 'Café Solo' appears to be both a 'brewing method' and a 'brand name' as well! 'Experts' say it, "*Brews like an upside-down French Press; with a built-in, convex filter… which descends into the brewing chamber.*" In reality, its glass 'brewing container' somewhat resembles a 'Chemex' brewer; and the whole thing is covered with a Neoprene cover. Some 'Coffee Snobs' I have met, even say, "*Coffee brewed with the Eva Solo brewer, tastes 'cleaner' than a SoftBrew or French Press.*" Personally, I cannot see or taste too much difference when served side by side! Nevertheless, it is an enjoyable way to brew – and looks attractive, sitting on a dining or breakfast table!

Surprisingly, some people are confused or 'intimidated' by its use; but it is not that complicated: using a 'Medium/Coarse' coffee grind, one tablespoon of grounds is added to the carafe for every <u>four</u> ounces of water. 198°F - 202°F water (depending upon personal taste, roast, and elevation) is poured into the device. The Neoprene cover serves two purposes; it helps to help keep the finished brew warm, and it allows the device to picked up after filling with hot water!

One minute into the brew, the coffee grounds are 'stirred' with a 'long-handled' spoon or paddle, which comes with the device. The 'Filter and Lid' are placed, securely, onto the carafe; and the brew 'steeps' for a minimum of four minutes. The coffee is, then, allowed to be 'poured' – which action, puts it through its 'Filter/Sleeve.' It is suggested that <u>all</u> the coffee be, immediately, 'poured' into a carafe. The coffee, usually, comes out clean, bright, and with its 'Oils' intact; so, it does not meet California's 'health' suggestions!

'Coffee Snobs' enjoy this method for both results and price – around $100.00. Plus, it is obscure enough to impress most people!

Technivorm®

'Hand-built' in the Netherlands, at this writing, this is one brewer that about every 'Coffee Snob' I know, would love to have... including, myself! Available in a multitude of colors (and sometimes large enough to qualify as furniture), Technivorms look something like a 'Drip' Coffee Maker with a 'thyroid condition' (so to speak)! It has hoppers, brewers, showerheads, drip chambers, water chambers... you name it! 'Coffee Snobs' have often told me; *"This is the best and only way to achieve full flavor, aroma, and body! Moreover, at only $350.00, the Technivorm 'Mochamaster' is a steal!"* Be that as it may... I do not own one; I would like to but cannot justify the expense!

'Restaurant' versions – with a much larger footprint – are available as well – but, for a much higher price! I will admit it, Technivorm <u>does</u> make a great cup of coffee – even with reasonably inexpensive grounds – and it is easy in which to 'standardize'... with commercial grinds, such as 'Farmers Brothers™' coffee! Not surprising, most people cannot tell the difference between a 'coffee house' brew and what a restaurant would make with their Technivorm. Moreover, 'like most people,' I have difficulty telling the difference between one *"Great cup of coffee,"* made with one device, and another *"Great cup"* made with a Technivorm as well! In fact, during one 'blind, taste tasting seminar,' I could not tell the difference between 'French Press' when compared with 'Technivorm!' I would suppose, one might wonder, *"How 'good is good;' if one cannot tell the difference between 'good' methods?"*

If one looks hard enough at restaurants like Denny's™, IHOP™, or any 'chain type' restaurant or 'diner,' one can still see some older, commercial units being used. They were great for large crowds – or to serve an abundance of customers all day long. Their whole idea was: *"Brew it fast... serve... moreover, store the rest while more is brewing!"* Larger restaurants or hotel convention centers might even have two or more of these!

Again, I do not own one... however, I would like to!

Siphon (Syphon or Vacuum) Brewer

Regardless of how one spells it – Siphon or Syphon – I have to say; *"Immersion brewing with a 'Syphon Brewer' does put on a good show!"* Many restaurants back in the 1960s, had 'table or cart' versions of these; and they fascinated me as a child (and frankly, still do)! I own a, small and simple,

'Hario' brand – as shown on the previous page. It is not 'fancy...' but it works! Prices start around $40.00 and 'hover' over $100.00. Other brands, however, can run into 'several hundred' dollars!

A 'relic method' from the 19th century (and yet another machine looking something like a 'science experiment' or a miniature, 'Moonshine Still') a 'Syphon Brewer' is essentially, <u>two</u> pots; temporarily, mounted to each other with a 'sealing' gasket. Often, models will have a 'mounting or holding' stand as well; which can be just as much as a 'piece of art' as the device itself... moreover, can be made from almost anything! If money were not a consideration, I would own one of these brewers with copper, brass, and glass – just to catch people attention at 'tastings!'

The process can be a bit more involved than just 'one-pot siphoning into another' – especially when considering the different forms, styles, and types, of brewers. Primarily, the 'Bottom Pot' is filled with pure water; while the coffee grounds are held in the 'Top Pot.' A 'siphon tube' is attached, connecting the two pots – and a cloth or paper <u>filter</u> goes 'in between' the two. A heat source, of one type or another, is placed under the 'Bottom Pot' to 'heat the water' for brewing. The heated water is, then, forced out of the 'Lower Pot' and up into the top 'ground chamber;' where the coffee is 'steeped,' then 'siphoned back out,' when the coffee begins to cool. The 'still hot,' but cooling, coffee 'refills' the Lower Pot! While 're-filling' the Pot, however, the coffee passes through a filter. The same heat source, which was used for brewing, now, keeps the coffee warm. It is fun to watch!

'Syphon Brewing,' scores very high with 'Coffee Snobs;' as water temperature can be more 'tightly controlled;' and 'taste and body' can, at least, somewhat, be controlled as well! Plus, it puts on a good show! Moreover, I have to say; it <u>does</u> create a great cup of coffee!

Is a 'Syphon Brewer' better than other Immersion methods? Well, that depends upon the consumer's taste!

'Pour-Over' (Filter) Brewing Cones:

I was recently in a group and asked, "*What <u>is</u> a Pour-Over Cone or Basket?*" My simple answer... "*A 'manual' Keurig... only better!*' This brewer comes in many diverse types and brands. It is, also, the most 'difficult brewer' to write about; as 'diverse types and brands' of Cones, equates to so many different forms,

shapes, sizes, styles, materials, designs, colors, drainage holes, and more! Surprisingly, 'Cones,' in various forms, are used by many 'Corporate Coffee Buyers' or Baristas; as a way to 'choose' the best beans for use, resale, or 'canning!'

The Cone, shown on the previous page, is an example of what some people are surprised to learn <u>is</u> 'Pour-Over' than Cone too! Yes, it is 'flat-bottomed,' Cone' shaped; but unlike a 'true Cone,' it is more of a 'Stand Alone' Filter – which simply 'sits' over a waiting cup or mug; and <u>works</u> like a standard Cone! However, like a 'Sowden SoftBrew,' rather than using a 'paper filter,' hit has a stainless-steel chamber/cone which has many small holes in it. Grounds go into the cone directly (although, some people may put in a 'secondary' paper filter within the cone) and hot water is 'poured over' them – either with or without 'Blooming.'

Some types/brands of 'Cones,' even attach to other types of 'major' brewers; and can be used in conjunction with different devices to (both) obtain clarity of the brew and to remove oils – through use of a separate or coupled 'paper or cloth' filters! However, unless like the Cone shown in the photograph, <u>all</u> Cones require 'filters' of some sort. Some require round filters; while others need 'pre-shaped' ones! Although, there are some Cones are 'wedge' or 'V' shaped – and need a 'wedge' shaped filter; while others (such as the Chemex) use what is more of a 'sheet' of paper, folded into a 'Cone' shape!

Some Cones might even use a 'nylon screen or netting' as a filter; while others may use a 'cloth' filter… which can be rinsed and reused. Still more people may use a piece of 'cotton' (or other material) placed in the bottom of their Cones; covering the drainage holes; and 'slowing down' drainage!

 Many Cones need a 'special holder or stand' of some sort; or have their own glass or plastic 'Cone within a Cone' system in which to brew. Others are used in conjunction with an attractive carafe; so, coffee may be served immediately after brewing… while still others (the majority of Cones) may fit on top of a cup or mug – and may have windows on the sides for beverage 'level' viewing. Moreover, some cones are even designed for 'double brewing' or 'specialty' types of coffees; and are inserted into some 'Automated' brewing machines – such as the Technivorm!

This previous Cone shown, is one of the 'simple,' type/single cup brewers which I own. It is designed for 'quick and easy,' single-cup brewing! The Cone is, first, placed over a mug (preferably, pre-heated), and a 'bleached or unbleached' 'V' shaped paper filter is placed into it. However, rather than using a 'paper' filter at all, with this cup shown, I used a 'fine mesh,' 'V' shaped filter; made out of wire and plastic! As soon as the filter is filled with hot water, it begins to drain into the mug. When finished, the 'Cone and filter' are removed; and the coffee is ready to drink.

However, before looking too closely, at various 'Cones,' let's have a short 'class' on 'comparing' the different methods. First, somehow, 'beg, borrow, or steal, a few different types of Cones – including, types like Chemex. This is where it pays to be a member of a 'Coffee Club' of some sort. For myself, I have never had trouble finding 'willing participants' for a 'Coffee Test!'

After assembling all the Cones, one would like to compare, 'standardize' on a few things – to keep everything 'fair; as this is how one will determine the brewing method, grind size, coffee/water ratio, temperature and more! With most of my tests, I start with 24 grams of 'medium' grounds, and 400 grams of pure water! In most cases, I use the same brand/weave 'paper filter' in each brewer – again, to keep things constant. Water temperature is brought up to a 'constant' 205°F, and when brewing (even though, every brewer recommends a different size grind and temperature) the grounds and water are 'pre-wet' with 205°F water for 30 seconds. The water kettle is replaced to restore heat. Then, depending upon the brewer, more hot water is added (poured in a circular motion) until the correct ratio is met. Only the smaller brewers are different when it comes to water and grounds, as they cannot hold as much.

In a test of these brewers, we found that some produced coffee which was weak and bitter; while brewers created 'full-bodied' cups – remember, all aspects of brewing were the same. After choosing the 'best of the best,' we then start to 'augment' each brew – adding or subtracting grounds. From there, the next step is to try different 'grinds;' but again, with everything else staying the same. However, if feeling ambitious, we can then, 'reverse' a few steps, and try different water temperatures with the same size grounds first! I, often, do this, as I prefer brewing with a 'hotter' temperature!

After determining our favorite 'augmented' brew, we then performed the same test once again; but this time, we compared different types of brewers; such as comparing our favorite 'Cone' to a favorite 'French Press,' or 'Percolator!' I cannot describe how surprised some people were after tasting their 'favorite' brewing method, and then, comparing it to a simple 'Cone!' Performing this test, not only allows the person brewing to determine their favorite 'Cone' for brewing, but 'how' to augment/fine tune their beans/brew even more!

Looking closer look at Melitta Cones:

Melitta Coffee Cones:

Melitta Cones were invented nearly 112 years ago (at this writing), by Melitta Bentz; and very little has changed since, other than 'size' and color! Although, some of Melitta's 'Signature Series' Cones have 'ridges' (or groves) on the sides – "*Ribbed for one's pleasure*" (if you will pardon the pun), as can be seen in this photograph. The actual reason for 'ribs,' however, is that many manufacturers feel that the grooves create a certain amount of 'space' between the paper filter and the cone; which will allow the coffee to pass through the filter and then 'flow' into the waiting cup or mug. If a cone does not have any ridges or channels, the brewed coffee is thought to 'well up' between the filter paper and the cone; and adversely affect brew time!

Years ago, when I first bought my first 'Melitta' Cone at a grocery store, there was little difference in size and shape; the smallest (a #2), just looked like a smaller version of the largest (a #6)! Not to mention, 'black' was the only color available! It was not too long, however, before Melitta added a 'Red' #6 color in which to choose! Of course, the manufacturer promptly threw 'Bleached or Unbleached' paper filters at me to choose from too. I decided 'Unbleached' was best for me... at least, it seemed like a good idea!

When one 'preps' for 'brewing,' a decision needs to be made as to 'pre-wetting' the filter, or not. Some Baristas claim this will help with "*More 'even' brewing; and eliminate some Paper taste.*" Also, it can help to 'pre-warm' (or, 're-warm') the cup as well; as with most Cones, the coffee passes directly through the filter and cone into the waiting cup or mug. However, as so little water is used during this process, 'pre-warming' the cup is best done after the 'pre-wetting' process – after the ounce or so of water passes through the grounds, into the cup, and the 'Blooming Water' disposed of. Brewing water may, then, be added.

Brewing water is, preferably, in the 195°F - 205°F range; and is 'poured over' the grounds in a circular manner. The water temperature has <u>everything</u> to do with brewing and taste but <u>is</u> just as subjective as the 'grind size!' I know people who <u>only</u> brew with 'low' temperatures with one 'grind;' while others – like myself – prefer to brew with 'higher' temperatures, while brewing with a 'coarser' grind.

As I have already stated several times, Professional Baristas will, most likely, tell you to "*Only use 205°F water.*" However, due to the small hole(s) in the bottom of the Cone, the extraction of the coffee will '<u>change</u>,' depending upon the temperature of the water, before slowly passing through the filter and 'draining' directly into the cup or carafe. This is where all the different 'brands and designs' of Cones come it! Some Cone have only one, 'big hole' in their bottom; where others, may have several small holes for coffee to drain.' Each 'varying' size and number of holes dictate the amount of time the coffee extracts – presuming, the person brewing, is using the proper filter and temperature of the water. That is, 'what is proper' for the particular brewer being used. Again, 'personal preference' takes preference over 'set' brewing times, water temperatures, and even 'grind' sizes! Therefore, it is so essential for one to '<u>standardize</u>' on whatever brewing method is being used – as well as all other factors!

The Melitta Cone 'drains' at the same rate as most other cones – taking approximately, three minutes to brew. Why does it (some models) have only 'one drain hole;' as opposed to two or more? The best answer is… that is how it was designed some 112 years ago! Some people think 'three or more' holes will permit "*Better extraction*" of the coffee; but, again, this is more of a 'matter of preference,' than fact! If it were not, then, one would never see some people putting 'toothpicks' into 'Bee Hive' brand 'Cone Brewers' cones – to 'slow down' the extraction process.

The facts of the matter are, the entire process (depending upon the cone) should only take a few minutes – hence, I wonder why some people 'have to have' a <u>fast</u>, K-Pod Brewer – as simple logic would dictate that a 'Cone' might be better! Plus, any brand 'Cone' can use '<u>fresh</u>' coffee; whereas, most commercial pods are already, somewhat, stale when purchased! However, all cones, even Melitta, need to have their 'grind, temperature, and time' adjusted accordingly; depending upon the 'drinkers' preferences!

Very little has changed over the years with the 'Melitta Cone;' except, the company, now, has many sizes, models, accessories, and colors in which to choose! Their Cones can be cast from plastics or ceramics. They even have their own 'Carafe' type coffee makers – as well as 'Pour-Over' stands for single or 'multiple cones' use in commercial settings.

In my opinion, one of the best brewing methods (short of, once again a 'French Press' or 'Clever Dripper') is 'Pour-Over, Cone Coffee!' I must stress *"One of the best;"* as there is a form of 'Pour-Over' which is a little different than the others – besides, just the holes in the bottom of the brewer; but more on that model later, along with the subject of 'Filters.'

'Coffee Snobs' (if they are willing to use a Cone) either love 'Melitta Cones' or hate them; as they are so inexpensive! I have no doubt that should Melitta 'tack on' $50.00 onto the cost; most 'Snobs' would love them!

However, as previously stated, the actual 'holes' in the bottom of the cones, are what makes the difference between most brands – and, Melitta is no different... okay, the cones 'shape' has something to do with it too... as do any 'ridges,' and the 'type' of filter the cone uses! However, other than 'size for brewing amounts,' it does not matter what shape the Cone is... round, 'V' shaped, flat, funnel-shaped, 'Wave' shaped, or anything else! Despite what anyone says, it is the 'holes in the bottom,' that dictate the 'speed' (and extraction) in which the coffee extracts.

'Cones' (even one as 'simple' to use as Melitta) can be very confusing to those new to them! Some have 'multiple holes;' while others have 'oddly shaped' holes. Some holes are tiny, while others, like the Melitta, are large! Holes can number as few as 'one,' or as many 160,000 or more!

The 'Melitta' works fine for me, should I simply wish a 'fast' cup of coffee; and as much as I enjoy the coffee it brews, I still do not think coffee tastes as good as 'full immersion' coffee! However, again, more on that later!

Let us talk a little bit about some subtle differences between 'Cones' in the brewers which follow! Remember, if using a 'paper filter' in a 'V' shaped Cone, one needs to 'fold over' the side and bottom seams of the filter; to aid in holding the in place and keeping it from collapsing.

The filters of 'Sieve' type (or round, pointed) brewers, do not require filters with 'seams;' nor, does a 'Chemex' – which uses a folded, flat paper to use as a filter.

Bee House/Hive,' Pour-Over Dripper/Brewer

Generally available in just two sizes (at this writing, and for the brand), in Japan, the 'Pour-Over Bee House' (or 'Bee Hive,' as it is sometimes called here in America) brewer manufacturers, claim that their method and design of Cones are *"The best way to brew coffee; as 'Bee House' produces a stronger, full bodied brew than other cones!"*  Here in America, however, these 'Cones' are just another 'effective way' to make a 'Pour-Over' brew! The photograph above, shows the 'small' version I own. As with the 'Melitta' and a few other Cones, it has 'channels' on the sides to 'enhance' brewing!

Known more as a 'Bee Hive Brewer' in Japan, the similarities between 'Cones' are somewhat confusing; when it comes to temperature, ground size, and brewing time. Many students have told me, *"All Cones are confusing,"* as there are so many types and brands… however, not all cones are the same; even if they look similar!

Some people might say, *"Japanese Bee Hive Cones are just a smaller way (sometimes) to make Chemex or Hario coffee;"* and they are correct, in a sense! Nonetheless, I have found the 'Bee Hive' to be more closely like a 'Melitta Coffee Cone;' in the fact that it is similar in shape and has 'vertical internal ridges;' the only 'big' difference being, the 'Bee House/Hive' has a handle on it, and has 'two' large drain holes, rather than 'one,' like the Melitta!

Brewing only takes *"Two minutes or so,"* according to the manufacturer – although, most directions recommend <u>four</u> minutes! A 'wire or paper filter' (Melitta Filters work fine) goes into the Cone, and both cone and filter are 'pre-heated' to 200°F – the same as the brewing water. Three tablespoons (or 22 grams) of 'medium-fine,' grounds go into the filter; and the Cone goes over a cup – no change here, over a Melitta' Cone. Of course, as with so many other brewers, an ounce of 'hot water' is poured into the 'Filter' to allow the coffee to 'Bloom;' although, the manufacturer does recommend 30 seconds for 'Blooming.'

After the drinkers' preference of 'seconds to minutes' are allowed for the 'Bloom,' additional hot water is poured into the filter – sometimes, in stages. The hot water passes through the grounds; and extracts the flavors, acids, oils, and colors, like any other cone. Remove the Bee House from the cup, and the coffee is ready to drink!

In theory (and the Japanese way), some say one is supposed to be able to *"Control water temperature, strength, color, and even taste' through the 'irregular' sized drain holes the brewer has;"* and it gives another way of exercising more control over temperature and brewing time! I am not exactly sure how one would do that; unless one has 'sealed off' one of the holes – thus, making it more like a 'Melitta' again!

Due to the size of the brewers 'large holes,' Bee Hives users have told me that they *"Need to use 'coarse grounds' like most French Presses;"* but, as with French Presses, 'grind size' does not really matter if a 'dense enough' filter is being used, and extraction time – coupled with water temperature – adjusted. Again, water should be poured in a slow, circular, or 'zig-zag' fashion, to thoroughly wet and cover the grind.

I, frankly, cannot taste any difference between the 'Hive' and the 'House' brands/models, once other considerations are made; nor, can I taste a difference between this or another brand 'Cone!' I am sure, however, I could find several 'Coffee Snobs' or experts, whom would disagree with me!

Typically, these brewers would, probably, 'throw off' an actual 'Coffee Snob;' as, like Melitta, they are so inexpensive. They do, however, attract some genuine 'Coffee Connoisseurs.' There is still hope for the 'Coffee Snob,' however; as cones like 'Bee Houses,' are available in 'expensive' glass, 'fancy' copper, or ceramic, models… besides plastic! Used ones, found online or in thrift shops, can be cheap; but for new models, the more 'ornate,' the 'more <u>expensive</u>' the consumer will find – 'fancy' does not brew better coffee, however!

Whatever type used, 'Cones' offer many options! Here is what one 'Coffee Snob' friend recently told me: *"If one is <u>forced</u> <u>to</u> brew their own coffee, especially a small amount, a <u>Cone</u> is one of the best ways… moreover, the 'Bee Hive' Cone is, certainly, the best cone!"* His statement might be debatable; considering so many people have different tastes (not to mention, other 'Snobs' whom dislike the brewer due to 'price!'

I can remember my first response to 'Pour-Over Cones,' and what I told students; *"Cone Coffee was so much better than 'Drip' Coffee, the first time I tried it, that I promptly went out to purchase one!"*

However, the next brewer, I have found to 'improve' upon a regular Cone!

[157]

<u>Clever</u> <u>Coffee</u> <u>Dripper</u>®

My 'all-time favorite' brewer (as I have mentioned at least twice before in this book), still, is something of a 'Cone;' but the, much emulated, 'Clever Dripper' is something else' as well – it's an 'Immersion Brewer' (meaning all of the coffee and all of the water 'meet' at the same time and temperature) – and is, undoubtedly, more practical (and 'forgiving') than a regular 'Cone' brewer!

The 'Clever Dripper' is a durable device; made from BPA-Free, Eastman Tritan Plastic; so, it is not going to transfer any adverse chemicals or flavor to one's coffee – and sells, for less than $30 in most places! It must be noted, however, that this device is neither Microwave nor Dishwasher safe! In time, however, I have found that the plastic will develop 'micro-fractures;' and not look very good. However, I have owned and used my 'Dripper' for, approximately, two years, and I have not seen any 'leaks' develop yet!

Many 'Coffee Snobs' may disagree with their fellow 'Snobs,' when it comes to their 'Cone' opinions… that is, if they <u>use</u> 'Cones' at all; but <u>almost all</u> are in agreement about the 'Clever Dripper;' and that is, if they have ever had an opportunity to taste coffee brewed with it, they would choose the 'Dripper' over any other cone! Why would anyone 'think' this? It is because, the 'Clever Coffee Dripper' may be a 'Pour-Over' brewer… however, is also, a 'full immersion' brewer (like a 'French Press')! Its 'cone' shape is just a 'happy coincidence'; as it could be almost any shape and still 'brew' the same way!

Known by other names as, 'Better Pour-Over, One Clever Brewer, Clever Dripper or 'The Clever Coffee Dripper,' the brewer is available in only two sizes – 11 and 18-fluid ounces – at this writing. The 11-ounce model is designed for only <u>one</u> cup of coffee; whereas the 'larger' version, can easily make two or three – depending upon the size of the cup or mug. A 'Metal or Mesh Filter' can be used, but the device is designed for use with paper ones! Often, if I am out of 'Clever Dripper Filters,' I will use a Melitta, #4 or #2, one!

As with other 'Cones,' a 'recommended' 25 grams of 'medium to coarse' grind coffee is added to the filter (a 1-18 ratio with water). The manufacturer recommends using 195°F to 206°F water. Frankly, I enjoy <u>208°F</u> best when I brew with it! As with other methods, 'temperature' is a matter of preference!

Special Note: I purchased my 'Clever Dripper' <u>before</u> I purchased a digital scale. However, as I know that a level coffee scoop of dry coffee grounds is, approximately, 10 grams, I used 'two scoops' of coffee for every 6 ounces of water. As I own the '18-fluid ounce model (and this is the equivalent of two large servings of coffee), I used three scoops of coffee in the brewer. Depending upon the 'type' of beans and the grind, I may use more or less grounds; depending upon me or my family's preference any given day; not to mention, this brewer is as 'forgiving' as they come! Any 'reasonable' amount of coffee grounds will still turn out an excellent cup of coffee)!

Because of the 'Valve' on the device, the consumer has 'more control' over how the brewer works! For example, if a 'sip' coffee is too weak, one might allow the coffee to extract for a minute longer before 'filling' their cup! Alternatively, all that might be needed the next time brewing, is to use 'more grounds!' Again, 'personal preference' is going to determine all aspects of brewing. Remember, the directions which come with the 'Clever Dripper' (as with any other brewer) are mere '<u>guidelines</u>' for brewing! Moreover, one <u>does not</u> have to own a digital scale to make coffee with this device unless determining 'coffee water' ratios; however, a full brewer – approximately ½ inch from the top of the filter, is close to 400 grams!

If one wishes to 'bloom,' the 'release valve' feature allows one to do so, if desired – and enables the 'choice' of either 'keeping or releasing' any excess water! The 'bitter' 'Blooming water' can be either allowed to stay in the brewer – and 'mix' with the brewing water – which, incidentally, will 'bring down' the brewing temperature, or be 'drained' into another cup or sink before the actual 'brewing water' is added. Once again, water can be added in stages (and the grounds stirred); in an attempt to keep the 'brewing temperature' constant. I cannot taste much difference in beans which have had time to 'degas;' so, I do not always bother with pouring out 'Blooming' water before adding my 'Brewing' water! I 'Bloom' with this device for 'pre-wetting' both the grounds and the filter!

Frankly, this method of brewing, is my favorite way to brew coffee (although, I do own another brand brewer, which brews the same way – but, doesn't, necessary, require a filter); and, I do not feel that 'measuring out grounds and water' (as was demonstrated to me by a Roaster) is all that important, after determining my 'bean and water temperature' preferences. I merely add a 'few tablespoons' of my favorite 'bean and grind;' and add water to the top of the cone! This way, I have two, large, cups of coffee… brewed the way I like it!

Of course, the longer the grounds 'steep,' the darker and the more caffeinated the brew becomes – not to mention, the 'colder' it becomes in temperature – so, a good 'troubleshooting tip,' may be, it might be best to pour hot water in stages over the grounds; and stir, once or twice, to break up any 'crust' (being careful not to 'tear' the delicate filter). As with other cones, both the 'Clever Dripper' and cup/mug should be 'pre-warmed.' This is easy for me, as I always 'rinse' my brewer and mug under 'hot' water in the sink while the coffee is brewing. Then, I place my mug on a 'pre-warmed,' electric 'Cup Warmer;' to keep it warm, if I still have some 'wait' time.

Many 'Coffee Snobs,' that I have asked for 'Clever Dripper' opinions, say they are "*Up in the air*" over this method; some absolutely hate it – as "*A 'true Barista' is not preparing the coffee*" (I have seen several in coffee shops, so "*Yes*," they are); nor, is it "*A 'highly expensive,' or complicated, piece of equipment!*" Nonetheless, many 'Snobs' like the idea of 'being their <u>own</u> Barista (of sorts);' and 'controlling their brew' through the grind, temperature, time and dose. Surprisingly, I have not had a single person, whom I have demonstrated this device to, say that they "*Did not like the taste of the coffee*;" even though, they may not have 'liked' the device itself! Frankly, I think it only takes a small 'taste' of the brew to decide 'positively,' upon a 'Clever Dripper!'

In this same sense, I know the owners of a professional 'Coffee Roasting Company and Restaurant Supply' in my town. They supply 'Roasted Beans' to many of the top coffee bars in our area – including one company, which 'resells' the beans all over the world under a famous name! These 'Professional Roasters' can easily be classified as 'Coffee Snobs;' as they have many 'conceived' and 'pre-conceived' ideas and opinions – and rightfully so, in many cases! After all, they have been at this business for many years; and are '<u>tops</u>' in their field. I believe one would be foolish <u>not</u> to 'value' their opinions! The <u>only</u> way they will, themselves, brew and drink coffee – or will perform 'tastings' for their 'buyers' or their customers – is with the 'Clever Dripper!' <u>That</u> <u>alone</u> should say something – should my word, alone, not mean anything!

Again, the 'Clever Dripper,' is only available in two sizes; but, other attractive styles, are available under assorted styles under other brands – such as

the patented, 'Zevro®' (by Honey-Can-Do) 'Incred-a-Brew' – as seen here – (of which I like the design and appearance, and which does not require a paper filter), or the Bonavita, Porcelain, 'Immersion' Dripper – as shown to the left. Rather than have a 'pressure plate/valve' on the bottom to 'drain' coffee, the Bonavita has an 'open/closed,' 'Release Lever' to serve coffee. There is never an 'accidental draining;' that is, unless the 'lever/valve' is forgotten open! Due to the Bonavita 'drain hole' size, brewing time is, approximately, one minute longer than the 'Clever Dripper!' Prices 'hover' between $18.00 to $50.00.

On a side note (and this should, probably, be listed under 'Cooking with one's Coffee Maker,' instead of here), my large 'Clever Dripper' or 'Bonavita' doubles as a handy 'cooking' tool! For example, after cooking chicken or turkey (or any 'oily' food for that matter), I use one of my 'Drippers' as an 'Oil/Fat' separator! After the 'meat,' for example, is removed from its cooking pan or kettle, I pour the remaining liquid into my 'Dripper' – allowing it to 'sit' for a few minutes. The majority of 'Fat/Oil' in the liquid rises to the top of the brewer – leaving the 'flavored liquid' in the bottom. This is, especially, handy when preparing something like gravy or soup. After placing the 'Brewer' over a measuring cup, the bottom plate is depressed, or 'lever/valve' opened, and the flavored liquid pours out; filling whatever container I wish. When the 'Fat' reaches the bottom of the brewer (which is easy to see with the 'Clever Dripper,' (as the brewer is 'clear'), I lift the brewer; closing the valve. The left-over 'Oil/Fat' is, appropriately, disposed of in my 'oil recycling' can; and my Brewer is then 'de-greased' and cleaned.

Hario® V60 Glass Brewers

The 'Hario V60,' tends to be more of a 'brand name' than a kind of Cone Brewer; but, most of their brewers tend to be more of a 'Pour-Over' type (and, what many other brand names, seem to model themselves after). The only reason I am listing them here is the fact that so many people ask about the differences between this and other 'Cones' during coffee 'tasting' classes!

Hario was founded in Japan in 1921; and catered, primarily, to the scientific world; making beautiful glassware. After years of precision glass making, the company expanded into coffee brewers; which tended to look

[161]

and work like other 'Pour-Over' cones. It was not long before Hario started developing tea kettles, double-walled coffee presses, 'American Presses,' Drip coffee brewers, bean grinders, pet products, glassware, kitchen/coffee scales, laboratory glassware, cookware, serving decanters, and accessories!

Looking something like an 'art' piece, 'Hario Brewers' are available in heat resistant plastic, glass, ceramic, and copper. Some brewers fit directly onto a cup; while others require a wooden or 'wire' holder/stand ('Coffee Snobs' love the expensive 'Stands')! The procedure is the same as with any other 'Pour-Over' Cone; the 'pre-heated' brewer is, then, placed over a preheated cup or mug – and a paper, metal, or mesh filter, is placed into the Cone. A decision to 'pre-wet' the filter (paper) is decided upon; then 'coarse-ground' coffee is added to it. Again, a determination is made to 'Bloom' or not. If decided upon, a small amount of hot water is poured in; usually, in a 'clockwise' motion – according to the directions, for some reason – to allow the grounds to 'Bloom.' After several to thirty seconds, the Cone is, then, filled with an appropriate amount of hot water. The water passes through the grounds, extracts the oils, essences and flavors, and immediately begins to fill to the cup below it. When the cup is full, or the Cone is devoid of water, the coffee is ready to drink; a process which is not much different than that of any other 'Cone' Brewer!

Fortunately, or unfortunately, most of the 'Coffee Snobs' I know, only buy the Hario due to its price, history, and bragging rights! After all, $60.00 or more for a 'visually pleasing,' Copper Cone, is something in which to brag… I guess!

Kalita Wave® Dripper

The 'Kalita Wave Dripper' is very much like the Hario V60… at least, in the fact that it too is a 'Cone;' and is available in a variety of materials – including, 'glass and wood' – which makes it look something like a 'Chemex;' but only from the 'wooden middle' up! However, more 'common' models look more like a metal or plastic 'cup with handle' resting on a saucer!

Rather than having a 'V' shape to it, it is rounder; and uses a 'flat-bed' filter – much like a standard or 'Automatic Drip Coffee Maker' might have; however, it does have a smaller diameter 'bed.' Because of its 'bed' size, it uses "*Special* (and expensive) *filters*" (or, so says the manufacturer); which must be ordered 'online,' or purchased from a coffee 'specialty' store…

however, they look amazingly like a standard, 'flat-bottom' filter, available at most grocery stores. I do know some people who use standard filters – either cone or flat bottom – and 'adapt/fold/cut/squeeze-in' them to work!

The device manufacturer states that it is "*Easier for the consumer to use and is more 'consistent' than a Standard Cone*;" as well as, "*There is less room for <u>consumer error</u> – thus, giving the drinker a 'better cup' every time!*" They also claim, "*The unique, 'flat-bottom' design of the Kalita Wave Drippers – and their unique 'wave shape' in the bottom* (which looks like a 'Y') *– is the 'secret' to what makes 'Kalita Pour-Over Coffee,' the best cup of, 'error-proof' coffee one will ever taste!*" Frankly, I must question, how much 'error' can one have with 'Pour-Over' coffee?

Instructions call for 'just covering' the grounds with, approximately, 205°F (allowing for altitude) hot water and allowing them to 'Bloom' for only 15 or 20 seconds… <u>never a 'second' more</u>! Then, fill the Cone with hot water, and allow the grounds to 'steep' for three minutes (while draining into a cup at the same time).

Some 'experts' say: "*Taste of the Kalita, is like that of a 'Clever Dripper' or 'Bonavita;' but without the trouble of having to 'time' ones brewing – as coffee drains, slowly, into the cup through three small holes*;" which, I am told, are "*Supposed to 'automatically time' the extraction of the coffee, through drainage!*" Frankly, I do not see much difference between the 'Kalita' and any standard cone! Moreover, as far as "*Tasting like a Clever Dripper or Bonavita*," they are both '<u>Immersion</u>' brewers; the Kalita is not. Water is going to 'drain,' approximately, in the same amount of time as any other Cone with 'similar sized' holes!

The 'Kalita Wave Dripper' <u>does</u> makes excellent coffee – providing, one 'standardizes' on all materials and time… again, just like any other brewer!

I do know one former 'Coffee Club' member, who uses one of these; and he has 'broken off' a toothpick in one of the holes to 'slow down' the brewing/filtering time – as he claims the Kalita "*Drains too fast.*" I guess that makes sense – as everyone 'taste' and 'coffee preferences' is different – and frankly, if one is looking for 'the taste of a Clever Dripper,' the more prolonged the coffee stays in the water, the 'closer in flavor,' it will become!

Also, rather than using an 'special ordered' paper filter (or even a Melitta or generic 'flat bottom' paper filter), he uses a 23K 'Gold,' Basket Filter – which looks amazingly like the 'Gold Tone,' Ground

[163]

Basket/Filter I use in my 'Drip' Coffee Maker! The only problem with this is, the 'Basket' is larger in diameter than the brewer; thus, it 'sits' taller (and farther above the drain holes) than the brewer filter itself; which, is not a problem, providing one is careful with pouring their water, and uses a small cup!

The price for a Kalita is excellent – generally, around $10.00 for a plastic one, or up to $60.00 for Stainless Steel or 'Wood/Glass' models; although, expensive 'Accessory Kits,' or 'Golden Ground Baskets,' may be purchased from 'Name' stores – like 'Bed, Bath and Beyond!'

'Snobs' will dislike the low 'Kalita Cone' price; but enjoy the high, multiple accessory price. They will also enjoy the 'convenience' as well as the brew!

Primula/Seneca, Pour-Over Coffee Dripper®

One of my favorite brewers, the 'Primula' has two features which are different from other cones. First, it does not need a 'paper filter' (but, one can be used with it to hold back oils or extend extraction time). Moreover, the permanent, 'Double-Lined,' Stainless Steel Cone, itself works very much like a 'Sowden Soft Brew' coffee maker; as it has 'countless, little holes' for the extracted coffee to pass through. One cannot see it well in the photograph, on the right-hand side of the brewer, there is a cut-out, 'Peek-a-boo' window; for easy 'coffee level viewing' – as not to 'overfill' the cup! After brewing, the entire brewer and 'spent' coffee, is removed from the cup, and set aside!

The Stainless-Steel Filter goes into a thin, BPA free, plastic or glass cone; which then fits over average to 'generous sized' cups or mugs. The traditional amount of coffee grounds – 'fine to coarse' grind, according to taste, go into the 'pre-warmed' filter, and two ounces of 200°F (or to taste, again, I prefer 208°F) water follows; providing, the cup has been 'pre-warmed' too!

The manufacturer suggests, "*Blooming' for 30-60 seconds!*" The rest of the water is poured into the filter (as always, in a circular motion); and the filter allows the color, flavor, and aroma, of the coffee to "*Develop through time*;" while extracting the oils from the grounds. This process will take around three to five minutes – or more if using an additional paper filter – to remove (in California) those *"Carefully extracted oils,"* of which the device advertises! This is one 'Cone' which I feel, 'especially,' needs 'standardization of grinds and temperatures;' to achieve consistent results!

Cost is about $25.00 online or in some stores (I bought mine at a discount market); and 'Coffee Snobs' seem to like them, as they appear 'higher-tech' than they are; at least, the device gets a lot of *"Oooo's and Ahhhs."* at my coffee tastings! Besides, I find the metal filter convenient; for just for a 'quick cup' of 'Pour-Over' coffee! However, just 'how' convenient is the question! The grounds still need to be 'dumped and the cone cleaned!

Many people, I have known, dislike the plastic cone… however, love the 'metal filter;' so, they, often, take the filter and use it with some other, more expensive, brand cone. I have seen some of my students, even use it with a Chemex – mostly, for its appearance! I recently had one 'unmarried' member of our 'Coffee Club' tell me at a 'tasting,' *"If I want to impress a 'date' with my 'brewing abilities and equipment,' I will use my 'Primula Filter' over my fanciest cone!"* Perhaps, it might 'impress' some people; my wife, however, would ask, *"Isn't that the brewer you bought at the discount market?"*

Vietnamese 'Phin' Coffee Filters/Strainer/Phin

Similar to several other types of brewers, many 'Coffee Snobs' call this brewer, *"Just another Cone;"* but they could not be more wrong! It <u>can</u> be called a 'Pour-Over' Brewer, however! In Vietnam, however, most people know of it as a 'Phin!'

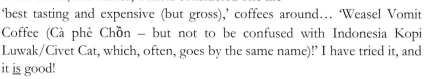

Vietnam is the second-largest Coffee Producer in the world; and makes, what is considered one the 'best tasting and expensive (but gross),' coffees around… 'Weasel Vomit Coffee (Cà phê Chồn – but not to be confused with Indonesia Kopi Luwak/Civet Cat, which, often, goes by the same name)!' I have tried it, and it <u>is</u> good!

'Weasel Vomit' aside, this brewer, makes coffee which is considered, *"Less concentrated than Espresso; but stronger/bolder than traditional 'Drip' brewed coffee…"* and many Vietnamese people enjoy using this device to brew their morning cup! It is simple to use, and both easy to clean and brew with – especially, when brewing 'Vietnamese Egg Coffee!'

[165]

These 'Filters' (if one can call it a 'Filter,' rather than 'Brewer'), can be made from ceramics, plastic, or the most popular version (as shown above), thin, stainless steel! It may not be a 'Cone,' but it is like a 'Primula/Seneca,' 'Pour-Over' coffee dripper; in the fact that it has many holes in its bottom, and it sits over a cup. 'Paper filters' are not needed; however, something like a 'Kalita' filter would work nicely, to 'filter out' any coffee 'oils!'

Often, being used to brew 'Weasel Coffee' – one of the most expensive, but unappetizing, coffees in the word (being that it comes from 'regurgitated' coffee beans, eaten by weasels) – a 'medium-fine grind' of coffee bean is recommended to be used; however, I have seen many people brew with a 'wide assortment' of grinds… which is the 'beauty' of the device, in my opinion! Brewing sounds complicated, but it is not! The first step, again as with any other brewer, is that one should 'pre-heat' both the cup/mug and brewer with 'boiling' (or the water used to 'brew' the coffee), then, the brewer is placed over the cup – as with most other cones!

Next, the 'lid' is opened, and three to four teaspoons of coffee are added to the 'Filter Cup/Basket.' The 'Basket' is shaken or 'tapped' on the side, to help 'settle' (flatten) the grounds. A 'flat plate' is, then, placed on top of the coffee grounds (usually, with a small handle for ease of use) to help 'flatten' the grounds some more; and, slightly, 'compress' them – much the same way as a 'tamper or leveler' would do. With some models, this plate may even 'screw' on. My 'pressure plate,' as shown in the photograph on the previous page, only 'sits' on top of the grounds – however, care needs to be made not to 'tighten or compress' too much!

'Placement,' of the pressure plate, needs to be held off until 'Blooming' is completed. To 'Bloom,' an ounce of 'Boiling Water' is added to the 'Basket.' After one minute of 'Blooming,' press (or screw) down the plate, slightly. This will help to 'compress' the, now 'swollen,' grounds; and help extract more flavor once the hot water is added.

The 'Basket' can now be filled with 'Boiling Water' – or, as much water as the cup or mug can hold (if using a 'large' Phin, then, a large container or carafe needs to be used). If the device has a 'lid,' it can be placed on after the water is poured. Allow for all the water to 'seep' through the device into the cup; it may take two to three minutes, depending upon the size and type of the device and the grounds. Add additional 'Boiling Water' to the brewer, if needed, to fill the cup. When all the coffee has drained, it is ready to drink – either 'black,' or the traditional 'Vietnamese' way; with condensed milk, sugar, and, sometimes, a touch of salt (if the coffee is slightly bitter, that is). Of course, any 'additive' can be used; but then, it is not, uniquely considered, 'Cà phê Chồn' (or, even regular) coffee!

I paid only $2.50 (which included shipping), online, for mine! 'Snobs' do not like the price; but they do like <u>one</u> of the 'coffees' recipes! Later in this book, I will talk about it; the, previously mentioned, '<u>Vietnamese</u>, <u>Egg</u> <u>Coffee</u>.' Be sure to give it a try!

Walkure Karlsbad®, Porcelain, Pour-Over Brewer

For 'Snob' value, there are fancy, 'Pour-Over' devices on the market; such as the German-made, Walkure Karlsbad, Porcelain, Pour-Over Brewer... at least, it would appear to be expensive! Whereas, a $10.00 Cone is not going to 'impress' many people while going from person to person during dinner party... for under $140.00 (for one of Walkure more expensive styles), the Walkure can undoubtedly make up the difference; and 'dress up' a dinner table! Walkure Karlsbads largest model, however at this writing, will serve up to 48 ounces (about the same as a standard size, 'Drip' machine) so, it is fine for a dinner party or family group. The device is very 'forgiving;' as directions call for up to <u>40 grams</u> of 'coarsely' ground coffee.

The manufacturer makes the following claims, "*It is quite an art to enjoy the 'absolute' aroma of coffee;*" and, "*This method of brewing, without any paper or metal filters, allows ones' coffee to develop its pure aroma, and keep its delicate oils... by being the 'gentlest way' of preparing coffee.*" They 'guarantee,' "*An unadulterated taste!*" Exactly, '<u>how</u>' they guarantee that... I do not know! The coffee does have more of a 'unique' taste about it than with other brewing methods!

Nevertheless, the device needs a 'coarse' grind; and as previously mentioned, does not use filters – although, some could be adapted for use! Its 'coffee basket' has a 'crisscross' pattern/grid of drainage holes! Walkure has a few styles and accessories available. It is worth a 'lookup' on the internet!

What is nice, is the 'pouring device (carafe) is very attractive; and will fit in, nicely, on an 'elegant' dining table!

[167]

Breville Precision Brewer®

"For the ultimate in 'Pour-Over' coffee, we can now 'mechanize' it – and serve a more significant number of people, than with the previously mentioned brewers;" or, so says the manufacturer of the Breville Precision Brewer!

Reminiscent of a 'Technivorm,' the 'Breville 'Precision Brewer' seems simple enough being mechanized; being that it is still something of a 'Pour-Over' brewer! However, this device is designed for much more precise, 'Mechanized' brewing! The machine looks like something of a cross between a 'Drip' Brewer and a 'Pour-Over' Cone. Coffee may be brewed by the cup, multiple cups, or by the pot, in a few unusual ways. For 8 or fewer cups, the manufacturer recommends one *"Use a 'Cone' shaped, ground holder; with a paper filter"* (and, that would mean <u>any</u> brand of cone); but for brewing '8 or more' cups, they recommend *"Using a 'flat bottomed,' 'Mesh' filter – '<u>still</u>,' along with a 'Paper' filter!"* Presumably, the 'paper filter' is to address the 'evil' oils! However, as previously mentioned, its primary brewing method entails placing its own (or another brand 'Coffee Cone' of some sort) on top of a 'brewing adapter.' The water dispersing 'nozzle (called a 'Showerhead') regulates 'how much' water enters the Brewing Cone – as well as having a 'precise,' dispersing pattern, for 'even' wetting of the grounds! Surprisingly, the machine may, additionally, adjust its water temperature and flow by itself.

Whereas I have seen many 'Coffee Snobs' swearing by various 'Pour-Over' methods, most would agree that the 'Breville' is the *"Ultimate"* in 'Pour-Over' Brewers! So, for we, so-called, *"Non-Snobs,"* we get to combine both 'favorite types' of cones (except 'Clever' types) with a 'favorite,' mechanical brewer – and, in many cases, have up to 12 cups of coffee, instead of the normal 'one or two' which Cones, usually, brew!!

Wood Chorreador

The 'Wood Chorreador' brewer, is one of the oldest ways to brew coffee – it is considered, basic 'Pour-Over' coffee – but, without a cone! People have been brewing this way for hundreds of years; and, many people, still, use it today; more for 'show' than anything else! It seems to be a cross between, 'Pour-Over, Immersion' (sometimes), and 'Sieve' brewing.

In the past, coffee drinkers would take a small bag or net, fill it with coffee, and hold it over a cup while pouring hot water into the bag. Of course, the water would, slowly, drain into the cup. It was not long, before some 'bright' person, invented a 'hanger' in which to 'hang' the bag (or dangle it) over or in a cup. Next, came a small net of some kind – which is still used by some people today.

Here is an image, to the left, of the 'Coffee Net' that I own. It works very much like using a 'Sieve' with a handkerchief in it (as we used to do back in the 1960s while camping); and the 'Net' looks something like a miniature 'Butterfly or Fish Net.' 'Medium-ground' coffee is placed inside the net, and hot water – of any temperature – is poured into it; filling a cup or mug!

Today, many Chorreadors, using a net, look something like a 'Lantern Mantel' hanging on a banana stand (which is exactly what I did in the photograph on the last page). A Wood or Metal 'Chorreador' is nothing more than a 'bag' or 'net' of coffee grounds that hot water is poured through.

The Chorreador is something a 'do-it-yourselfer' might even enjoy making… I know I would; but ordinary, everyday items (such as a banana stand) can be 'pressed into service' as well!

Just remember, a 'bag or net' will not stop any coffee oils – so, a 'paper filter' would have to be placed between the cup and the bag; and this, probably, will affect the way one's coffee tastes, and be considered 'safer' by some scientists. However, one more thing to remember (especially, when a 'study' states that they test on "*Lab Rats*") with few exceptions, a person is <u>not</u> a rat; and most people, likely, will not be consuming the 'quantities and strengths' of coffee (in proportion to size and weight) that the 'Lab Rats' do!

Moreover, even if the oils '<u>were</u> <u>to</u> <u>be</u>' bad for human consumption (which California has recently announced "*They are not,*") a 'little bit,' once in a while, will **<u>PROBABLY</u>** be okay! I have to say 'probably,' as everyone is different; and will react to substances 'differently!'

Chorreador prices run, 'online,' from just a few dollars for a small 'Net,' to $70.00 or more for a wood or metal 'stand;' in which to hang the 'Bag' or 'Net.' However, <u>anything</u> to 'hang' the 'Bag' can be used; in fact, I had an Asian friend who used a small, 'Bonsai Tree' as a stand for his 'Bag Chorreador!' The tree was small enough to be easily transported to functions.

[169]

To prepare and serve, he would 'tie' his 'Coffee Bag' to a branch on his beautiful, little, 'leaning' tree, place a 'Fine-China' cup under it, and pour hot water from his 'Gooseneck' kettle into the small opening of the bag. People would always gather to watch him brew a cup of coffee! His coffee was not any better than any other method; but it put on a 'good show' and looked elegant on a table with his 'fine china!'

Of course, like other methods, the 'Coffee Snobs,' whom enjoy this method, claim, "*It only makes the <u>best</u> cup of coffee in the world; and, is the only way one can achieve aroma, boldness, full-body, and smooth taste, together!*" Generally, 'Coffee Snobs' hate the 'homemade' versions (but loved the 'Bonsai tree')… moreover, I have even heard negative comments about $59.95 'professional' versions; but I have never heard anything 'negative' about the fancy, $150.00 or more, handmade, Chorreadors… created by true artisans!

 I am afraid that I must question, "*Why*" bother with a Chorreador at all; other, than the purpose of '<u>putting on a good show</u>?' Yes, I have, previously mentioned, I have used 'versions' of Chorreadors out on boats, or while camping, back in the 1960's; when no other coffee brewers were available. Today, however, if one wants 'bagged' coffee, it can be purchased 'handy packs' (like Tea Bags). They can be dropped into a 'Cone' or 'Carafe;' or placed directly into a cup or mug! Again, however, if wanting to 'hold back' some of the 'fines/mud/oils' (which would seep through the bag into the cup), why not just use a standard, 'Pour-Over' Brewer?

<u>Hario</u> (Wood Neck) <u>Drip</u> <u>Pot</u>® or <u>Nel</u> <u>Drip</u>

Another model of 'Hario' brewer, this method is still a style of Chorreador… alternatively, perhaps, a 'Pour-Over, Chemex, Handkerchief,' or 'Sieve.' In fact, it is similar to <u>many</u> different types of brewing methods – with the manufacturer taking the best of several, brewing features and putting them together into a single brewer!

'Drip Pots' are available in two sizes and used by many 'specialty' Baristas… moreover, the 'Wood Neck' model makes it look like a 'Chemex' brewer! In fact, the most expensive cup of coffee in the world (at this writing – which costs somewhere around $950.00 per cup at 'The Münch,' in the southeast side of Osaka in Japan), is brewed by this method; but, with a similar brand brewer – 'Nel Drip.' Years of 'storage' aside (for The Münch), coffee brewed with this method, comes out tasting reminiscent of Cold Brew.

Brewing at home with the 'Wood Neck, Drip Pot,' is similar to many other brewers for most people; however, for 'The Münch…' going from green beans to roasting, to brewing, to storage in Oak barrels, to the cup, takes upwards of 22 years… moreover, the coffee is very black, thick, and pours very much like syrup!

However, brewing with the Hario 'Drip Pot' (or Nel Drip) can be very simple, or unbelievably complicated; with scales, 'stirring sticks,' mounds of 'coffee with indentations,' 170°F water, 'boiled' cloth bags/filters, Gooseneck Kettles, water, and more. Filters are reusable and replaceable; and brewing can use several different grinds! However, brewing times, in my opinion, still work best with water, heated to just 'one degree' below boiling; and poured over a 'Medium Grind/Dark Roasted/Chocolate Coffee.' However, the brewer is perfect for 'fruity' roasts as well!

Frankly, if one is looking for an 'old style' form of brewing, this method is, probably, one of the world's oldest!

Some experts say something to the effect of, *"Coffee can be thick and incredibly sweet – like a 'Mulled Wine.' However, it can be incredibly fragile, too; should the water be 'too hot' or the coffee 'brewed' too quickly – plus, the coffee will lack 'complexity.' Only expert Baristas should attempt to brew this way!"* Now, what 'Coffee Snob' could resist a recommendation like that?

Cost? Between $30.00 and $50.00; depending upon style and size. Of the few people I know who brew this way, none are considered 'Coffee Snobs…' just, 'experts!' It is not called or considered *"Very technical"* by 'Snobs' (mostly, because few know about it); but to others, there is 'ultra' control in brewing this way (and, I have yet to hear anyone who has tried 'The Münch' coffee in Japan, complain about it… other than 'price')!

Turkish 'Cezve' Coffee

Sometimes, 'true snobs' take their coffee to the extreme; by buying expensive, Brass Cezves (a.k.a. Ibrik, Briki, Turka) Pots, to brew their coffee in… moreover, some people, even 'boil' (almost/sometimes) coffee in those pots, in 'heated sand' pits or bowls. Technically, brewing in a 'Cezve' is along the line of making an Espresso –

as 'Extra-Fine,' ground beans are used. In fact, in many cases, the grounds go one step beyond (to 'Extra, Extra-Fine'); as many commercial and home grinders have a 'Turkish' setting for grinding beans.

Cezves are, generally, found in 8, 10, and 14-ounce versions – technically speaking, 'any sized' pot made of any material can be used. Ideally, 'Pots' should have an extended handle on them; for safe handling over a fire; or, while moving, or pouring.

Again, true connoisseurs, claim *"Turkish Coffee* (again, as with every other brewing method), *is the ultimate in coffees;"* which is something of a surprise, as many people have considered it something of a 'boiled' coffee (which is a *"No, no"* among 'Coffee Snobs')!

'Ultra-fine' grounds are put into the Cezve, and it is placed over low heat – or, maybe high heat – depending, upon the Barista! Some may call the temperature 'boiling' (and it may be… due to altitude); but, the water, supposedly, is not allowed to 'quite boil!' Generally, only 1/3 of the number of coffee grinds are required, as opposed to other brewing methods; as 'almost boiling' will extract more flavor, caffeine, and color. Sugar, cinnamon, and cardamom are often added during the heating process as well; and some drinkers claim that this mixture can even *"Help with digestion!"* In theory, the grounds are supposed to 'sink to the bottom' of the Cezve; and then the coffee can be poured into a cup – leaving a clean, brew. I have not always found this to be the case, however; and have ended up with a cup full of grounds!

It seems, only 'true aficionados' even know what 'Turkish Coffee' is (at least, in the coffee groups I have been associated with) – but once they learn… they love it; especially, when the 'Coffee Snobs' find the 'Cezves' can be purchased in ornate Copper, Brass, or Ceramic! Prices start around $40.00 and go up from there; to even, the hundreds of dollars!

Frankly, I am surprised that 'Coffee Snobs' might like 'Turkish Coffee' so well; as it is so much like boiled, 'Cowboy or 'Percolator' coffee! However, lately, in some 'specialized' Coffee Bars, some Baristas attempt to 'put on a show' (as what one would find in other countries), when it comes to brewing Turkish Coffee. Expensive 'Sand Pits' are made in some coffee bars; covering a fire underneath, and the Barista works to keep the Cezve from 'boiling' over the heat. I have seen it done, and it is something of a 'good show' to watch. It is good coffee too – providing, one enjoys a strong, 'Espresso-like,' seasoned coffee!

More 'Hot Water' options for 'Cones' and other brewing methods:

All 'Pour-Overs' require hot water to use – which is the chief complaint by many 'Coffee Snobs,' when comparing 'Pour-Overs' to 'K-Pod' brewers! They, also, require a 'heat source' of some sort; like a stovetop, electric tea kettle, or microwave oven to heat water; not to mention, keep the brewed coffee warm! 'Keeping the coffee warm,' aside, not surprising, there are many methods to 'heat' water – and, some seem more effective than others!

For myself, I use <u>several</u> ways to heat my water; and one favorite is a portable, 'Instant Hot Water Dispenser…' that I can use with many brewers – as shown here! This 'Hot Water Dispenser' makes 'Pour-Over' coffee almost as fast as my 'Electric Bonavita Gooseneck Kettle' or 'Keurig;' providing, the water is 'heated' and ready!

At home, I use an 'upright' model – which dispenses up to 5-gallons of both 'Hot and Coldwater;' and, I keep it at a temperature suitable for brewing. For 'portability,' however, I use this one, above. It dispenses 'Hot' water one degree 'under 'boiling;' plus, it works like a 'Thermos,' in the fact that it will keep water hot for an extended period, even 'unplugged!' It has, both, an electric 'Dispensing Button' and a 'Hand Pump' (like an 'Airpot)! It, also, has a convenient 'handle;' for transporting the dispenser from one location to another! I do not like the fact that it does not have an 'on/off' button, but it does keep water 'hot' for an extended period – again, just like an 'Airpot!' Moreover, if I am going to have access to electricity, I can merely 'plug it in' once again to 'bring the water back up' to temperature!

The price is certainly reasonable on these; as they can, easily, be bought in stores or online. What is nice about this type of 'Hot Water Dispensers' is, when coupled with a 'Pour-Over' cone of any kind, one can take it to parties or outside on picnics; and the water will continue to stay warm enough for brewing for an extended period, without electricity. Remember, I prefer to use water one degree <u>under</u> boiling; whereas many other people prefer to use water which is 205°F. In this 'insulated' device, water will take quite a while to drop in temperature (unplugged) to 205°F; so, water of an 'adequate brewing temperature' will be available for hours without electricity!

'K-Pod' brewers can be used to make 'Hot Water' in a short period, like the above Dispenser; just as a standard 'Drip' Coffee Maker – just leave out the grounds in either case! Unfortunately, they are not as 'practical;' as most 'Cones' cannot be placed under them for easy filling – at least, with my 'Drip' maker! Also, as they are not insulated, water is not going to stay warm for a extended period – unless, the 'Drip' device is left 'plugged in' and turned on to 'keep warm!' Plus, neither device will create a substantial amount of hot water; again, however, the 'Drip' device will, at least, create 10-12 cups, where as the best a K-Pod Brewer can do at one time, is only 1-2 cups, before needing to 'cycle' the machine once again.

When I am 'teaching' or 'experimenting,' however, I find that either a 'Tea kettle' or a 'Gooseneck' kettle works best; as they are easier to handle. I prefer the 'Gooseneck' kettle over most methods; as pouring small amounts of water is easier for 'pre-wetting' grounds, 'pre-warming cups,' or 'pouring' water in a circular or 'zig-zag' fashion!

Again, despite what some 'Coffee Snobs' might insist, there is no 'right or wrong ways' to heat water – or pour it over coffee grounds! Methods are, totally, at the discretion of the person doing the brewing – and whereas, I might find I prefer one method, and a 'Coffee Snob' another… the end result is always the same; a, hopefully, delicious cup of coffee!

More Brewing Methods – which can be used at home; but more often, used while camping:

"Our culture runs on coffee and gasoline, the first often tasting like the second."

~ (Attributed to) Edward Abbey

Percolators

'Percolators,' almost, went into 'general' Brewing Methods; as it is still prevalent here in the United States! However, it would seem that more Americans than ever, are looking to use a Percolator while camping. This is surprising, as so many other 'modern' brewing methods are available! Worldwide, however, it is quite another matter. Yes, some people may use Percolators while camping; but still more use  Percolators on an 'every day' basis – and, I am seeing more and more people in my 'online' coffee groups, who say they "*Love to use them*;" as Percolators (a 'step up' from a 'Cowboy Coffee Pot') are available in all assorted sizes, materials, styles, brands, and kinds!

My family did not purchase their first 'Percolator' until the middle of the last century! However, (for a little history) Percolators, incidentally, were invented (technically) in the year 1810 or 1814; but were not patented until 1865 by James Nason! However, it was not until 1889, that a version, like what we still use today, was invented and patented by Hanson Goodrich!

I was born in the early 1950s, and I grew up seeing and smelling my Mothers coffee being brewed on the 'gas stove' in a Percolator every morning. There was no such thing as 'fresh ground beans' for her to purchase; as coffee (by the 1950's), generally, only came from a can, for the average consumer, and, there were not many choices of that! Of course, there were some places where 'beans' could be purchased, by my family no longer knew where! So, they and other people bought what was advertised in the newspaper, heard about in commercials on the radio or television, or by 'grocery store' display!

Two of the first radio and television commercials I can remember, as a child, were for 'Maxwell House Coffee' (with Maxwell House claiming it was "*Good to the last drop...*" and having a distinctive 'jingle)!' By 1960, the commercial 'jingle' became so popular, that Trumpeter, Al Hirt, recorded a hit, 'Top 40' version (vinyl record) of the Maxwell House Coffee, 'Percolator' commercial – of which, I was fortunate enough to hear him play while vising his famous 'jazz club' in New Orleans. I am sure his recording increased coffee sales; and Maxwell House used this 'jingle' for decades... they still do, occasionally – and, anyone my age or older would surely recognize it if heard!

It was not too long before my mother bought an Electric Percolator – keeping up with the times. It worked much the same as the stovetop version; as water in the Percolator was brought to a boil – but over its own heating element – rather than a stovetop. The 'boiling water' traveled up a hollow stem and out; hitting the top of the Percolator's lid or 'knob,' and falling back on top of the basket which held the grounds. The lid 'knob' (which was always clear) could be watched for both 'action' and 'coffee color.' After bouncing off the 'knob,' then upon falling back down (via, gravity) on top of the basket plate, the water, then, 'seeped' into the ground chamber; passing through the coffee grounds, and then going back into the pot. The 'darker' water/coffee… with added flavor, aroma, and color, then traveled back up the stem again! Each trip 'up the stem, and down through the brewing basket, making the coffee richer and darker! The result being, what one 'Coffee Snob' told me, was *"Both 'boiled' water and 'boiled' coffee (not to mention 'scalded/burnt' beans… meaning, certain death";* however, many people love 'Percolator Coffee!'

'Percolators' have not changed much; today, just as with when I was a child, the longer the water 'boils' in the Percolator, the more flavor, oils, color, and caffeine is extracted. To reiterate what many experts have stated, *"This method is one of the easiest ways to 'burn' or 'scald' coffee"* (leaving the door 'open' to numerous and perilous issues). Moreover, many 'Coffee Snobs' feel *"Percolator Coffee is not worthy of drinking…"* as both the water and coffee have been 'Boiled;' and thus, have become 'inferior' in some way! Also, to make matters worse, 'Electric Percolators' will keep coffee warm for hours – yet, another reason for 'Snobs' to leave it alone! My mother's 'Percolator' would sit and 'simmer' all day – except when needing to brew more – and neither she nor my father ever complained or 'worried' about the coffee! So frankly, I would doubt anyone who brews with a 'Percolator,' would complain about 'taste or quality,' now!

Most 'Coffee Snobs,' in my groups, would not 'lower themselves' to drink such a brew… that is, unless it proves, somehow, to be a 'Specialty' coffee, brewed by a known Barista. However, I must admit, that there is a particular 'charm and taste' to old fashioned, 'Percolator' Coffee… and, I consider it a 'Specialty' coffee in itself – drinking it often! Moreover, surprisingly, when serving it 'unbeknownst' to 'Coffee Snobs,' they have appeared to enjoy it… that is, until they discover 'how' the coffee was made!

I recently bought a replacement 'Pot' for my old, clear, Pyrex® Percolator; as I enjoy the 'boiled' taste and enjoy seeing both the action and the color of the brew changing! Plus, I often use it for things like 'Egg Coffees!'

Percolators can still be bought in most stores – but these days, few Americans, other than those camping, tend to brew with them; and, with the onset of portable, 'K-Pod' brewers, even <u>that</u> is dimming… except, for those wishing to 'rough it!'

'Campfire' Brewing (Cowboy Coffee)

Another form of 'roughing it' (and method of brewing, which, surprisingly, does <u>not</u> have to be done over a campfire), is 'Campfire Coffee;' which, is appreciated by few people younger than the author's age. However, I 'grew up' with it; and have learned to enjoy its unique taste! In fact, on an upcoming page, I have a photograph of some I made on my home, stovetop – using my 'Pyrex' Percolator – but, without its 'guts!'

Usually, coffee is 'boiled' in an enameled pot – whether over a campfire, camp stove, BBQ, or kitchen stove – the 'Pot' not having any 'internal' parts! Even just a standard pot or kettle could do the same thing! However, 'Boiled, Cowboy Coffee' is, today, considered *"The worst way,* (or *"The 'worst of the worst' coffees"*) to brew coffee, by 'Coffee Snobs – with 'Percolator Coffee,' coming in a close second! What is the 'absolute truth'? Well, think about it; sometime between the 10th the 18th centuries, coffee was exclusively 'boiled in pots, and the liquid drunk!' To reiterate, after 800 to 900 years of this method (before Percolators), 'how bad' could 'boiled' coffee be? I often tell my students, *"Surely, people would have stopped drinking 'boiled' coffee by now, if it is 'so bad'!"*

Campfire Coffee has the same kind of 'charm and flavor' that regular 'Percolator' coffee has – but still has 'free-floating' grounds… plus, may have 'floating egg or eggshells' in it too! I grew up camping most summers in Canada, the Yukon, and in the wilds of Alaska (with an occasional summer in Mexico). We did not have 'Drip Coffee Makers' back then – and, did not own a 'Camping Percolator'; so, coffee started off being brewed over a campfire, in a simple, enameled 'Coffee Pot!' The aroma of 'Cowboy Coffee,' today, still brings back memories for me; some 60 years later!

While only 'Canned Coffee' was, usually, only available for my Mom at the local grocery store near home, for my Dad up in Canada, it was a different matter! Canned Coffee did not seem to be available too often in some of the

'Native' Trading Posts we would find out in the wilderness; but, the Trading Posts, did, usually, have a barrel (or large, burlap bags) <u>filled</u> full of 'Green' Coffee Beans. If we visited the Trading Post at the right time of year, we might have found a smaller barrel next to the 'Raw Beans;' filled with 5-pound, burlap sacks of Roasted! The Trading Post proprietors would, usually, roast beans once or twice per year – and sell, mostly, to trappers, foresters, loggers, or the local 'Native Canadian' Reservations! When we would pass by, my Dad always stopped to pick up any 'last-minute' rations we might need. This, usually, came in the form of 'Jerky and Powdered Milk;' however, some fresh meat, if available, would be purchased too… along with matches, used newspaper, and 'freshly' <u>Roasted</u> <u>Coffee</u> <u>Beans</u>!

When he was 'brewing outside,' Dad's 'first-morning chore' would be to build a campfire – and over it, would place a wire, cooking rack. He filled his 'Enameled Coffee Pot' with lake or river water and added few 'purifying tablets' to it; before placing it over the campfire. While the water was heating, he would search his camper for a small, 'Mortar and Pestle' (grinding bowl) he had purchased in Mexico, during one of his fishing trips. He would then, he me 'grind' a, large, handful of beans into what would look like a 'medium/coarse' grind. When the water started to boil, he would open the Pots 'Metal Lid' and pour in the grounds. The mixture would 'sit and boil' for several minutes (depending upon what else Dad was doing to prepare breakfast). Then, the Pot would be moved to a part of the grill which did not have any direct heat under it; or placed directly in the campfire's warm coals to 'keep it hot.' As the coffee, often, spilled or 'boiled' out onto the fire, the camp air would smell of Pine Trees, Quaking Asp, and 'burnt/boiled' coffee; I can still remember the smell today!

Sometimes, when finished boiling, Dad would open the top lid of the Pot to pour a little cold water over the grounds – causing most to sink to the bottom (and to help dilute the 'overly-boiled,' strong coffee). More often, he would take a clean handkerchief or a paper towel (they were much thicker in those days) and place it over one of the Stainless Steel or 'Enameled' mugs we used; to <u>filter</u> <u>out</u> the grounds. However, when camping with one, Norwegian uncle, Dad would allow him to 'pour a beaten, raw egg' into the coffee (along with its crushed shell), to remove any perceived bitterness. The 'scrambled egg' would cook, and the mixture would adhere to the grounds;

so, they would sink, or be easily removed by pouring through a strainer or handkerchief. However, Dad, 'still' pouring a bit of cold water into the Pot, caused even the eggs to sink to the bottom of the Pot! It made for a very 'smooth' cup of coffee.

I recently made some 'Stovetop/Cowboy/Egg Coffee' for myself and family, in the photographs below, with my Pyrex Percolator, without its

ground basket; only, I used my stovetop at home, and a 'Pour-Over Filter' to catch the 'left-over' grounds and egg. I did try pouring in a touch of cold water first, but it did not work near as well as I had hoped – even, after coffee grounds were added 'after' the eggs!

The coffee in the Pot looked revolting, with an egg floating on the top of coffee; and, it did not look much better after I poured a little 'cold' water in to make the egg mixture sink to the bottom! I then, placed a filter over my cup. I did not 'have to' pour it through a filter; but when I did… it insured that I had a 'clean' cup of coffee! It tasted great! I, also, poured cups for my unsuspecting family; without telling them how I brewed it. They loved it; claiming, "*The coffee was clean, bold and pure*;" and were greatly impressed when they were informed 'how' it was made!

As 'Pour-Over' Cones did not seem to exist back in the late 1950's or 1960's, when 'hard-pressed' for filtering, Dad would use 'left-over,' metal, window screen (from making shelves for our Smoke House); stretched over a wire, coat hanger. When that was not available, he used the aforementioned 'handkerchief' or some other article of clothing… such as one of my mother's nylon stockings (but, I do not remember him doing that more than once, after Mom found out). What he, more often, used was a 'Kitchen Sieve' of some sort, in which to filter!

I did the same thing, after making another Pot of 'Egg Coffee;' rather than using a 'Pour-Over' Cone and Filter. The reason there is so much 'volume of egg and grounds,' shown in the photograph, is because the Coffee Pot I used was quite large; and, I had poured out the remaining coffee into the cup shown. Again, the result was a 'clean' cup of coffee – but, still with its 'oils.'

'Cowboy Coffee Pots' are still available in some stores (like Walmart) but any pot or 'Percolator' (without its ground basket) can be used. Cost? The cheapest 'Campfire Pot' I found in thrift stores, was $.30 cents (however, I did find a rusty one, like my fathers, in a Consignment shop; and it was 'on sale' for $160.00... the store calling it "*An antique!*" In other stores, (again, like Walmart, online stores, or a 'Sporting Goods' stores), a new 'Enameled Pot' can be purchased new, for less than $20.00 – and, it can 'double' as a Percolator as well!

If someone is, genuinely, a 'Coffee Aficionado,' I would recommend that they try 'Campfire Coffee' at least once! I have yet to find anyone trying it (with or without an egg) who did not enjoy it – even when it might have had a few grounds in it! Alternatively, as one 'student' told me, "*Campfire coffee helps to make camping special!*" I would have to agree!

I cannot close this heading, without adding a few 'alternate ways' to make coffee without a 'mechanical, coffee maker,' while camping. My family has tried all of the methods, on the following pages, from time to time; that is, when we had a 'heat source' with us in our tent, camper, or boat (hikers' stove), and had a 'commercial' can of coffee, or some freshly ground beans from a Trading Post, with us.

Invariably, I will be asked by someone in a 'tasting class,' "*Is there an easier way to make 'Campfire Coffee?*'" The answer would have to be, "*There must be countless ways;*' but the easiest way for me, is to:

1. Fill a 1.0 liter, 'Automatic, Variable Temperature, Bonavita Gooseneck Kettle' with 'Pure Water;' and set its temperature for what is desired. In my case, I enjoy 212°F (or higher) – 'boiling.'

2. Add the appropriate amount of dry, freshly ground coffee (Coarse Grind) to the kettle. No pre-wetting (Blooming) is needed.

3. Allow the water/coffee to 'boil' for as long as you wish; by removing the top of the kettle and viewing the darkness of the coffee. One may wish to 'pour out' a tablespoon or so, to view/judge in a 'more lighted' area.

4. When completed brewing, turn off brewer, and add an ounce, or two, of cold water to the kettle. Hopefully, the grounds will settle to the bottom of the kettle. **Optional**: 'Reset' the kettle to a 'keep warm' setting – for drinking over an hour or two!

5. Pour and serve!

Here are a few more, so-called, 'modern camping/glamping' ways in which to brew coffee without an actual, commercial brewer:

"Good communication is just as stimulating as black coffee, and just as hard to sleep after."

~ (Attributed to) Anne Morrow Lindbergh

Handkerchief

As mentioned before, just as my Dad would 'filter' the grounds from his 'Campfire Coffee,' he would sometimes make a version of 'Pour-Over' coffee; just by taking one of our short, 'enameled' cups, fill it with lake water (considered 'wilderness safe' to drink back in the 1950s), and place it over our little Sterno® powered, hiking stove. Dad would still 'boil' the water to purify it, however. He, then, would 'drape' a clean  handkerchief over the top of another cup; and having me hold it (he would, later, change to clothespins or rubber bands after I had spilled a few cups from being scalded), place the equivalent of two tablespoons of ground coffee in it. Using another handkerchief, he would lift, the now 'boiling,' cup of water and pour it over the grounds in the other cup.

The water 'washed over' the grounds; and it would work like a 'Pour-Over' Cone – slowly, seeping into the cup! I have done it by myself in the photograph above; by using, boiling water, from a measuring cup… however, heated in my microwave oven!

Of course, it does not have to be a handkerchief that one uses; it can be a sock, a scarf, the sleeve of a shirt, a T-shirt, cotton balls… anything; which will allow water to flow through it; while holding back <u>most</u> of the coffee grounds.

What was the opinion by my 'Coffee Snob' friends when I showed them the previous photograph: a resounding "*No way*!" However, I would expect a "*Yes*," by those needing or wanting a cup of coffee… I liked it; especially, when I added my coffee creamer to it!

<u>Metal</u> <u>or</u> <u>Plastic</u> <u>Sieve,</u> <u>Homemade</u> <u>Pour-Over</u> <u>Coffee</u>

Much like the last method, another form of 'Pour-Over' is to use a metal or plastic Sieve (of any size) to hold ones' grounds; and, merely pour 'hot water' over them while holding the 'Sieve' over a cup!

Of course, if one wants a longer 'brew time,' a handkerchief or paper towel could be added to slow down the 'water flow' through the Sieve; or, to brew multiple cups. Just use a larger Sieve – as I showed with the 'Egg' Coffee, to brew a larger amount of coffee. A 'larger Sieve,' over a pot, was often used in our 'early' camping days – as smaller sieves were not available!

Perhaps, if this method were used over a piece of 'fine china,' it would be accepted more by 'Coffee Snobs;' but, I always found it to be a 'natural' for 'Tin Cup' coffee, while camping. Of course, one does not have to hold the 'Sieve' above the cup, if the cup is big enough. The Sieve can just sit on top of the cup (dangling in), as in this photograph! This method is still considered 'Pour-Over;' but in actuality, it is a form of 'Steeping' (which I will discuss in later paragraphs).

My family often did this while fishing; while we were 'too busy' reeling in a fish, to finish brewing. The brewing starts like a 'Pour-Over;' but ends up, becoming more like a 'Steeped or Immersion Brew' – as the grounds, eventually, end up soaking in the coffee! If making a single cup like this, it is best to use the same size or smaller diameter Sieve, with the cup. Surprisingly, there can be quite a difference in taste between this and the previous method!

For more than one cup of coffee, however, a 'whole pot' of coffee could be made the same way; again, by using an 'extra-large' Sieve over a large Pot, Carafe, or Pitcher of some sort.

Naturally, this would not be a popular method with 'Coffee Snobs,' either! However, let us take a closer look at it!

'Steeped' Coffee

As previously mentioned, 'Steeping' (designed for tea), can work just as well for coffee! My father often 'steeped' while traveling or fishing… moreover, in various ways! One of my Dads favorite ways, involved filling a 'Steeping Ball' with coffee grounds; while heating some water directly in his cup over a can of Sterno, then dropping the ball in. While driving (should his Thermos bottle be empty)

he would put his metal cup in the dashboard cup holder, drop in a 'Steeping ball' filled with coffee, add water, then drop in his 'Cigarette Lighter, Immersion Heater!" The coffee would heat and brew while he drove his RV!

When we were in his boat, however, and after a few minutes of 'boiling water' over his 'Sterno' stove, Dad's coffee was finished; and he did not even need to filter it – and, it gave him plenty of time to continue his fishing!

'Steeping' does not have to be done with a metal 'ball;' <u>anything</u> can be used to hold the coffee grounds. For myself, I prefer to use small, cloth bags; that I used to use for prospecting – something, along the line of what some other person might use to 'cook with' spices. One of my brothers-in-law liked to use one for his chewing tobacco; rather than the 'foil pouch,' it came in! Small cloth bags are very versatile!

The Ball shown here, is 3 inches in diameter; and less than half-filled with grounds, to brew a large cup of 'strong' coffee. When fully filled, it can 'steep' a ten or twelve cup pot! Just reduce the amount of coffee for smaller vessels or cups. This is an efficient, cheap, yet uncomplicated way, to 'Cold Brew' coffee as well. Just take a pitcher full of water and drop in the 'Steeping Ball' – filled with a 'coarse grind' coffee; then, refrigerate.

When I have done so, however, I have found a lot of 'fines' in the coffee – even though I used a 'coarse' grind! I would still recommend pouring the 'cold coffee' through a filter, of some sort, to catch 'fines' and oils.

This photograph shows an alternative way to 'Steep' coffee; by finding a way to 'hang' a cloth bag in a cup of hot water; where it can sit and 'steep' for several minutes. Of course, 'fines' (or mud) is rarer!

The 'Coffee Snob' response from my former, coffee group? A resounding, "*No...*" except, from some of 'Cold Brew' lovers; who… 'loved it (there is always somebody)!' Of course, there are 'unique holders' (which are expensive) for 'steeping' by the cup or by the pot; and for many 'Snobs,' cost is what coffee is all about!

There is one more way to 'Steep' coffee (actually, I am sure there are countless ways to do it). This method is just one of the ways 'my family' has used – a 'Steeping/Infusing Spoon!'

Similar to a 'Loose Leaf, Tea Infuser' spoon, this device, after being filled with ground coffee, 'sits' in a cup of hot water; where the water slowly extracts flavor and color. It can be used in a home or recreational vehicle 'Microwave Oven' as well!

Collapsible Pour-Over Brewer

There is not any reason to go into any detail on this; as it works exactly like any other, primary, 'Pour-Over' brewer – except, it has <u>five</u>, huge (in my opinion), drainage holes in it. It is made of soft 'Bakers  Silicon;' so, it 'collapses' to fit into a backpack, pocket, purse, or suitcase! However, it still needs a very difficult to find, #1 Filter to work correctly! Luckily, I have an 'all in one' Cooker/Brewer; which has a removable, 'nylon' filter basket. I can take the 'filter basket' out of the brewer and put it into the Collapsible Cone. It stands a bit taller than the Cone, but a #2 paper filter would stand taller – although, it could still be 'pressed' into service!

In the past, when I have been backpacking or camping without too much in the way of equipment, I have always taken with me a 'Collapsible Brewer' – and, even collapsible cups. Often, they have come in quite handy; even, if no filter could be found to use in it. Usually, however, I would take cotton balls out of our 'First Aid Kit,' use a 'paper towel,' or use a spare, 'handkerchief' as a filter!

However, 'collapsible' brewers do not always just come in 'Silicon Cone' form. Sometimes, they look like the one in this photograph – a 'Primula Coffee Brew, Buddy.' There is nothing to 'fold up,' except the 'netting;' which holds the coffee grounds.

Technically, it is a 'Camping' brewer... even though it can be used at home, as this photograph shows. It is perfect for a single person – and can even be used as a 'steeping/immersion' filter! The device is not a 'French Press,' as there is no

plunger; but it <u>does</u> make excellent 'Immersion' Coffee – at least, partially…
as the 'netting/grounds holder/filter' can, possibly, 'sit' in the coffee for at
least 'half' the brewing time. For this reason, some people enjoy using the
device at home – with a tall mug – as shown on the previous page. If stopping
'halfway,' in the brewing, one has 'Pour-Over' coffee.

Surprisingly, some people like to suspend the device over a cup or mug;
claiming, *"It works more like a Wood Chorreador!"* Alternatively, at least, it
would be… if it had anything 'wooden' about it!

So, the best description of it would be that of a 'Pour-Over' brewer;
which has a 'net' for a 'ground filter.' Coffee can be made in *"As little
as 30 seconds,"* according to Primula. The average time, for most people,
is about 3 minutes, I have found.

Microwave Brewers

Back in the 1950s and 1960s, 'Microwave Brewing'
was not possible; as the Microwave Oven had not
been commercially released yet. Nevertheless, we can,
routinely, use this method today at home or while
camping; as most 'RV's' have microwave ovens in
them.

'Microwave Percolators' – made from safe, BPA-free, polypropylene –
are available in several brands and styles. I had family who used to have one
in their Motorhome; after 'Microwave Ovens' first came out. Its main
problem then, was the same as it is currently; it only brews 'one or two cups'
at a time.

There is very little which can go wrong with 'Microwave Brewers;' as most
have a 'built-in,' Mesh Filter. No 'paper filters' are required to brew. 'Too
full,' however, they may still 'boil over;' as my families did, some 30 years ago.
Coffee can be made multiple ways with similar 'home devices' – such as
microwave safe, measuring cups or bowls. Technically, I would suppose this
method could be called a form of 'Cowboy Coffee!'

Again, I asked a few 'Coffee Snobs' for their opinion; and they have told
me, *"Oh, God no! They all must make burnt coffee!"* The 'average' coffee drinker's
opinion was somewhat different; *"Well, in a pinch – as long as someone else is doing
it – especially, while camping!"* Of course, the old myth 'pops up' again: *"Boiled*

water or coffee will kill you!" What coffee drinker has never 'reheated' a cup of coffee in the Microwave oven… moreover, had it ever become hot enough to boil – and drank it anyway? Statistically, I think one would find a 'Coffee Snob' would be more likely to drink 'Instant Coffee;' rather than, take the time to brew in a microwave oven. So even then, why not just brew it in a standard brewer – like a French Press or Drip? It is almost as fast; and certainly better!

There is still one more way to make 'Microwave' Coffee; and that is to use a plastic (microwave safe) spoon/container filled with 'medium-fine' ground coffee (as I showed a few paragraphs back).

It is placed into a cup of water, then both placed into a microwave oven; and the oven switched on. When the water starts to boil, the coffee 'steeps' into the water.

Instant Coffee

Is there anything else for brewing besides a microwave oven for, so-called, 'quick' brewing? Probably, 'Instant Coffee' is the leading way – either in or out of a microwave oven! 'Instant Coffee' is so varied; I cannot even go into it here; other than to say, it can be produced 'cheaply;' and, it is available in 'powdered, flake, and crystal' forms. This bottle shown; is the brand I use for cooking! Few 'Snobs' will find it drinkable; although, I do know some 'everyday'  people who seem to love it! For me, I will not drink it – but I <u>will</u> cook and 'season' with it! Well, as I always say (and <u>George Washington</u> proved), "*Where there is a will, there is always a way;*" and people seem to accept 'Instant Coffee' for varies reasons. 'George,' by the way, (not Juan Valdez) invented one of the first versions of 'marketable,' Instant Coffee (George Constant Louis Washington – a Belgium/American inventor and businessman, that is); 'way back' around 1910! In actuality, true 'Instant Coffee' was first patented, and used, by the British government, around 1771!

'Instant,' still holds quite a 'vital' place in the travel industry – and was very big back in the 1960s; both at home and in 'Vending Machine Servers.' In fact, for camping or travel, it is <u>still</u> popular; except, with 'Coffee Snobs,' that is! Whereas, I do not drink or enjoy it (as fast/fresh brewing is so easy –

and Keurig has simplified brewing so much with 'Pods'). I do, however, use 'Instant Coffee' for cooking purposes – and, for making 'Coffee Additives;' such as homemade, Kahlúa, or Tia Maria (coffee liqueur).

Getting, back to brewing, 'brewing invention' can be done by anyone – if someone has forgotten to bring their brewing equipment with them while traveling. In my family, we have, always, just 'built our own' brewers when 'spur of the moment' camping – as I have, previously, mentioned, with some of my father's methods! 'Obscure methods' are not as difficult as they sound. 'Pour-Over,' of one sort or another, can always be performed somehow!

I was recently asked about, *"Making an Emergency Brewer,"* by one of my coffee students. I explained a 'Pour-Over' method, which I had used weeks before; after being 'evacuated' from my home because of a Wildfire! As it happened, many of my coffee students wound up at the same, local evacuation center during the first hours of the fire; and through sharing coffee supplies, and watching me 'make' a brewer, many used this same method to brew coffee.

Unfortunately, the Red Cross had not arrived yet at the shelter to supply food and drink for we 'early arriving' survivors. As it happened, I had some #2 Coffee Filters in my car; along with some 'freshly ground' beans, purchased in a grocery store, earlier, that morning! Luckily, large bottles of 'Pure Water' for the survivors had arrived from some source; and had been stacked up on wooden pallets for people to help themselves to. I took one 'bottle' poured it into the clean and empty, 'Travel Mugs' with us. Someone else, then, took the water, and poured it into a metal cups they had, and placed it on top of their, small, 'hiking' burner.

I took my pocketknife and 'cut off' the top of the bottle; down, several inches, as shown below, in the 'recreated' photographs. The top of the 'water bottle' had, now, turned into a 'Cone/Funnel' with a cap on it; and, resembled a 'Hario' brewer, with its 'twisted; cone! After inverting the cone and placing it on top of one of my mugs, I took one of the #4 filters I had with me and

put it into the 'makeshift' funnel/cone. A #6 would have worked better, but this was an 'emergency' situation! I, then, added the equivalent (my best guess) of two tablespoons of 'coffee grounds' into the filter; then, added an approximate ounce of newly, heated water.

After allowing the grounds to 'Bloom' for 30 or so seconds, I removed the bottle cap from the cone; and any 'left-over' water flow into the mug. Replacing the cap, I poured in the remaining hot water – filling the 'filter;' and allowed the coffee to 'steep' for three minutes; before, once again, removing the bottle cap and allowing the coffee to 'pour through' the grounds, into the waiting mug below. What I had done, was, effectively, make a 'Pour-Over' Cone, Immersion Brewer. I repeated the process for each person in attendance; until the Red Cross arrived with their 'coffee machines!'

Our coffee tasted great; especially, under the circumstances! It was not long before I had a line of people (not entirely my students) waiting to use my 'Cone' brewer; or making their own.

As it happened, I had filters (although, the wrong size) with me; but anything might have been used to filter the coffee – such as cotton balls, a handkerchief, cheesecloth, paper, a sock, or paper towel!

Special Note: I visited one of the major, 'Coffee Roasters' in our state capitol recently, and we went over this process – showing them the photograph above (but in color), on my Cell Phone. They gave me, what I consider, a great compliment – by calling my brewing method: "*MacGyver Coffee*;" named, after the television character, 'MacGyver;' whom, seemed, to be able to make 'valuable, life-saving tools,' out of, virtually, anything! Moreover, in this 'time of emergency,' for myself, family, and students, my 'MacGyver Coffee' was more than welcome and enjoyed!

An empty one or two-liter bottle of 'Soda Pop (or any other liquid)' can make just as good a 'Pour-Over' Cone as the 'water bottle' did; or anything else, for that matter, which can work as a funnel… including an actual 'Funnel!' A regular 'paper or metal' (or, even 'Mini') filter may be used – and I keep a filter in my emergency, 'Go' bag – along with, a 'vacuum sealed,' bag of Coffee Beans, and a small, hand grinder!

Still More, Brewing Methods for Travel, Home, or Emergency:

12 Volt Auto Drip Brewers

Again for 'Camping or Glamping,' of course, it is a simple enough matter to make coffee with any of the earlier methods I mentioned – providing one can find some 'hot' water. However, some people 'must-have' their 'Morning Drip!' Luckily, the internet, most sporting goods stores, and Truck Stops, carry '12-volt, Drip Coffee Makers;' and, they can be found in many unique styles – some of which, only brew by the single cup! There are even 'handheld' models which brew  Espresso – in Pod, form! I happen to own the one shown above; and have used it for over 20 years, while traveling! However, most 12-volt Brewers are similar in 'style and size' to what many motels and hotels might have – small, 'two to four cups, Drip Brewers' (but, even these are starting to be replaced by, single serving, 'Keurig' type brewers)!

Truckers used to love these models; as they would plug into a cigarette lighter; and work just like the 'electric' Drip Brewer, they owned at home. Now, however, most 'long-haul' trucks (or even camp trailers or motorhomes) have gas-powered, generators; or large, 'Power Inverters' – which convert 12-volts into 110-volts (not to be confused with a 'converter;' which converts 110 volts, down to 12 volts) – so almost any appliance can be used. This one, in the photograph, is the 2000-watt model I own – along, with a large, 'Marine, Deep Cycle' battery. Since its purchase, I seldom use my little, '12-volt brewer,' anymore!

However, I own several 'Inverters,' of assorted sizes (from 150-watts to 3000-watts), for use in my cars, RV, and even in my house for 'emergency' power outages. In fact, in our area, our 'utility provider' (Pacific Gas and Electric) just announced (due to the 2018 Camp Fire) that they will be *"Cutting off power to many people in, extra-dry, 'danger' zones – for up to five days!"* My 'Inverter' should come in very handy to run some electrical lights, small coolers, and my small, 'chest' freezer for a short period! Moreover, should my 'Marine Battery' run out of power, I can run and electrical cord from my car's battery; and start and run the car, periodically, to keep the batter charged!

Surprisingly, there are other, older, devices which some people still use. I have a 'Long Haul Trucker' friend, for example, whom still makes his 'Instant Coffee, Packet Soups,' and a few other liquids, with what my dad used to use back in the 1940s, 1950s, and 1960s; a 12-volt, Immersion Coil.

I loved the device as a kid (and, probably still would, if I owned one); as I was able to make myself 'Potato Soup' or 'Hot Chocolate' from 'instant packets,' while my Dad drove!

My friend told me just this morning, that he *"Does not know how long"* he has owned his! *"Some 45 years,"* he estimated! He fills a cup with water, adds 'Instant Coffee,' or something else, to it, 'plugs in' his 'Immersion Coil' to his trucks 'Cigarette Lighter,' and starts driving. After a brief time, he has a cup of 'hot' coffee, soup, or some other liquid! He likes to use 'Instant Coffee;' but he could, just as quickly, make fresh, 'Immersion' coffee with his Immersion Coil; if he were to drop in something like a 'steeping' ball or 'coffee bag' into his mug!

The only reason 'Coffee Snobs' might like 12-volt devices, is if they love to 'Glamp' (camping, but still with luxury items); then, any 12-Volt, cigarette lighter in a car, truck, or emergency power device will work. In fact, I use both 'multiple outlet' 12-volt cords(for multiple appliances); and a 'Smart Power,' Marine Battery Box – with a 'Deep Cycle' Battery… which has <u>both</u> USB and 12-volt outlets. This way, many appliances – such as Espresso Machines – can be used in the woods while 'Glamping' – providing, one has enough 'Wattage' available!

Frankly, since it is so easy to make 'hot water' with 12-volt devices or power inverters these days, I would, still, prefer to use a 'French Press' or a 'Clever Dripper' when I travel; and forget about the 'fancy' 12-volt brewers – except, for making 'hot' water, that is!

Camp <u>Stove</u>, <u>Drip</u> <u>Coffee</u> <u>Makers</u>

As earlier mentioned, some people say they *"Simply <u>must</u> have their 'Morning Drip' to get 'started' each day."* However, many people, also, say they: *"Hate change;"* and, *"Need, what they are 'used to' at home"*… and that, usually, is a 'Drip,' Coffee Maker. As many of these same people consider themselves, 'Outdoorsy' people, they are not about to use a 12-Volt coffee maker – as they say, "*It does not taste the same*" as their 'Home Drip!' In actuality, it is 'exactly' the same as their 'Home Drip;' as 'electricity is electricity!' Let's face it, how would anyone 'know' the 'coffee water' was being heated with '12-volts' rather than '110-volts?' Not to mention, 'Drip Coffee Makers,' are 'Drip Coffee Makers...' regardless of the 'power' operating them!

Surprisingly, however, some 'Snobs' will put a 'Percolator' or something else on their camp stove – with the rationalization, that the device is for 'Glamping/Camping!' Luckily, however, Coleman, also, makes a 'Drip Coffee Maker' which fits directly over a burner of a camp stove or a campfire – as seen in the last photograph on the previous page! Again, it is just like any other 'Drip' device, electric or not; but I must admit, it is 'impressive' to see what looks like a regular, 'Drip' coffee maker sitting over a flame!

'First,' observations by those witnessing the use of this brewer, would be that "*Someone is melting their coffee maker over a fire!*" At least, that is what people thought of mine, while camping! For fun, I would, also, cook Waffles over an open fire, BBQ, or camp stove, with a specialized 'Waffle Iron...' designed for such use! Unfortunately, both items were lost in the November 2018, town of Paradise, 'Camp Fire' fire as well! Perhaps, one day I will replace them new ones!

As with these type of 'home' devices, coffee grounds are placed in a standard 'brew basket' along with a mesh or paper filter; and 10 cups of water go into the bottom reservoir! When the water begins to 'boil' (something a 'Coffee Snob' will not like), it is pumped up to the ground basket; where the coffee 'brews' like a regular, 'Drip' machine. It then, 'drips down' into a carafe for serving. One nice feature with this type of brewer is, if one cannot wait to brew a whole pot – as with a Percolator or some other devices – there is a 'Pause and Serve' feature built-in – for pouring out 'a quick cup;' just like on many 'home' Drip brewers.

After performing a quick 'internet search,' one can find several assorted brands and models like the 'Coleman' – to use with various heat sources; to help 'bring the indoors,' outdoors! If one loves both 'coffee and camping,' the following types of brewing, on the next pages, can be fun (even, when used at home):

AeroPress™ (a.k.a. EuroPress™)

The 'AeroPress' is just as easy to take camping as it is to use at home, but a bit 'too involved' for some people; due to all its 'pieces parts!'

Sometimes known, a 'EuroPress,' this device makes a great cup of coffee – and several different ways as well, by using varied 'grinds' of beans! This is why it would be so versatile while camping; one could brew with whatever coffee they happened to bring along with them!

Some 'Coffee Snobs' feel that the AeroPress is more of a 'hands-on' type of brewing method; and it gives them 'a lot' of control during brewing with so many different options! To reiterate what I just said, many of the 'Coffee Snob' users I know, claim: "*AeroPress, is the 'only way' to brew at home or in the woods; as it uses any grind of coffee beans or temperature of water!* " The 'Snobs' are correct; and it does brew a delicious cup... moreover, I "*Used the hell*" out of mine... until I found, what I felt were, 'more effective' ways of brewing! However, I found with mine – 'stained' and 'cracked' from use and age – filters were, sometimes, difficult to find! However, with the internet, now, that has all changed!

Looking like it came out of an Elementary School Science Fair, the 'AeroPress' uses air pressure to 'speed up' the brewing of both hot and cold coffees – and, one would think that the "*Higher one's altitude, the better the coffee might be!*" Although I have never seen such a study, I can certainly believe this! Also, some claim that the 'AeroPress,' "*Helps to cut any bitterness from the coffee,*" as well; but my experience is, bitterness depends more upon the 'grind' of the coffee – and luckily, 'multiple grinds' can be used in the 'AeroPress!'

Still, others believe and claim, "*This device brews coffee similar in taste to that of a 'Pour-Over' device;*" while more still say, "*It is closer to that of a 'French Press...' in, both, brewing action and flavor!*" My own opinion, is that it does taste more like coffee brewed in a 'French Press!'

In any event, where 'any grind' of coffee grounds may be used in the device (according to taste), brewing times and water temperature is going to be different for each 'type' of brewing; however, generally, 'medium-grind' grounds are, most often, used with 200°F water. However, overall, 'hot water' is poured into the device, so the grounds 'steep' for three or more minutes.

[193]

The top half of the device is, then, 'pressed down' (regardless of the grind); moreover, the coffee is 'forced' through a filter – similar, to a French Press – directly into the consumers 'waiting' cup or mug! The only actual difference, being, any 'left-over' coffee grounds, do not just 'sit' in the coffee!

Prices hover in the $30.00 to $40.00 range (it just looks like it might be more expensive, for those wishing to impress; however, some 'Snobs,' think and have said to me, as it is all plastic, "*It looks Cheap*!" However, there are many accessories one can buy, including bags to carry everything in, that can help to 'drive up' the cost!

Most true 'Snobs,' like the 'AeroPress;' as it makes 'Immersion' coffee! I have one; but, never use it anymore! It is too involved for my taste, and I do not have the patience first thing in the morning to 'work and wait' for my coffee – and, as more and more consumers are purchasing K-Pod brewers, this type of brewing is falling by the wayside!

Upcoming Methods

After all of the previously mentioned brewing methods, one would think I have mentioned <u>all</u> the ways to brew coffee available! In actuality, I have 'neglected' to comment on many more methods, than I have mentioned! What is more, there are <u>new</u> methods of brewing being invented every day! Even if someone is not looking for a 'Coffee Brewer,' they may get one with other purchases; such as with a 'Bottled Water Dispenser' I recently purchased. It dispenses, not only 'chilled' and 'hot' water but has a 'built-in' Keurig coffee brewer as well; taking water directly out of a three or five-gallon 'pure water' jug as needed!

Other forms of 'Drip' coffee makers (and upcoming methods) are too numerous even to list! Moreover, when it comes to 'Cones,' well, I do not have the time or space to list them all! Not surprisingly, there is very little difference between 'Cones;' besides, 'shape, ribs, or drainage holes.' However, one new promising way is a 'Pour-Over' method called 'Lindkind.' Currently, an 'Indiegogo' project; as of this writing, one can still go to the 'Indiegogo' web pages and contribute to the development of the Lindkind – and, achieve a substantial discount upon its distribution! It is, truly, a very interesting device; not to mention, appears to be a great brewer!

The 'Lindkind' is a unique form of 'Pour-Over.' First, it is not a Cone – but, it 'brews' like one! Secondly, it has a 'DC' powered, motorized Showerhead/Water Chamber! This allows the 'Grounds' to 'pre-wet or brew' in a most effective method – something, along the same line as a 'Sowden SoftBrew' or a 'Primula/Seneca, Pour-Over Coffee Dripper®!' The 'brewing chamber' is metal; and filled with, what I would guess to be, 'thousands' of drainage holes! Its Automatic, 360° 'water chamber,' revolves while allowing <u>all</u> the grounds to evenly wet; then, the water, slowly, extracts the color and flavor from the coffee – draining directly into the waiting (preferably pre-warmed), cup or mug.

The manufacturer claims, "*According to the SCAA (Specialty Coffee Association of America), achieving the 'Golden Cup Standard' requires the perfect 'coffee-to-water' ratio, accurate water temperature, the precise time for the coffee-to-water contact, as well as 'special water pouring' methods.*" It would appear to me that this device does all that and more! I know I plan on purchasing one, when available; not just for the fact that it is going to brew a <u>great</u> cup of coffee; but due to it using 'Triple-A' batteries, being so easy to clean, it it is going to be <u>perfect</u> for when I Travel!

I should think that 'Coffee Snobs' will love this method of brewing; I know I am, undoubtedly, looking forward to it!

Next Question:

Question: "*My extra-large, 'Cafetière à piston' brews 12 cups. How do I keep brewed coffee 'hot' long enough to drink it all? I ruined my last press by placing it on the stove, and the Press before it, 'sparked' in my Microwave Oven!*"

Answer: "*Cafetière à piston…*" well, the name you used, tells me something in itself! Most people in America call this type of brewer, a "*French Press;*" but, you <u>are</u> correct in the use of the name! The answer is simple enough, with multiple solutions; either, 'drink fast,' or invite eleven other people over to enjoy the 'twelve cups' of coffee while hot! However, as the 'Press' <u>is</u> <u>not</u> 'microwave safe,' one can '<u>reheat</u>' the coffee, in a "<u>microwave</u>-<u>safe</u> bowl, in the microwave oven – of course, no 'Coffee Snob or Expert' would ever agree to do that!

However, the simplest solution is; brew a smaller amount! Just because ones' brewer will <u>make</u> 12 cups, does not mean that one "*<u>Must</u> <u>brew</u> <u>12</u> <u>cups</u>*" at a time! Just adjust the amount of 'hot water and grounds' you wish to use!

Remember to 'pre-heat' the 'Press' before using; as it will help to keep the coffee warm longer – and help with the brewing too! Just do not place it on a stove; as it is not designed to go over a burner any more than it is designed to go directly into a Microwave Oven!

Smaller presses are cheap; and a 2-cup version can cost as little as $20 or less! Unless having guests, or hosting a 'Coffee Tasting' party, I use a smaller 'French Press' myself. Presses are available in 1 – 12 cups sizes; and are not very expensive. I even own a 'Bodum Travel Press (as seen here);' which holds only 12 ounces... and it doubles as a 'Travel Mug!' My 'Travel Press' is '<u>more</u>' than well used; as it is almost 'worn out' – the top seal is beginning to leak!

Four heaping teaspoons of 'medium/coarse' grounds (or to the consumers' preference) are placed in it; and an ounce of 205°F water is added to allow 'Bloom.' After 30 seconds, I fill the rest of the device. The coffee 'sits' for three minutes – as with a regular French Press. The top is 'screwed on,' and the plunger is depressed – pushing the grounds down to the bottom; extracting all the flavor and aroma! The coffee is, then, ready to drink; right out of the press or poured into a cup – however, if one wishes to add cream, sugar, or something else, it is a bit awkward to do so through the 'drinking' spout... but it <u>can</u> be done! Perhaps, the best time to do this is before the Plunger/Top is placed on, or after the coffee is 'poured' into a 'pre-heated' cup or mug! The problem of doing this, however, is it will 'lower' the temperature of the brewing water – unless, any 'additive' is 'heated' before adding it to the 'Press.' In any event, it is a very handy device!

I taught 'Alternative High School' for 'teen offenders' for several years, before going into 'Alternative Health Care;' and daily, used this device so I could have coffee during class. Unfortunately, due to the nature of the students (mostly gang members), an actual 'heating device' with 'coffee pot' or 'coffee machine' was forbidden! However, as I had an instant, hot/pure, water dispenser in my classroom, brewing in my 'Travel Press' (which I kept in my desk), was quick and easy! Moreover, I could easily 'pre-heat' the Press before class just by 'rinsing it out' with hot water in the sink; then use 'fresh roasted/ground coffee,' I brought each week from home!

Getting back to the question, of 'larger servings,' one might consider buying an 'Insulated Carafe' in which to pour the hot coffee. Being 'insulated,' the carafe will 'hold heat' for a more extended period – especially, if it too, has been 'pre-heated!' In fact, 'pouring into the insulated carafe,' is my, personal, choice. Most carafes will hold two, medium-sized 'Presses' full of coffee – minus, the first poured cup, that is! This way, I have hours to enjoy my 'French Press' coffee! I do the same thing for, large, 'Coffee Tasting' parties; where 'French Press' coffee is being served; only, I use an even larger, 'pre-heated, Airpot' as a decanter! Oddly enough, many 'Coffee Shops' will 'pour out' any coffee which is over one hour old, replacing it with fresh; even if being stored/served in an Airpot. For myself, 'one-hour old' coffee does not seem 'old' to me!

Another thing one might do, when buying a new 'French Press,' is to purchase one which is 'Double Insulated or Double Walled!' This should help keep ones' coffee hot for a much longer period – again, especially, if it is 'pre-heated (inside and out) before brewing. Ones' budget is, often, the only limit to style, and size used! Let's look at some more 'French Press' information:

French Press (Cafetière à piston)

'French Press – American Press – Cafeteria – Press Pot – Coffee Plunger – French Plunger – Coffee Press – Piston Press – Plunger Pot…' whatever one calls them, 'Presses' are one of the 'tastiest' ways to 'Immersion' brew coffee! In fact, throughout this book, I keep comparing brewers and 'taste,' to 'French Presses;' as I find it 'tastes best' to many people… 'Coffee Snobs,' included! However, I do, personally, think there is one more way of brewing, which is better; and that is with a 'Clever Dripper' – of which I have mentioned earlier.

As previously stated, 'Presses' are available in many assorted styles, materials, sizes, and colors; and are a much easier/cleaner way to brew than other, popular, methods… such as an 'AeroPress.'

'French Presses' are containers in which a 'filtered' metal or nylon/plastic screen on a metal plunger, travels from the pot top to, almost, the bottom – 'pushing down' grounds after they have been allowed to 'steep' in the hot water. 'Forcing down' the plunger, also, 'forces out' the grounds flavor, color, oils, and essence; and is often compared to that of a 'pressure' device, like an Espresso machine!

Think of it this way; with an 'Espresso Machine,' water is 'forced' through the grounds under pressure. The water 'pulls' the flavor, color, and oils out of the grind. With a 'French Press,' however, the reverse is true; the beans/grind (after having time to soak in hot water and releasing their flavors) are 'forced' through the water by the Presses 'plunger' being depressed; and a filter, keeps most 'small particles' out of the coffee. It is a fact, that 'additional flavors' are 'brought out' of the grounds, via water pressure – in other words, again, the act of 'pushing down' the plunger!

With some 'French Presses,' however, rather than have a 'screen' to filter and 'push' the grounds down, they have an attached basket to put the grounds. The 'flavor' is still 'forced' out of the grounds, but the device is easier to clean later – as the grounds stay in the removable basket. I like this method; as it makes it easier to 'dispose' of the grounds. There is no 'digging out' compressed grounds from the bottom!

Some 'Presses' may even have a secondary holder; to hold a paper filter, as well. This additional filtering helps with 'added clarity' of the coffee, and to help filter out unwanted or unhealthy substances; like 'fines,' or oils! One other brand of 'Press,' even has a bottom which 'screws' on and off; allowing the grounds to be easily removed. I dislike having to 'dig out' compressed grounds out of my press; so, a 'removable' bottom is undoubtedly an attractive advantage!

So, as one can easily see, 'French Presses' have features to suit just about any tastes!

Any size grind of coffee may be used, according to taste and filter; however, 'Standard Presses' are <u>designed</u> for use with 'medium/coarse' grounds; to extract the most flavor – anything 'finer' may result in a 'cloudy' or 'muddy' brew. One tablespoon of grounds should be used per 4 ounces of water (or to taste); I use fewer grounds with my 'dark roast.' As said before, one should 'pre-warm' the Press with hot water before brewing. I use a bit of the same water I am brewing with, 'swish' it around, and pour it out before adding my grounds. Then, the 'Press' continues to stay warm when I 'Bloom' the grounds (allowing them to off-gas) for 30 seconds! Typically, the water used should be 195°F to 205°F; but I enjoy using 205°F - 210°F water for the taste I enjoy best, at my, particular, 'home' altitude.

After the 'Bloom,' and the 'Press' filled with hot water, the grounds 'steep' (Immersion) for three minutes or more minutes (according to taste) before the plunger is depressed; pushing the coffee grounds down to the bottom of the container. However, some like to think that before putting the lid/plunger on, and midway through the steeping, the grounds should be lightly 'stirred' to break up any 'crust' forming – I do this myself, with my larger Press. The longer the coffee steeps, the darker and 'bolder' it becomes; as well as the most caffeine, presumably, 'drawn out!'

The major drawback to the 'French Press' (as mentioned previously, and, if not using a Press with a ground basket), is 'cleaning out' the press after the coffee has been poured. Sadly, the grounds do not come out easily into a garbage can; and they should not be washed down the sink or garbage disposal; especially, mine; as I have a Septic Tank!

What I do, is to add a little water to the Press, 'swirl it around,' or use a 'long-handled' spoon, Bamboo stirring stick – or 'photographic' chemical stirring stick, in my case – to 'break up' the grounds if compacted too tightly; then pour them on my yard plants or into our small vineyard!

The earthworms seem to love coffee grounds; my tomato plants do too!

On the 'Snobby Coffee' scale, 'French Press' brewers rank very highly; as one can control a lot of the brewing aspects (if they know the tricks)! Plus, although 'Presses' like 'Mr. Coffee' (or some 'off-brand'), can be very inexpensive, other brands (depending upon their features) can be quite costly! Again, the brewers all work, basically, the same (except for 'Reverse Presses' – like the 'AeroPress'); and in some cases, one is, mostly, 'paying' for 'how pretty' the Press can appear on a table!

Frankly, other than removing the used grounds, the 'French Press,' is one of the best tasting, and easiest, ways to brew coffee; as well as one of the best ways to 'test' different roasts and brands of beans! I have, usually, found that 'Roasters' (if they don't use a 'Clever Dripper') will use a 'French Press' to test their different coffees and roasts!

Types of Presses are countless; and some, even can go into the Microwave Oven! However, they are not much different from the 'Individual Cup' Presses; which are available. This one, in the photograph, is what I own. I like the idea of it; but it, often, is more trouble than it is worth! I would suppose that this model could, probably, go into a Microwave Oven as well as being placed into a cup of hot

[199]

water. However, for some reason, it does not make as 'good a cup' of coffee, as one would expect! As with other devices, one needs to 'standardize' on the Press – which I have not done. I'm sure I could get a 'good cup' if I just 'experimented' with different grinds, water temperatures, and steeping times!

Alpha Dominche®, ('Steampunk' Craft Brewing)

Frankly, I would not expect to find this method at home or camping/glamping!

An ultimate form of 'French Press,' although, some 'Coffee Snobs' and Baristas alike would say *"This method is not similar at all,"* is the 'Alpha Dominche;' and it certainly looks like something a 'Mad Scientist' would use! Surprisingly, it is 'all the rage' on the East coast! It is only now, at this writing, starting to take hold on the West coast; especially, with 'Tea or Craft Beer Bars!'

This unique form of 'French Press' (but, I use that term very loosely) brewing is said to be the *"Absolute, ultimate in coffee brewing!"* Of course, in reality, the 'Alpha Dominche' is not a 'French Press' at all! However, it does use a 'plunger' (along with pressure) to 'press down' the coffee grounds!

Often called a 'Steampunk brewer,' 'Alpha Dominche' devices are designed for 'state of the art' coffee or teas; and come in a broad range of styles! I have seen some photographs of 'banks' of 'Steampunk Brewers;' each, staffed by an expert Barista, to extract the coffee – and, these people, put on quite a show! I would recommend, if ever finding a Coffee Bar using one, give it a try; even, as expensive, as it will, no doubt, be! One student told me that they found one being used in Las Vegas, Nevada; and coffee was being sold for $23.00 per cup!

Brewing is a lot more complicated than what I am going to state here; but these are the 'basic' facts: the 'Alpha Dominche,' is a fancy, commercial, 'Full Immersion' brewer; and, it looks and works like a cross between 'Syphon, Forced Pressure, and French Press' devices. All aspects of brewing are adjustable – time, temperature, volume, steam, grounds, and more. The brewers operate something like this: the device 'heats' its own water – having four different brewing temperatures, (or, according to the bean roasters, consumers, Baristas, or consumers personal taste). Before any brewing can begin, however, the device 'Crucible' (water/brew holder) must, first, be 'pre-warmed' with pure water. This process is performed, by running a 'cycle' of hot water through it without actual brewing!

The grounds are put in the 'top' of the brewing chamber; then 'tampered down.' 'Hot' water, in the bottom of the device, is 'forced upwards' with steam; to help 'pull' (extract), the flavor and essences from the grounds (again, strong, medium, weak, et cetera, are extracted according to the Barista's or customers preferences). However, a small amount of hot water can be introduced to the grounds for a 'pre-infusion' (Bloom), if desired.

Steam is added, during brewing, to help 'break up' the coffee crust (like 'stirring' other devices), and 'encourage' it to fall to the bottom of the chamber; while 'extracting' <u>most</u> of the flavors at the same time. A valve, automatically, opens when the desired 'steeping' time has been met – again, everything depends upon 'someone's personal preferences. When the steam is forced out – which causes a 'natural vacuum' – the brew is 'pulled down' through a filter and placed into a holding tank; looking, very much, like a 'French Press' or ''Syphon Brewer' working.

The finished brew, 'gravity fills' a waiting cup; and this allows for a 'unique tasting' cup of coffee – full-bodied and <u>very</u> clean! Filters may be chosen according to the preference of the drinker – as far as 'pore size' for the coffee to extract through – again, for 'body and cleanliness.' Oils and 'grit' can be either totally removed, left in, or, only <u>partially</u> left in – again, according to the preference of the Barista or drinker! In other words, the 'finished' coffee beverage can be <u>manipulated</u> to suit 'whomever!'

Assorted brewing methods do not begin to have as many options to choose from as this device! However, I do tend to remember the old saying, *"The more one overtakes the plumbing, the easier it is to 'stop up' the drain;"* and this method has 'tons' of options – many of which, can create a great cup of coffee… at least, when compared to a 'standard' brewing method! I can only imagine the 'problems' all these options may create, or the 'mechanical' breakdowns the equipment may experience with time!

Still, I have yet to hear of any 'negative aspects' of the device; other than two issues… the device price – some $15,000 - $40,000, or the '<u>$18.00</u> <u>per cup</u> <u>served</u> (or more)'… as charged in some Coffee Bars!

Still, I would be willing to try it… once!

More methods:

<u>Moka</u> <u>Pots</u> a.k.a. <u>Machine</u> <u>À</u> <u>Espresso</u>

Not to be confused with 'Mocha Coffee' (which is a beverage), 'Moka' (or what is considered 'Italian or Cuban' style coffee,) comes from a 'Moka Pot' – which is a type of Aluminum, Espresso Brewer… of sorts! Of course, many people think this method is just another way in which to make coffee confusing. 'Moka Pots' and available in brewer sizes of 1 to 12 cups! I own several 'Pots' of assorted sizes, styles, and colors.

Frankly, when it comes to 'Espresso,' I believe I enjoy 'Moka Espresso' better, than what is prepared in my, actual, 'Espresso Machine.' Moreover, if asked to 'taste the difference' between the two different beverages, when 'mixed' in beverages, I would very much doubt I could tell much difference without seeing it brewed. However, let me 'qualify' that last statement; <u>both</u> the 'Moka Pot' and the 'Espresso Machine' must be 'standardized' on when it comes to all aspects of the coffee! If not, then, it is easy to taste and see the difference! I like to think, 'Moka Pots' are all about 'convenience!'

To me, 'Moka' tastes like a 'high grade' Espresso – only, generally, not quite as 'bitter.' In fact, I have been to some (so-called) 'parties,' in which both an 'expensive' Espresso Machine and a Moka Pot were in attendance; and assorted 'Coffee Drinks' served. From what I could observe, the so-called 'Coffee Snobs' could not taste any difference between actual Espresso, and the Moka Pots 'Espresso-like' brew, either – but then, both devices had been 'standardized' upon, by someone who 'knew' what they were doing!

Frankly, it is much easier to use the 'Moka Pot' than my 'Espresso Machine' – and, certainly faster and more convenient. The Espresso Machine must be cleaned, have its' 'ground cup/portafilter' filled with 'ultra-fine' grounds, stirred, tampered down (sometimes, with expensive accessories), and installed on the machine. Plus, 'all aspects' of the machine must be 'pre-warmed' for at least 20 minutes before brewing! In addition, I have, often felt (and have said before), that if I 'pulled my left earlobe three times' (and the Espresso came out good, with acceptable 'creama,' then I had damn well better 'pull' my left earlobe the <u>next</u> <u>time</u> I make Espresso; or I won't find the same appearing and tasting brew! I love my Espresso machine; but I find it difficult to achieve the same results twice!

The 'Moka Pot' (which is, usually, made from aluminum to help 'hold in' heat), can use 'ultra-fine to medium-grind' grounds; which are put into the 'middle' of what looks like a 'Percolator' type container (most 'Moka Pots' have their own, removable, 'funnel-like' ground chamber; located between the top and bottom sections). However, they do not need to be 'tampered down' as with a standard, 'Espresso Machine.' None the less, I do tend to 'smooth' the grounds over and depress slightly with my 'filling spoon' or thumb! The holder is placed into the lower chamber; which has been filled with pure water. Once inserted, and the top ring/edge wiped off to remove any 'stray' grounds which would interfere with screwing on the upper pot, both 'pots' are 'screwed together.'

There is a 'stem,' of sorts, for the 'Espresso' to pass through when brewing… like a 'Percolator' – except, it is not on a 'hollow rod' which sits in the brewer; it is 'built into' the top/serving part of the 'Moka Pot' (as can be seen in this photograph to the right). However, unlike a 'Percolator,' the brewed coffee does not 'fall back' into the lower 'Pot…' where it would continue to boil; it is, merely, 'held' within the upper 'Pot!' Once

put over an electric or gas burner, the water 'boils' ("*Bad Word*" according to some 'Snobs'), and is forced 'up' through the grounds through pressure; which, incidentally, travels up the 'stem,' and fills the 'pouring chamber' of the Moka Pot – as the photograph, above indicates. When the 'Upper Pot' is filled with coffee, all the water will have been used from the bottom chamber – so, there is no danger of 'over-filling' the upper 'Pot.' The device is removed from the heat source and is ready for serving.

Unfortunately, most 'Moka Pots' are manufactured from cast aluminum – at least, the bottom part; which is not, necessarily, the 'healthiest' to brew in (again, California – and a few other states – feel aluminum is carcinogenic). Nor, are there any 'paper filters' to catch any oils – so, if 'filtering' is desired, the coffee must be 'poured through' a filter separately.

'Moka Pot' prices will fit almost every budget; running from $10.00 to hundreds of dollars – depending upon size, and style… such as enameled, anodized, part glass, part ceramic, et cetera. Best of all, when finished using, the 'Moka Pot' is easy to clean! I just cleaned mine after brewing this morning, and found it took less than a minute. Simply 'unscrew' the top pot, remove the 'gasket' (if needed), remove the 'brewing basket,' and rinse/wash all parts! I always give mine a 'quick dip' in Colloidal Silver too –to kill any pathogens which may be lingering on the pot or parts.

'Coffee Snobs' – at least, the ones I know – consider this method, *"Poor-man's Espresso;"* and (as previously mentioned), *"<u>Boiled</u>!"* Those enjoying it, however, prefer this method; as one can make a 'more substantial' amount of Espresso at a time (depending upon the size of the Moka Pot); both faster and without, an 'expensive machine' and clean-up!

Whereas, I have already mentioned that 'Moka Pots' are inexpensive, for a bit more 'elegance' than a simple, aluminum one, plan on spending up to $200.00 or more for a fancy, display type. The photograph to the right is about as 'fancy' as I get (the 'poor, old thing…' but it still works)! It is an excellent example of a 'Combination Pot;' aluminum on the bottom, as well as the ground basket; while having a stylish, 'Ceramic Top Pot' for multiple cups of 'Moka.'  I think I recall paying about $60 for it, several years ago, as a 'discontinued' model!

For 'serving,' one has the options of either 'pouring/serving' directly out of the pot with the 'bottom' still connected, as shown above, (this is advised, as it won't leak), removing the bottom for a more attractive 'Pot' in which to serve, or 'pouring' the coffee into a serving carafe of some sort – which, frankly, in my opinion, 'defeats the purpose' of having an attractive, ceramic Moka Pot' to begin with!

At least the 'Coffee Snobs' I know, are willing to drink this form of Espresso (at least, when served attractively), and appreciate it; that is… as long as they see the grounds being 'compacted' before brewing (even though, 'compression' is not necessary). That is why, with some groups of people (and for show), I will make sure they see me (at least, slightly) 'tampering down' the grind with my regular Tamper; or, what appears to be expensive, 'Mini Tamper' – which I keep on my keyring! To some 'Snobs,' however, *"Just the right Tamper"* can, *"Make all the difference in the world, regarding taste"*… even, with a 'Moka Pot!'

I am often asked, *"Can I make Cappuccinos or Lattes with Moka Pot Espresso?"* My answer has to be… *"Why not; in fact, I prefer it!"* 'Moka Pots' are simply an 'alternative' to using an Espresso Machine; and, I really should not say 'alternative!' I prefer to view 'Moka Pots,' as just another <u>way</u> to make coffee!

Let us start looking at 'Tampers' and other paraphernalia!

"When my blood runs black as the moonless night, and my heartbeat sounds as the warriors' march… only then may you say, I've had enough coffee!"

~ (Attributed to) Unknown

EXTRA – TAMPERS, FORCED TAMPERS, LEVELERS, AND GROUND-DISTRIBUTION TOOLS

I could write a book just about 'Coffee Tampers' alone, as there are so many distinctive styles and types; wood, glass, plastic, stainless steel or other metals, combination and adjustable 'Tampers,' et cetera. However, they are, also, available in 'automatic impact' styles, 'power-hammer, palm, grooved, trimming, forced, shaped, rotating, miniature, multiple-size, keyring, chromed, multiple color, anodized, leveling, depth setting, pressure sensitive, center-weighted, lever bar, piston, hydraulic, electric styles…' the list is endless!

All these different styles of 'Tampers,' stem from some, so-called 'expert,' somewhere, saying: *"There is more to 'Espresso Grounds' than just the surface of the grind… it is what is 'below' the surface of the grounds that truly matters!"*

Frankly, I think 'pulling time, ground size, roasting, dosing, and water/equipment temperature' are far more crucial than the 'type or price' of Tamper one uses; or even, 'the amount of pressure' on the grounds!

Stepping back a bit, 'Espresso Machines' (or any device which uses pressure to help brew), generally need an 'accessory' to compress the grounds; as water will take longer to 'force' its way through, extracting flavor. Decades ago, all that was 'needed' was a 'thumb!' However, today, 'something more' is needed to, not only 'compress' the grounds to the correct 'packing,' but 'level' them as well!

'Moka Pots' do not need this, as I stated earlier; as 'time' and temperature (boiling) is more of a factor. However, some people, like myself, still 'compress' the grounds to a certain degree to obtain 'better' extraction. In other words, the 'Pot' is going to 'boil' until <u>all</u> the water has been forced through the grounds; regardless of 'how compacted' they are. If the grounds are just 'laying' in the 'basket,' the water can quickly and easily 'pass through' to the upper Pot – and extract only a minimum amount of color and flavor. However, if the grounds are slightly 'tampered,' it is going take the water longer to pass through; thus, extracting more flavor, aroma, and texture. The same is true when using an 'Espresso' machine! However, unless comparing two cups brewed 'with and without' ground compression, one is not going to taste much difference – especially, with the 'Moka Pot!' However, one might 'see' a bit more difference, as 'compressed' grounds, may create more 'Crema!' However, 'observances' could still register as 'false;' due to 'grind' coarseness and water/brewing temperature!

First, came the 'Thumb' to 'compress and level' the grounds on early 'Espresso' machines; then quickly, came actual 'Coffee Tampers' made from carved wood, then glass or metal, and then, later, plastic. Today, however, 'Tamper' styles can be as varied as there are brewing methods – and different brewing methods, may call for 'different' types of 'Tampers!'

Once considered a 'freebie' when purchasing coffee beans or machines, today, some 'Tampers' can cost, upwards, of $200.00 or more! They still can come in glass, wood, metal, plastic, nylon, or a combination of all; and some are indeed a 'piece of art' and craftsmanship! Some brands even come with 'alternative shaped or adjustable bases;' so they can be used with different machines. Even though, 'Tampers' are designed for just one, simple purpose – compressing grounds – their styles and functions come straight out of the imagination!

The only thing most 'Tampers' have in common is that the actual 'pressure plates' (the Tamper base) are, usually (but not always), the same size! The reason for this is to fit 'most' Espresso Machines. 'Portafilters/grind baskets' – which, are somewhat standard in size – with **58mm** being average for most professional machines; even my 'Moka Pots' ground baskets are 58mm. However, 'Portafilters' can start as small as 51mm; and, my Breville 'Espresso Machine' uses a 54mm one – so, needless to say, a generic 'Electric Tamper,' probably, would not work with it! The 'Puqpress' company, however, has an 'adjustable' model which will accommodate 54mm – 58.3mm Portafilters; which will take in a lot (but not all) of machines!

Looking something like a old style 'Soda Fountain' milkshake maker, the 'Puqpress' is available for purchase by anyone – in a range of $1000 to $4000 (Coffee Snobs should love it); however, the devices (in my opinion) are really designed for 'Coffee Shop' use; where 'standardization' is important! The device can 'compact,' the grounds exactly the same, every time it is used – regardless of 'multiple' users! Some models even have 'built-in' coffee grinders as well! Coffee shops should be very interested in these!

Frankly, any size flat surface will help to 'compact' the grounds; and, as previously stated, when the grounds are adequately compacted, water – powered by pressure, is <u>forced</u> through them at a slower rate. In other words, the more 'compressed' the coffee grounds, the slower the extraction... moreover, more flavor extracted as well! Just remember, 'overly compressed' grounds, however, will result in 'too slow' an extraction – and, possibly, a 'bitter' Espresso – whereas, 'too slow' an extraction results in a 'sour' brew. Incidentally, water which is 'too hot' can result in bitterness as well; whereas, 'too cold' water results in 'sour' Espresso.

Grounds do not have to be 'compacted;' as long as the person brewing enjoys the taste of the brew. But, a 'much better cup' of Espresso – with more Crema – will be created if they are! So, 'compacting/tampering,' is significant for 'ultra-fine' grinds; but, more importantly, is using 'time' to brew (or 'pull a shot'); say, 25–35 seconds (depending upon the machine), per 2 ounces of Espresso, to achieve the most significant extraction from the coffee grounds. However, the 'grind size' is, also, responsible for 'how long' it takes the water to be 'forced' through them. In other words, if the grounds are not compacted, or the grounds are too coarse, the machines 'pressurized water' will be 'shot straight through' the grinds (like a K-Pod brewer), extracting little; and resulting in a rather 'nasty,' under-extracted tasting brew.

However, if using an inexpensive 'Espresso' maker, without adjustable 'pull times,' one may be looking at buying a useful timer; in which to 'stretch' ones 'Pulls,' as well. One can experiment with grinds and compacting; to further 'fine-tune' just the right combination with the 'Tamper' and the machine! However, one must remember, that 'times' and 'grinds' are going to be different for every bag of coffee purchased – even if it is the same brand as the previous bag!

However, 'Professional Baristas' (and 'Professional Coffee Snobs') do not have many choices as far as the machine 'Base' is concerned – but, that <u>is</u> changing, slowly! Right now, it is the 'Base of the Portafilter' that many Baristas are concerned with – that is why 'multiple-sized and shaped Portafilters' can be bought for specific machines. When purchasing a new device, this should not be too much of a problem; but matching a 'Tamper' to an older machines base, could become one!

The professionals state: *"The best Tampers are ergonomically designed to have a handle which fits comfortably in the brewer's hand; but might not fit the base of the machine – but, will fit the diameter of the Portafilter."* Well, that <u>can be</u> somewhat confusing for the average consumer! That is why they, also, claim, *"The 'Base' of the*

Tamper should <u>match</u> the bottom of the 'Base' of the 'Espresso Basket' (where one places the grounds, not the base where the Portafilter goes) in shape." It gets, still more, confusing the farther we research this!

What the previous paragraph is saying, is whereas all the 'standard size' 'Tampers' may fit a 58mm basket, the bottom of the '<u>Inside Tamper Base</u>,' might have a 'curve' to it! It might have what is known as an 'American Curve;' or be 'Flat, C-Flat, C-Ripple, Rippled,' have a 'Euro Curve' – or, who knows, what else! 'Coffee Snobs' love this… as it, again, not only scores high in 'bragging rights,' but few people, other than Baristas, have a clue of 'what the hell they are talking about!' Again, the 'Base' (bottom or foot) of the 'Tampers,' according to the experts, "*Need to match the 'curve' of the basket*;" which makes me wonder, as the Espresso Machine was first patented in 1884, what did Baristas use for a 'Tamper' back then? Probably, it was the aforementioned, 'Thumb…' if anything! Plus, owning a 'Leveler or Razor' on the top of the grounds, becomes, rather, 'moot!'

Come the early 1900's, the newly invented 'Tamper,' could, again, be made from just about anything available; as long as it could 'fit' within a brewing Basket. Generally, it was carved from wood in those days. Unfortunately, few examples have survived! Soon, blacksmiths started to 'cast' or fabricate metal 'Tampers' – which, are still popular today – although, 'blacksmiths' no longer seem to make them. However, with the 'invention' of plastic in the last century, many commercial 'Tampers' (especially for home use) were made of molded plastic – although, metal and wood were still favorites! Some 'cheaper' Espresso Machines (like mine) still come with 'Plastic Tampers' – and in my opinion, there is nothing wrong with using them, as they 'work!'

As of late (within the last few years), the 'Tamper trend,' has returned to mostly, metal – but with a wooden or plastic 'handle/grip.' Although, most 'Tampers' (plastic or not) have been considered "*Under-sized, under-weight*" and "*Inefficient*" by Barista and 'Coffee Snob' alike, combination and specialty 'Tampers' have come about! In fact, some experts state "*Flat plastic or wood is 'not good enough' to compress coffee grounds; the proper size, curve, weight, and 'pound pressure' of the Tamper is needed… as they can increase an 'Espresso' yield, by as much as <u>2%</u>… the average person is unable to determine '30 pounds' of pressure by themselves accurately! Moreover, and fortunately, some Tampers come with a built-in 'leveling' blade as well – unless (and better still) it comes with the proper-sized 'curved' base!*"

So, 'guessing' pound pressure is now, "*Simply out of the question*," as stated by some people; and, <u>who</u> would not wish to increase the amount of 'Espresso' extraction in their 2 or 4-ounce, Demitasse cup, by an additional **2%**?

2% would equal, approximately 0.08% of a 4-ounce, 'Demitasse' cup! Frankly, I must wonder, if 0.08% more liquid in my cup, would be worth paying up to $<u>200.00</u> for a 'Tamper!'

So, (we must assume) for the past 100 or so years, Baristas say, we have all been "*Wasting 2% yield*," and "*Drinking 'very poor' Espresso*," without even knowing it! Honestly, the 'experts' might argue this one; as the most popular coffee shop in my town (which always has a line waiting at its 'drive-through') uses a standard, non-adjustable, 'Metal Tamper' with a flat base – just like what I use at home – and they purchased it at exactly the same store I did – the local, 'Restaurant Supply Store!' Frankly, the coffee shop owners say, they "*Do not have the 'time' to 'adjust' Tampers; or use 'fancy' Bases, specialized Funnels, Rings, or Holders!*" They need to "*Tamper down coffee grounds as fast as possible; to 'get on' with the 'next' Coffee or Espresso order!*"

If they were to use anything besides a 'Standard Tamper,' it would be a 'Leveling' or 'Trimming' tool (and some Tampers have them 'built-in') – since the 'old fashioned' idea of having 'flat grounds' is still used by many Baristas. This one shown here, is the model I have; and, which came with my Espresso machine, along with a standard 'Tamper!'

Although many 'Tamper/Levelers' look like small, 'Hockey Pucks,' having small ridges on their base, many 'unique designs' (supposedly to help water to pass through the grounds easier), also have a 'blade' to smooth the grounds.

The entire idea of a 'Razor' or 'Leveler,' is best described by the Breville corporation (who makes the 'Razor™' which came with my Espresso machine); "*The Razor: is a 'twisted blade' that trims down the puck to the right level to keep a constant extraction.*" Breville does not seem to put much stock into 'Tampers with built-in' levelers; and their separate 'Tamper' (which, also, came with the device has a 'flat' Base… so, I have to ask again, *"How important is a 'curved' Base on a Tamper if the grounds are going to be 'leveled,' after tampering, anyway?"*

Apparently, Breville feels that an estimated '30-pound Tampering' – and then 'Leveling' – is quite adequate!

However, still the discussion goes on; some Baristas (at major coffee chains), now claim: *"Use of an improper Tamper can not only ruin an Espresso, but can cause hand/finger, limb, and spine damage to the Barista; and negatively affect 'water posture'!"* *"Water posture?"* What the hell is that? I looked it up on the internet, and the closest thing I could find, was perhaps, *"A Study on the Coffee Spilling Phenomena in the Low Impulse Regime,"* (oscillating, cups of coffee to see how much is spilled)!

Frankly, I call *"BS"* on these statements by 'Coffee Snobs' or Baristas! Considering history, if *"Improperly tampered"* 'Espresso Grounds' have been used over the past 100+ years, and Espresso has been so *"Awful, to drink,"* why is it so popular now? One would think, that 'Espresso,' as a beverage, would have 'died off' generations ago! Moreover, if an *"Improper Tamper"* is so 'hazardous' for *"Hands/Fingers, Limbs, and Spines,"* why would anyone want to become a Barista or own a Coffee Bar?

Summing up, if one pays any attention to the 'Coffee Snobs,' then 'Espresso,' *"Has not been fit to drink, for the past 100+ years, due to improper Tampers!"* I am sorry, but, again, I do not buy this line of thought! So, I will continue to use my 'sub-standard' Tamper to brew my Espresso… 'risking' my limbs, back, and 'water posture!'

The plastic, combination, 'Scoop and Tamper,' shown here, and the metal Tamper shown on upcoming pages, are what I use with my Espresso maker; and some people (right or wrong… probably, right) call me a something of a *"Coffee Snob!"* As I have said so many times in this book, I would doubt very seriously, that there are very many people who can 'genuinely' taste the difference between tampers, razors, brewing materials, water temperatures, types or brands of devices, sizes, features, colors or styles – especially, the Espresso made, if 'part' of a beverage, filled with 'tasty additives;' and, I seldom drink, 'Espresso,' alone!

However, everyone is different – and some people do have much more of a developed palate than I. For example, I know of yet another member of a former 'Coffee Club,' who claimed he could "*Taste the difference between Tampers as well as machines*;" so, he brews his own 'Espresso' (as no one else is, apparently, capable) in a $2000+ Espresso Machine; stating, "*Starbucks does not use a 'Euro-Curved,' center-weighted* (whatever that is), *Tamper; so I only make my own Espresso… so it can be adequately prepared!*" He would even bring coffee from home in a travel mug to club 'functions' in Coffee Bars – frankly, if I would have owned the Coffee Bar, I would have 'tossed him out!' Just as 'bringing one's own food to eat into a restaurant' is improper… it is just as inappropriate to bring one's 'home-brewed' coffee into a Coffee Bar!

Was his 'home' Espresso/Coffee good? Yes! I have tasted it; but it was no better than what I could get from any coffee shop; nor, is it any better than what I can make with my own, 'cheapy,' 'Espresso' maker – using my 'Plastic Tamper!' Out of the styles of Tampers I mentioned previously, I would bet if I had multiple cups of Espresso, 'tampered individually' with each device, he would not be able to taste any difference! However, I know he and others claim, and believe, they "*Can*!" Perhaps, I should give him the benefit of the doubt – at least, until the day I can run an actual test!

In the past, it was 'enough' to just 'smooth and press down' the grounds for an 'Espresso' machine. Today, however, some 'Tampers' are 'Spring Loaded' or 'Forced' – as not to compress the grounds 'too much' or 'too little' – as with a solid 'Tamper!' Can anyone accurately 'gauge,' say, 30 pounds of pressure with a simple, non-adjustable, flat 'Tamper?' Perhaps, at least, they could come close, with years of experience. For myself, I can come 'close enough' for the beverages I make and enjoy! However, a 'true Barista,' might even 'calibrate' their 'Custom' Tampers, according to the 'Espresso' device they are using; and brand/type/roast of beans! Some of these 'calibrated tampers,' make a 'click' when pressing down on the coffee – which triggers a piston, when the proper pressure (about 30 pounds) has been met. The 'Piston,' with a 54 or 58mm foot (with the appropriate curve), 'stomps' on the beans; compressing them, with no more or less than 30 pounds of pressure! One might think, that 'Tampering' on a digital scale, might solve the 'pressure' issue; but, so far, I have not found anyone who would agree with that practice!

Of course, just holding a 'Portafilter and Custom Tamper' can affect pressure as well; as my arm/hand might 'give' a little against the pressure! This would cause the grounds to have 'less' than 30 pounds of force applied to them... in theory! If one is going to 'standardize' on equipment, then do not throw in any 'variables' such as 'opposite arm strength!' One must use what is known as a 'Tampering Station;' to hold constant, 'upward' pressure against the Tamper. This device cannot be 'handheld;' as one would be back to their 'arm or hand' moving – and thus, reducing the amount of 'reverse pressure' applied to the beans! What would this 'look like' if one could see it? I had it explained to me by a 'Coffee Snob' once; *"Think about an 'immovable object' hitting an 'irresistible force!' Then, think back to when you were a kid; watching 'Superman' movies, TV shows, or cartoons. A 'bad guy/criminal' would approach Superman and 'punch' him in the face. Superman never flinched, and the 'bad guy' always walked away with a sore or broken hand/wrist. If Superman hit the 'bad guy,' however, the criminal would be 'thrown backward;' often, careening into another person, knocking* <u>*them*</u> *down too! 'Tampering' coffee, using a 'Tampering Station' is much the same; although, the 'Superman' example is a bit extreme!*

In the same sense, if you were holding a 'Portafilter' full of coffee grounds, and someone 'pushed' your arm/hand down, your arm would move, at least somewhat, in a downward motion. It would not matter if the arm were 'pushed' by the wrist, the hand, or the 'Portafilter' held within the hand... the 'arm would move downwards because you (or ones arm) are not an 'immovable object!' So, any 'grounds' being kept in a 'Portafilter' would (in theory) have less pressure 'applied' to them, than if the arm/hand holding the Portafilter, even, if the pressure were applied to only the grounds" (this is all 'headache material' for me... when I want a cup of coffee)!

I'm sure 'physicists' could argue this 'theory' back and forth as to its value; but the simple fact is, if using a 'Tampering Station,' it should be used on a 'hard surface' (like a countertop) so that any grounds being 'compressed from above,' will all be affected by the same pressure set... as always, <u>30</u> <u>pounds</u>!

A 'Tampering Station' is nothing more than a stand (or 'mini' table) which holds the 'Portafilter,' firmly and level! The 'set' 'Tamper' is placed on top of the grounds (and sometimes, within a Distribution Ring, which I will talk about later), and slight pressure is applied to '<u>trigger</u>' the tampering mechanism! <u>Precisely</u>, 30 pounds of weight/pressure

(providing the 'Tamper' is accurate) is then applied to the coffee grounds – evenly, every time (providing, both the 'Tamper and Portafilter Base' have the same 'curve,' so all things are equal)! The Portafilter is, then, ready to be placed into the 'Espresso' machine!

'Coffee Snobs' love all this 'extra' detail to the grounds!

For me, until I started writing this book, I had never heard of a 'Tampering Station!' I would, however, often place the 'Portafilter' down on my kitchen counter, holding it in place, and use my 'Tamper' – but, that was more or less, an effort to help 'steady' the 'Portafilter;' and not 'spill' any grounds!

Some Baristas, and/or 'Coffee Snobs,' like to say that, *"Different 'Espresso' machines – and different beans – plus, the <u>freshness</u> of the beans, the degree of 'fineness of the grind,' the 'temperature of the water, and the humidity of the air,' require different amounts of pressure on their baskets – so different designs, or 'Adjustable Tampers,' are necessary for each bean type, age, roast, and grind;"* so, these people do not use even generic, 'Calibrated Tampers!' They must use '<u>Custom</u>, <u>Calibrated</u>, <u>Adjustable</u> <u>Tampers</u>;' claiming, *"One must always check a Barometer and weather before tampering one's grounds; then adjust the Tamper for the appropriate 'humidity!"* Oh please… this is going too far! I cannot even find these 'Adjustable Tampers,' easily, online; as they are so new – and, *"Adjust the Tampers for humidity…"* how? So far, nobody has been able to tell me 'what' pressure to set an adjustable 'Tamper' at, on, say… a 'rainy day' as opposed to a 'sunny' one! These same people claim, *"These tools are the <u>only</u> <u>way</u> to achieve perfection in one's Espresso – and, to save ones back, arms, and hands!"* Funny, I do not see Starbucks or Dutch Brothers 'checking the weather' before brewing each 'Espresso!'

Try going to a 'high end' Coffee Bar sometime and look around the 'Espresso' machines. If you see an assortment of 'Custom Tampers;' ask *"Does anyone's back hurt?"* Chances are, anyone who has been standing for an extended period – regardless of the 'Tamper' they use – is going to say they, *"Have a sore back!"* I get a 'sore back' in Starbucks, just 'standing and waiting' for my coffee order to arrive!

Again, with many 'Coffee Snobs,' <u>price</u> has more to do with 'Bragging Rights' than 'function' or 'perfection!' As, somewhat, stated before: I give the same advice to my 'Snobby' (but on a budget) coffee friends as I do for friends who say that they can *"Only can purchase furniture from the most expensive store in town"*… "***LIE***" about your purchase; if 'image' is <u>so</u> <u>important</u> to you!

Why waste money, when one does not have to? For my money, I use what works – and <u>works</u> <u>well</u>! When I need to make a cup of 'Espresso''– '<u>now</u>,' I do not need 'style and grace, song and dance, or hopes and prayers' for the most part! I just use, 'what works!'

This premise may be seen throughout this book – as, I tend to look like an 'advertisement' for inexpensive, 'Mr. Coffee' or 'Primula' brands. It is not that I am so 'sold' on these 'particular' brands; it is just that in my small town, there are few outlets to buy coffee equipment or supplies! 'Mr. Coffee' and 'Primula' are the brands most of the stores (notably, the 'discount' grocery stores) carry!

When it comes to 'Tampers,' the <u>only</u> 'Restaurant Supply' store in town, carries the ones like in the photograph here! They do not sell 'fancy…' just, 'what works!' This one, shown, cost me only $7.00 from the Restaurant Supply store! I see it used in many, local, coffee shops! It may be 'generalized'… however, it works fine; and, as one Barista told me, "*It is still considered a 'Forced' Tamper; as it is <u>one's</u> <u>arm</u>, which is 'forcing' the pressure!*" Moreover, it is 'fancy enough' to have 'two sizes' of Tampers on it! It is heavy and 'feels good' in hand! My old, 'Plastic Tamper,' however, still works too – and, I will use whichever I happen to find first! When teaching or demonstrating, however, students are more accepting of this metal one!

So, how much are the 'Specialized' Tampers?' Anywhere from $50.00 to $200.00 for the 'fancy' ones; or less than $20.00 for the 'generalized or generic' brands.

Overall, how much does it cost to make ones 'first cup' of 'Espresso' at home these days? A 'Coffee Snob' might spend several hundred or thousands of dollars on an 'Espresso' maker. Then, up to $200.00 for a good 'Tamper!'

Then, up to $200.00 for 'Funnel and Distribution Tool,' $20 - $100 or more for a 'Coffee Station,' at least $50.00 for a 'good,' 'Digital' Scale, $15.00 or more per pound for Coffee, and '<u>whatever</u>' more on cups, mugs, glasses, and other paraphernalia! So, it is conceivable, that one would spend upwards of $2600.00 or more (providing an inexpensive 'Espresso' machine was purchased), just to pour their '<u>first</u> <u>cup</u>!'

I, however, spent under $100.00, for my first Espresso Machine; (and, considerably less, if one considers using a 'Moka Pot' rather than an 'Espresso' maker); and, I cannot taste much difference 'dollar-wise;' especially, when the Espresso is mixed with steamed milk, flavored creamer, foam, chocolate, caramel, syrups, cinnamon, sprinkles, whipped cream, or other additives! I will admit, however, that my 'every day Espresso' maker, shown on the previous page, cost me around$500.00! However, honestly, I only purchased it, as my son and I were taking 'Barista classes;' and we needed a, rather manual, machine to practice on!

Scales:

Most present-day Baristas (and, every 'Coffee Snob' who makes their own 'Espresso') are going to want to have the 'top of the line' equipment; and, that might include 'Espresso, Grounds Distribution Tools… alternatively, 'other accessories!'

"What 'other' accessories," one might ask? First, a 'Digital Scale;' to accurately 'measure out' the correct weight of 'Espresso' grounds and water for the brewer; in other words, establishing, 'ratio!' Scales should be used if one wishes to, time after time, always have their coffee 'look, brew, and taste' the same! Of course, 'trial and error' is how most people (new to coffee) determine their coffee ratios.

With this 'Digital Scale' shown; I did not purchase it because I needed for 'brewing coffee;' I bought it because I wanted a photographic example for this book – so, one can see, I do not place too much importance in 'Scales!' I have only used it twice, since – and even then, it was for 'classes!' However, it can be used for postage or in the kitchen for other weight measurements! I learned to brew coffee like most 'average' people – through 'trial and error!' I took what the brewer recommended and changed the 'coffee to water ratio' up or down until I achieved the taste, I enjoyed most… no 'scale' required!

How is a 'Scale' used? An empty bowl, Portafilter, or piece of paper is placed on the weight plate of the 'Digital Scale;' and the scale turned on. A decision to use 'ounces or grams' is made, and the device 'zeros' out; meaning, where it usually starts with a reading of 'zero,' it considers the weight of, say, a bowl-like in the photograph above, and returns the readout to '**0.0**' once again. In other words, the bowl and 'Scale' are now one! It does not matter what is used to hold the grounds. I have friends who use a dry, flat bottomed, coffee filter; while others use a, glass, measuring cup. Still more people, enjoy just using a piece of paper – then, dumping it into their 'Portafilter!' In some cases, however, the 'Portafilter or brew basket' may sit on the 'Scale;' and coffee 'ground' directly into it!

The 'Scale' may even be used with certain brewing devices to 'weigh' both water and grounds together; to determine the correct 'water to grounds' ratios!

Some 'Snobs' even do this when using their 'K-Pod' brewer; with refillable 'Pods.' However, weighing grounds to go into a 'Pod' is rather useless. Just fill the reusable 'Pod' to the fill line! If one requires 'more extraction,' then add a 'paper filter' next time in the 'Pod.' If still <u>more</u> is needed, lightly 'tamper down' the grounds before placing the 'Pod' into the device! Of course, if the coffee is 'too strong,' one can always 'cut down' on the amount of grounds used. Moreover, when it comes to water, no 'weighing' is necessary; as most 'brewers' have 'cup mark' on their water tank; so, one knows 'how many' cups they may brew. It does not do any good to 'weigh,' say, '10-ounces of water,' because the consumer is going to want to have a 'cup or mug' <u>full</u>! I merely, 'fill a mug' with pure water, then pour '<u>that</u>' amount into the machine. I never have 'too much' water for the mug – and, it allows me to 'fine tune' the brew by adding more or less water for the next cup! 'Weighing' 10-ounces, would be useless! However, if I were using a 'Pour-Over' or 'French Press' brewer, 'weighing' could come in quite handy!

Special Note: Many 'coffee brewing' companies have their own brands of professional, 'Scales' to purchase – starting around $50 – and going up to $200.00 or more… for what one would call, a truly 'scientific' scale. However, the one shown here (and on the previous page), was only $12.99 (plus sales tax) at a local 'discount,' grocery store. I have compared it side by side with a $100 model; and it is every bit as accurate!

Getting back to Espresso, after the proper coffee weight (Dosing) has been achieved on the Scale (say, 17 grams for ones' Espresso maker settings, or 43 grams for my coffee maker, as the photograph on the previous page shows), it is carefully poured into the Espresso Machines Portafilter (ground basket); and the Espresso is ready for Tampering. This is where a standard piece of paper comes in handy – as it can be folded; to, safely, 'pour out' the entire grind. This makes the paper, something, of a 'Distribution Tool!' However, actual 'Distribution Tools,' now come into play… that is, if desired; because apparently, one cannot just 'pour in' grounds into a 'Portafilter' before 'tampering' them down in a certain way, anymore!

Distribution Tools:

'Before' the grounds can be placed into the brewing basket, a specialized 'Funnel' (which looks like a Chrome or Tungsten, Escutcheon (a flat/thick piece of metal for protection or ornamentation, around a keyhole, door handle, or light switch – in this case, a Portafilter Basket, or Automotive Spacer, 'flange' – what is called a 'Bell Flange – or, sometimes, even an 'adult' sex device… go figure) must be placed into or 'over' the 'Portafilter' basket. The real trick is, finding something with a 58mm (or another size) diameter on one end – or something which can be 'cut' easily. The best 'Distribution Tools' come in, slight, 'funnel' shapes. Therefore, in later paragraphs, I demonstrate with an 'easy to cut,' Yogurt Cup or 'hard plastic' Funnel!

I, often, fill my 'Portafilter' by pouring grounds directly from the bag the grounds come in (if not grinding myself); then, 'tamper' them down, slightly. Nobody has ever noticed or tasted any difference between me using (or not using) a Distribution Tool! However, some people simply have to use a special tool to 'pour and tamper' their grounds!

So, the 'Funnel/Escutcheon' is used before pouring the grounds into the basket (if possible); as not to 'spill' a single grain of coffee; as it comes out the paper, bowl, scoop, spoon, measuring cup, or grinder. However, that brings us to owning a 'fancy grinder' – which can 'measure out grounds while grinding too – eliminating the need for a 'Scale!' The 'Portafilter' with the 'Distribution Ring' (funnel/spacer) can be placed directly on or under the grinder in many cases; not on my 'Espresso' maker, but, if it could, it would be of help; as sometimes my 'Portafilter' overfills! Again, in theory, a 'ring or tool' should help to prevent even a single grain of coffee from being spilled or lost! For me, however, it just creates 'more' of a headache; as my machine will 'start and stop' on demand; so, I can keep from 'overfilling' it.

'Spilling the beans,' while pouring into the 'Portafilter' basket aside, another primary function of the 'Funnel,' however, is so a 'Stirring Stick' (which looks amazingly like a toothpick, dental tool, or 'Martini Olive/Onion Holder' (shown here), to 'evenly stir' the grounds in the basket – eliminating any 'air pockets' or 'clumps' of coffee grounds. In other words, preparing, and evenly 'distributing,' the grounds before 'tampering.' Apparently, this is the essence behind a 'Distribution Tool!' 'Stirring,' assures 'even distribution' of the coffee grounds; for 'fuller' extraction of flavors and essences. It, also, 'aids' in 'tampering;' as, the 'ring,' serves 'double duty,' in keeping grounds <u>in</u> the 'Portafilter!' I have to question 'how important' this is to 'spare' even a 'single grain' of coffee; as if changing grinds on machines with automatic grinders, a small amount (up to a 'puck') of coffee is wasted before grinding to the proper size, and inserting into the Espresso Maker! Fresh grounds can, just as quickly, be 'brushed off' or 'tampered' over a can or small bucket to 'catch' any spillage – then, reused!

Since I have some friends who feel 'Distribution Tools' are an 'essential step' to brewing 'fine coffee,' (but can't afford a real, 'Distribution Tool') I feel as if I need to offer a 'choice' to the 'Tools' – which, again, can cost hundreds of dollars; even though, since the invention of 'Espresso,' these tools were never needed. Humanity has made 'Espresso' (Italian, for 'forced out… meaning, under pressure) for over 100 years without such tools – and most people enjoyed it (at least, I have never heard anyone say, *"Gee, I wish the Barista would have run the grounds through a funnel or stirred them with a 'stick' before mechanically tampering, leveling, and brewing"*)! These tools are innovative ideas – and 'Coffee Snobs' will love the price… needed or not. However, the 'Funnel' is just designed to keep one from 'spilling the beans;' both in pouring them into the basket, and with the 'stirring' or 'distribution' of the grounds. Often, it is kept in place to help 'guide' the 'Tamper' into – that, apparently, 'hard to find and navigate' – 'Portafilter Basket!'

The 'Coffee Snob' may wish to buy one or more of these expensive devices (regardless of how 'useful' they are); if only by the fact of their 'price' and 'bragging rights!' Let us presume, the fact that 'Distribution Tools' <u>are</u> useful; but one does not have one hundred dollars or more to spend on them… however, feel they simply '<u>have to</u>' use them! There is an easy solution; one can 'make' a device to use. It may not be very 'pretty;' but again… it works!

Even an inexperienced 'Coffee Snob' can 'make' an acceptable version of a 'Distribution Tool' – should they feel they need one! An acceptable 'Funnel' can be made easily… moreover, most spouses, will not complain about the price! Of course, there probably is not a 'Coffee Snob' in the world who would do this, but it works for we 'average' people. However, most likely, nobody really needs this type of tool; and, I certainly cannot 'taste' any difference between using one or not – as some people may claim!

One of the most practical 'Funnels' that one can make, is made from an empty Yogurt cup – as shown here.

The bottom of the 'tapered,' plastic cup is cut off, and the cup inverted. The top part (which is, now, the bottom) – which is shaped like a wide 'Funnel' – is placed into the basket. Coffee Beans can be either ground directly into the 'Portafilter,' through the 'Funnel,' or 'measured and weighed' safely; then added to the basket. Depending upon the 'Grinder' and the 'Scale,' sometimes the 'Portafilter and Funnel' can be placed on the 'Scale' together; or placed under the Grinder, and coffee ground directly into the 'Portafilter Basket' – thus, serving the useful purpose of 'helping to keep every grain of coffee' in the 'Portafilter.' The beauty here is that the 'Funnel' may be cut to any height for ease of use! There is no difference between a 'Yogurt cup' and a 'Chrome Ring/Tool;' except appearance, weight, and <u>cost</u>!

If one does not like the looks of the 'Homemade Filter,' or the printing on the side of it, then, 'paint it' any color you would like – how about, 'Professional Black' for 'a touch of class!' There is even 'Shiny Chrome' color paint; available at 'home stores' and hobby shops, which will make a 'homemade' Ring/Distribution Tool look professional! Any 'color' may be used; for example, I have a friend who loves Copper – so he painted his 'copper-colored' to match his kitchen appliances, pots and pans! Just make sure the paint used, is 'non-toxic!'

If one does not like the above design and wants a 'firmer' tool, an actual, plastic, 'Kitchen Funnel' can be modified. Cut off the stem at the proper diameter; 57mm (which is slightly smaller than the standard, 58mm Portafilter). This image is of a 'small' Funnel; with a 'crudely drawn,' guideline, on which to cut. The 'angle' of the funnel will be 'strong' enough to fit into the 'Portafilter;' and not 'fall out' when moved. Plus,

there is a 'handy' tab on the 'Funnel' and its 'lip;' which is along the top, to ease handling! Again, should the color of the funnel 'offend,' paint it the desired color! Again, 'chrome colored paint' is very impressive!

After grinding the beans, and filling the 'Portafilter,' a toothpick, dental tool, bamboo skewer, a thin stick, rod, meat thermometer, or even a hairpin can be used (and work just as well), as a 'Distribution Stick,' to get rid of any 'offending air pockets' trapped between grounds! Anything which can 'stir' the grounds (as long as it is 'pointy and small' enough to use with the Funnel on) can be used. In other words, what one student expressed, "*A, tiny, pointed stick of some sort!*" I prefer long-handled, metal, 'dental tools,' myself!

One of my 'Coffee Enthusiast' friends, recently, asked me if there was "*Anything else*" that could be used as a 'Funnel' – as his wife will not allow him to spend $200.00 on a Distribution Tool Set – and he didn't like the 'Yogurt Cup' or 'Plastic Funnel' ideas! There are many other things one could do when it comes to 'making' a funnel – besides what I just wrote. 'Fruit Cups,' 'Pudding Cups,' or 'Styrofoam Cups' come to mind. However, Funnels do not even have to be 'that' fancy! For example, I recently bought a 'Hand Crank, Burr Grinder;' to take on trips with me. This allows me to 'grind' 18 different degrees of coffee – everything from 'Ultra-fine' to 'Ultra-Coarse.' Pouring the ground beans into a Portafilter is not too much of a problem, due to the small size of the device ground holder. However, providing I had a piece of construction paper, acetate, or a magazine with me, I can easily make a Funnel/Distribution Funnel out of a piece of paper or acetate. I did this, recently, on a business trip; where I happened to have my old, portable, Espresso Machine with me.

In this case (as shown in this photograph below), I used a hotel brochure, found in my room, from my travels. It was printed on heavy paper; and one side was 'slick' for print, while the other side, gray construction paper. Hotel rooms, generally, have some 'brochures' left for their guests. If not, then one can, often, be found in the Hotel lobby, in a display rack for 'nearby' attractions!

Using an ink pen and two 'caps/lids' from a coffee can, and a water bottle, I traced two circles (of varied sizes) onto the paper side of the brochure. Then, I outlined two more (but smaller circles); one within the other as a 'guide' for 'cutting.' Cutting them out, then 'taping' them together from the inside, I created 'Funnels,' so to speak. The tape, also, made up for any 'shortcomings' of the funnel – as the photograph below shows! The 'Funnel' does not have to be perfect, just 'functional' – that is, should one feel they need one at all!

By doing this, I could choose 'which funnel' fit my Portafilter best! Coffee grounds were, then, 'poured' into my Portafilter... without spilling a single grain of coffee! Although difficult to see here, a simple 'toothpick' worked for a 'Distribution Stick;' and my thumb worked as a Tamper. After placing the Portafilter onto the Espresso Machine, I had a great-tasting cup of Espresso after only a few minutes; and I did not have to bring along any 'real,' Distribution Tools, besides my scissors and some tape; which are always in my briefcase! However, there is still an, even more, straightforward way to do this; and that is, to take a brochure or postcard, roll it into a 'Funnel,' and pour the grounds through it into the Portafilter; and forgetting about 'stirring!' 'Tamper down' the grounds with a 'thumb' or anything else, and brew!

I can hear the 'Coffee Snobs' mouths, collectively, 'falling open' right now – but, 'non-snob' groups I speak before, love this! It is crude... however, it works – that is, unless one 'needs' to be impressed! Frankly, I never found a need to use a 'Funnel!' I like to think I am 'clever' enough to pour a small amount of ground coffee into a Portafilter basket without help! Besides, my 'Hand Coffee Grinders' ground cup, is similar in size to my Portafilter basket – and works great as a 'Tamper!'

That is, unless one is pouring their grounds into a 'K-Pod' brewer or 'Moka Pot.' In the 'old days,' I would use my thumb to 'smooth and compress' the grind; but when I became a bit more sophisticated, I started using the long 'combination,' Plastic Scoop/Tamper' which came with my, Espresso Machine. So, wanting to achieve 'better brewing with my 'K-Pod,' I purchased a small 'Tamper' to use with my, refillable, 'K-Pods!' It is, more or less, just for fun, but it does serve a useful purpose – and looks better than my thumb!

Is it worth the extra steps and cost to make a cup of Espresso? Some people might say "*Yes*;" but I cannot justify the cost or taste any difference… moreover, neither can my '<u>regular</u>' Barista! So, if all this 'Tampering, Distribution Tools, and Tamper Stations' can be eliminated just by 'lightly compressing' and 'leveling' the grounds with a 'simple' tool or thumb… the whole 'Tampering' issue becomes 'moot!'

I would suggest, if one owns their own 'Espresso Machine,' is to 'pull' two cups; but with different tampering methods. Make sure <u>everything</u> else is the same, however… pre-warmed machines and cups, ground coffee, the same dosing, time, et cetera. 'Tamper' the first Portafilter with a standard Tamper. If you own a 'Forced,' automatic, or other type of Tamper, you might try 'pulling' a shot, using it as well – and use it as a 'control;' as <u>one</u> <u>knows</u> it will use only, 30 pounds of pressure! Then, filling yet another Portafilter, use a 'thumb;' with an estimate of what one would think would be an adequate amount of pressure. Just make sure, that the top of the grounds, in each case, are of even/matching height, and smooth.

Taste each Espresso; and compare to see which one 'tastes best' to you. Don't be surprised, if you cannot taste much difference between cups! The last test I performed, I could not tell any difference in taste between using a 'Forced Tamper' and 'Standard Tamper;' especially, when the Espresso was served in a cup, with other ingredients added to it, to make a 'Latte Macchiato.'

Let's take a closer look at Espresso:

"Coffee and love are best when they are <u>hot</u>!"

~ (Attributed to) German Proverb

HOME ESPRESSO MACHINES

"Pulling a Shot..." some 'Coffee Snobs' are determined to have the same (or better) Espresso than the local 'coffee hang-out' has – and, the current, 'upwardly mobile Snob' – is willing to 'pay through the nose' for their own Espresso Machines (and tools) to use at home! Many 'Home' type machines can cost upwards of $8,000.00 or more; but, can save close to $1000.00 over 'store bought,' cups of Espresso!

However, a 'reasonable' machine can cost, under, $500.00 – that that is what my machine – shown here – cost me. I purchased this Breville as a 'learning machine' for my family and students – after first owning a $40.00 Mr. Coffee Espresso Maker! Although the Breville can create an 'automatic' brew, it allows for many 'grinding' and brewing options. And, if one can 'save' $1000 with the more expensive machines, one is looking at several thousand dollars in savings; that is, providing one drinks a lot of Espresso!

'Dollar' savings aside, and unless 'teaching' or 'selling' Espresso, I do not know why someone would want an <u>expensive</u> Machine; when they could just go to a Coffee Bar for a good cup or purchase a 'cheaper machine' like I have. Alternatively, if nothing else, I do not understand why someone might not be willing to own a 'Moka Pot;' which would perform, <u>close</u>, to the same task, for a fraction of the money... at least, to start! Who knows... status? Bragging rights? Perhaps, they merely like 'Machine Espresso;' and <u>want</u> to make their own!

When buying an Espresso Machine, one needs to take several things under consideration; surprisingly, the primary concern by many people is the amount of <u>counter space</u> it takes up! Some machines have a 'footprint' smaller than a coffee maker – making one, small, single-serving cup of Espresso. Other devices may even look and act like 'K-Pod' brewers! Still more machines, however, might take up <u>much</u> of a countertop – and make several servings all at once... not to mention, have 'built-in,' Coffee Grinders and Milk Steaming features! In any event, one needs an Espresso Machine (or Moka Pot) if they are going to create <u>authentic</u> Cappuccinos, Lattes, or other coffee beverages.

Most home Espresso Machines require a 'fine' or 'extra-fine' coffee grind – and both manufacturers and Baristas suggest using an *"Espresso (dark) Roast;"* but, any 'roast' may be used as long as the 'grind' is 'fine' enough.

Some machines (like mine) will even 'grind the beans' directly into the device Portafilter – and when using the machines 'recommended' settings, one is more likely to 'pull' the type of cup desired… at least, have a good starting point! Incidentally, and contrary to popular belief, not all 'Espresso Roasts' are of 'one type' of bean. Many Baristas use an '80/200 or 70/30' ratio of both Arabica and Robusta. I prefer 100% Arabica beans; sometimes, with a 'chocolate' flavoring.

Unless a 'Pod' type 'Espresso' brewer (as shown on the next page), 'small' devices (Mr. Coffee type) start around $40.00 for a 'basic' machine; which, generally, includes a 'Steamer/Frother' for milk – but more on 'Steaming and Frothing' in the next section. Typical, and as stated previously, higher end, 'home type' machines can 'hover' somewhere around $300.00 and can run upwards as high as $8000.00… not bad prices, considering 'professional' machines can run $18,000.00 or more! Frankly, I do expect 'more' from an $18,000.00 device than a $40.00 one; but I have been disappointed too many times! Realistically speaking, when purchasing a 'Home Espresso Machine' (a good one, which will not only give the consumer great 'Crema' but excellent tasting coffee as well), one should expect to pay between $350.00 and $600.00 – there is no reason to spend more, unless looking for a particular brand, or 'features' which don't appear on less expensive machines. However, if 'great crema' is not an issue – and one is using the Espresso for Lattes, Cappuccinos, or other beverages, sometimes, less expensive machines are just as good; and for me, again… 'Moka Pot Espresso' is undoubtedly, 'more than acceptable;' as it tends to be less bitter.

There are a lot of 'bragging rights' for 'Coffee Snobs' when it comes to 'Espresso Machines!' Because I, seldom, drink a 'cup' of Espresso alone, choosing to 'mix' assorted beverages or ingredients, it does not do me much good to 'brag! Even though my Espresso Machine only cost around $500 (on sale), I have not found any 'Snob' yet, whom could taste much difference between my Espresso, and one from a local, Coffee Bar; using an $18,000 device. But, perhaps, people are just being polite! I am sure a 'true expert' could tell the difference – especially if I were serving only a cup of Espresso – but not myself, or the general public; when it comes to Cappuccinos and Lattes! If I had to purchase an Espresso Machine again, however, I would, probably, buy one slightly more 'automatic' than the one I have!

Some people are a bit more 'particular' when it comes to 'time and convenience' than they are 'top-quality tasting' Espresso; and I even purchased a 'quick and easy' device for myself when traveling (for use when I do not wish to 'lug around' my 'Big,' Espresso Machine). Often, I will have a 'blender' with me when I camp; so, this small box (shown) is not unreasonable to carry along – although, it does come with its own 'bag' for transporting. The device is a 'Portable' Espresso, 'hand-held brewer' – which uses 'Pods' like a Nespresso™. The only thing one needs is hot water and a 'Nespresso' Pod!

There are many brands and types of 'Single Pod' brewers available – and, many, start in price around $200.00 or less. However, I like the 'Simpresso™' brand, Portable, (19 Bars) Travel Espresso Maker; as it makes quite an exceptional Espresso, for under $100.00… moreover, even with its own 'Travel Bag,' it only 'weighs in' just over 3/4 pound; so, it fits into my camping gear just as easily as my 'French Press/Travel Mug.' It even fits within my briefcase! I wish my Blender were as easy to carry!

Reusable, and included, 'Pods' ('Smart Capsule') are filled to 8-9 grams (or filled to 'sight, once experienced) with 'medium ground' Espresso beans of one's choice! The 'Pod' is placed into the device, and hot water is added. The device is then placed over a cup – or its own (attachable) cup is placed under it – while a 'Leverage/Handle' is 'pressed' down. This action moves a piston, downward – to 'pressure force' the hot water through the 'Pod;' with approximately 20 pounds of pressure. The newly brewed 'Espresso,' drains into the waiting cup.

Grounds can be of any type roast may be used; but a 'Dark Roast' is recommended. The reason the beans are ground to a 'Medium-fine' grind is, so they will not 'block' filter holes of the device or interfere with 'Pump' action. Grounds should be only slightly 'Tampered;' again, as not to interfere with the Pump. 'Pre-filled Pods' may be purchased at many grocery stores; of course, again, using the 'Smart Capsules' can help to 'save' our landfills!

Again, the 'bonus' with filling one's own 'Pods,' are, any type or roast of beans can be used! I do recommend, when starting, use of a 'Scale' to determine just 'how much' 7, 8 or 9 grams. Just fill one of the included 'Smart

Capsules;' and make a note of results for future Espressos, should the brew be too strong. However, different beans and roasts will have different weights to consider; and (along with water temperature) determine the taste of the brewed Espresso.

The 'Simpresso' can create 'pre-measured,' Espressos, Ristrettos & Lungos at home, in the car, or the woods, while camping (with or without an RV) – providing, some boiling water can be found! What is the difference between beverages made with it? Not too much; as each drink is based on the same ingredients and processes as one makes with a 'powered' machine; but they do differ in how the 'process' is completed. The device does not come with a 'Mild Frother;' but a separate, battery-operated, 'pocket' Frother is easy to 'pack' along!

Perhaps, the following should be placed under 'Beverages made with Espresso; but I believe in keeping 'like items' together – especially when it comes to 'purchasing devices' to serve different issues. So, let us look at a bit of the beverages made by 'Simpresso' now… then, more on 'Espressos' later!

Espresso: Dark Roast, Espresso Beans/Grounds are not very different from what we put in our 'Drip' coffee makers at home; except, they are 'milled,' somewhat, 'finer' for use in the 'Simpresso!' General 'Espresso Machines,' use a much 'finer' grind!

Espresso may be drunk by itself; or be used as an ingredient of another beverage. Depending upon the Barista or the machine, variable amounts of water are used. However, if prepared properly, the result should be very similar from one device to another; with a concentrated, 'dose' of coffee – with delicious 'Crema' on the surface of the shot. It is served, generally, in single or double 'shots.' Depending upon the Barista or the machine, again, (not to mention personal tastes) most Baristas call for a 'recommended,' "7 *grams of finely ground coffee per 25-30ml of water.*" (The Simpresso brand, shown on the previous page, recommends 8 grams).

Ristretto: Ristretto made the same way as Espresso; but hot water is 'restricted' (hence, part of the root of the name). Ristretto often requires 'half' the water that one would, typically, use in an Espresso. As 'less water' saturates the coffee grounds, the caffeine content is lowered. However, the coffee may show more 'aromatic' traits; and most people prefer Espresso to Ristretto, due to its caffeine count.

Ristretto (American brew, that is) calls for, approximately, 7 grams of coffee grounds per 12.5-15ml of water. However, some Baristas (as everyone is different) enjoy using 8 grams of coffee.

Lungo: Lungo uses 'double the water' per 7 grams of coffee. This is so more caffeine will be extracted; and stronger 'flavor essences' can be pulled from the coffee. 'Lungo' can be very popular with 'Coffee Snobs!' Most are made using 7-8 grams of coffee per 50ml of water.

Back to topic: what is the next step in brewing with any of the methods listed so far? Sometimes, the 'next step' is maintenance! One cannot brew if their equipment is not clean or maintained; and 'poorly' cleaned equipment can, undoubtedly, perform a '<u>disservice</u>' to the coffee!

Let us look at some ways to 'maintain' not only Espresso Machines but Coffee Makers in general.

"A cup of coffee shared with a friend is, both, happiness tasted... and time well spent."

~ (Attributed to) Unknown

HOW TO 'DESCALE' ONE'S COFFEE MAKER

As a 'rule of thumb,' if ones' coffee tastes odd, and a change of grind does not seem to make much difference, perhaps, it is time to 'clean' the coffee maker; and use a 'Descaling Solution' to remove any 'left-over' minerals.

A change of water might be in order too! This is, especially, important when using 'Pod Brewers.' If using 'Tap' water in them, they can very quickly build up both scale and bacteria! Plus, their 'needles' (where the pressurized water comes through into the coffee) can become 'clogged/plugged!' I clean my 'Pod' brewer, after every 10 cups! However, I have had a few *Snobs' tell me, "Oh no... never clean out the interior of the machines, as it 'seasons' the machine; creating the best flavors."* Think of it this way; would you like to drink coffee served in a 'dirty cup?' If not, why not? Just look at all the flavor leftover in the bottom of a cup; especially, if there is dried creamer, old grounds, or 'sour' milk in it!

Regardless of 'popular belief,' the truth of the matter is: the brewing device needs to have any of its machine 'pieces/parts,' which are removable, 'rinsed' with a mild soap and water solution to remove old dust and oils. Use a moist sponge, dishrag, or paper towel, to wipe down the parts. This action is, primarily, necessary should the brewer have a 'window' for viewing water or coffee levels. In most cases, the person 'cleaning' will find that coffee oils adhere to those transparent panels – and not only that, but 'cloud/stain' them as well!

Then, if the brewer still looks a bit 'cruddy,' consider using a proper 'Descaling' Solution – (which, often contains White Vinegar) found, in most grocery stores; in their 'coffee departments.' Just follow the directions on the bottle to clean most automatic brewers; but, generally, a 'Descaler' requires 1 ounce of 'cleaner' per 8 ounces of water to fill the coffee maker. So, most of a bottle, as shown here, will be  used to clean! Sometimes, however, just a bit of cleaner on a sponge or rag is enough to remove some scale. Descalers/Cleaners are available many different devices – including, 'Pod Brewers' as well! For Espresso Machines, however, 'Descaling Tablets' are, generally, used.

If 'designer brands' are wanted – such as 'Keurig' or 'Bar Keepers Friend' – they are, sometimes, found next to the 'generic' brands too; or more often, at stores like 'Bed, Bath, and Beyond,' who specialize in 'designer' coffee makers! I recommend regularly cleaning (and running a little 'Colloidal Silver' through brewers to kill any bacteria); especially when it comes to 'K-Pod' brewers! However, there are other brands of 'Descaler/Cleaners' which work very well too. And, if a 'tool' of some sort is required, surprisingly, I have found a simple 'paperclip,' or 'small gauge' wire, can become handy for cleaning a 'K-Pod' brewer, when the 'jet' become 'clogged!'

However, 'Do-it-yourself' solutions may be made easily. If one uses citric acid for canning or other purposes, they will need an 'acid-to-water' ratio, of about one-part acid to 20 parts water. Pour the mixture into the machine and run a cycle! However, this can be done just as quickly with 'Vinegar or Lemon Juice;' the combination is a 50/50 ratio. As Lemon Juice is rather expensive, I use White Vinegar – which I can purchase at the grocery store in gallon bottles.

Again, pour the mixed solution into the water reservoir of the machine and switch on; as one would when brewing. Just do not use any coffee grounds or paper filters. I do keep my 'metal mesh' filter in my 'Drip' device, however, as it can build up with scale too – plugging the mesh!

However, 'descaling' can be even 'easier' still! There are many generic and name brand 'cleaning' liquids available; which are safe for food or beverage machines. Moreover, there is minimal 'mixing' that one must do with many of them! Some are so easy, all that is necessary is to 'pour in' the cleaner.

Here is a method I like to use. Several local stores sell 'Cleaning, White Vinegar' (usually, a weaker solution of straight Vinegar) by the gallon; in fact, I just purchased the 'Cleaning Vinegar,' shown here, at the local 'Dollar' store – so, it's very inexpensive, when compared to the '12-ounce' bottle of 'professional' product. I must admit, that if my coffee maker is full of 'scale,' the 'Cleaning Vinegar' does not seem to work near as well as just plain, White Vinegar – but works fine if used regularly! I run two cycles through my coffee maker; pouring the same solution through the device, twice (filtered if necessary, the second time)!

If I do not have any 'Cleaning' Vinegar, I will, often, make a '50/50' solution with regular, 'White Vinegar' and pure water. After mixing, I pour it into the water chamber (the water chamber, usually, shows the first sign that I need to 'de-scale' – as it starts to drip/leak from the bottom when scale begins to form). Since 'Scale' forms on the valves, seals, needles, and vents first, the water 'inlet' is the best place to start cleaning! If this does not work, then, I will resort to 'using a wire or pin' to clean the Jets – then, run the Cleaning Vinegar through a second time!

For especially 'heavy' scale, however, I might use the Vinegar straight – and, I still run the machine through two cycles! Sometimes, if especially full of sediment or scale, I will stop the brewing cycle mid-way; to allow the parts to 'soak' for an hour or two. Either way – or if using a commercial 'descaler' – after I pour out the 'Descaler/Vinegar,' and run two or three cycles of freshwater through the machine; to remove any 'loose' scale, and to get rid of the 'Vinegar' taste and smell.

Again, if 'scrubbing' is necessary, I can then, quickly, 'scrub down' any built-up sediment from the screen, window, or heating element, with a sponge, 'scrunge,' small toothbrush, or stiff cleaning/soldering brush.

Different brewing methods – such as 'French Press' or 'Pour-Over Cones' – do not need cleaning with 'de-scalers' or even vinegar – as they can be easily washed, immediately, after use. However, sometimes – especially, when using Tap Water – pouring a bit of White Vinegar on a sponge is good to get rid of a few mineral deposits on the brewers, remove any 'water spots,' and, 'clean' the sponge. Alternatively, depending upon the brewer, if it is 'dishwasher safe,' running the brewer through a 'spot-free' rinse, can often 'clean' as well as get rid of 'water spots!'

Now, presuming that all brewing machines and devices are clean – and this includes all brewing accessories as well – and, ones' coffee beans are accurately ground, and the water is pure and brought up to proper temperature, one should be, almost, ready to brew!

It is time to look at Filters!

"Coffee is the common man's Gold. And like Gold, it brings to every person the feeling of 'Luxury and Nobility!'

~ (Attributed to) Sheik-ABD-Kadir

[231]

FILTERS

Some people call them, *"Coffee Filters,"* while others call them, *"Coffee Strainers."* Does everybody use them? No! Do you need them? No… that is, not if one enjoys their coffee 'gritty,' to have an 'oily' surface, or be full of '<u>whatever</u>!'

Some people have even told me that they *"Prefer to brew without filters; as they enjoy the taste of the oils and 'mud' left in the coffee!"* I would doubt they 'truly' *"Enjoy"* the oils and 'mud,'… probably, they have just become accustomed to the taste of them! After all, my parents, grandparents, great-grandparents, and other past ancestors, 'got used to' unfiltered, 'boiled' coffee from 'crushed' beans – and, enjoyed it, thusly! However, regardless of one's 'reason' for using a 'Filter or Strainer,' its primary purpose is, not only, to 'filter or strain' the 'large chunks' of Coffee Beans from ones brewed coffee, but to do the same with 'fine coffee dust' as well! It has only been in recent years, that 'filters' have had 'other purposes' to them, regarding coffee!

No matter what kind of brewer one uses, a 'filtration system,' probably, is going to be needed – except for 'Boiled,' Turkish, or Egg Coffee, specifically; and with today's 'health warnings…' even more so! Depending upon the brewing method, some 'coffee makers and devices,' have 'built-in' filters/screens/strainers/et cetera, to 'keep out' small particles of coffee from the cup; but other devices, or coffee 'grinds,' may require additional, 'special filtering' to be used. Even more, some devices might need a 'combination' of filters!

For example, I use both a 'Mesh Filter' and a, fine weave, 'Paper Filter' in my 'Drip' brewers; which also has a small, built-in 'wire mesh' filter to help catch small particles of coffee from entering a cup too. I, first, put in the 'Paper Filter;' then add my 'Mesh Basket Filter;' then, coffee grounds go into the Basket. Water is added, and 'seeps' through the grounds, until the coffee is brewed!

I do something similar when using my 'K-Pod' brewers as well! As I do not use 'pre-filled' Pods, I fill my own; but 'trial and error' has taught me, that I enjoy the flavor of a 'slightly coarser' grind than what I could purchase in a 'readymade' Pod. My 'reusable' Pods have a very 'fine' mesh/screen on them for the brewed coffee to pass through. But between the 'fine Mesh' and the 'coarser grounds,' there are still a few 'small particles' which get through;

to either 'clog' my brewer needle or to 'sink' to the bottom of my cup. However, I put a 'Paper Filter' inside the Pod before filling. This catches anything which 'might' pass through the Mesh! Plus, it helps to filter out the 'dangerous in California' oils from the coffee! Plus, it gives my coffee the advantage of having a 'longer' brewing time – as water cannot pass through the grounds quite as quickly – with the result being a 'tastier' cup of coffee, with <u>more</u> caffeine!

Call it a filter, screen, sock, sieve, or sleeve, '<u>something</u>' should come between ones brewed coffee and their cup – and 'that something' (filters) have been used with coffee since Melitta Benz came up with the idea in 1908; when 'filters' are thought to have been, first, invented. However, I am sure that over the centuries, someone, somewhere, used a cloth or something to 'filter out' grounds from their brew!

Some filters are 'specifically designed' for use with 'specific' brewers – as this stainless-steel one, shown here. Moreover, in actuality, it <u>is</u> the brewer itself! No additional filtration is needed – unless, otherwise desired, that is! Other 'Paper Filters' could be put either inside the 'Cone,' or inside the Metal Filter. The 'Metal Filter,' alone, makes great-tasting coffee; but when using a 'Paper' filter with it, will not only filter  out all the 'evils' of 'California Coffee,' but sometimes improve its flavor; making it, sometimes, taste sweeter or fruitier. However, adding a 'paper filter' to a brewer can be used to 'fine-tune' one's brewing time as well... as 'steeping time' will be increased!

Professional, commercial, or homemade filters, can be made of paper towels, brown paper, bleached paper, bamboo, hemp, cloth, cotton, metal wire, nylon mesh, window screen, cheesecloth, burlap, kitchen strainers, or about anything; including, as I previously mentioned, a 'clean' handkerchief!

'Ingenuity comes out of necessity;' for example, back some 50 years ago, after a fishing trip, my father and I were transporting a lot of Canadian, Smoked, Rainbow Trout. We needed something to wrap them in; so, we brought a large roll of 'Cheesecloth (loosely woven, cotton cloth which resembles medical gauze)' with us for wrapping. We not only used the Cheesecloth to 'wrap' the Trout, but we would, also, use 'layers of it' for 'filtering' our water and 'Cowboy Coffee' as well – in both 'cup' or 'pot!'

Of course, a coffee filters original purpose was to 'strain out' the grounds from brewed coffee; but people soon learned, 'Paper Filters,' also, performed other essential functions – as the 'Cheesecloth' did for us:

- The 'oily' substances found in brewed coffee – 'Cafestol' and 'Kahweol' (diterpenes) – are stopped from entering the cup by the paper filter! This helps the consumer from ingesting significant amounts of the oil; which can elevate bad, (LDL) blood cholesterol levels – if one worries about such things.

- Filters can help to regulate (slow down) the drainage of 'Pour-Over' and other brewers; and increase the amount of 'steep' time.

- Sediment (mud) found in the bottom of the cup is reduced – resulting in a 'clearer cup!'

- Use of a 'Paper Filter' can make some coffees taste more, 'sweet or fruity' – and some say, even 'improve' the taste of 'canned' coffee!

- Filters can remove (debatable) acids, which can 'bitter' a cup of coffee! This could be a matter of 'taste' for the consumer.

- Paper Filters can help reduce or eliminate the 'newly determined health hazard' (in some states) of the potential, 'cancer-causing' agent of <u>Acrylamide</u>; which is produced during the coffee bean roasting process.

- Paper Filters (notably, the 'unbleached' ones), are suitable for 'Composting;' and earthworms like them.

- And More!

Of course, it is very challenging to be 'Snobby' when it comes to something as simple as a 'filter.' So, not to be left out, some of my 'Snobby' friends use a device to, not only store or hold their excess 'Cone, Paper, Coffee Filters' (in the form of a 'flip box' like mine shown here); or what looks like a miniature 'hatbox' to keep their round/flat filters.

For regular, flat bottomed, 'Drip' filters, I just keep them in their own 'bag' in a drawer; or in a small, empty 'coffee can;' if storing in our RV!

However, no 'Self-Respecting Coffee Snob' is going to be without the 'proper tools' to help 'simplify' the undaunting task of <u>separating</u> stacks of, flat bottom, coffee filters; mainly, in the form of what they call, a "*Séparateur Pour Filtres à Café…*" in other words, 'Coffee Filter Tongs' (a 'French named' product, manufactured in China… go figure)! Surprisingly, these 'Tongs' really work…  however, let's face it, exactly 'how difficult' is it to separate and 'pick up' a Coffee Filter?

I own a set – as seen above – just to 'rub the noses in it' of certain 'Coffee Snobs' in classes, when they start feeling 'a bit full of themselves.' I generally, end up asking them, "*What… you do not use a Séparateur Pour Filtres à Café,*" when they start getting a bit 'Snobby' with me. It may sound a bit 'nasty' of me, but I enjoy watching the 'Snobs' attempting to use the 'Tongs' for the first time – trying to determine 'how' to use them (unknown to most, the Tongs are very simple; and one, only, needs a 'stack' of filters for them to work)! Are 'Filter Tongs' truly necessary? Certainly not. I only learned about them while performing research for my previous book on coffee. However, there have been occasions, in which my hands either 'hurt' too much for various reasons (or the coffee filters behaved like plastic, vegetable bags in the grocery store) for me to separate them – of which, I used the Tongs!

 Some people enjoy using 'two' filters when they brew – including, some manufactures. Why would a manufacturer recommend the use of two filters? Well, it is just as I previously mentioned – it can be a 'health' issue! Some people think that if "*One filter is good, two or more have got to be better*!" Two filters are never needed unless one of the filters is made of metal, nylon, or plastic – and even then, the 'Paper Filter,' could, probably, take the place of a 'solid' one. The role of the 'Paper Filter,' is only going to be for 'filtering' out 'the nasties' which might in the coffee – and some 'mud;' or, 'slowing down' the brewing in some brewing methods – such as 'Pour-Over.' Or, as I previously mentioned, I use a Paper Filter in my 'K-Pod' brewer for the same reasons – especially, as I use only 'fresh' coffee, of a 'finer that average grind,' in my 'refillable' Pods!

[235]

I hate repeating myself, especially in print, but remember – when brewing coffee (at least in California) there is now a 'Health Warning' posted about Coffee and Cancer in many stores – even though, health organizations have 'annulled' such warnings! But, even with Coffees 'cancer-preventing' agents, it still contains compounds, besides caffeine, which can be of concern; namely, 'Acrylamide' – which is a, presumed, 'potential carcinogen'… at least, in Lab Rats; who drink an <u>overabundance</u> of coffee. What is supposed to happen is, the body, presumably, converts Acrylamide to Glycidamide – which can damage DNA, and cause cancer. Studies are inconclusive, in my opinion; especially, as Rats assimilate chemicals differently than humans!

When I use a 'Paper Filter' in addition to the 'Mesh Filter,' Acrylamide is all but eliminated; but, frankly, I my original idea was to help return some coffees to its original 'fruity' flavor, slow down the brewing, and to 'catch' any small, coffee particles, which would end up in my cup!

Question: *"Do Filters need to be 'pre-wet or warmed' before use?"*

Answer: No. 'Filters' do not have to be 'pre-wet.' However, 'prewetting' can either help or hinder the brewing process; as a 'wet' filter, will extract faster than a dry one – but, is more prone to 'tearing.' Also, 'pre-wetting' a filter can get rid of a nasty, 'paper taste' that some filters have.

Question: *"Is there any advantage to using 'bleached or unbleached' filters?"*

Answer: There are many opinions on this, but 'bleached or unbleached' filters do not make <u>any</u> <u>difference</u> in brewing a cup or pot of coffee. However, 'Unbleached Filters,' are 'less processed' than 'Bleached' ones; and thus, are more 'environmentally friendly…' at least, in theory. I, also, for some reason, seem to get a 'clearer' liquid with 'Bleached' filters; when using them to filter Colloidal Silver. I have not been able to determine if my coffee is any 'clearer' or not!

Question: *"Are all filters, essentially, the same?"*

Answer: No, filters can be very different; besides, the obvious, shape, size, or brand. Some filters are metal, some nylon, some cloth, and others paper; and each type have various 'degrees of weaves' (or pore sizes); which can help 'regulate' the flow of brewing coffee (thus, extending brewing time). Sometimes, if one is dissatisfied with their coffee, just a change of type of 'filter weave' can make all the difference in the world; even with 'K-Pod' brewers. For example, this afternoon, I used a 'reusable Pod' with some freshly, ground coffee. Whereas it would make a satisfactory, regular-sized cup of coffee, it makes a very weak 'mug full' – due to a larger amount of water used. By putting a small, 'Paper Filter' into the Pod, before filling with coffee grounds, 'brewing time' was extended by, approximately, 30 or more seconds – thus, brewing a <u>stronger</u>, bolder, coffee!

Question: *"Can I use a 'Kitchen Strainer' as a Coffee Filter?"*

Answer: Absolutely! In fact, I cover that very issue within this book. Any kind of 'strainer' can be used as a Coffee Filter – even items which are not strainers – including cotton balls, handkerchiefs, shirt sleeves, hats, cheesecloth, window screen and more! The only difference between any of the above (and an actual Coffee Filter), will the number of coffee grounds which will 'slip through' the strainer and end up in the cup. In other words, 'mud!'

Also, no 'coffee oils' (or other agents) will be filtered out of the coffee; as a 'strainer' (or sieve) does not have a 'tight enough' weave to capture something like 'oil.' If this is not an 'issue' for you, then, by all means, use a 'Kitchen Strainer!'

"Coffee is like sex; even when it is rather bad… it's still damn good!"

~ (Attributed to) Unknown

FROTHING/FOAMING/MICRO-FOAMING/CANNED FOAM/STEAMING MILK AND COFFEE CREAMERS

'Cream, Milk, Froth, Foam, Micro-Foam, Canned Foam, and Steamed Milk' are not to be confused with 'Flavored' Coffee Creamers… alternatively, even 'Flavored Foams;' not to mention, cans of 'pre-processed,' powdered Cappuccino or other mixes. However, these products can become part of the same coffee beverage… even an important part!

Some people (not Baristas or 'Coffee Snobs,') also use these products to create certain drinks – like 'make-shift' Cappuccinos; bypassing all foams of steamed milk and such. They add a teaspoon (of 'whatever powder') into their cup of Coffee or Espresso; and, maybe, add some milk or cream. I do this myself, sometimes, just for the taste – not to make a Cappuccino, but to add a 'Mocha' flavor to my coffee! In fact, at 3:00 a.m., getting up to write, I am a lot more inclined to put in a spoon of 'sugar-free,' Cappuccino Mix (or 'squirt in' a shot of Chocolate Latte Foam) into my mug of coffee than I am to make a real Cappuccino with my Espresso machine!

Nonetheless, this same reason is 'why' I might use my 'Keurig!' I can have my coffee within a few minutes – even with 'filling' my own Pods (but, I do, generally, fill my Pods the night before)! Do I have a 'true cup of Cappuccino?' Not in the least! I have a 'Cappuccino Flavored Beverage!' As long as I do not think (or attempt to pass it off to someone) as a 'true' Cappuccino, I am okay! Sometimes, I might even add a 'spoonful' to my Espresso; instead of 'Foam or Milk' – as the brand of <u>Cappuccino Mix,</u> I use, has 'powdered milk' as one of its ingredients. However, nothing takes the place of actual Milk or Foam! Therefore, even with a 'makeshift' Cappuccino, adding Foam to it is only going to make it better!

Actual 'Milk Foam' ('Frothed Milk, or Latte Foam,' as it is, also, known) goes directly on top of the cup of Coffee, Espresso, or a mixture of ingredients; and, it sometimes even goes on the top of Steamed Milk! However, a 'Flavored Creamer' might go into the coffee itself before the Steamed Milk, or Froth, is added; to help 'accent' flavor! Of course, any other 'augmentation' can be done to the coffee too (like one of my friends who likes to add Rum to his); or something like 'Cinnamon or Chocolate

Sprinkles' put on the top (in fact, some drinks <u>need</u> a 'little bit of everything')! The 'order' in the Foams or other ingredients are put into the cup, are what makes certain <u>types</u> of drinks!

Another confusing fact is that some people – such as me, again – not only use 'Foam or Froth' on top of their coffees but 'Flavored Foam' – layered – as well! Sometimes, I might forego any 'flavored creamer;' and use the 'Flavored Foam' as a 'Creamer/Sweetener.' For example, I might pour myself a cup of coffee in the morning and add some 'Mocha Latte Foam' to it; rather than a little 2% milk… to make the coffee a 'bit' richer and creamier!'

Other times, I might put one flavor of Foam on top of my mug, then a 'full layer 'of foam down deep into the coffee – using yet another flavored foam; as these photographs, below, indicate!

Of course, for a 'decadent' dessert coffee, I could always pour some Chocolate Syrup down the 'inside' of the glass, then put some Whipped Cream and 'chocolate shavings' on top – which, is something I tend to do when we have company (this makes a considerable variation of an Irish Coffee if Whiskey is added)! Generally, I will use a 'decaf' coffee, as 'desserts' are often served after dinner!

Fortunately, nobody I serve this concoction to notices that the foam comes out of a can – thinking, I am 'terribly clever' to 'flavor' my foam! It does tend to separate too quickly, however; so smaller cups should be used! Also, 'foaming below the surface,' with this kind of product, however, often, means putting one's fingers into the coffee. It is not necessarily the most 'hygienic' way to make a Latte – especially, for others – but I do enjoy the taste better when the foam 'squirts through' the coffee! If doing this, make sure you have 'washed' one's hands!

Back to Milks and Steams:

[239]

Whatever one might want to call their Espresso/Coffee's 'Thick Milk' (including boxed brands), most 'Home Espresso Machines' have 'built-in,' Milk Steamers on them; to make 'Steamed' Milk – technically, 'canned' foam is not necessary for most beverages… it is just a happy 'add-on!' It is best to follow the manufacturer's guidelines, to produce the best 'Steamed' Milk for one's machine! However, some devices – like my first (inexpensive) machine – neglected to come with any directions – so, for me, it was 'trial and error' to create 'Steamed Milk;' so I always used 'other methods' to create a 'foam.' However, there is something of a difference in making 'Steamed or Frothed' Milk with a 'Steamer,' as compared to other methods! What do they all have in common? They all start with <u>Ice Cold Milk</u>!

Depending upon the 'foaming' device, there are several different 'kinds' of milk one can use – however, the 'recommended milk,' should be ice-cold, <u>1%</u>, 'Low Fat' Milk; as it 'foams' easier. However, accepted results can, often, be achieved using a 2%, 'Reduced Fat' Milk – again, providing, that the milk is 'ice-cold' once again!

Surprisingly, 'canned' or 'boxed' brand, as seen here, (for a longer, non-refrigerated shelf life) can be used as well – but, perhaps, not as effectively as with fresh. I enjoy these 'Boxed Milks' – especially, for travel; and, always keep an unopened box in my home, Coffee Bar Refrigerator… just in case I run out of

regular milk! 'Boxed Milk' is available in many various brands; but the ones in the above photograph are an example of the brands I use… and they, often, are available at 'Dollar' stores! Again, the 1% 'froths' best… however, it <u>must be</u> very cold!

Besides just wanting to add some 'boxed milk' to a brew – and/or, be able to create a bit of 'Artwork' on the top of it – what the 'Home Barista' is looking for, is to turn 'Steamed Milk' into, the aforementioned, 'Micro-Foam (confusingly, <u>not</u> compared to an actual Froth);' which some Baristas say, *"Should be smooth like velvet"* and *"Akin to something like 'wet paint' to draw with!"*

I prefer it for the 'flavor and the texture' of the brew after the Foam/Milk has been added; rather than any 'artwork.' 'Steamed Milk' is <u>heavier</u> than Frothed Milk; because it does not have as much 'froth,' and contains less air! Therefore, it is put into beverages '<u>before</u>' Foamed Milk. The 'Steamed Milk' will float on top of the coffee; while the 'Foam,' will float on top of the Steamed Milk. Again, for something extra-rich, Baristas might put 'Whipped Cream' on top of the 'Foamed Milk!'

For some preferences, it is not uncommon to 'layer' Steamed Milk, over coffee, already, with an <u>additive</u> in it (as in the picture here). This mug has its coffee added, then a flavored, creamer, then a carefully poured (as not to mix), 'double shot' of Espresso. The next step will be adding 'Foamed Milk' on top of it – or, if it was not already full, one could add a 'Frothed Milk' on top of that; along with 'Whipped Cream' on  top of the Milk, and 'Sprinkles,' on top of the Whipped Cream! As a habit, I 'overfill' my mugs, so I must take a drink first… to make room for the Foam and Whipped; Cream!

If the Foam or Froth is going to be used as 'Artwork' (and who has not admired some of the art on top of some cups, drawn in the Foam) the key to creating the artwork is <u>practice</u>! Frankly, I have never gotten too creative when trying this – but, 'Coffee Snobs' love it!

Speaking of Artwork… well, some of us are not that artistic (or steady of hand) enough to pour a 'design' in the top of the foam! Making a leaf or something simple is not that difficult, but it can be somewhat intimidating. So, there is a way to '<u>cheat</u>' at this!

There is a product called a 'Spice Pen' (sometimes known, as an Electric Spice Pen)! 'Coffee Snobs' hate it – as it is not considered, *"True, Coffee Art;"* But I like it – as it allows 'non-artistic' people like myself, to 'decorate' their 'specialty' coffee!

This is the first and only kitchen gadget designed to make creative messages and drawings with all -natural materials found in food, such as cinnamon, instant cocoa powder, Hungarian paprika, ground parsley, ground sugar, and more. This offers a great way to surprise loved ones with a thoughtful message written in their favorite spice, and it's perfect for adding a little extra spice to parties and gatherings

Initially designed for use with cake decorating, Baristas have started using 'Pens' for 'decorating' the tops of coffee beverages – for when 'foam alone' is not enough! I have found it handy for when I am making the same (but slightly different coffee drinks) with foam or whipped cream on top, and I 'write the name of the person' in the foam with the Pen – which, is handy when I have prepared multiple coffees, with different additives!

The 'Spice Pen' is a 'vibrating' device; shaped, somewhat, like a banana. Some companies even sell it in various colors… especially yellow (making it look even more like a small, banana). Mine is white. A panel opens on its back, revealing a chamber to place Cinnamon, Chocolate Powder, Powdered Sugar, Spice, or 'fine-ground' Coffee. Turning it on, and facing its 'nose' downward, the chosen powder 'vibrates' out. The person holding the pen, now, has a choice to make; whether to 'write, draw a design,' or make a 'pile of powder' on the top of their foam. Some powders, however, might be too 'fine or coarse' to work well!

As one can see from the photographs on the previous page, it does not take much talent to draw a Flower, 'Jack-O'-Lantern, or a 'write a name;' and, I could see this device, easily, used in a 'pastry department' of a bakery, coffee shop, club, or classroom. From my experience, everyone seems to get a 'kick' out of being served a Cappuccino with their name on it, written in foam! However, there is still another way to 'cheat' at this (for those of us, which are even more 'talentless!' The way I prefer is to find a decorative paper template (available at art supply stores) and hold it over my 'foamed' cup. Then, it is a simple matter to 'sprinkle' Chocolate or Cinnamon powder on top – thus, making a creative design!

Getting back to Foams, unless ones Espresso Machine states something 'different and better,' Steamed Milk/Micro-Foam should be made this way:

1. Start with ice-cold, Non-fat Milk (about 34°F) in an ice-cold pitcher – mine, is Stainless Steel, and I store it in the freezer until use!

2. 'Steam' the milk, starting with the bottom of the pitcher, with the machines 'milk Steamer;' and by 'spin' the liquid, clockwise, with the 'Steam Wand.' Then, work the 'Wand' upwards to the surface of the milk – then, working just the top of the milk, 'steam' for at least 20 or more seconds. When working on the top of the liquid, have the 'Steam Wand' Tip just barely on the surface of the milk – so it can 'suck in' both 'air and milk' at the same time! Continue this action until the liquid is thick.

3. If it is possible, check the temperature of the milk. It should measure between 140°F – 170°F. However, with experience, one will be able to judge temperature by the texture and thickness of the milk. It does

not seem logical, that one would need 'ice-cold' milk to start with; when bringing it up to a high temperature… but it does seem to make a huge difference! Just do not allow the liquid to become too hot; as 'scalded' milk does not work well in coffee, espresso, or lattes! In the same sense, one does not want 'chalky' milk; from it being too cold from lack of steaming!

4. Slowly and carefully, pour the Steamed Milk/Foam into your cup or mug over the liquid coffee (designs can be 'poured' at this time). Decorate, if you wish, with 'Sprinkles, Chocolate Shavings, Cinnamon,' or other spices; or if creative, 'draw' pictures or designs on the top of the Foam with more finely ground coffee or Espresso grounds or spices. Sometimes, a Bamboo Skewer or Toothpick can help draw designs; or, a 'Spice Pen' as previously mentioned.

Other Frothing:

When not using steamed milk, canned foam, whipped cream, or just milk in my coffee, I will use one of my 'Milk Frothers!'

There are numerous styles of 'Frothers' on the market – and many different devices can be used <u>as</u> a 'Frother;' such as a blender, food processor, or even a 'Self-Stirring Mug!' I own this one in the photograph, myself! I have even been known to add a little fresh 'Whipping Cream' to the mug, first, or 'top' with it later! In this photograph, I am making an entire cup of 'Chocolate Froth!' I filled the mug, roughly, **1/3** full of 'Non-Fat' milk, and pressed the button the handle. When the milk had 'tripled' in size, I put in a few drops of 'Chocolate Cooking Extract,' sprinkled in a touch of Sugar, and turned on the mug once again. When ready, I poured half of it into my coffee cup. With the remaining Cream/Foam, I poured coffee over it for someone else!

When traveling, I might not have my 'Self-Stirring Mug with me; but I generally will have a small, Milk Frother! Working as a small blender – but without a carafe – I pour milk into whatever mug I will be using; then 'plunge in' the Frother and turn it on. In just a few seconds (rising and lowering

the spinning wand), the milk will double or triple in size! Again, should I want any added flavor, such as chocolate, it is a simple matter to add a 'drop or two' of Extract to the, almost finished, Froth. A touch of sweetener can, also, be added at this time. The Froth is, then, ready to use with any coffee drink!

However, for fun with students (and being something of a 'good, Coffee Snob,' myself), I will use my actual 'Milk Frother' – as shown to the left. Milk Frothers look very much like 'French Presses' – in fact, I have been known to use my French Press to 'froth' milk when in a pinch! Moreover, there are even models of French Press which 'advertise' that they *"Do both;"* 'Brew and Froth!'

Surprisingly, a bit less 'milk' is used when 'Frothing' than when 'Steaming.' On most 'Frothers' (although, it cannot, easily, be seen here) there is a 'white line' drawn on the glass carafe (at the milk level) – this is a 'Fill' line. Many people tell me that *"This is not enough milk to Froth"* – however, the volume of the 'Froth' usually is three or four times the amount of the milk poured; as one starts with 1/3 of a carafe of milk, and ends up with a full carafe of 'Froth.'

I know I have said previously, that one should *"Only use ice-cold, 'Non-Fat' Milk to make Froth/Foam;"* but this is just a guideline! I have friends who enjoy using Raw Milk, Soy Milk, Hemp Milk, Almond Milk, 'Boxed' Milk, Evaporated Milk, Powdered Milk, Goats Milk, Camels Milk, or just 'Whole Milk' straight out of the refrigerator; as just about anything will 'whip/froth' to a certain degree – because 'air' is added to the liquid by the 'frothing' action.

Again, use what you enjoy most; and, if one wants a 'sweetener' in it, do that as well! But, just a 'special note' here: if adding a 'sweetener' to your 'Homemade Froth,' froth it first – as one would with the previous methods I mentioned; then, when 'frothy,' add your 'pinch of sugar' or drops of 'flavored extract' to it… then, 'froth' a few times more to mix.

Any sweetener, flavorings, or other ingredients must be put into the 'Frother' after any 'frothing;' otherwise, the milk will not froth much! Just do not add too much of 'any' ingredient! If using a Flavored Extract (such as Chocolate) one or two drops is more than enough! Froth the milk first; then, when it appears to be 'fully frothed,' add your 'drop or two' of Flavored Extract; and 'froth' two or three more times. The milk, most likely, will not lose much of its 'froth;' but will be flavored and 'colored.' If the Flavored

Extract is 'alcohol-based (as most are),' using more than one or two drops may cause the 'Froth' to lose its 'air bubbles;' much in the same way, as adding alcohol to 'soda pop' my cause it to lose some of its carbonization. Generally, I suggest, if using any alcohol in one's coffee, put it into the coffee before adding the foam; to keep most of the foam intact!

The same is to be said when it comes to adding 'Sugar' (or a 'Sugar Substitute') to the 'Frother.' Add a 'pinch' of sweetener after 'frothing;' and 'froth' some more to thoroughly mix! If using 'powered' milk in a Frother, or blender, it is still best to 'froth' first; then add any other ingredients afterward!

Let's look, more, at Espresso:

"Espresso is to Italy, what Champagne is to France!"

~ (Attributed to) Charles Maurice de Talleyrand

BEVERAGES MADE WITH ESPRESSO

Food and dessert recipes aside, I do not have a clue, exactly, how many 'different drinks' can be made with Espresso – although, I am sure, it would be countless. However, I do know, that to 'make' Espresso… usually, no more that 45-55 Coffee Beans are 'ground' to 'fill' the average sized 'Portafilter!'

As with all forms of coffee, the most important factor is 'Pure Water' in which to brew. However, many individuals enjoy putting their own 'spin' on each recipe – such as one local 'Coffee Kiosk' I know, which uses Red Bull™, instead of water, in their beverages; and my 'health club…' which uses 'Vitamin Water' in their beverages – both, what I would consider, would 'gum up' an Espresso Machine! Most likely, the 'Espresso' part of a beverage is made with 'Pure Water,' and any other 'coffee-type' beverage which is used to 'mix' with the Espresso, has had Red Bull or something else added to it… thus, the reason for the word 'Infused;' that so many coffee shops tend to use for their 'unique' blends!

However, I might not use 'Espresso' made by my Espresso Maker at all in my drinks; choosing to use my 'Moka Pot,' instead – which would be less prone, to 'gum ups.'

Other times, however, I might do the exact opposite with my Espresso; and put it into my regular coffee – just to improve the taste (no Red Bull or anything like that). Sometimes, I will even make 'Turkish' coffee; but, if I (or my guests) do not care for the 'Turkish' brew for some reason, I may use the 'brew' as a 'Base Espresso' in some beverages. If nothing else, I will make and use some 'extra strong' coffee in a 'Percolator' to use; and add my 'Espresso or Turkish brew' to it! Everyone's 'tastes' are different, and options are countless.

Different growers, roasters, and retailers, sometimes, do the same! I am, often asked, "*How do all the drinks differ?*" Other than 'bean brands/types and roasts,' there is not too much difference; as, most commonly known beverages use the same ingredients: espresso, steamed milk, foam, and whipped cream. Besides, there might be a few other ingredients; such as cinnamon, chocolate sprinkles, or syrups which might be used. However, the list on the next page shows some of the more 'common beverages' which most Baristas agree to; and, which should be available and understood in most Coffee Bars – thus, the 'Coffee Snob' should know them as well!

However, do not be surprised if the same beverage ordered in different shops, might taste a 'bit different' than the previous drink, ordered someplace else – as every Barista will have their 'own spin' (choice of beans, grinds, brewers, and water temperatures):

Americano	Black Eye	Bonbon	Borgia
Breve	Ca phe sua da	Café / Bombõm	Café Affogato
Café au Lait	Café con Hielo	Café con Leche	Café Crema
Café Cubano	Café del Tiempo	Café Noisette	Café Panna
Cappuccino	Chai Latte	Cortadito	Cortado
Doppio	Double Latte	Dry Cappuccino	Espressino
Espresso	Espresso Romano	Flat White	Frappé
Galão	Irish Coffee	Latte	Lazy Eye
Long Black	Lungo	Macchiato	Mazagran
Mocha	Mocha Breve	Piccolo Latte	Red Eye
Ristretto	Turkish Coffee	Vienna	And More…

The actual 'ratios' of 'Espresso to Steamed or Foamed Milk' – or any additive – are so numinous, that I cannot put them all here in this book; and if brewing at home, it is best to simply 'lookup' on the internet, 'recipe directions' for each beverage; and make variations according to taste.

When buying an 'Espresso Machine,' expect to receive a 'recipe book' of some kind; which, should give several of the 'basic' beverage ratios. The main thing to remember is when brewing or 'pulling' for yourself… start with the 'basic guideline' of 'Espresso, Milk, and Foam' – and then, 'augment,' as to what you happen to enjoy most – as it is foolish to drink something that one

does not enjoy! I do know some 'Coffee Snobs,' however, who do just that…
as they want to 'stay in fashion,' keep with tradition, or not go against the
'wishes/recommendations' of their Barista or 'peer group!'

Honestly, I would doubt that any Barista would care, one way or another,
'how' anyone drank their Espresso! And, I am not about to drink something
which does not appeal to me; only to please someone else… whom, only
hours to days from the event, will even remember it!

Again, the thing to remember here is (and, I cannot say this enough), go
ahead and follow the 'recommended recipes;' but drink what <u>you</u> like – or,
augment with whatever 'extras,' <u>you</u> might enjoy! For example, an elderly
friend of mine (who was my sons 'adopted' Grandfather) used to enjoy 'trying
to copy' what the local Baristas would make… at least, when it came to
Espressos, Cappuccinos, or Lattes. 'Carl,' would end up adding a shot of
Whiskey to each of his beverages – regardless of what he made, or 'attempted'
to make. His 'Lattes' (or 'Caffe lattes' as he called them) were not even close
to what the Barista in the Coffee Shop made (especially, when one considered
that he didn't use an Espresso Machine, but only 'Espresso Beans' to brew
with); but still, his beverages were delicious!

*"Our culture runs on coffee and gasoline; the first, often,
tasting like the second!"*

~ (Attributed to) Edward Abbey, Essayist

EXTRA – ESPRESSO SHOT GLASSES

Just as there are countless 'Espresso Tampers,' and even more Espresso drinks, there are just as many 'Espresso Shot Glasses,' or, actual serving cups!

Some, like this one shown, come with 'measuring marks' all around it; to aid in the creation of beverages. The shot glass can be used to measure grind or liquid in teaspoons, tablespoons, milliliters, or ounces – unfortunately, this one does not list grams; as grams are considered a 'variable' unit of measure, according to the density/weight/humidity of the grind! In other words, one 'grind' of a particular roast, may weigh more than another of the same volume. So, if not using a Scale, each grind becomes more of a 'measure of volume' than of weight.

Some 'Shot Glasses' become 'Serving Glasses.' They can be as simple as a standard, shot glass – with no markings – or can be of various shapes, styles, and sizes, for attractiveness. The 'fancier' the glass, the more 'bragging rights' the consumer might have.

Personally, for serving, I use an Italian style (Bormioli Rocco, as seen in this photograph), for my 'bragging rights.' They come in assorted sizes (and can be seen throughout this book). I like them, as they have a removable handle; so, a 'too hot cup/glass' is not an issue. I paid $6.99 for each set of <u>four</u> glasses; and I use them, primarily, for serving Espresso or 'dessert' drinks. I have sets of them in 4, 6, and 8-ounce sizes; but I will use other types of cups, as etiquette dictates, that <u>are</u> the 'appropriate size and style' for serving. It does not matter in what one 'serves' their beverages; as long as one uses what <u>they</u> want!

Back to questions:

Question: *"Is a Coffee Cherry anything like a regular Cherry? What or where are the beans? Do they have pits which turn into beans?"*

Answer: 'Coffee Cherries' are different from the 'regular' Cherries we buy at the grocery store; but they are close in the fact that the Cherries or 'Berries' <u>did</u> start off being eaten! The 'seeds' or 'pits' are <u>different</u> from the pits one would find in a regular Cherry; and probably why, we do not refer to them as 'Coffee Pits,' but 'Beans' instead. They may form in numerous shapes and sizes; according to species.

People have 'eaten' Coffee Cherries for centuries; and, some people may eat, cook, or make wine with the Cherries today; however – by themselves, they are not very tasty!

As mentioned in the 'Introduction' of this book, legend has it that 'Goat Herders' first noticed their animals eating the fruit from the trees, then, 'behaving strangely' afterward. It was not long before people (including the clergy) started eating them themselves – and found, like the goat, they 'had more energy' after doing so. The actual reason of 'how and why' someone started making beverages out of the 'beans,' as well as the cherries, is anyone's guess. It was, probably, something along the line of: "*Waste not, want not!*"

One can only presume that somewhere, after starting as a 'wine' of some sort, someone 'boiled' the cherries or the beans separately; and somehow, the beans were considered 'something of a brew,' in itself; with the same or more 'energy' that the Cherries had, alone! In any event, consuming the cherries or 'Boiling the Beans,' and drinking the liquid (then or still today), would have been considered an 'acquired taste!'

Another theory is that the beans/seeds were 'accidentally' spilled into a fire – or, water 'boiled out' of a pot – and the 'forgotten' beans ended up 'roasted.' Again, "*Waste not, want not,*" probably came into play! The now, roasted, beans were (apparently) 'boiled once again' – to, perhaps, soften or 'rehydrate' them – and the dark liquid, was either cooked with or drunk. People liked it; and started 'roasting' beans on purpose! Then, someone came along and found that if the beans were crushed, they could make an even better, and darker, brew; plus, 'crushing beans,' to various degrees, seemed to, still, make the beverage taste different! Coffee – as a beverage – was born!

Question: "*What is 'Earthy' coffee?*"

Answer: 'Earthy' or 'Natural' tasting coffee, tends to be from a 'defect in processing' the coffee cherries or beans. Often, in more impoverished coffee-growing countries, or on 'second-rate' farms, the coffee cherries/beans are spread out onto the ground. Often, that ground may be somewhat 'wet' as well; from earlier batches of beans, or harsh weather.

Unfortunately, beans will absorb the 'flavor or smell' of the dirt they are laying one (just as they might absorb flavors and smells from a freezer). Oddly enough, this trait can be 'sought' by some coffee 'aficionados!'

Question: *"What does it mean if the coffee is 'Grassy – or, do I mean 'Gassy'?"*

Answer: *"Gassy,"* refers to a 'fresh beans/roast…' and they are still 'Degassing' after the roast. Most probably, what you mean is *"Grassy;"* another processing term, 'Bean Buyers' or Baristas use; meaning that the *"Coffee Cherries were picked too early or too green."* Some Baristas refer to this flavor as a *"Front Lawn Brew."*

Question: *"What does 'Musty Coffee' mean? Is it a flavor or an aroma; and is it in the beans or the cup?"*

Answer: *"Musty,"* is not so much of a flavor, but a 'smell;' leftover from the improper storage of the beans in a barn, the storage area, or even burlap bags, which were kept 'too wet' or humid. The aroma can occur in the beans, the grounds, or even be transferred to the cup!

Question: *"What can I do if I receive a 'crappy' cup of coffee from a coffee shop or vendor? What if I make my own 'crappy' coffee?"*

Answer: Let me answer that question with another question; if you went to a restaurant, and received a 'crappy' meal (perhaps, undercooked), what would you do? Would you eat it or send it back, to have the chef 'try again?' Alternatively, maybe, would you order something different? Most people would send the meal back; although I must admit, it must be 'pretty awful' before I do… however, my wife is quick to speak up on my behalf! 'Lousy' Coffee is no different – and, an assortment of reasons can cause it – in a Coffee Bar or at home. For example;

- The equipment is not clean (this happens a lot with 'Pod type' brewers).
- The coffee grounds are stale or old.
- The coffee is a 'bad blend;' created by the shop owner or 'Bean Buyer;' thinking they have created a *"Taste Treat."*
- The Barista does not know or care what he/she is doing.
- You have 'really pissed off' the Barista for some reason.

- There are 'fines/mud' (grounds) in the cup; from the 'wrong' or 'too fine' a grind – in other words, poor filtering.

- Whoever brewing the coffee attempted to 'reuse' grounds; or, mixed 'old grounds with fresh,' to 'save money.'

- Reusing cups or mugs – again, a 'cleanliness' issue.

- And, 'countless' more!

I recently had this happen to me; I went to a local Coffee Bar, 'drive-thru;' and, ordered a *"Large, Double Shot, Mocha, Caramel Macchiato – with Whipped Cream on top"* (their version of just Chocolate/Caramel Coffee)! I drove off to my first 'patient' appointment of the day; waiting for it to cool, somewhat, before tasting it. After pulling into my 'appointment' location, I 'turned back' the cups 'drinking tab' and took a sip – and practically spit the brew across the dash! I do not know what the mixture was; but it certainly was not a 'Double Mocha, Caramel Macchiato with Whipped Cream on top!' I was not even sure it was coffee! I opened it up to look at it. First, the cup was only three-quarters full – which I have had shops tell it, *"It is a safety measure; so, customers do not, accidentally, spill on themselves."* I call *"BS"* on this one too! Most shops do not reduce what is served if one is drinking inside the shop! Not serving ¼ of what is ordered, is just a crooked, 'cost-cutting' method by many, failing, 'Coffee Bars' with 'drive-throughs;' and just another way to 'rip off' the consumer! However, I digress!

Getting back to the drink, secondly, the coffee I ordered did not have any whipped cream; but had what looked, and tasted like, some 'left-over foam' on top. It did have some Caramel Syrup – which was 'poured' down the insides of the cup – but not mixed at all. Moreover, I cannot tell you what the coffee was – but, I am rather sure it did not have a 'Double or Single Shot' of Espresso in it – it was just 'coffee;' which tasted slightly old, weak, 'fishy and 'soapy!' I do not even think it had any milk in it – with the Barista, choosing to use only 'leftover foam' – instead of milk or whipped cream! It tasted, as I would imagine, being made with 'yesterday's dishwater; or, was some watered-down, leftover, generic coffee, of some inferior bean. It was awful, and I should have thrown it away!

I am pretty sure I was not given somebody else's order; as, other than myself and the shop employees, the place was deserted; and, I was the only one in the 'drive-thru' line. I may not have drunk it – but thought, *"Perhaps, it could be saved…"* at least, somewhat! When I returned home, I decided to 'experiment' for the sake of this book; and divided the, now cold coffee, between three large cups, added some caramel syrup, put a dash of chocolate syrup, then, added some fresh 'Moka Pot' Espresso – which I made with, 'freshly roasted', Chocolate/Caramel Coffee Beans. I 'topped off' each cup of coffee with a little 'Chocolate Whipped Cream' and 'Chocolate Sprinkles' on top. The coffee, was now, 'very drinkable;' and my family (whom I shared the coffee with) liked it just fine – as it no longer tasted of 'fish and dishwater!'

I did send an email complaint to the company; but they responded with, *"You should have brought it back immediately; we are not going to take your word for it, now, that the coffee was bad!"* Maybe, their attitude is why there were no other customers there that morning! I know, I will not be returning as a customer again! I had to reply to the shops' comment to me: *"Is it worth losing a customer forever – who is not going to give a good review to anyone – over a single cup of coffee?"* I had no return answer. I did notice, recently, the shop was, now, under 'new management;' with a new name – with 'girls in bikinis' to serve – perhaps, a reason to give it 'one more try!'

So, to answer more of the question of *"What to do…"*:

- Do like I did (if salvageable); and mix the 'poor' coffee with good coffee to make 'fair' coffee.

- Send the coffee back to be remade (and take a chance on the Barista spitting in the new coffee – as a friend, recently, told me has witnessed happening to him more than once).

- Give it to a friend, family member, or co-worker ('tacky' thing to do).

- Throw it away, taking a loss… (being, the most popular choice with people I have discussed this with)!

Question: *"Do I need to use 'fresh beans' for my 'Pod' or 'Drip' Coffee… alternatively, can 'canned coffee' be made just as good? Can I mix both canned and fresh beans in the same brewer?"*

Answer: 'Fresh beans' are always the best way to go to ensure flavor – as any Barista or 'Coffee Snob' will tell you! However, the taste of coffee depends upon many factors; the type of beans, their processing, their age, the roastery, how long the grind has been sitting around, if they have been 'nitrogen-flushed,' the type of decaffeination, the brewing process, have they 'degassed'… and more! Moreover, *"Yes,"* you can mix 'canned' with 'fresh;' as no laws are stating that you cannot! It might not make a 'great' cup of coffee, but it very well might improve an older grind. I would suppose it matters more about 'how discriminating' ('Snobby or cheap') one might be about the age and type of ones' coffee! If you still enjoy the taste… do it! I have some friends who, also, do this; but only serve the mixture to guests; or use the coffee in 'mixed' beverages!

Question: *"What water temperature should be used to brew? Is it true that different 'purities of water' require different temperatures?"*

Answer: As said earlier, there is much controversy over water and temperature; and, most of it is nonsense! The 'cold,' fact is, one only wants to use clean, pure, fresh, and hot (over 200°F) water to brew their coffee. However, to make the 'best-tasting' coffee, one might wish to 'fine-tune' their water temperature; to extract the most flavor from the beans and grind! Also, there is something to be said about the 'minerals' found in 'Tap Water.' If one makes old fashioned, 'Percolator' coffee, chances are they are 'used to' the taste of 'Tap' water – and, there is not anything wrong with that! I prefer to use 'Purified Spring Water' in my brewers, including Percolators – but, I did get used to drinking coffee from my 'Drip' machine brewed with 'Steam Distilled Water' once. I think one will find that most 'Coffee Bars' use only 'pure water' in their equipment, for the best-tasting brews. However, again, water temperature might depend upon the 'type' of brewer one is using – rather, than the 'type' of purity of the water! Even though, most coffee is advertised to "Brew at 205°F," the owners of the 'Roastery' I purchase from, only 'test and serve' their coffee at 189°F… and it is good!

When and using a 'Mr. Coffee' type, 'Drip' or a 'Pod' brewer, the device controls the 'water temperature' itself – so, it is not an issue. However, if using a 'French Press' or 'Pour-Over' device, the water temperature can make all the difference in the world! The same is true with other brewers; as every brewer manufacturer has their preference on 'what temperature will work best with their device!' In reality, water temperature 'boils down' to personal preference! I bring my water (whatever type or degree of water purity) to the beginning of a boil (211°F for my, current elevation) and then, remove it from the heat; and, by the time I reach the coffee brewer with it, the water has cooled down to just the right temperature; at least, for what I enjoy drinking! As far as *"Different degrees of water purity…"* temperature will not make any difference; except to help 'purify,' if brought to a boil!

Yes, I can taste the difference between some temperatures – generally 'high' temperatures, as opposed to 'low;' but frankly, for coffee served other than 'black,' I have found most people cannot taste much difference in temperature in any event – especially, once chocolate, caramel, creamer, sugar, foam, whipped cream, whiskey, and more is added to the cup!

Question: *"How much ground coffee (bean or canned) should I use in my Coffee Maker?"*

Answer: This is a very 'personal preference' type of question! The easy answer comes from the brands or machinery: *"Just follow the directions on the 'Can' or what came with the Coffee Maker."* Most likely, however, the two directions <u>will</u> <u>be</u> different! My advice is to try brewing with both recommendations; then choose from that – but, augmenting to suit your own, personal taste.

However, 'Coffee Snobs' may tell you, that there is an *"Exact ratio,"* as to 'water to grounds' when making coffee... except, when using a 'Pod' brewer. Then, the rule is, use a 'reusable' Pod, fill it with 4-grams of coffee, slightly tamper it down, then brew. Then, experiment with it – using a paper filter, somewhat 'more or fewer' grounds, more or less 'firm' tampering, or 'pre-warming' the machine before brewing!

The general rule with 'Drip' Makers is 'two tablespoons' of grounds for every '6 ounces' of water. However, many 'Coffee Aficionados,' claim that the *"Only way to make coffee, is to use a digital scale to 'measure out,' exactly, the correct amount of grind every time, in relation to water and cups brewed."* This technique is 'exceptional;' providing, one always uses the same beans, roasts, grinds, filters, and brewers – which is impossible, as beans and roast will 'change' from batch to batch! However, I have found an easy way to determine what to use, if traveling; I might only have 'one liter' (33.8140226 ounces) bottles of water available to use. I start with 60 grams of coffee grounds; for a 'full' pot of 'Drip' coffee (or half that amount (30 grams) if only brewing a 'half-pot.' Just remember, this <u>my</u> <u>own</u>, personal preference! I might change the amount of grounds, from pot to pot, depending upon my preferences!

A good experiment is to make coffee in one's own, every day, coffee brewer; using the 'usual' amount of grounds. Then, using a 'French Press' or 'Pour-Over' brewer, use the same amount of water and grounds. Chances are, one is going to find two 'different tasting' cups of coffee in comparison! This is, primarily, because different devices need different grinds, filters, and water temperatures; even if the roast and the ratio to water is the same!

Various techniques are going to give different results! Most likely, one will find they need to add 'more grounds' to the 'Pour-Over,' or 'French Press,' devices the next time they brew; and, perhaps, use a different 'temperature' of water!

Try it yourself with both 'canned' and 'freshly ground' coffee, also; but, note if the coffee is 'too weak, too strong,' if it is 'rich,' or has a 'fruity' or 'nutty' flavor, is 'too bold' – or perhaps, 'not bold enough,' et cetera. Make another pot – but this time, add or subtract, a small amount of dry 'grounds' (maybe, one tablespoon to start) to make the coffee taste the way you 'suspect' you might like best (or, to taste more like what you would find in your favorite Coffee House). Be sure to taste the coffee; before adding creamers or additives, so, <u>you</u> can 'get to know' your coffee! Use different temperatures if possible, as well as different brewing methods. Do not forget to try different 'water temperatures' as well as 'pre-wetting' your grounds and paper filters! This is what we do in my 'coffee classes;' we 'taste' every variation… however, there is no reason why one cannot do this themselves in their own home!

This is, also, where one needs to keep 'accurate notes' as to 'what' one has done to 'brew' their coffee; to achieve the <u>same</u> results, the next time. For myself, if I do not have the proper grind, I might find that I need to use almost <u>double</u> the number of grounds in my 'French Press' to approximate the 'richness' and color from my 'Drip' coffee maker! However, this is <u>only</u> if I am using 'canned' coffee; which I do not like doing! However, if I do use canned grounds, depending upon the roast, I might put them through my 'hand' grinder once again. This has the effect of, not only, grinding the coffee to the proper size for the device, but it helps to 'refresh' the grind (somewhat, if it is not too old) by reducing grind size and exposing more area to extract flavor!

Question: *"I only purchase fresh, Organic, 'Free Trade' Coffee Beans, because it 'helps' people; but I do not enjoy the taste of what I brew! Any suggestions?"*

Answer: Yes, I have some suggestions/observations: *"Fresh"* is always a good sign, *"Organic"* is great, and *"Free Trade"* is excellent… however, is the purchase of the coffee 'any savings' – or, 'will it help' anyone – if the drinker does not enjoy it; and, thus, limits or eliminates ones' future purchases?

In theory, if one does not enjoy a 'particular' coffee, they are not going to be purchasing, or drinking much of it, again! With some of my 'Coffee Tasting Class' students, I will recommend 'mixing' a blend of 'Free Trade' with other coffees – to help alleviate some 'guilt' associated with <u>not buying only</u> 'Free Trade Coffee.' Finding 'Organic' coffee beans is not that difficult; so, 'mixing/blending' flavors, roasts, and such, is not that difficult, either. So, if 'mixing' beans, one is '<u>still</u> <u>helping</u>' some people, in theory; but as one student told me… *"Sometimes, we have to be a bit selfish; and think about our <u>own</u> 'wants and desires' first… moreover, find a way to 'save the world' some other way!"* Well… that is true! I have told classes, as a whole, *"Drink what <u>you</u> enjoy… also, one can donate cash <u>directly</u> to the Free Trade Organizations; or to some other charity, individual, or family that needs it!"*

To reiterate, drinking what one <u>does</u> <u>not</u> enjoy, really does not help anyone; as the consumer, probably, will <u>not</u> be purchasing and drinking it again!

Question: *"Why is my coffee always bitter?"*

Answer: Bitterness is another 'subjective' thing. What is 'bitter' to one person, might taste 'sweet' to another! First, one must <u>choose</u>, not only the proper coffee, roast, grind, and water temperature, but determine if the method of brewing – and even storage – have had something to do with 'bitterness' too.

Coffee, which is '<u>over-cooked</u>,' tends to be 'bitter.' By 'over-cooked,' I mean, 'Coffee which sits over a burner, or heating element, for an extended period!'

However, there are things to do about that as well! First, 'bitterness' can be an 'acquired' taste (pro or con) – being, only, 'something different' than what one is 'used to' drinking – and, one can 'get used to' drinking, anything!

However, today, with all the 'flavored coffees, creamers, additives, whipped cream,' and such, finding a 'truly bitter' coffee is rather difficult! Most people would need to drink their coffee 'black' before they would notice much 'bitterness;' once all the 'stuff and junk' has been added to the cup! Once again, 'standardizing' on a 'particular' coffee and 'methods' are, often, the 'key to a good cup;' when it comes to 'bitterness' – but then, one can place a 'touch of salt' or even 'eggshells' into the grounds while brewing, to reduce some bitterness… if one is, already, sure that a particular 'coffee and method' is going to result in a 'bitter' cup! These actions are known as 'troubleshooting' the brew! Moreover, besides 'salt or eggshells,' there are many methods/options one can follow, to reduce (or hide) 'bitterness!'

Of course, the 'Old Standby,' of 'sugar, sweet cream, or whipped cream,' can 'sweeten up' some 'bitterness' – or at least, give that appearance (masking the bitterness). However, sometimes, if coffee is genuinely 'bitter,' going the opposite route can create an 'observed difference;' which can become part of the drink itself!

Some 'coffee additives' (powders or liquids) can become so 'overwhelming;' they become more of a dessert than a beverage; as in this photograph. It is called by Baristas, "*Meringue Coffee*;" and besides the 'Meringue,' it may even be topped with 'Raw Sugar' or some other ingredient! This is where, in my opinion, the coffee 'leaves' the 'beverage' category, and moves into a 'dessert' one!

Even if the coffee is 'highly bitter,' few people are going to notice it with this type of coffee (I suggest the reader look 'Meringue Coffee' up on the internet)! In keeping with 'a touch of egg' in one's coffee to control bitterness, this option takes matters to new extremes! Imagine, a cup of Coffee or Espresso; but, rather than a 'sweet creamer' or a 'topping' of 'Whipped Cream' on top (which can be an inch or two high), the coffee has 'several inches' of 'Sweet Meringue' on top... like a pie! Moreover, to top it off, 'Raw Sugar' crystals – or other toppings – are 'sprinkled' over the Meringue! The Meringue may even be 'scorched' just a touch (as a Meringue Pie might be).

Unlike 'Whipped Cream,' Meringue does not melt into the coffee; but, depending upon how thick – and if it is sugared, sprinkled, or 'scorched' with a kitchen torch – it can be 'dunked' into the coffee; and eaten like a doughnut! The 'Meringue' can take the place of 'sugar' or other 'flavorings' – especially when it has its own 'flavorings' on it! The best thing about it is, 'Meringue' is perfect for my 'lactose-intolerant' friends – who are unable to eat whipped cream or frothed milk (it does not help we people with diabetes, however).

Getting back to 'bitterness,' often, however, people confuse 'bitter tasting' coffee, with 'strong!' If one's coffee is 'bitter,' try using a 'coarser' grind – especially, with Espresso! Look at the coffee grinders in most grocery stores; 'Medium-Grind,' will have two or three different settings – depending upon the type of brewing method used! Try moving the 'adjustment dial' up one or two 'coarser grind settings;' to see if the coffee is less bitter when brewed. Most people will find that the coffee <u>will</u> <u>be</u> less bitter!

However, this is not to be confused with 'too weak' coffee. 'Too weak' coffee, as previously mentioned, is often confused for 'bitter' coffee also; but it is merely 'too diluted' a brew! Try adding a bit more grounds to the brewer; but, do not 'over-extract' – as <u>that</u> can add to 'bitterness' as well! It can all become very confusing!

A good example of coffee, which is often 'bitter' is '<u>boiled</u>' coffee! Unfortunately, some of my students have thought that 'bitterness' makes coffee *"Too complicated to deal with;"* moreover, they go to Starbucks, or some other Coffee Shop, to purchase their coffee 'ready-made' instead of dealing with the problem! When one realizes that it might only take 'one more click' on the 'grinder setting knob' to eliminate the problem… where is the *"Complication?"* Unfortunately, too many people 'give up' too quickly; and resort to having someone else (a Barista) brew their coffee for them. If one has the 'time and money' to go to 'Coffee Bars,' then I would suppose this is okay. However, for those us who might wish to 'watch' our money… then brewing own coffee, is the way to go – for the 'cheapest' and 'best tasting' brew!

Question; *"I have seen pictures of Coffee Beans on the Coffee Trees, and they do not look anything like the ones in the stores. Are they the same; or just dehydrated?"*

Answer: Yes, they are the same; but what you are looking at is the 'Coffee Cherry' (fruit of the plant), not the bean! The 'Cherry' looks like a 'Bing' or another type of Cherry; but rather than just having a 'pit' inside, it has a 'green/beige,' 'Coffee Bean.' However, unlike 'Cherry Pits,' the 'Coffee Bean' can be eaten; as well as processed, roasted, and turned into a beverage! It is only after 'processing and roasting,' that the beans 'look' like what we are familiar with in stores. The green coffee beans <u>are</u> dried first, however!

When it comes to *"Coffee Trees,"* there is some debate from the experts; that Arabica coffee beans *"Do not grow on trees"* – they *"Grow on 'shrub-like' bushes – known as the plant species of 'Coffea!"* *"Robusta coffee,"* on the other hand, many experts say, *"Only grows on 'trees;' and not bushes!"*

Surprisingly, Arabica plants tend to develop cherries; having <u>two</u> beans/seeds – each with a flat side, which face the other. When a plant produces only 'one bean' in the Cherry, it is called a 'Peaberry' – as their 'shape and size' are like that of a 'Pea;' (not in my opinion, but by the experts). Oddly enough, this 'deformity' is considered one of the 'tastiest' of the coffee beans; and is, often, sold in stores as 'high end,' Hawaiian, or other types/brands of coffee.

For a little more information, and, as mentioned before, Arabica plants grow best at higher altitudes; and tend to be more 'disease' resistant – as well as costing more… thus, many people consider Arabica to be the 'superior' bean – I know, I enjoy its taste more.

Robusta trees, however, grow more in the lower altitudes – in hotter (and more hostile) conditions – including sea level. These beans do not have the same rich taste as the 'higher altitude' beans – but they are 'cheaper' to both grow and harvest; and produce a larger yield… thus, they sell at a much lower price. Most consumers, who drink coffee made from 'canned' grounds, are drinking a blend of both beans; so that <u>both</u> flavor and cost can be enjoyed. Most Coffee Bars, however, primarily use 'Arabica beans' for a 'distinctive' taste.

There is a third type of beans, which few have even tried – called 'Coffea Liberica;' and it grows, primarily, in the country of Liberia. As of this writing, this species is not' given much attention or significance! There are a few companies, and farms, which sell 'Liberian' or 'Malaysian Specialty Coffee;' and it is considered an 'acquired taste' by some coffee drinkers! However, some 'Roastery's' are starting to 'mix in' a small percentage of 'Liberian Beans' into their 'Specialty Roasts;' again, for a 'distinctive' taste! I have to admit, the first time I tasted it, I was not told it was 'Liberian' coffee; and I told the person serving it, when asked for my opinion, *"Well, this does not taste very good!"* I am sure, if 'mixed' with other beans, it would taste a lot better!

Question: *"Should I worry about the 'processing' my coffee beans have undergone? Should they have been 'Wet or Dry' processed?"*

Answer: There is, really, not much in which to *"Worry"* when it comes to 'processing!' My experience has been, only coffee drinkers of 'extreme experience' (such as professional 'buyers/tasters' for coffee companies) can tell any difference between 'Wet, Dry,' or even 'Semi-washed,' beans. However, the actual difference is:

'Dry Processing:' some feel, enhances 'body and complexity.'

'Wet Processing:' enhances 'clarity and acidity.'

'Semi-washed:' tend to combine the two enhancements.

Frankly, I cannot tell the difference; especially, when creamers, Kahlúa™, or other additives, are added! If you <u>enjoy</u> your choice of coffee; do not worry about how it was processed… except when comparing growers or brands!

Question: *"What are 'Flavor Terms? Do I need to know anything more than what I like to drink?"*

Answer: Technically and realistically, one does not need to know <u>anything</u> more than *"What they like!"* I know some coffee drinkers who <u>never</u> change their orders in Coffee Bars – or ever prepare anything different than the 'same thing,' every day at home! However, one can never, continually, brew the same, every time, year after year. Yearly crops, beans, roasts, grinds, and even 'home' waters, temperatures, and brewers, all change… and often! What matters is what the <u>experts</u> call 'Coffee Terms;' which are 'general' terms, for judging most coffee. However, to press a point, there are 'terms' are that the 'average coffee drinker' should know and understand, when purchasing beans or drinking coffee.

The following terms, on the next pages, are some of the more familiar words/terms that one might hear 'Baristas' or coffee experts using:

"If this is coffee, please bring me some tea; but if this is tea, please bring me some coffee."

~ (Attributed to) Abraham Lincoln

COFFEE 'TASTING' TERMS

The list of 'Coffee Terms' seems endless – and, I have already addressed some of the 'terms' along the way in 'Questions.' However, one would expect 'Terms' to appear at the end of a book as a 'glossary' of sorts; but, in reference to the previous question, here are some of the most common, professional terms:

Acidity: This term relates to both 'roast and variety;' meaning, surprisingly, 'taste,' rather than acid content. Some 'Coffee Snobs' may refer to acidity as "*Lively or bright.*" However, the term of 'acidity' is more of a 'sensation on the tongue' and 'the roof of the mouth,' than a taste. Acidity can appear like the sensation of 'sweetness' on the tongue.

Acrid: A harsh, tart, sharp, 'biting,' or sour taste.

Aftertaste: Often, the way the coffee tastes or feels on the tongue when the 'vapors' are released after swallowing. Sometimes, 'Aftertaste,' can even be a different aroma left in the nostrils; or a taste in the back of the mouth after swallowing.

Alkaline: Another 'taste term,' for the sensation felt on the back of the tongue. 'Alkaline,' can feel dry and taste bitter; and is often found with some Indonesian, dark roasts.

Aroma: Aroma can refer to the 'smell' of any roast, variety, or mixture of beans. However, the term 'Aroma' can include 'brewing' as well; after all, who have not ever heard the phrase, "*Wake up and smell the coffee?*" It can smell, 'flowery, winey, like chocolate,' or more; and can even make some people hungry.

Ashy: Coffee has an odor like that of a fireplace or cigarette ash – and, (if one will pardon the example), causes urine to smell that way! This is caused, generally, by a dark roast; with a 'carbon-like' flavor.

Astringent: A 'salty' or 'sour taste;' sometimes leaving a 'dry' sensation on the sides of the tongue.

Baggy: A 'Coffee Bag' like flavor; from beans being stored for 'too long' in bags. Some people even sense a 'burlap' or 'feed store' type flavor or smell.

Baked or Bready: This is more of a 'roasting' term – at least, according to many Baristas. 'Baked or Bready' refers to beans which have been roasted over 'too low' a temperature, for 'too long' a time; resulting in 'flat' tasting coffee. When this happens, not all the 'chemical changes' in the beans happen; thus, they become, 'Baked or Bready' – with 'Bready,' being more of an 'under-roasted' term! This is an essential term for those who 'home roast!'

Balanced or Smooth: A term referring to both 'roasting and variety;' when 'appearance and flavor' do not compete.

Bitter: A 'Roasting' and/or preparation issue. With some beans, bitterness can be desirable. Robusta beans are 'more bitter' than Arabica; but 'mild' coffees can become bitter as well, if 'over-roasted' or 'over-extracted' during brewing.

Bittersweet: Stemming from 'roasting' once again; and sometimes, mistaken for 'strong.' Often, 'bittersweet' comes from 'poorly roasted beans;' and 'over-caramelizing' of the sugars within them. When the sugars are 'burnt,' it gives the coffee something of 'charcoal' taste.

Body: Mostly, but not entirely, relating to the roast. 'Body,' can be a 'textural quality;' or a 'perception' of viscosity (thickness or fullness) on the tongue. The Body develops with the degree of roast; and with 'over-roasted' coffee. It can, also, vary by the coffee's variety and origin. 'Body' can easily be noticed by brewing methods – as with coffee from a ''French Press;' where fine particulates may remain suspended in the liquid… or an 'Espresso;' which holds emulsified, coffee oils. Also, 'Body' will be noticed, when coffee is 'under-extracted;' as it will have a 'light' body.

Bright: 'Wine-like;' with a pleasant, tangy flavor.

Briny: Coffee which has been left over a burner too long – and has developed a rather 'brine-like' taste and smell – it is easier seen in coffee brewed with a little salt.

Burnt: Some people enjoy this aspect – or, a slightly 'burnt taste' to their coffee; when it is mixed with creamer, milk, or sugar. Sometimes, it is mistaken for 'tasting closer' to what one might receive in a Coffee Shop. Brewed Coffee may even have a 'burnt' aftertaste or leave a 'burnt aroma' in the nose.

[263]

Clean: 'Clean-tasting' coffee beans, and brews, have perfect caramelization of sugars; and are free of any other defects.

Complexity: When coffee is 'Complex;' this refers not only aromas, but textures, and tastes as well. However, 'Coffee Roasteries' often change the style of the roast; according to the region of the bean. This way, different beans can have different profiles – or, can be 'forced' to taste like other beans of different roasts through manipulation.

Crust: A layer (or 'crust') of coffee grounds; which float to the surface of a cone, bowl, or brewer, when first being 'pre-wet' and 'off-gassing.'

Earthy or Natural: Within limits, *"Earthy* or *Natural'* can have a pleasant note; but more commonly, it is a '<u>defect</u>;' in which the brewed coffee has an 'after-taste,' reminding one of 'soil.' It relates to poor processing; such as when the beans absorb flavor from the dirt, on which they were spread to dry. In some cases, this quality can add interesting characters to a coffee; and can even be 'sought after' by some drinkers.

Flat: Lacking in taste, aroma, and having low acidity. This, often, occurs when the coffee goes stale, the brewing temperature is 'too low,' or there is a lack of minerals in the water – as with 'Steamed Distilled.'

Floral or Fruity: Coffee having the 'scent' of flowers. Sometimes, this type of coffee is called 'fruity' as well.

Grassy: Picking/Processing related. The coffee may have the aroma, taste, or aftertaste, of hay, herbs, or a 'newly mown lawn.' 'Grassy,' most commonly, results from prematurely (unripe) picked Coffee Cherries. Most of the 'aroma' develops in the coffee during the roasting process – which is not surprising; as roasting, coffee smells quite strong. If one is not careful, the aroma and taste of 'burning' can easily be transferred to the beans!

Harsh: Coffee, which is bitter, disagreeable, or of low quality.

Hidey: A 'leather-like' taste – usually, found in East African coffees.

Malt-like: Coffee beans having the aroma of malt or cereal.

Medicinal: Coffee having a 'medicine like' taste or smell of iodine – usually, found with cherries which have been allowed to dry while still on the bush.

Mellow: 'Higher altitude' coffee; which does not have a strong aftertaste. Generally, found in a 'medium' roast. Most people do not realize this, but roasting can affect acidity – by either increasing or decreasing bitterness. However, without a certain amount of acidity in the coffee, when brewed, it would taste 'flat!' Too much acidity, however, can cause a 'puckering' of the mouth – as with a lemon – and make the mouth feel 'parched.' Acidity can be a complicated term!

Musty: Coffee tasting moldy or of mildew; often this is the result of poor storage conditions. Improper aging also can cause 'mustiness;' while proper aging can contribute a 'desirable' flavoring.

Neutral: Coffee beans with no predominant taste sensation; which are, often, used in blending.

Nutty: An aroma of fresh nuts.

Papery: Coffee beans which have been stored in 'poor quality' paper sacks or bags; or, coffee which has picked up the flavor of a paper filter – which, has not been 'pre-wet' before brewing – often, flavors found in 'old' or poorly made filters.

Quakery: A 'peanut-like' flavor from 'under-ripe' or 'under-developed' coffee beans. These, generally, come from smaller farms.

Rancid: The taste or smell to describe old or 'decomposing' coffee.

Rubbery: An aroma or taste of Rubber; sometimes, associated with Robusta beans.

Scorched: Just as the name implies; beans which have been 'scorched' by roasting 'too hot;' or by a grinder which has been 'over-worked!' Often, one knows they have 'scorched' beans just from the smell, once cooled.

Skunky: An aroma left, when 'roasted beans' are 'heated' to quickly; leaving an unpleasant 'Fishy' or 'Skunky' smell or taste. Sometimes a similar condition is seen with 'unclean' equipment or 'poor' quality water.

Sour: Not to be confused with Acidity, 'Sour' is an unpleasant, sharp, or 'tangy,' sensation; caused by cherries which have begun to ferment before processing. Alternatively, unpleasant-tasting, 'Acrid' (an unpleasant taste or smell) – as if contaminated by vinegar. This taste can occur in low-growing, or poorly washed, coffees; but it more commonly occurs with 'under-roasting.' 'Sourness' can, also, happen when brewing with water, which is 'too cool' in temperature.

Tainted Coffee: An unpleasant flavor caused by too much 'pulp' in fermenting parchment.

Tobacco: Similar to 'Ashy;' but with a somewhat 'burnt tobacco' taste or smell to the coffee. Again, 'smell' can turn up in urine; by drinking too much of the coffee.

Watery: 'Watery Coffee' is just as it sounds… Coffee which is too 'weak;' in other words, a mediocre 'coffee to water' ratio in brewing.

Winey: An 'acidy and fruity' taste, smell, and mouth sensation; similar, to drinking wine.

Woody: 'Old tasting' coffee; often, with the taste or smell of 'dry wood.' This 'taste' is, often, caused by improper storage.

Back to Questions:

Question: *"Cups… what kind of cup or mug should I use? What kind is 'proper?' Is cardboard, okay; that is what I get at the coffee shop?"*

Answer: *"Proper"* cups or mugs?" There is no such thing! Of course, we all know people who say, they will *"Only drink coffee out of their Royal Doulton China, with the hand-painted Periwinkles;"* as a character in one of my favorite BBC shows used to say. In my case, however, my mother's *"Hand-painted, 'Royal Doulton, Old Country Roses."* Still, others think 'Styrofoam' or 'Cardboard' cups are fine. Some people do not appear 'too adverse' to drinking straight out of the coffee pot – as my photograph on the cover of this book, indicates!

It does not matter what one drinks their coffee from; and, the people I 'hang' with, generally, think: *"Who cares?"* Ideally, the more insulated the cup or mug, the longer the coffee will stay warm – 'that,' is all, many of us care about! Some 'Snobs' will say, *"Only pour your coffee into 'pre-heated,' ceramic, cups or mugs; that is… if 'fine china' cannot be used."* Surprisingly, if 'brewing' directly <u>into</u> a cup, the 'Snobs' <u>are</u> correct about 'pre-heating' the cup or mug!

It does not matter 'into what' the coffee is poured; keeping it 'warm enough,' until it is fully drunk, is far more critical than the appearance of the cup or mug! Nonetheless, there <u>are</u> things one can do. For example, when waiting at a tire shop, automotive garage, or my wife's hairdresser (when 'Complimentary Coffee' is being served to patrons), I will take <u>two</u> of their 'Styrofoam Cups;' place one inside the other, and then fill the inside cup with coffee – in other words, making my own 'insulated,' Styrofoam cup!

A "*Proper Cup*" is going to be in the 'eyes of the beholder;' so, one should try to do their best with a mug (possibly, insulated) which will keep their coffee warm for an extended period! Moreover, remember, never pour any more coffee than one can drink in a reasonable amount of time; or if you have to, use an electric 'Cup Warmer!'

Let's look at some more 'Cup' Sizes:"

"Coffee makes us severe, and grave and philosophical."

~ (Attributed to) Jonathan Swift

COFFEE BAR CUP SIZES

As varied as types of coffee beverages, 'Disposable Cups' are just 'as varied' in coffee bars, restaurants, and gas stations! Ceramic cups are easy enough; as they tend to be 4, 8, 12, or 16-ounces in size; that is, in most 'drink in' Coffee Bars. However, several people in one of my Coffee Groups once complained, that they *"Cannot get a small 'take out' cup of coffee, the same size in every shop they go to – at least… to go;"* and, *"No disposable sizes match 'ceramic' sizes!"* I have seen many 'ceramic and disposable' cups which are similar in size, but people in my Coffee Group are correct… *"Sometimes, it is difficult to order the same size, 'take out' cup in every coffee bar."*

For example, rather than a size called 'small,' they are often given a choice between what would be a 'regular' or a 'large,' cardboard, fiber cup! It seems that every coffee bar has their 'own version' of what 'sizes' are; and, unfortunately, many 'so-called' Baristas are not aware of the size difference or different names associated with 'competitive' shops… moreover, why should they? The reverse is true as well; as I cannot tell you how many times, I have ordered a 'large' cup of coffee and received just a 6 or 10-ounce cup! For example, my favorite 'Coffee House' (which is, also, a 'Fresh Bread,' Bakery) serves only 6 and 10-ounce sizes – whereas, I can get 16-ounces (or more, if I bring my cup) at my local ARCO am/pm!

This is not surprising, as some, coffee bars 'rename' assorted sizes to suit themselves – and to confuse the customer; such as: *"Primo, Medio"* or *"Tassimo…"* meaning, small, medium, and large. Some might call a 'large' cup, a *"Grande,"* or a *"Texas Cup!"* Alternatively, they might use something else entirely – like a 'European' method of measurement; meaning, a number, such as, "225, 336, 460," and sometimes "570…" for 'milliliters;' and thus, confuse we Americans more!

However, still more Coffee Bars, like a new place I, recently, visited, might use the cups 'order numbers;' like a *"22043"* (complicating matters that much more). As I did not know what a *"22043"* was, they had to, begrudgingly, explain it to me… when I just wanted an 'Extra Large' coffee. In other words, what would be an 'Extra Large' in one coffee bar, might be something entirely 'different' in another bar; or called something which would either be misleading to the 'uninformed,' or 'confusing' to someone else… such as a 'number!' Of course, 'numbers,' instead of 'common size names,' confuses the issue that much more!

Another, popular, 'Coffee Bar' in my town, calls their 'Extra Large,' a "Big Gulp;' like what one would find in a 'convenience store' when purchasing a soda pop! Moreover, even more of these 'Coffee Bars' are having 'custom' sizes made; to, not only, look <u>bigger</u> by being tall, but be narrower to hold less! This idea came from some restaurants and liquor bars, which have custom, bar glasses; designed to look large, but, often, hold the same amount, or less, than a standard bar glass. I recently tested both beverages at a bar; and found that <u>both</u> their coffee and beer, served in 'regular' sizes, were only 2-ounces smaller than their 'Extra Large!' I checked again at another Coffee Shop, and found their, standard, 'Large' – was only 1.5-ounces different from their 'regular!' 1.5-ounces is the equivalent to only 'one' swallow more of coffee; and frankly, paying up to a dollar more for only 'one swallow,' really 'rubs me the wrong way!' There is getting to be much deception, apparently, in coffee!

My advice, when visiting a 'new' coffee shop, look to see if there might be a display of 'sizes' on the wall or countertop; and note their names. Otherwise, when in doubt, instruct the clerk to, "*Show me your sizes!*"

'Disposable' cup sizes:

4-ounce Disposable Cups – Sometimes called 'Extra-Small, Mouse, or Demitasse (French, for half-cup).' These are the 'smallest size' of what coffee bar lids come with – which serve more than most Ceramic, Demitasse cups; which hold 2 to 3 fluid ounces.

8.45-ounce Disposable Cups – Often, called a 'Small, Short, Demi' (but not short for Demitasse) or simply… 'Cup.' This size is 'popular' for events, festivals, and exhibitions – as they are the closest in proportion to what a 'standard' cup of coffee at home would be… 8.45-ounces. Lids are advisable for this size; especially if they are going to be used in a car or an environment with lots of movement. Sometimes, cups may even have two 'wings' on them; so, when folded together, they form something of a 'handle' (or 'Ear' – as it is known in many cultures). Lids might even have a 'plug,' of sorts, for the 'drink' opening, when 'carrying' (luckily, 'plugs' will fit most sizes of cups).

12-ounce Disposable Cups – Most coffee bars will consider these to be "*Tall*." However, in some 'Coffee Bars' like Starbucks, it could be considered a "*Small*." However, still, others call this size a "*Medium*" or a "*Double/Double*."

This is the standard industry <u>size</u> for most 'store-purchased' coffees. Of course, it comes with a lid and 'plug' in some places! Surprisingly, in some, smaller, stores, 12-ounce is the largest they sell.

16-ounce Disposable Cups – Perhaps, the most confusing size, this cup is known as a *"Grande"* in many shops, or a 'medium' at some shops like Starbucks. Just as the names can vary, 'sizes' do as well – and, they are not all 16-ounces… when one would think they would be! In some coffee shops, 16–31 ounces can, also, be called a 'Trenta.' However, it might be called a 'Venti' – which, sometimes, is 16 ounces; but generally, 20–24 ounces in other stores. A 'Sedici,' is 16-ounces… unless more; as, with a 'Large Double/Double,' an 'Extra-Large,' a 'Supreme,' a 'Premium,' an 'Abe Lincoln,' a 'Big,' 'Big Mo,' a 'Big Guy,' a 'Griffin,' or an 'Alto;' which (confusingly) all can be of <u>any</u> size besides 16-ounces, apparently, when given 'special' names! As one can see, unless one specifies, *"16-Ounces of Coffee,"* they are liable to receive any size – and, very confusing!

20 – 24-ounce Disposable Cups – This cup size is, also, often called the *"Venti"* at some bars like Starbucks, but just a 'Large' or 'Extra-large' in most others. Many 'Coffee Snobs' enjoy the fact that some bars have 'special names' for this size. This cup, also, happens to be the same size as a standard 'British Pint' glass. Some of the names, also for this size, can include an 'Extra Large,' a 'Paul Bunion,' 'Super-Sized' or 'Big-Gulp' – which is anything more substantial than a 20-ounce!

Are you confused by reading all this nonsense? I know I am! I wish there were only four sizes, with no 'special' names, terms, or numbers; such as a 'Small, Medium, Large, and Extra Large;' that everyone would follow!

Another Question:

Question: *"What is a Peaberry? Is it Coffee or a brand?"*

Answer: 'Peaberry' (a.k.a. Caracolillo), as mentioned previously, is a type of coffee bean – in either Arabica or Robusta. Typically, the 'Coffee Cherry' has two, 'oval-shaped,' seeds/beans; and, those seeds (by growing side by side) each develop with one flat side, facing each other. Sometimes, however, only one of the seeds is fertilized; so, only one 'mutant,' seed develops. The seed grows more into a 'pea-shaped and sized' oval – but <u>without</u> a flat side; which gives the bean its name, 'Peaberry.'

Some people feel that 'Peaberry' coffee, not only roasts better – as their 'more rounded' shape can 'roll' in the roaster easier; thus, creating a 'better roast,' which tastes better as well! An excellent example of a 'Peaberry' bean would be 'Kona' Coffee, from Hawaii. Traditionally, Peaberry Beans are roasted to a 'Dark Roast!'

'Coffee Snobs' enjoy Peaberry Beans; as they are rarer; and, generally, more expensive (high-end) than other types… which is, sadly, sometimes more important than flavor! Personally, 'high-end' aside, I do think Peaberry Coffee tastes best when comparing types.

"What on earth could be more luxurious than a sofa, a book, and a cup of coffee?"

~ (Attributed to) Anthony Trollope

[271]

'COFFEE SNOBS' AND MONEY

'Snobs…' we all know at least one; (or, perhaps, we are one)! As I stated previously, I know people who will buy furniture at a 'designer' furniture stores, and pay a fortune for it; when, they could purchase the same brand, dye lot, and style, at a store like Sears®, Walmart® or on the internet… just so that they can 'brag' about cost and where they purchased the furniture! 'Coffee Snobs,' are a lot like that; and some will only purchase 'certain coffees,' from 'certain stores, certain farms, certain roasters, or certain coffee bars!' Unless coffee is a 'Designer Coffee,' some 'Snobs' will not buy it at all! Until recently, even I did not even know there is such a thing, as 'Designer Coffee' – but, this type, is all some 'Snobs' are willing to buy – and, at a 'high price!'

Of course, there are brands of designer, 'Canned Coffee,' too; which cost more than other brands. When I was a kid, the only 'designer' or 'high-end' type of coffee (although, it was never called that) was 'Yuban' coffee. My Dad considered Yuban to be the '*Best*;" but only drank 'Sanka brand' for its lack of caffeine. However, my Mom would, sometimes, buy a 'Caffeinated Coffee' at 'Woolworths;' to keep her awake in the afternoons. Mom (as not to tempt Dad) would buy Folgers or Hills Brothers, but never the more expensive Yuban! She liked it well enough; but did not like the 'higher price,' over a 'generic' brand; stating that she, "*Could not taste the difference!*" But, she could, indeed, 'taste the difference' between her 'Folgers' and 'Yuban.' So, the only time she would purchase Yuban, was if she were hosting a party or wedding; and only wanted the 'best' for her friends and guests. After my father died, however, she did start purchasing Yuban; as she was 'only' brewing for herself; and never had more than one or two cups of coffee in the morning – with only one in the afternoon as well, to help 'stay awake!'

Today, even less expensive, 'packaged coffee' – such as Folgers – have their own 'high and low' end coffees in 'Traditional, Regular, Gold, Original, Dark, Pacific Coast, 'Café,' Electra-Matic, Special Delivery, Private Reserve, Black Silk, and countless 'decaffeinated' other roasts. However, there is a distinct difference between these coffees! The difference is found in both the 'roast' and 'bean mix;' rather than anything else. The same thing can be found with 'Fresh' beans and roasts; and many 'name brand' coffee bars, sell nothing less, for a much 'higher price' than what one could buy themselves to brew! This has surprised many people; but, look at the 'fresh roasted' coffee beans available in most grocery stores! My local store sells (what they call) "*Fresh Beans*," for only $6.99 per pound. However, they advertise they sell other *"Bagged Beans,"* such as Kona – from Hawaii (Peaberry), for $19.00 per bag! However, then, they might sell a 'generic type' of 'designer beans' – such as Chocolate, Macadamia Nut, Hawaiian Kona Beans – for a discount price ($9.95 per 12-ounce bag) as well; which are, surprisingly, and sometimes, <u>fresher</u>! Moreover, I will not even go into the 'Pod' issue with price and brand at this point!

'Designer Bean' names aside, often, these beans could even be considered 'factory seconds;' meaning, they were *"Too low grade,"* to make a 'high end,' or, what is known as a 'Private Reserve,' brand of coffee. Is this considered, 'misleading the public?' You bet it is!

Many of the stores capitalizing upon the term, 'Hawaiian, Kona,' do so, just so they can charge a 'higher price,' for a 'poorer' product! However, the consumer can 'educate' themselves regarding these beans! If one looks at the bins of 'Fresh Beans' in the store dispensers, often 'Peaberry' beans will be in a bin marked *"Hawaiian Kona;"* as opposed to any other bean. Nevertheless, one needs to look closely at them! If all the beans are 'rounded,' then, they are a true <u>Peaberry</u>. If they have one flat side, then they are not; and if 'some are and some are not,' then the bin is a 'mixture' or 'blend' of beans – which might taste good… however, is not what is 'advertised' – and, certainly not 'worth the high price' that 'Peaberry' commands! Surprisingly, some people will pay this price 'regardless' of what they are purchasing! From what I understand, right or wrong, stores can 'get away' with this practice, because they are calling the coffee, *"Hawaiian Kona"* rather than Peaberry!

In the same sense, many of the 'deals' that consumers get on 'Designer' beans, in 'Discount' Grocery Stores, may be good beans… however, they are in the store for one reason only; the store '<u>buyer</u>' received a 'great deal' on them from the wholesaler… because they were getting old!

Try this experiment, yourself, for fun. Purchase a small bag of beans (few bags are sold in pounds anymore – but in 8 or 12-ounce sizes) and grind them yourself. At the same time, purchase some, similar, '<u>fresh</u>' beans from one of the overhead bins and grind them. You might even buy some 'pre-ground' coffee of a similar type or brand if available. Take them home, and immediately make two or three 'Pour-Over' brews; and, observe the 'Bloom' in each one! The 'pre-bagged' beans/grind, probably, will not have much of a 'Bloom;' whereas, the 'Bin Beans' should 'Bloom,' nicely. 'Blooming,' is an indication that the 'bagged beans' are older; and have, already, 'de-gassed.'

Perhaps, they could even be somewhat stale – if they have 'sat around' in the store or warehouse for an extended period. The same thing can be found with 'pre-ground' beans; but, the 'lack of 'Bloom' will be noticed even more! Of course, there is an argument as to 'how long' the roasted beans can stay 'fresh;' but we will save that for some other venue.

I ran yet another test at my local market a few months ago; I had a 'Marking Pen' in my pocket; and I picked an 'obscure,' ground coffee for sale – of which I could easily remember the name. I reached back to the 'last bag' on the rack; and with my marking pen, made a small 'dot' in the upper, right-hand corner of the bag – something that nobody, besides me, would ever notice!

I checked the shelf and bags, again, a few days later; and one or two bags were gone from the front of the shelf; but the bag with the dot, was still in the back. One week later, I checked once again; and there were one or two more bags gone – but, my 'marked' bag still there in the back! A few more weeks went by, and I happened to check the rack once again; and the rack was <u>full</u> again; but the bag I had marked was still in the back, in the same spot I had left it – meaning, the supplier <u>had</u> come in, and had replaced the 'sold' products with new; but had not 'rotated' the bags on the shelf, as he should have.

A month later, I checked again; a few bags were missing, but my marked bag by was still in the same spot in the back of the shelf. One more month went by; and again, the 'marked' bag was still on the shelf! This coffee, had become 'old' without ever being opened; not to mention, there was no way of knowing 'how old' the coffee was when the store had purchased it, or how long it had sat on the shelf before I found it, but I did know that at least 'three full months' had passed since I had marked it! The coffee <u>was</u> <u>not</u> 'fresh!' Had I purchased it and compared it to a similar type/brand of what I knew was 'fresh' (designer or not), I am sure I would have both 'seen' and 'tasted' a difference!

The moral of this tale is (for the money), it is hard to beat 'fresh roasted,' and 'freshly ground' beans!

However, freshness is not the only 'story' to watch for; there are other factors to consider when purchasing fresh or canned coffee – as, not all brands are alike; and other brands of beans, may be 'just as good' as the 'top of the line' brands! For example, I was lucky enough to sit in on a 'Jamaican, Blue Mountain Coffee' test, several years back, while on vacation in Jamaica.

Although, there are only a couple of 'high end' coffee plantations there, 'low end' (or smaller) coffee plantations are abundant (if one can say that… as Jamaica is a small island).

Early one morning, the bartender of the resort, of which I was staying, served me, and a few other 'early risers,' coffee from a 'French Press…' prepared, right in front of us, with the most 'expensive brand' of 'Blue Mountain' available. The bartender, however, appeared to be drinking a coffee from a different 'Press.' When questioned, he informed me, that *"High-end, Blue Mountain brands were reserved for the guests – but the employees could drink all they wanted of the 'regular and cheaper' Jamaican brands. It is not bad, in fact,"* he said, *"Technically, the coffees are identical! Only the 'tins' (Cans) are different,"* and he offered the group of us a taste from his Press to compare the difference.

He poured us each '¼ cup' from his 'Press;' and sat it down next to our cups of Blue Mountain. None of us in attendance could taste, see, or smell, any difference; just as the bartender had suggested to us! He told us there was *"No difference in 'High Mountain,' and regular (mountain) Jamaican beans…"* and he was correct (although, I am sure many 'experts' would disagree with me) – at least, with what he was serving! The so-called, 'Blue Mountain' was a 'Designer Brand,' in name only… at least, there in Jamaica; where it is common! The only things which could have been different were the Plantation names (brands), 'picking' (which was probably the same), and the 'processing' (which too, was perhaps the same as other brands)! The altitude/elevation of the grower we tasted was, relatively, the same as the 'Blue Mountain.' Both brands we tasted, were made from Arabica Beans! I wish I could have tasted and compared several Plantations beans – especially, the lower altitude beans… but no such luck!

From what the Bartender told me, the truth of the matter is, *"There are three 'grades/kinds' of 'High Mountain' coffee grown in Jamaica; which, are 'graded' on size, shape, and defects. Tourists expect to purchase and drink 'only the best,' high priced brand; but we 'locals' think we are drinking the best too – as we do not see or taste any difference!"* I would have to agree with him, from our short test!

The 'Coffee Experts' tend to judge the coffees elevations; with beans grown between 1,500 feet and 3,000 feet, being called *"Jamaica, High Mountain,"* (which is what the resorts serve; and is bagged and sold in American stores). Some Arabica Coffee is grown below 1,500 feet – which is what most of the locals drink – but usually, mixed with the 'Blue Mountain' or 'High Mountain,' – and called 'Jamaica Supreme, or Semi-Low Mountain'

[275]

(not, 'Green Mountain,' which is a popular misconception). True, 'Low Mountain,' we found, could be either Arabica or Robusta grown. Some of the 'local' coffee was a mixture of the two beans; and unless served each type, side by side, I have enjoyed all coffees – even the 'cheapest brand' of what some of the 'locals' enjoy – and frankly, if it is brewed well, I cannot taste to much difference between most coffees! When coffee is good, the only 'primary' difference... is in price!

Here, on the West coast of California, 'Blue Mountain' is an imported, 'High End,' expensive coffee (from the Eastern, Blue Mountains of Jamaica); which, mostly, 'well off,' true "Coffee Aficionados, or 'Coffee Snobs' purchase! One does have to be aware of 'Scams,' however; and sometimes, even experts are, unwittingly, 'scammed.' Stores are only as good as the 'buyers' who pick out the beans. As a warning, many brands of 'Jamaican' coffee may pass themselves off as being "*High Mountain*;" but, are in reality, the 'Lower Mountain;' or more likely, a mixture... like what some of the 'Jamaican locals' drink.

I am often asked, "*Is it possible to be on a 'tight budget;' and to 'cut back' on cost... while still enjoying good coffee... even if you cannot afford 'Jamaican High Mountain?*" You bet... even if one is something of a 'Coffee Snob!' For example, I have friends who greatly enjoy 'flavored' coffees, macchiatos, cappuccinos, and lattes; but did not have very 'discriminating' taste! They merely went to the nearest 'Starbucks' in which to 'order' every day... <u>multiple</u> <u>times</u> per day, in fact! They did not care about 'brand names,' or particular stores... they just knew what they enjoyed drinking – more or less as a hobby – and Starbucks was nearby! They were always wondering "*Where*" their money had gone, by the middle of the month!

After taking a good, close look at their finances one day, they <u>quit</u> going to Starbucks every morning, afternoon, and evenings (for 'dessert' coffee) and started going – of all places – to their local ARCO am/pm™ gas stations; where, they could make 'flavored coffees,' of multiple sizes, for less than <u>half the price</u> of Starbucks (this is where I had first learned of ARCO!)! They did not mind the 'change in flavors – as they already found 'change' enjoyable; in comparing "Starbucks, to 'Dutch Bros.,' or 'Peets Coffee!'

In other words, they did not 'give up' any favorite, coffee; they just '<u>cut back</u>' on the amount they were spending... in other words, they were 'giving up' the 'Designer' or 'Name Brand' coffee; not to mention, the 'added snacks and desserts' they would, sometimes, purchase to go along with their coffee order!

They had tried, quite by accident, 'ARCO am/pm coffee' and liked it; at least, enough to purchase it again! Then, they found they could have 'many different coffees' to choose from – and, if they still wanted a 'snack,' could get one as well… moreover, they <u>still</u> were able to 'save money' over going to Starbucks! Eventually, they even started bringing in 'Travel Mugs,' like mine, to fill; so, they could purchase a 'larger' coffee and save even more money… as the station would give a 'substantial discount' to those not using 'Cardboard Cups!' Apparently, gas stations would like everyone to believe, that 'cardboard cups' are 'unbelievably,' expensive; while the coffee is not!

Some of my friends who do the same, and previously 'frequented' Coffee Bars,' have claimed to me that *"Over the course of a year, we were able to save the 'down payment' on a new car just by 'cutting back,' and buying a cheaper (in price) coffee!"* I would have to think, they must drink a lot of coffee to do this; but I do know there can be quite a savings by <u>avoiding</u> 'Designer' coffee and 'Name Brand' coffee bars! Of course, in any event, the coffee is only as good as its Barista (in this case, a store clerk). Frankly, I have not received as many 'weak or nasty tasting' coffees at ARCO, as I have in some coffee bars!

The wonderful thing about this type of coffee is, not only can one put <u>all kinds</u> of additives in it, for a 'custom' flavor, but they have a large assortment of sizes (if not bringing one's own container) as well – all defined by 'how many ounces!' In other words, if I am on my way to treat a patient, and I know I will not have time to 'drink' all my coffee before it goes cold, I can quickly get a 'small' cup of coffee in a fraction of the time it would take me at a coffee shop; and it's cost it would be, approximately, half that of Starbucks or even McDonalds; and, I know it is not going to be only ¾ full!

Let's look at some more 'Troubleshooting;'

"A day without coffee is like… well, I have no idea."

~ (Attributed to) Unknown

TROUBLESHOOTING AND TIPS

Troubleshooting coffee? Is that even possible? Yes, it is possible – and even probable – when it comes to roasting, grinding, temperatures, brewing, and also filtering. However, 'troubleshooting,' cannot <u>only</u> apply to ones' coffee, but water, grounds, and even the cups ones' coffee is poured in as well! In fact, even the 'appearance' of purchased coffee can be 'troubleshot' – so to speak!

Again, when I was working with the County, I would run into 'Coffee Snobs,' who would look at my 'ARCO am/pm' cups and make 'snotty' remarks. I watched others, experience the similar things; the only difference was, 'they too,' were something of 'Coffee Snobs' – even though, they were 'saving' money, by buying their coffee at ARCO am/pm™! However, they had a unique way to, somewhat, 'hide' the fact: many of them purchased paper, plastic, or leather sleeves – which would be 'custom imprinted' to say their name or something 'clever' on them. These sleeves would cover (at least, at the time) the ARCO am/pm logo… moreover, presumably, save the person some embarrassment; thus, proving the adage, *"Out of sight, out of mind."* Frankly, I never cared what anyone else thought about my coffee!

In my opinion, they would have been better off doing as I did…use an insulated, 'Travel Mug!' But, the 'Coffee Snobs' would turn their noses up at that as well – not viewing it as a 'status symbol' (if there can be such a thing, coming from a Kiosk)! For myself, I just wanted a 'large,' coffee; which would stay hot for an extended period! Using an insulated, travel mug, 'troubleshot' my 'keeping my coffee warm long enough,' problem. Of course, I could have used a 'Cup Warmer;' but I did not want it 'walking off' at work!

The 'Travel Mug' I own – as shown here – even has an optional, 'color-coded,' handle to use, to 'tell it apart' from others. I have an 'orange-colored' handle on my mug; while my wife has a 'purple' one, and my son has a 'green' handle on his! Being 'well insulated,' it will keep a beverage hot or cold all day. Although I do not like to advertise or promote <u>any</u> particular product, I have been able to drive from Northern California to Reno, Nevada – some three hours away

– with the beverage staying hot – spend some time walking around, and then

travel back again in the same day; with the coffee remaining, at least, 'lukewarm.' Of course, that was a 'test' of the mug – as coffee never lasts that long for me! 'Snobs,' may or may not like them; but they are practical and fit within my cars cup holder!

However, after losing one of our cars, and badly damaging the other, in the devastating, Paradise, 'Camp Fire' (named after 'Camp Creek Road,' where the fire started… not an actual 'campfire') we have since purchased a new Mini-Van; with multiple, tighter-fitting, cup holders. Although my 'Travel Mugs' will fit, they do not fit as well as I would like. So, I have replaced them with this smaller, non-spill mug! It keeps my coffee just as warm, for just as long a period – it just isn't quite as large!

Of course, insulated cups come in many types, colors, and styles – again, depending upon ones' budget. 'Insulated' is not always necessary; as 'Electric Cups' are available. In the same sense, there are '12-volt' models for use in a car, RV, or boat too. However, for desktop/home use, a simple 'Cup/Mug Warmer' (or 'heater,' in the form of a 'Mini-Hot Plate') is entirely proper. The one I use, turns 'on and off,' automatically, with cup weight! Often, however, I have left my desk, only to return hours later, to find a 'heavy skinned' cup of coffee; evaporated down, to almost empty! Again, when it comes to the 'Coffee Snobs' that I know, many will not go for something like a 'Desktop Warmer;' as that would be too much like *"Cooking"* one's coffee!

Other Troubleshooting Issues:

Oddly enough, with 'types of filters' as numerous as they are, I receive many questions regarding *"Grounds in my coffee!"* 'Getting rid of them'… alternatively, 'preventing them, to begin with,' is yet another form of 'Troubleshooting!'

Preventing grounds (or mud), is really, simple! I did it myself, just this morning; before writing this. I made a pot of 'Percolator Coffee' on the stove; to photograph for this book. Not wanting to 'waste' the coffee after photographing it (and, personally, enjoying 'boiled' coffee), I poured myself a mug. However, I could see that it had some 'floating grounds!' So, not wanting to waste anything, I

'pressed' my 'Single-cup, Pour-Over Brewer,' with a 'Wire Mesh Filter' in it (of course, a paper filter could have been used just as easily), into service. I set it over a new mug (as seen in the previous photograph); then, 'poured' the first mug into it – going through the Mesh Filter! The Mesh Filter caught all the loose grounds and 'mud;' and the coffee came out 'clean and clear!' I, then, topped it off with my favorite creamer, and it was ready to drink. Problem... 'troubleshot!' 'Coffee Oils' were not 'filtered' out; but one can't have everything!

There are other ways to 'troubleshoot' a 'lousy' cup of coffee – as, seldom, have I ever seen a cup or a pot which could not be made 'drinkable' somehow – besides, merely throwing it out! Sometimes, all it takes to 'save a cup' is to use a 'Flavored Creamer;' or, to mix the 'poorly tasting' coffee with an 'excellent' brand! Basically speaking, 'troubleshooting bad coffee' can be 'frightfully simple!' For example (and to reiterate what I have previously mentioned elsewhere in this book), if the coffee tastes consistently weak, most likely, the grind is 'too coarse' for the brewer used. Alternatively, perhaps, there are 'not enough' grounds being used. Try adding another tablespoon of grounds when brewing the next time; or 'grinding' the coffee 'finer.' Also, 'steeping time' or water temperature might be increased or decreased; or, add an 'extra filter,' if possible, to 'slow' brewing time.

One more option, to make the coffee 'taste better,' is to add a shot of Espresso to it; and create a 'make-shift' Latte or Cappuccino. Of course, if time is not an issue, there is 'Double Brewing' coffee as well – which will hide a 'multitude of sins!' 'Double Brewing,' is, actually, yet another form of 'brewing' coffee in itself – for a 'unique' taste (and achieve more caffeine).

If the coffee tastes 'bitter,' then perhaps the beans have been ground 'too fine.' A 'coarser' grind might be tried the next time. However, if the coffee is a 'Dark Roast,' try lowering the brewing temperature to 195°F.

If the coffee is 'too strong,' try a shorter steeping time; or using less grind; and, if using a 'French Press,' do not allow the brewed coffee to 'just sit' in its carafe and continue to 'brew.' Pour it into an insulated or 'pre-warmed' carafe of some sort, immediately. For an 'instant' fix (not instant coffee), if the coffee is 'too strong,' dilute it, slightly, with some water or creamer! If all else fails, 'cook' with the coffee; or save it for 'drinking cold" – with, perhaps, a 'weaker' brewed coffee... frozen into ice cubes. As the cubes melt, the 'overly strong' coffee will 'weaken' as well. However, often 'too strong' coffee is 'just a matter of taste;' and those drinking it, 'get used to it' very quickly!

If the brew of a 'French Press' is 'Thick or Gritty' (or leaves sentiment in the bottom of a cup), the 'Press Filter' is not fitting 'snug enough' against the glass of the press carafe; and needs to be replaced. Another choice would be to use a different type of brewer; such as an 'AeroPress, EuroPress,' or 'EsproPress' (which have 'smaller weave filters); or, use a 'built-in,' cone filter of some sort, in conjunction with the 'Press.' One last possibility, depending upon ones' Coffee Press, is to cut, and custom fit, a paper filter to place on top of the grounds; before inserting the metal filter/plunger.

When it comes to brewing, again as previously mentioned, it does not matter what kind or brand of 'Coffee Maker' one uses; as 'brewing good coffee' has more to do with 'how' one brews it (and the water) than the coffee or device itself! The main issue, for my money, is to keep the machinery clean – both, inside and out! 'Coffee Oil' tends to build up in carafes – so, make sure to always start with a clean 'Coffee Brewer.' Nevertheless, take exceptional care not to leave any soap residue in the carafe!

When using a standard or electric 'Percolator,' do not allow the coffee to 'sit' on the burner (or, be left 'turned on' if electric) for very long – unless, one enjoys the taste of 'smoky' or 'burnt' coffee! The same thing with 'Automatic/Drip' machines – as grounds sitting in the device too long before drinking, can ruin the coffee (therefore, most 'Drip' brewers have separate 'grounds' and coffee chambers)! If the 'Drip' machine has an adjustable 'keep warm' timer, set it for just as long as you think you will be drinking coffee. Do not allow the coffee to 'warm' indefinitely! If need be, again, 'pour the coffee' into an insulated carafe; for 'slower' drinking.

Another, related, 'Troubleshooting Tip…' only brew enough coffee to drink at the time; but then, brew more coffee, if 'seconds' or 'thirds' are needed! However, do not add new grounds to the existing/used coffee grounds – or, one will end up, most likely, with a 'bitter' pot or cup of coffee!

'Coffee Grounds' are best used once; however, I do know people who have 'fine-tuned' this process to achieve consistent results with a mixture of fresh and 'once used' grounds for 'smoothness' – proving, 'anything' is possible! I watched one of my students do this one day, when he brought his own 'Drip,' coffee maker to class; to compare to other brewing methods. After brewing and drinking one pot, he added 2/3 of the amount of fresh grounds to the previously used ones; and brewed as usual. Comparing one cup of the previous coffee to the new, there was only a slight difference in flavor and body.

Of course, one can always use a small 'Desktop Mug Warmer' – as I, previously, mentioned, to extend their 'drinking' time. This is how my coffee stays hot (but, not too hot) the whole time I am drinking it (to be honest, as I am writing at the same time, I do tend to 'forget' that I have coffee waiting for me)! Using a 'Mug Warmer' keeps my coffee from becoming cold before I can drink it! Typically, coffee temperature never drops below 'drinking' level – and, it is not so 'hot,' as to 'cook' the coffee – at least, for a short period! Space permitting, my 'Warmer' sat directly to the left or the right of my Laptop keyboard -as shown above! It now sits to the right of my computer; as I am righthanded, the electrical plugin on the right side of my desk, and I had a 'close call' when it came to 'almost' spilling on my laptop keyboard!

It is best to start with a 'scorching' cup or mug of coffee – preferably, in a 'pre-warmed' cup or mug; as the coffee will stay 'hot' for a much longer time if it starts hot! Just do not plan on 'reheating' the coffee with a Cup Warmer! I will, often, 'pre-heat' my cup by directly 'pouring' a bit of hot coffee into the cup and 'swirling' it around a bit before filling; or rinsing my cup under hot water in the sink! Once filled, the coffee temperature stays in the 'drinking' range longer.

Another option, if adding 'cold creamers' or 'powders' to a cup, one might wish to 'heat' the coffee a bit more in a microwave; so, when the additives are put in, the coffee does not get too cold. I, often, do this with my 'Drip' coffee; as it does not come out of my old device 'hot enough' for my taste… moreover, is not 'hot enough' to, quickly, dissolve a 'powdered,' sugar-free creamer. This, also, tends to heat the cup as well – at least, with older cups or mugs. Then, it is an easy matter for a 'Cup Warmer' to keep the coffee hot!

Brands of 'Mug Warmers' are countless; some plug into the wall outlet, while others use a USB cord; which can plug, directly, into a Laptop or Desktop computer – which is handy for writers my like me! I have seen a few 'battery operated' versions; but I do not recommend them for anything other than, perhaps, camping; as since the device is 'making heat,' it is going to 'use up' the batteries quickly! If using one, do not plan on using it more than a day or two before having to replace the batteries; and the USB models (which seem to be increasingly difficult to find) 'wear down' laptop batteries fast too!

To keep a larger volume of coffee warm, consider using an 'insulated' serving carafe; as shown here. However, then, what should one do with 'left-over' coffee in the carafe? Well, first, do not 're-heat' it, that is for sure (however, we have <u>all</u> done it)! Moreover, do not add it to the coffee maker to help make 'new brew;' however, as mentioned before, there are many delicious recipes for 'Double-Brew' coffee on the internet!

If one is going to try to 'save' some left-over coffee, consider placing it into a carafe of some sort; and, storing in the refrigerator – drinking it as a 'Cold Brew.' Alternatively, pouring it into ice cube trays and freezing; to use later in 'Blender' drinks, or for cooking/baking recipes, works well too! One more way, is to freeze the left-over coffee into 'large blocks or rings;' which can be used in a 'coffee punch' of some kind. As the punch is depleted, the frozen 'coffee chunk,' will 'replace' the drunk coffee – allowing the punch bowl to be 'full' for a longer period. I use either a 'bread pan' or a 'Gelatin Ring' to 'freeze' my coffee in – depending, upon the 'shape' I am looking for!

As previously written, I usually end up 'brewing <u>fresh</u> coffee for cooking or baking purposes;' however, there is nothing wrong with using 'day-old,' refrigerated coffee in ones' recipes. Stronger coffees, usually, work better in most desserts; where a predominant 'coffee flavor' is needed. In some cases, one might wish to use a few drops of 'Coffee Extract' as well. 'Watkins™' makes an excellent tasting product! However, in most cases, strong coffee, alone, should suffice! For something different, 'ultra-fine,' ground coffee can be used as a <u>dry</u> <u>ingredient</u> as well – in fact, I often use it as a 'Rub' on meat! Alternatively, as a 'worst case' scenario, 'Instant Coffee' can be used.

Getting back to 'troubleshooting,' if using '<u>Decaffeinated</u> <u>Beans</u>,' try only to use a quality, 'naturally decaffeinated' product! There are many good brands, in both 'fresh' and 'canned' versions, in which to choose! It even comes in 'Pod' form now; however, as I do not enjoy filling up our local landfill with 'Plastic Pods,' I purchase good, 'Decaffeinated Beans,' grind them, then put it into my 'reusable' Pods. That way, plastic Pods do not end up at the dump… where they will last decades! I do not even have to do this now; as I have 'K-Pod' brewer which has a 'removable/replaceable,' ground basket. This way, I can make up to two cups (or fill my Travel Mug) with decaf coffee; and, eliminate even the 'reusable' Pod!

Many brands of coffees are decaffeinated by using chemicals – which cannot be good for anyone! However, the 'best tasting' decaffeinated coffees, are those who only use 'water' (or a 'Swiss Water' process) to decaffeinate. Watch for 'Naturally Decaffeinated' signs or symbols when buying ground coffee or beans. However, if purchasing at a 'Coffee Bar' or 'Coffee Broker,' the counter person or Barista, should be able to help in choosing a good, 'Naturally Decaffeinated,' coffee for you. As far as 'taste' goes, the same recommendations for grinds, amounts, or brewing times apply! Just do not be surprised if your 'Decaf Folgers' does not taste like your 'Regular' Folgers! A lot of 'troubleshooting' may go into making a good, 'standardized' decaffeinated coffee!

For 'cooking' with 'bean grinds,' one may grind the beans in either a coffee grinder, blender, or food processor; as the ground size is not that critical when it comes to cooking. However, 'fine to medium' grinds are, usually, best for most baking needs; unless the coffee is used as a topping. Then, coarsely ground coffee tends to be best. However, this is a matter of taste! I prefer my 'coffee toppings' to have the consistency of ground Cinnamon!

For the most coffee flavor, however, 'freshly grinding' whole beans will add the most <u>intense</u> flavor. If not using a blender, whole beans may be placed in a plastic 'zip-lock' bag and crushed with a rolling pin or even hammer. I, personally, use a marble (for pastry) rolling pin on a marble slab for this purpose – especially, with 'Chocolate Coated Espresso Beans' – where 'crushed' beans, are used as a topping (I enjoy big, chewable, chunks)!

Coffee mills, brewers, and recipes aside, there is one main thing people can do to 'troubleshoot,' or improve, the taste of their coffee… and that is, to 'doctor up' the taste for themselves with a 'flavored' liquid or powdered creamer – that is unless they only drink their coffee, 'black.'

In theory (and, providing one enjoys putting 'additives' in their coffee), once we make the 'best coffee' we can, pouring in a 'flavored creamer' is going to make the coffee 'taste better' (hopefully)! I, always, enjoy a bit of 'Sweet Cream' or simply, milk in my coffee; but personally (especially, with 'generic, canned coffee'), I like to use a bit of 'French Vanilla' or 'Sugar-free, Powdered,  Chocolate/Caramel Creamer' in mine – to make it more of a dessert, coffee. Moreover, this time of year, (Fall/Winter, when this is written) there are many diverse types of creamers available; such as 'Chocolate Peppermint' or

'Pumpkin Spice;' as well as 'Hazelnut, Candy Bar,' and many more – and, these can all become part of a good 'food or dessert' recipe as well! Unfortunately, many people get 'hooked,' (so to speak) on 'flavored creamers;' and use them regardless of how good the coffee truly is! Sometimes, we need to 'retrain' ourselves to enjoy just a cup of plain, black coffee… alternatively, at least, enjoy one with only a little plain, cream or sugar in it! Those are the kind of people I enjoy having at 'Coffee Tasting' classes or parties – those who can learn to truly enjoy coffee, without filling it full of 'stuff and junk!'

Of course, I keep saying, the primary purpose of one's coffee is to enjoy it; so, consumers should put whatever they enjoy into it! However, I ask that people do not discount the simplicity and sweetness of plain, black coffee; and hope most people will, at least, 'taste their coffee' before augmenting it!

So, many different variables will begin to come into play as one brews – and the coffee drinker is going to have to make decisions as to 'how' they enjoy their coffee… besides, just adding a 'flavored creamer!' One needs to experiment with their brew; for example, directions might call for three tablespoons of a specific grind per 6-ounces cup of water… however, one might prefer four or five tablespoons instead, just because, they might enjoy their coffee darker, 'bolder,' and with more caffeine. This action is nothing more than 'troubleshooting,' once again! Of course, the reverse is also true; especially, when brewing with different beans, roasts, and brewing methods.

Depending upon the type of bean, one might find that 'fewer' grounds may make for a 'smoother' coffee. For further example, I enjoy my freshly ground, Dark Roast, 'Black Silk' Coffee… extra dark and strong; but, enjoy more of a 'Medium/Dark Coffee' when brewing Hawaiian Kona. Also, just a 'Medium Roast/Medium Brew' seems to be best for me, when it comes to generic, canned, breakfast, or 'restaurant' coffee! Of course, everything needs to be 'standardized' upon, and proper notes taken to 'keep track!' 'Choices…' are all about 'troubleshooting!'

Other people might do what would be considered 'strange things' to improve (troubleshoot) the taste of their coffee. Again, as I mentioned before, I had an elderly and widowed, Norwegian uncle whom would 'scramble an egg' into his coffee before brewing; but then, another uncle who held back the egg; but would put broken eggshells into his pots 'ground basket.' As a child, I found both methods, somewhat, revolting – as, neither ever 'filtered' their brew. Moreover, I never considered 'cooking' an egg in coffee, as part of 'troubleshooting!'

What 'revolted' me more, was when, yet a third, Norwegian uncle would not only 'crack an egg' into his Percolator, but place the eggshells into his ground basket too – to not only take some of the acids out of his coffee – but to end up with a 'coffee-flavored,' and gritty 'Poached Egg' to eat for breakfast as well. He used to say, he *"Had the best of both worlds this way… good coffee and, 'a uniquely flavored,' Poached Egg for breakfast!"* As he, also, put 'a lot' of salt in his brewing coffee, (again, removing some bitterness from the coffee), the egg was *"Pre-salted for him,"* he would claim!

I never tried his 'Coffee Eggs!' However, 'Salt and Eggs' were as far as his 'troubleshooting' would go! He always let whatever brand of 'canned coffee' tell him 'how many tablespoons' of grounds to put into his Percolator – and his tablespoons, were always 'heaping!' *"The Hills Brothers must know how much coffee to use, or they wouldn't be in business,"* he would, often, say!

He, sometimes, would do a similar thing with 'Hardboiled Eggs;' dropping one or two, room temperature, fresh eggs, into his brewing coffee, then eating them later in the day for lunch or with a dinner salad. The eggshells (supposedly) removed any bitterness and acid from the coffee, while the eggs 'hard-boiled' in the Percolator. Even if they were not 'done enough' to begin with, they would sit over heat and 'boil' all day while he, slowly, drank his coffee. These eggs, I did try, once; and 'Coffee Flavored, Hardboiled Eggs,' indeed, were different; although, sometimes a bit 'salty.' His coffee had no 'bitterness,' either – but again, it was 'too salty' for my taste! Perhaps, he was onto something; and should have reduced the amount of salt he used!

He, incidentally, drank (slurped) his 'boiled' coffee, what he called, *"The Norwegian way;"* which was from a saucer, rather than the cup – allowing him to drink the coffee *"More quickly;"* as he said it would *"Cool faster!"* I have yet to try this method!

My uncle seemed to cook everything in his Percolator – just because it seemed 'easier' to him, being 'widowed!' *"No dirty pots and pans for me,"* he used to tell me. I could understand the 'coffee thing,' (as he achieved – in theory – less bitter coffee) but he cooked other things <u>without</u> any coffee – and, he taught me 'how' to do it, as well, while in college! It made sense to me at the time!

On the following pages, are some of what 'we kids' in college used to do (but, what no 'self-respecting, Coffee Snob' would ever try); cooking in their coffee makers… moreover, many people, aside from college, still do to this day, just like my uncle used to do! Just look at the internet; it is full of recipes! Here are a few recipes of what we used to do in college:

"Coffee, the favorite drink of the civilized world."

~ (Attributed to) Thomas Jefferson

EXTRA – 'COOKING' WITH COFFEE MAKERS

Even though this section does not have anything to do with coffee, it does pertain to individual coffee makers; and I would be remiss if I did not at least touch upon 'Cooking' with Coffee Makers.

The best 'Coffee Maker Cooker,' is an 'Automatic Drip,' Coffee Maker. However, with a little experimentation, other coffee makers may be used as well. For example, I have a patient who uses her 'Pour-Over' brewer, to make 'Coddled Eggs;' much the way my uncle used to with his Percolator. Whereas, if he wanted a 'Coddled Egg,' he would either leave the lid off the Percolator and make (in essence) 'Campfire' coffee – just using the Coffee Pot; or, brew his coffee, then remove the Percolators lid and ground holder. He would drop in an uncracked, fresh egg; allowing it to 'boil' for a minute or two in the coffee. Then, upon removing the egg from the pot with a tablespoon, he would have a 'Coddled (slightly cooked) Egg' – and, perhaps, slightly milder coffee… at least, in his mind!

My patient, as previously stated, uses her 'Pour-Over Brewer,' with coffee grounds; and places a 'room temperature' egg into it. Then, slowly, pours boiling water into the brewer, over the egg. The egg is exposed to both the coffee and the boiling water for approximately three minutes; at which time, the coffee is made, and the egg is 'Coddled' (lightly cooked) to her perfection; not to mention, her belief that her coffee is 'smoother' as well. This, also, 'pasteurizes' the egg! She, then, places her egg into a 'special serving holder,' cracks off the top, then 'dips' her toast or 'English Muffin' into it!

A more natural way is for one to use a 'Drip' maker like mine; which is 'carafe-less,' or a 'Keurig device' – to brew hot water, for hot cereal, coddled eggs, or soup. However, it is just about as easy to combine brewers – such as a 'Keurig' brewer and a 'French Press.'

For example, early one recent morning, while staying in a hotel suite (and having a few grocery's and my 'French Press' handy), I decided to have a 'poached egg' for breakfast. Unfortunately, there were no cooking utensils or equipment for cooking, besides a small, 'Keurig' type coffee maker. I carefully cracked an egg into my 'French Press,' filled it with 'close to' boiling water from the 'Pod Brewer,' and allowed the egg to 'just sit' for 3 minutes in the water. I, then, put the 'Press Strainer' (plunger) on the top of the 'Press;' but did not press it down. Carefully, I poured the water into the sink. With all the water gone, I turned the egg out onto a plate, added some salt, pepper, and some 'real' Bacon Bits (from a package, I had with me). It was delicious (and did not mess up my hotel suite). Mentioning it to someone at the hotel, they asked, "*How did you ever come up with an idea like that?*" I informed them that it was, "*Simply, something I used to do back in college!*"

Of course, I made some 'French Press' coffee, first, to go with the egg; even though, there was a 'Keurig type' brewer in the room! I did the same thing this morning, at home, (but using my 'Instant, Hot Water Dispenser') for photographs for this book – it is a shame that the photographs below are not in color!

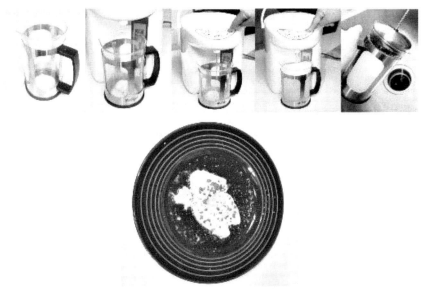

Although, a 'French Press' is considered, 'sophisticated,' this 'cooking process' was, probably, started many years before – with the early Europeans! The 'poor' might have had only one pot to put over a fire; and everything went into it for cooking – and when coffee, as a food or beverage came about, that went into the pot as well! Sometimes, the container had not been washed too well (if any), and food was mixed with the coffee. The food was eaten, and the coffee was drunk!

Bringing us up to, more modern times – such as the Civil War, then World War 1 – 'Pot' brewing/cooking continued; with soldiers not owning a cooking pot, but a 'Campfire Type,' Coffee Pot… so they would make coffee, soup, boiled meat, eggs, or cook vegetables in it, over an open fire.

[289]

As 'war technology,' and food packaging progressed, soldiers were able to receive 'Coffee Rations' at the front. This did not always mean, they had a 'Coffee Pot,' of some kind; and sometimes, they did not even have a cooking pot! Many soldiers used their metal helmets to cook or brew in! Luckily, for those wanting coffee, 'Military Helmets' were not 'vented' in those days. If the soldiers killed a rabbit or chicken 'wandering' somewhere, it would quickly make it into the 'Cooking/Coffee Pot Helmet' as well!

When the next war came about, 'canned' foods and coffee had become common; and, 'Canned Chicken' was often prepared – but, still, just within a single, Coffee Pot! However, many <u>more</u> things were prepared besides coffee in it! This is not as strange as it may sound; but to many of my younger readers, remember, a Coffee Pot is 'just a tall pot!' There was not (nor still is), anything 'magic' about it to say, *"Only use this pot to brew coffee in!"* Soldiers were forced to use what they had!

Technology moved on; and, the public and soldiers began to own some form of 'Percolator.' However, for soldiers, if no Percolators were available to put over a fire or can of 'Steno' (jellied alcohol), an empty 'tin can,' or 'found pot' of some sort could be used – anything, which would 'hold water' (yet not melt or burn up) while over a campfire. This was, simply, 'Campfire' coffee. My Dad, in World War II, used tall, 'Stainless Steel' cups to 'brew or cook' in; and continued to do so, until his death in the mid-1970s. I can still remember using them with him – and mentioned using them earlier in this book, under 'Brewing Methods.'

Springing forward to even more modern times, but before the Microwave Oven, college students would use a Percolator – to cook within their small, college 'Dormitory' rooms. I can remember my friends, living in 'Dorms,' having 'contraband,' small refrigerators and hot plates 'squirreled away' all over their rooms – behind curtains, under or behind furniture, hidden with blankets, under pillows, in drawers, under dirty laundry, and such… <u>all</u> fire hazards! 'Dormitory Officials' were always catching someone with 'contraband' cooking items, it would seem! The 'smart' students would use 'Electric Coffee Percolators;' as no hot plate was required, and if 'caught by officials,' they 'stood a lessor chance' of being punished!

Once 'Automatic, Drip' coffee makers were invented; however, 'small space' cooking in Dormitories took off! Whereas 'hot plates' might not have been 'officially' allowed in some college rooms, a 'Drip Coffee Maker,' usually, would be 'overlooked; as most students, and 'Officials' alike, felt that they *"Needed coffee, to get by!"* As it happens, 'college kids' – again, proved, 'where there is a will there is a way' – and started using their 'Drip Coffee Makers' to cook in… just as they did, previously, with 'hot plates and coffee pots!' And, when Microwaves ovens became available, students could create some 'clever' meals; when they combined the two devices!

I do not know why most of the people I knew were never caught by the 'Dormitory Officials;' as the smell of food cooking seemed to permeate the entire building. Perhaps, as the 'Officials' had, probably, done this themselves at one time with a 'coffee maker' of some sort, they were willing to turn a 'blind eye' to the students!

Limited only by the imagination, as to '<u>what</u>' to cook, in this following section, I am only going to touch upon a few things; as this subject, could take up an entire 'recipe book' of its own! Even though many 'Coffee Snobs' may have done this in college, I would doubt they would be willing to try eating any of the following, now; as I call it *"Dorm Room Cooking!"*

Dorm Room Cooking
An entire breakfast made with one coffee maker!

A typical breakfast for myself and friends in dorms, was 'coffee, sausage (in various forms), bacon, hash browns, fried eggs, and pancakes; all of which are shown above; and all being prepared with a 'Drip' Coffee Maker!

Of course, Spam, frozen waffles, stir/fried potatoes, or almost anything which could be cooked in a frying pan, can be cooked on top of the coffee makers 'mini' hot plate! The carafe is used, not just for coffee, but as a 'pot or kettle' for anything else; as the previously mentioned, 'hard or soft-boiled' eggs. Even 'Scrambled Eggs' can be prepared in the 'Drip' carafe; although, they do take longer to make than over a stove or in a microwave oven. However, 'Coffee Maker Food' can be much more 'exotic' than just Eggs!

Hot Cereal or Oatmeal

As mentioned before, something I might prepare when traveling, this is one recipe that I know a 'Coffee Snob' from my former group, to prepare while he's traveling too; or sometimes, at home as well – because, he only needs 'packaged,' Instant Oatmeal, and some hot water!' He pours his Oatmeal in a bowl, makes some 'pure and hot water' in his Keurig coffee maker and adds it to the

Oatmeal! If no 'Instant' Oatmeal is available, then by using his 'Drip Coffee Maker,' he can fill the carafe with pure water and cook 'regular' Oatmeal.

In the same sense, an elderly patient of mine does this same thing every morning with her 'Keurig' coffee maker; using it, not only to make her morning coffee, but to make 'hot water' for her 'Cream of Wheat,' Grits, Quinoa, Flax, or Porridge! As her Keurig device has a large water reservoir (which 'home health care' workers keep filled for my patient), she can make coffee, soup, or hot cereal, any time she wishes!

Hot Dogs (Frankfurters)

As with the early settlers whom would place the meat into their 'Coffee Pots' (after their invention), college kids and others will do the same today; and take a 'Drip' coffee maker and fill it with water – of course, excluding, the coffee grounds. After placing defrosted 'Franks' into the carafe of the maker, the device is turned on; and 'close to boiling water' is created and drained into the carafe; just as

'brewed coffee' would. The 'Franks,' now sitting in a pot of hot water, cook for 20 to 30 minutes over the warmer. Just as with cooking in a pan over a stove, the hot dogs are, soon, ready to eat! Maybe, it is not 'boiling' water, but it is close enough! Some people may 'pre-heat' the carafe first or make the hot water in stages to keep water as 'hot' as possible – this is what I did in the photograph above! After initially covering the 'Frankfurters' with hot water from the brewer, every two or three minutes I would add a little more water to the coffee maker; allowing more hot water to 'pour into' the carafe – keeping it very hot. The warming place below the carafe, merely helps keep the water hot!

Of course, cut hot dogs (or Vienna sausage) can be placed into the coffee makers 'ground holder;' and the hot water is run over them… they are, then, 'steamed' (somewhat) for 30 minutes. Again, adding a 'little water at a time' seems to be the best way to cook. A paper filter can be added, if desired, to 'slow' the draining process – thus, cooking the hot dogs 'faster,' by 'soaking' them a bit in the 'basket!'

However, why stop there? A can of chili, and some cheese, could be added after the hot water in the carafe is poured off; and allowed to heat/cook with the hot dogs! Buns can be 'warmed' on top of the coffee maker – or, even cut in half, and placed into 'water hopper' or basket to 'warm and steam.' Few 'Coffee Snobs,' I am afraid, would ever do such a thing… however, I must admit if one enjoys 'Boiled Hot Dogs…' these are not too bad; and, I would be surprised to find that today's 'Coffee Snob,' might not have done this while in college themselves! I would suppose, sometimes, some 'Coffee Snobs' might forget what it was like to be a 'kid' in college!

'Drip' coffee maker carafes are not the only kind of coffee makers capable of preparing 'Hot Dogs' – as previously, stated! A standard 'Coffee Pot' can be placed over a hot plate, stovetop, or even camp stove or fire just as quickly and easily – and used as a 'pot!'

I have already mentioned 'steaming' in a 'Drip' maker, ground basket; but, one can use the 'heating element' as a 'griddle,' so to speak; and, 'cut' Hot Dogs/Frankfurters, placed directly on it. Even a 'tiny' frying pan could be placed on it – although, it will cut down on heat, initially! If using a small 'frying pan,' be sure to allow it to 'warm' on the 'heating element/plate' for at least 20 or more minutes before cooking in it.

As the 'heating plate' is, generally, only 4-inches in diameter, the 'Franks' should be 'cut in half' to fit entirely on the plate; frankly, I enjoyed, small, 'Cocktail Weenies' and 'Vienna Sausage' prepared this way when I was in college – my friends called them *"Dorm Room Hors d'oeuvres!"* Of course, 'Coffee Snobs' are not going to be any more likely to eat these than they would 'boiled,' Hot Dogs!

Grilled Cheese Sandwich

Another 'favorite food' for college kids (and myself too) is the 'Grilled Cheese' sandwich. Again, a coffee maker, with a warming plate, is required for this one. Aluminum foil can be placed over the plate for easy clean up; but, the sandwich can just as easily, 'sit directly' on the heating plate (frankly, I enjoyed eating this sandwich, after 'creating and photographing' it)! The sandwich consisted of:

- Two slices of Buttered (both sides) Sourdough Bread
- Two Individually Wrapped, Cheese Slices
- Mayonnaise
- Horseradish
- Dijon Mustard
- Any other Condiment – Bell Peppers, Pickles or Relish

After assembled, the sandwich is placed over the 'heating plate' – and 'grilled' until the Cheese has melted, and the Bread is toasted. It takes a little time, but it is worth it! Aluminum Foil may slow cooking down a bit, however.

Of course, this sandwich can be augmented in many ways; including the addition of onion, bacon, multiple kinds of cheese, et cetera.

Ramen Noodles

This is the easiest recipe of all; however, I have known people who have augmented products with chives, seasonings, onions, meat, and more – and I did this myself while in college (and, again, enjoyed eating this one for lunch after photographing it). Preparation is simple – and can be done with most coffee makers... one way or another.

In a 'standard Drip device,' place the 'Ramon Noodles' in the carafe and allow hot water from the machine fill it. Let it 'sit' for several minutes; until the noodles are soft. Optionally, the noodles can go into a bowl; then hot water, created by the coffee maker, is poured over them! 'Seasoning' packets, additional seasonings, or cooked/canned meat can be added before the water is introduced or directly before serving.

The absolute, most straightforward way is to buy a 'Noodles in a Cup' type of Ramon. Remove the top from the cup and run the proper amount of water through ones 'Carafe-less' or 'Pod' Coffee Maker – sans, the coffee pod. I, also, do this with 'Instant, Beef Chow Mein' boxes, for a quick lunch! **Optional**: Break up the noodles, and place them in a 'Drip' brewer, ground basket; then, run a whole pot of water through. This way, one has 'cooked noodles' to put in another dish – such as a salad – without the seasoning or 'soup.'

The same thing can be done with other noodles – especially, in a carafe; such as spaghetti, macaroni, or other pasta. Sauces or toppings can be added after the water is poured off; and kept warm over the device hot plate!

Dinner – Poached or Grilled Salmon

Another 'super easy,' yet elegant, recipe is for 'Poached or Grilled Salmon' (and I did impress a few 'dates' by preparing this for them, back in the 1970s). Most of my 'girlfriends,' thought I was an excellent cook; but I will admit now, that I never told any of them exactly 'how' I 'poached' or 'grilled' my fish! In fact, 'grilling or poaching' any fish is as varied as one's imagination can handle!  For example, I would even run beer through my coffee maker to 'poach' fish like Halibut or Red Snapper!

Again, using a standard, carafe-type, 'Drip' coffee maker, place one or more servings of cut Salmon into the carafe. First, if needed, the Salmon may be 'marinated' – right in the same carafe! Marinating can be 'sped up' somewhat, by diluting the 'Marinade' with a bit of warm water from the coffee maker; and allowing the fish to soak for 20 or more minutes. The heat from the 'warming plate' helps to 'speed' the marinating process as well. Just be careful not to 'cook' the Salmon during this process – that is, not unless you <u>want</u> your Salmon cooked this way! I have found, that 'cooking' in a marinade, can be an excellent way to help 'flavor' the fish!

For cooking, making sure that the device is clean, and there are no coffee grounds left in it; then, place the Salmon into the carafe along with rosemary, basil, garlic, a slice of lemon or orange, or other seasonings. Pour water into the coffee maker and allow the appropriate amount of 'hot water' to cover the fish; wait a few minutes, then add more to keep the water hot. Continue the process until the carafe is full of water. This will keep the water hot through the cooking process. Of course, to keep the 'plate' hot the whole time, water can be added, a little at a time to the coffee maker – to allow both the plate and water to stay their warmest. Then, allow the pot to sit on the hot plate for ten or more minutes; depending upon the device and thickness of the fish. When cooked, feel free to start 'plating' your fish and preparing your side dishes.

Additional seasonings, such as garlic salt, butter, lemon juice, and such, may be added to the carafe after the water has drained into it! Serve with garnishments – such as parsley or cilantro; or 'more' melted butter, lime juice, or whatever! I prepared a box of 'Instant, Seasoned Rice' (again, prepared in the coffee maker) and served it with applesauce and the Salmon – as seen in this photograph to the left!

An alternate way to cook Salmon is to use the 'heating plate' as a grill or 'frying pan;' in fact, a small, frying pan can be placed on the plate – but, as mentioned before, it will take a bit longer to heat the pan to 'cooking' temperature. If 'time' is not an issue, then use of a small frying pan is an excellent way to go – as it 'cleans up' so quickly and easily. Frankly, I would rather do this, as I do not like  having to 'clean up' the plate of my coffee maker – generally because I am always looking at making some fresh coffee! So, if not using a small, frying pan, I will use a piece of Aluminum Foil over the plate for, again, 'easy' cleanup!

The way I prepared the above Salmon, was to place the fish on some Aluminum Foil, skin side down, covering the heating plate. I added a bit of 'rosemary, garlic salt, and pepper,' and a teaspoon of butter, to the top of the

Salmon. I 'fried' it for several minutes – rotating the fish, on the warming tray. After frying for several minutes, I, carefully, turned the fish over with a spatula, and 'grilled' it on the other side – but only for a few minutes.

Optional: a bowl or metal covering can be placed over the fish to make something of an oven – or the fish could be wrapped in Aluminum Foil after seasoning! Again, serve with something like Rice Pilaf or Scalloped Potatoes; which can, also, be cooked in the carafe of the coffee maker! Look at the many products which come 'boxed' and ready to cook at the store. If they can be cooked over a stove in a kettle or frying pan, they can be cooked in a coffee maker!

Frankly, if one is willing to spend a few dollars, it is possible to get a combination, 'Brewing/Cooking' unit for ones' dorm room or even at home. I know an elderly woman with one of the units; as she lives by herself, she finds it cooks just the *"Right amount"* of food and beverage for one person! It brews, fry's, boils, broils, and bakes… perfect for her
needs – and she chooses as many 'instant' foods as she can for variety! I was so impressed with her 'cooking, baking, and brewing' abilities, I bought one myself – and keep it next to my 'BBQing' station!

Do not be afraid to cook anything with a coffee maker! One is only limited by imagination! Even to this day – a world away from college – I still use my coffee maker for things like 'melting chocolate chips' for sauces – as it will not 'burn'!

Back to Coffee: is there anything else for cooking?

Coffee can not only can be 'drunk black' or 'augmented' with liquors, creamers, syrups, or other additives, but may become an important part of many recipes – either 'wet' or 'dry.' For myself, I often use coffee a 'Marinade' for meat; or a 'Dry Rub' for beef ribs, pork, or chicken. I just add some
'coffee grounds' to whatever spices chosen to be used as a 'Rub!' Above is a photograph of a couple of small steaks for baking.

[297]

Moreover, 'Rubs' are just the 'half of it!' Coffee and Caffeine can even be found in many 'non-edibles' too; such as 'Inhalable Coffee/Caffeine Stix,' Chewing Gum, Toothpaste, Shampoo, Face Scrubs, Deodorants, Soap, Enemas, Douches, Eye Drops, Bronchial Inhalers, 'Pants,' or 'Coffee-Infused' Cigars. However, when we think of 'anything else' for coffee, in the form of an 'additive,' we think of many other things besides 'Sugar and Cream!'

Few people seem to 'get past' coffee as a beverage! However, it can be used for many other things besides 'products' or drinking! For example, some people, such as myself, it becomes an intricate part of many recipes! I cook with 'liquid coffee,' and even use 'Ground Coffee' as a 'topping' for anything 'frosted!' Moreover, 'finely ground' 'Coffee' is delicious when sprinkled on top desserts, cakes, ice cream, or cheesecakes, as a delicious 'additive!'

Let's take a look at 'Additives – beyond, Sugar and Cream!'

"I have measured out my life with Coffee Spoons!"

~ (Attributed to) TS Eliot

ADDITIVES – BEYOND SUGAR AND CREAM

Cream and Sugar? Most people do not think of them this way, but, "*Yes,*" Cream and Sugar are 'Additives;' and up until a brief time back, they were just about the <u>only</u> things 'added' to coffee – besides, 'foamed or steamed' milk, or liquor. At this point, I must list some of the things that people put in their coffee – again, many of these have, already, been listed before within this book; but the following is more of a definitive list. People may use cinnamon, turmeric, honey, artificial sweeteners, flavored vitamins, proteins, and assorted 'flavored' creamers in their coffee – to make it taste more like a Latte or a Cappuccino; and, many 'Coffee Snobs' will use creamers like 'Pumpkin Spice' in their coffee, as it is, currently, <u>fashionable</u>. However, one would not believe the number of people who put 'flavors' into coffee that one has never considered!

I am sure, making some of these 'specialized' creamers came about from people cooking with their coffee makers! Someone, probably, did not clean out their coffee maker after cooking something (presumably, a candy) – and the previous substance, 'tainted' the coffee when they brewed it! Not wanting to waste anything, they drank it anyway; and, some people <u>liked</u> <u>it</u>! From that, people started putting all kind of things in their coffee – as they enjoyed the taste. In fact, people have been putting different 'foodstuffs' in their coffee since the dawn of coffee – for unusual flavors! For example, I once had a friend whom 'boiled,' bloody, 'Elk' or 'Moose' meat in his coffee while on hunting trips; however, he <u>drank</u> the coffee afterwards – not so much for 'waste not, want not…' but because he enjoyed 'Elk or Moose Flavored Coffee;' claiming, the animal blood, "*Gave more boldness to the brew!*"

Of course, there liquid, powdered, and even dehydrated commercial creamers available in stores; in regular, sugar-free, natural, organic, kosher, or 'artificial,' flavors – but few 'meat' flavored ones, thankfully.

Different flavored creamers are plentiful in many stores – in both 'regular' and 'sugar-free' versions. For examples, just take a 'quick look' at the 'limited' list I compiled, by going to the three, 'nearest' grocery stores to my home: 'Dove Bar' Chocolate, Almond, Almond Cream, Almond Joy, Amaretto, Apple Cream, Baileys Irish Cream, Belgian Chocolate, Butter Pecan, Cacao Chocolate (Super Food), Café Latte, Caramel, Caramel Latte, Caramel Macchiato, Caramel Marshmallow, Chili Cream, Chocolate, Chocolate Caramel, Chocolate Chip Coffee, Chocolate Fudge, Chocolate Hazelnut, Chocolate Mocha, Chocolate Peanut Butter, Chocolate Peppermint,

Chocolate Raspberry, Chocolate Truffle, Cinnabon, Cinnamon Vanilla Cream, Coconut, Coconut Caramel Latte, Coconut Cream, Cookie Dough, Cream Brulée, Dark Chocolate, Dark Chocolate Macadamia Nut, Dehydrated Honey, Eggnog Cream, Eggnog Latte, Espresso Chocolate, French Vanilla, Gingerbread Cream, Girl Scouts Thin Mint, Hazelnut, Hershey's Smores, Irish Cream, Italian Sweet Cream, Ketogenic – of assorted flavors, 'Lite' creams or assorted flavors, Milk Chocolate Macadamia Nut, Mocha, Mocha Almond Fudge, Mocha Mudslide, Mudslide, Nestles Chocolate, Orange Cream, Oreo Chocolate, Oreo Cookie & Cream, Peppermint Mocha Chocolate, Peppermint Patty, Pumpkin Spice, Red Velvet Cupcake, Reese's Candy Bar, Salted Caramel Chocolate, Snickers Candy Bar, Snickerdoodle Cream, Spiced Latte, Strawberry, Strawberry Cheesecake, Sugar Cookie, Suisse Cream Chai, Southern Butter Pecan, Tiramisu, Toasted Marshmallow Mocha, Toffee Nut, Vanilla, Vanilla Bean, Vanilla Caramel, Vanilla Caramel Mocha, Vanilla Chai Spice, Vanilla Heat, Vanilla Nut, White Chocolate, White Chocolate Frappé, White Chocolate Latte, White Chocolate, Macadamia Nut, White Chocolate/Raspberry… moreover, the list goes on and on; I am surprised, in fact, of 'how many' different 'additives' just three stores could carry!

Surprisingly, the above list does not even include the flavors and 'additives' – like 'extra caffeine' or different 'syrups;' which can be added to each cup! It surprises me, that some 'Coffee Snobs' will not try something like 'different waters or temperatures' – as it will 'disflavor' their coffee; but, will be quick to use various 'creamers, powders, and syrups;' such as those listed above!

However, here some more 'additives,' some 'Coffee Snobs,' will try! I must admit that I have tried and enjoyed, many myself!

Alcohol in Coffee – Sure… why not! This 'additive' is older than anything else! Moreover, I will admit that I have enjoyed a good, 'Irish Coffee' – especially during cold, winter nights… or even 'snowy,' holiday mornings! Moreover, certainly, some 'Snobs' enjoy Kahlúa, Tia Maria, or other Liqueurs in their coffees – not to mention Whiskey, Brandy, Rum or other liquors.

Unless a 'Coffee Snob,' only enjoys 'black coffee,' most will enjoy something like Baileys Irish Cream; or something else, which is mildly alcoholic – although, they might not like to admit it… that is unless they make their own; then, there are 'massive bragging rights!' For example, I make my Kahlúa (coffee-flavored Liqueur); and it impresses most people.

Added Caffeine – There are a few 'natural' ways to increase the caffeine in a cup of coffee. First, choose a bean which is a 'Light Roast;' as Light Roasts contain more caffeine. Secondly, use a 'Finer Grind;' as in an Espresso, for example. Thirdly, smaller cups of 'Espresso or Coffee' have more caffeine than larger ones! This sounds confusing; but the 'larger the coffee,' the <u>more</u> water it has – this is especially seen with some 'K-Pod' brewers. With my 'Pod Brewer,' for example, if watched closely, the coffee comes out dark, to begin with; then gets 'lighter,' changing to 'clear,' as it progresses. If I want 'more caffeine,' I'll stop the process, drain the 'clear' water into another cup, then 'brew' a second 'Pod' into my larger cup.

For more Caffeine, it is, sometimes, better to start with a 'Caffeinated Water' for begin brewing; or, add a 'shot' of Caffeinated Syrup' to the cup!

Another thing to try, when purchasing at a 'serve yourself' shop, is to choose a 'High Caffeine/High Voltage,' or 'High Octane' (as some vendors call it) coffee. These can, often, be found in 'pre-brewed' coffee, or as a 'Cappuccino;' which can be added to the cup from a bottle or machine.

Many gas stations, truck stops, and even 'specialty stores,' have 'Coffee Stations;' which give the consumer the possibility of adding many different 'additives' to their Coffees, Lattes, Frappuccino's or Cappuccinos – besides just cream and sugar! Of course, they may 'sell' these as well, for the consumer to take home! Moreover, I have mixed a number of these different additives – for, custom flavors in the  coffee bar – or purchased assorted syrups to take home! Usually, they are in a 'serving rack,' along with different brands of syrups which are popular; including, a 'bottled syrup' which is 'high' in Caffeine! The beauty of a choice of 'multiple syrups' is, one can put one, or many as desired, into their coffee! However, one must 'experiment' to discover 'what' they might enjoy. For example, this morning, while writing this, I tried a 'Sugar-Free' Caramel Creamer, with some 'Sugar-Free' Mocha powder, and some 'Sugar-Free' Chocolate Coffee Syrup in my coffee. It sounded good… but, was awful – and had a nasty, after-taste; but some people with diabetes, like me, do not have many choices when it comes to 'Coffee Additives…' we have to use 'what' is available!

My actual recommendation for a 'high caffeine' content is: *"If brewing ones' own, coffee, start with a 'high caffeine,' bean/brand such as 'Deathwish' coffee!"* Of course, 'Ultra-High Caffeine Coffees,' can be dangerous to some people. One needs to make sure they are healthy enough to drink such a beverage. Even if one finds a coffee bar which serves something of a 'High' or 'Ultra-High Caffeinated Coffee,' it might be best to make sure they are healthy enough to handle it first – in other words, if one's doctor recommends *"Avoiding caffeine,"* then a 'Deathwish' type of coffee might not be a good option! For myself, if I want enough caffeine to give me a minor 'boost,' and keep me awake when I need it, I might pour myself a 'regular' cup of coffee with creamer in it – but put in an 'extra shot' of Espresso or 'liquid caffeine' as well!

What else can be considered 'an additive?' Sometimes, it is just a 'specialty' water.

Ionized, Alkaline Water – Why stop with one of the earlier mentioned 'pure' waters, when 'Alkaline Water' can be an 'add on' just like a 'Pre-caffeinated' Water? Some people feel that they already have 'too much acid' in their body; so, they drink 'Alkaline Water,' brewed Coffee to reduce the bodies 'acidity!' They might even add some extra caffeine to it as well! However, they mistakenly think and say that *"Ionized water will help reduce the 'acid' within the cup of coffee!"* Personally, I would not drink it – as I have seen more devices which were more likely to 'ruin' the coffee than improve it! In the same sense, some people add other 'Alkaline' products to their coffee – or, just drink the water alone; thinking it will help to 'neutralize' the 'excess acid' in their bodies!

As a 'health care professional,' I can tell you that *"There is little need for 'Alkaline Water' to help 'reduce' the amount of acid in one's body; as the stomach is 'full of acid;' and 'that acid,' will 'neutralize' any 'light Alkaline' put into it. Plus, the stomach drains into the intestine; where a natural 'Alkaline mixture' of digestive juices, come from the Pancreas, Liver, and Gallbladder! So, drinking 'Alkaline' water is something akin to trying to 'sweeten a lake' by adding a teaspoon full of sugar!"* A 'small amount' (a cup or two) of 'Alkaline Coffee,' is not going to make a noticeable difference in the body's acidity – nor, is it going to reduce a substantial amount of 'acidity' in a cup of coffee! Remember, acidity/bitterness, is coming from the 'roasted beans' themselves – and can be an 'important' part of ones' coffee!

If one wants more 'Alkaline' in their system, they would be better off drinking an 'Alka-Seltzer®' to reduce acidity; and not, ruin their coffee! However, I have seen 'Coffee or Health Snobs, do just that too; and actually 'drop' an Alka-Seltzer directly into their brewed coffee, carafe, or coffee maker. I will admit that I have not tried this coffee; so, it is difficult to say that I "*Would not like it.*" In the same sense, however, I have not put 'gasoline' into my coffee either; but I am relatively sure I would not like that either!

"*Coffee is a beverage which puts one to sleep when not drunk!*"

~ (Attributed to) Alphonse Allais

COFFEE CREAMERS AND MORE ADDITIVES:

Of course, when serving coffee to a large crowd, one is going to <u>have to</u> serve a certain amount of 'coffee additives' for people to use! This might seem simple; but, if one is usually a 'black coffee' drinker, keep in mind that other people may not be! It is always good to have some sugar, cream, and even a non-dairy creamer choice on hand; if one is having  guests over! That way, one can accommodate all or most coffee needs, for most people. As one can see from the, above, photograph, from one of my coffee tastings, when serving a large group, I will put out a moderate selection of sugar, substitute sweetener, milk, cream, non-dairy creamer, soy milk, almond milk, chocolate syrup, caramel syrup, powdered sweeteners, and more. However, the 'Scandinavians' in my family, used to take this a bit farther; and rather than adding 'artificial cream,' they only used 'dairy' (of sorts) in their coffee… in the form of 'Reindeer Cream or Milk!' Luckily, or unluckily, few stores, in this country, carry such 'creamers for coffee,' these days!

However, I do know a few 'Snobs' who purchase 'Raw Camels Milk' at their, local, health food store; and in some 'scientific circles,' a few people do believe that 'Camels Milk' <u>does</u> have some medicinal benefits! 'Vegans,' however, are no more likely to consume this, than they are 'Cows' milk or cream! Therefore, it is always a good practice to keep a 'non-dairy' creamer around for any persons watching their Lactose intake, or do not consume any animal products!

The Creamer list on an earlier page is what brings me to the next section; which is about, more <u>detailed</u> 'Coffee Creamers and Additives.' Whereas, this book is not really a 'recipe' book, there are so many 'Coffee Additives and Creamers' which cannot be found in, standard, grocery stores, I feel obliged, at this point, to put in a few 'recipes' for some basic 'Coffee Flavorings;' that can be the 'starting point' of making ones' flavorings and creamers!

First, let us look at the fundamental 'Additives!'

'Additives' can be made of almost anything: such as 'readymade 'products or 'homemade' ones. In my family, most of us enjoy a 'Chocolate' flavoring in our coffee – especially, if we are not using 'Chocolate' Flavored, Coffee

Beans (our favorite coffee is a 'Hawaiian, Chocolate Macadamia Nut bean'). While, that is enough for my 'Chocolate Fix', along with a little milk, others in my family enjoy putting a teaspoon of sweetened, 'Hot Cocoa Mix' in their coffee – sometimes, combined with a 'Cappuccino Powder' as  well! If we are all out, they may use a spoon of 'Unsweetened' Bakers Chocolate; along with a spoon of sugar, dehydrated honey, a touch of milk, or, perhaps, a shot of chocolate syrup!

As previously said, additives/sweeteners come in many different forms; such as, sugar-free syrups, liquid creamers, powdered flavors or creamers, 'ultra-sweet' syrups, candy bars, proteins, and such… however, there is no reason one cannot make a 'similar version,' themselves! Also, if that is not good enough, the consumer can combine creamers, powders, and syrups, to create their own, 'custom,' flavors – flavors, of which, nobody has ever heard! It starts with a good, 'basic creamer;' which can be 'stored' in the refrigerator and 'augmented' as needed! I started making my own, when I found that not all of my 'favorite' additives were readily available in stores when I traveled! By 'making' creamer and additives, I am 'set' for wherever I travel!

Other than 'natural' extracts, most flavorings come in multiple types, including 'Sugar-Free.' They can each be used alone in coffee or mixed for a 'custom' taste! For example, when I am traveling, I will often go into a gas station or truck stop (surprisingly, many truck stops have amazingly good, Arabica beans) to get a cup of coffee. I will pour myself a tall – usually, a 'High Caffeine' Roast – coffee and mix it with some other roast (typically, a dark one); but I leave room in the cup for other additives. Of course, what I put in depends upon several issues; i.e., time of day, rainy, hot, cold, night time, my blood sugar levels, et cetera.

Sometimes, I will add some hot chocolate or 'Machine Cappuccino' to my cup! Then, I will pour in a bit of 'Sugar-free,' Caramel Syrup – if available (at least, it is a 'low sugar' additive for me). What follows, might add a few 'Caffeine' or 'Energy' (as some places call it) drops. Then, perhaps, a creamer – usually, a 'Chocolate Creamer,' if not using hot chocolate. I, sometimes, top it off, with some 'real cream,' for richness. Alternatively, for an added flavor, I might add some 'Almond' or some other 'Flavored Syrup.' Other times, I might add a bit of 'Foam;' should the 'Station Coffee Bar' have a

'Latte Foam' machine. Some places even have a few interesting 'Specialty Creamers' to add to coffee! What I end up with, is a 'unique' cup of coffee – something I am going to enjoy every bit as much (if not more) than what I would if I had gone somewhere like 'Starbucks' to get a Latte – but, at half the price! Best of all, as I often travel at night, I can get a coffee, the way I like it… <u>long</u> after most other 'Coffee Bars' are closed!

However, just as there are some there are 'Coffee Snobs' who will not drink a creamer other than actual 'Cream' or 'Raw Milk' in their coffee, there are some people who feel they have to have their 'daily vitamins' <u>in</u> their coffee!

Other than swallowing some vitamins with coffee – or dropping some vitamins and minerals into a cup (which, again, is going to create a 'nasty tasting' brew), there are 'Designer Products,' which are very good, and healthy for the drinker – such as 'Laird, Superfood Creamer.' This would be a 'specialized' additive that most people would not want – but with other people I know… it is the <u>only</u> way they will drink coffee! In the same sense, flavored 'Protein Drinks' can be used as a creamer too – thus, offering not only flavor and 'creaminess,' but nutrition as well! Even some diabetics can do something similar; by adding a bit of 'Glucose Control,' nutritional drink to their coffee; instead of using a 'Flavored Creamer!' I have tried using 'Boost™' brand (a Nestles product) myself, and the best I could say was, *"Meh… it is better than no creamer at all!"*

Then, there are other types of 'Educated Additives,' similar, to the 'Superfood' Creamers, to enhance coffee – and, I have tried one… 'Smart Coffee™!' It was, actually, pretty good! Some of these products may even promote weight loss or other health benefits! The inventors of these products seem to have taken the 'taste' of coffee into consideration when creating their additives; and have found more people will enjoy a 'natural' tasting cup, as opposed to one 'tasting and reeking' of vitamins!

Many products can be added to coffee; however, the results can vary greatly! So, this is where it pays to follow the recommendations of the 'product' manufacturers. The 'Smart Coffee' company I tried, advertises, *"Use this product mixed in Coffee or Tea for enjoyable results;"* and, *"Requires one scoop"* per 8 ounces per coffee!" The manufacturer states, that the product, supposedly, *"Enhances hormones, endorphins, dopamine, serotonin, oxytocin, and will, especially, enhance happiness… through 'natural and botanical' Nootropics"* (which are considered drugs, supplements, or other substances). They, also advertise that their product may, *"Positively, improve cognitive function, memory, focus, and creativity!"* I did not notice any of that while drinking, but the coffee did taste good!

If nothing else, some people enjoy brewing with 'Smart' or 'Vitamin' water. I don't know, exactly, how 'smart' it is to take a 'vitamin charged' water, and brew with it; but I do know, that the 'taste' of vitamins, can often 'over-power' the taste of other ingredients; especially, when 'B-Vitamins' are concerned. My recommendations would be, drink 'Vitamin Water' separately; and enjoy 'good' coffee!

Sometimes, it is just best to forget the 'designer' or 'fancy' additives… moreover, make ones' own, 'better' creamers:

MAKE YOUR OWN COFFEE SYRUPS AND CREAMERS

Not all 'Coffee Snobs' are 'purists;' and not everyone is unwilling to put 'additives' (of any kind) in their coffee! 'Coffee Snobs' come in various versions – some, like me – can 'talk' a good game; while others 'live coffee' as a lifestyle! Here are two different examples:

I know a woman who says, *"I will only drink my coffee, 'creamy and sweet…' but not too hot;"* So, she drops in a scoop of 'French Vanilla, Ice Cream' into her cup before filling it! I would have to say; her coffee would be *"Creamy, sweet,"* and *"Not too hot;"* and, I will admit that I, often, do the same with 'Soft Serve' in my coffee, at a particular, Buffet my family goes to, for a dessert!

My Dad, on the other hand (although, 'Coffee Snobs' did not seem to exist, or were not quite so obvious, back in his day), would never think to drink his coffee any way except 'Black!' I can remember him lecturing me one 'icy' morning in our fishing boat, on the *"Evils of polluting coffee;"* after my complaining, that I *"Did not have any milk to put in my coffee!"* Dad, usually, put nothing in his coffee; and, often said, when asked his preference, he *"Liked his coffee, black, hot, and strong enough to 'crawl out of the cup' on its own!"* He would, often, add, however, he: *"Preferred to drink his coffee the way he would drink his whiskey… Neat;"* meaning… with nothing added! However, he was known to put a 'shot' of Whiskey in his coffee, on cold mornings on the boat, or late night, sitting around a campfire!

"Why the hell do you want to dilute it? What do you think it is… hot chocolate," he would lecture me (to this day, I still enjoy a bit of 'hot chocolate' in my coffee)! And, back then, I would have preferred 'hot chocolate' over Dads Sanka! Dad was a 'purist,' even, way back then; but I still know, today, both 'Coffee Snobs' and 'Roasters' who <u>still</u> think the way he did! *"Anything other than 'black,' is a waste of good coffee,"* they tell me; and, perhaps, they are correct… as 'black' is how <u>they</u> enjoy <u>their</u> coffee best! There is no 'right or wrong' to drink coffee… just different ways – and 'black,' is the best way to taste all of the 'essences' that coffee has to offer!

Surprisingly, just as my father said he would *"Only"* drink his coffee black; I know people who say they will *"Only drink, name brand, 'Designer-type,' Coffee Syrups or Creamers!"* Once again, these thoughts can 'distill down' to '<u>certain</u>' types of 'Sweeteners!'

"I will only drink coffee with Blue Agave Nectar (syrup) in it," one of my fellow Coffee Club members tells me – and, she carries a small bottle of it in her purse. As it happens, the woman, usually, sitting next to her '<u>only</u>' puts 'Raw Honey' in hers; and, I have seen another person, often, sitting nearby, with bakers, 'Powdered Honey' – and <u>never</u> changes her choice of 'sweetener!'

In the same sense, I often hear people preach; *"I will only drink 'Hershey®' brand creamer… alternatively, I will only drink 'Torani®' brand syrups… I will only drink 'DaVinci®' gourmet syrups… I will only drink my coffee with a few drops 'J. R. Watkins®' brand extract in it…"* or, *"I will only drink 'Williams Sonoma®' brand coffee syrups…"* from many 'Coffee Snobs;' and they, greatly, 'look down their noses,' at anyone drinking anything else!

The fact is, these people are not 'Coffee Snobs…' they are 'Additive Snobs;' who enjoy forcing their preferences on others!

When it comes to taste, there is only a slight difference between syrups or creamers; other than flavor essences, the kind of bottles, their cost, and the fact that one is a 'cream!' That is, except for the 'Sugar-Free' brands… moreover, I have yet to find one of those brands that I truly enjoy – even with the 'powdered' brands!

Therefore, people – who are unimpressed with name brands – might shop more for the price (many stores have their own brands; which, are just the 'name brands' repackaged) or they make their own! Having once owned a beverage company, I prefer to make my flavors; and believe me, nobody can taste the difference – except, to ask *"What brand"* it might be!

Being diabetic, whenever I make creamers or syrups, I might use 'Blue Agave' syrup as a sweetener; or, a mixture of 'Brown Sugar and Stevia®' to sweeten my Coffee Syrups; I have even tried 'Dehydrated Honey' as a sweetener! Unfortunately, there are only a few 'Sugar-Free' creamers available for people with diabetes! However, there are many 'Sugar-Free' syrups which are available; unfortunately, many have a very 'artificial' taste to them… and, a 'nasty' aftertaste as well! Sometimes, when 'making' my creamers, I will use one of these 'syrups' as the 'sweetener' for the creamer – and it does not have a 'lingering' after taste. However, why not just make a 'syrup' and bypass any creamer?

Here is the 'starting point' for making Syrups:

BASIC SYRUP

For use as a 'sweetener' in coffee, teas, or for cooking.

Ingredients:

- 1 or more cups of Sugar – any type – or, Corn Syrup, Honey or any combination of sweetener ingredients. **Optional**: use an equivalent amount of an 'Artificial Sweetener' – to taste.
- 1 or more cups of Pure Water – an equal amount of Water to Sugar.

Directions:

1. Mix 'Sugar and Water' together, in a large pot, over medium heat; stirring constantly. Bring to a light boil for 15 minutes. Continue to boil and stir; until the syrup has the desired viscosity (thickness).
2. Allow to cool; then, pour into clean, serving bottles or jars.

FLAVORED SYRUPS

To make a 'Flavored Syrup,' add flavorings – in the form of extracts, seasonings, or even fresh fruit – to the 'boiling' syrup. **Special Note**: heat, sometimes, changes the way extracts perform (especially, with artificially flavored extracts) – so, one might wish to add them to cold syrup! Brown

Sugar – or, a mixture of 'White and Brown,' or Sugar Substitutes – may be used to make a different base in flavored recipes. For example, this one below:

CINNAMON, BROWN SUGAR SYRUP

Ingredients:

- Use a mixture of White and Brown Sugar when making the 'Base' – 1-cup each, for a small batch.
- **Optional**: A few drops of Cinnamon Extract.

Directions:

1. Prepare 'Base' using Brown Sugar.
2. Remove from heat and allow to slightly cool.
3. Add Cinnamon or Extract and stir.
4. Pour into bottles or jars.

Other Flavors:

For different flavors, add fresh fruit – such as Strawberries or Blueberries – to the boiling syrup. Continue to boil, until the desired thickness is achieved.

Alternatively, for other flavors, remove the syrup from the burner, and allow to cool slightly; then stir in other seasonings or flavor extracts – such as Pure Vanilla Extract, Peach Extract, Chocolate Syrup or Extract, Peppermint Extract, or any combination of all flavorings.

CREAMERS

Creamers may be as 'sweet' as the consumer wishes; or, also, prepared with a 'Sugar Substitute.' The same can be said, for 'lactose-free' or 'non-dairy' milk and creams. Even 'Gluten-Free' products may be substituted if desired.

Any type of milk may be used. Try using 'Almond Milk, Soymilk, Evaporated Milk, Powdered Milk, Hemp Milk, Pea Milk, Organic Milk, Goats Milk…' whatever one thinks they might enjoy! I do draw the line (for myself) at one 'creamer' used by a friend: Ensure® Nutritional, 'Chocolate

Shakes.' My friend says, "*I love coffee, I love chocolate, I need nutrition… it is 'a natural*!*'*" In actuality, I would suppose it would not be any worse than using the 'Glucose Control' product I mentioned earlier! I have tried 'Ensure Coffee…' but didn't enjoy it!

I also, as previously mentioned, recommend <u>saving</u> old/clean 'Creamer Bottles' in which to put 'Homemade Creamers!' This is, primarily, for the sake of convenience – and, the fact that most of us are 'used to' seeing creamers served a certain way; and, the fact that certain 'Coffee Snobs,' might not be willing to try a 'homemade' creamer… however, they might try a 'Name Brand…' if they think it is one!

<u>COFFEE</u> <u>CREAMER</u> <u>BASE</u>

Take 1%, 2%, 'Whole' milk, 'lactose-free' milk, 'non-dairy' milk, 'creamer,' or anything 'milk-like' (raw milk, soy, hemp, or almond milk), and mix equal amounts with a 'sweetened condensed' milk – or, a 'non-dairy' substitute. In other words, if using two cans of 'sweetened condensed' milk – which are 14 ounces in size, mix with 28 ounces of some other kind of milk. Add or subtract the amount totals, for bottling constraints.

Any flavorings may be added – I prefer a few drops of J.R. Watkins® brand extracts… especially their chocolate, caramel, or coconut extracts. The same is to be said about seasonings – such as cinnamon, nutmeg, or 'alcoholic' additives… such as brandy, rum, whiskey, et cetera. Just add enough of 'whatever preference,' to taste! This recipe may be altered or augmented easily.

Here are a few samples of 'augments:'

<u>CANDY</u> <u>BAR</u> <u>CREAMER</u>

Ingredients:

- 1 or more, cups of 'Creamer Base.'
- 1 or more, of any flavor, regular-sized, 'Candy Bar.'
- **Optional**: If using a 'Peanut or Almond Candy Bar,' use a few drops of flavor extracts to bring out even more flavor; for example, add some Chocolate flavoring or extract, some Peanut, Almond, Coconut, or other extracts to the 'Base' and 'ground-up' candy bar.

If wishing to forego the candy, use the proper 'flavor essences' – for example, chocolate, coconut or almond extracts. My son enjoys mixing peanut butter extract along with chocolate extract in his creamer; to make something like 'Reese's Peanut Butter' creamer.

Directions:

1. Place all ingredients in a blender or large food processor; and mix well. This will make a 'frothy' (at least to start) type creamer – and, solve the issue of 'putting additional foam or whipped cream' in the coffee... as 'technically,' one, already, has it with the coffee creamer.
2. For less 'foam,' blend your 'Candy Bar' with just a little of the 'Creamer Base.' Blend until the bar is pulverized! Add back to Creamer Base and lightly mix again.
3. Pour into a bottle or jar, seal, and refrigerate until used.

CARAMEL BRULEE COFFEE CREAMER

Ingredients:

- 1-3 tablespoons melted Butter.
- ¼ cup Brown Sugar – either light or dark; or 'Brown Sugar Substitute.'
- 4 tablespoons Heavy Cream.
- 1/8 teaspoon Sea Salt – for more of a 'Salted Caramel' creamer, double the Sea Salt; and reduce the 'Vanilla Extract' (listed below) by half.
- 1 cup Whole Milk or Half-and-Half – try to buy the 'latest' expiration date (freshest) available; unless one does not expect to be storing the mixture for very long.
- 2 teaspoons pure 'White Vanilla' Extract – as 'White Vanilla' is challenging to find in stores, Dark Vanilla may be substituted.
- **Optional**: A few drops of Caramel Extract or Caramel Syrup.

Directions:

1. Melt the butter, over medium heat, in a saucepan.
2. Mix in brown sugar; continually stirring until melted.
3. Add in the heavy cream and stir for two more minutes.

4. Stir in the sea salt; and, any other ingredients – except vanilla – this is especially important if using an 'artificial' vanilla.
5. Stir, until the liquid begins to lightly bubble/boil.
6. Remove from heat.
7. Stir in the vanilla and allow to cool.
8. Pour into a sealable bottle or jar and refrigerate until use.

POWDERED COFFEE CREAMERS

It is not that difficult to find a 'Powdered Creamer,' like Coffee-Mate® - and just about every grocery store has their own 'store brand;' and, that can be the 'Base' of a lot of 'homemade,' flavored creamers if one wants. I shop at places like Costco; and I get 'huge' containers of a 'generic brand,' powdered creamer! Frankly, this still could be 'Coffee-Mate;' as many manufacturers, often, 'package and label' under many generic or store brands. I cannot see or taste any difference when comparing!

For the record, 'Homemade Powders' are often better tasting (lacking the 'aftertaste' that many creamers have) than what can be bought in a store; and frankly, I like that! As an added benefit, 'homemade' powders are often sweeter, creamer, and 'froth' better than the commercial brands. One would think 'Coffee Snobs' would be interested in this aspect… unfortunately, I have found, most taking my classes, are not!

Here is a good 'Powdered Creamer' starting point:

BASIC POWDERED COFFEE CREAMER

Ingredients:

- 4 cups 'Whole or Non-Fat' Milk Powder (Whole, Powdered Milk will make a 'richer' creamer).
- 1 cup Powdered Sugar (or, to taste). **Optional**: use a 'Sugar-Free' Sweetener; or, a mixture of 'Sugars and Sugar-Free Sweeteners.'
- 1 tablespoon Vanilla Powder. **Optional**: one teaspoon of Vanilla Extract. **Optional**: For a slightly Chocolate flavor, add 1 teaspoon Cocoa Powder; or, a drop or two of Chocolate Extract. 'Flavored

Powders' – in place of flavored extracts – are mostly found in 'beverage supply' shops.

- **Optional:** Mix 'powdered milks' with a flavored or unflavored, powdered creamer, to 'augment' or 'extend' the amount! The result will be a creamier, 'Powdered Creamer!'

Directions:

1. Combine the milk powder, sugar(s), and any 'optional' ingredient in a large bowl with a mixer; or, mix in a blender set to 'low' speed. (Blenders work well, when a liquid extract is used, or when preparing a large amount).
2. When combined, pour into a sealable bottle. I, often, use an old coffee can with the label removed. Should there being any 'lingering' coffee flavor to the can, it will 'blend nicely' with the ingredients!
3. Put one or two teaspoons of your 'new creamer' into your morning coffee or tea; or mix with water to make a 'liquid' to use in recipes.

Here is one of my wife's favorite variations:

POWDERED, COCONUT COFFEE CREAMER

Ingredients:

- 4 cups Whole or Non-Fat Milk Powder.
- 1 cup Powdered/Confectioners' Sugar (or to taste).
- 3 tablespoons melted Coconut Oil (**Optional:** 1 or more teaspoons of Coconut Extract. **Optional:** 'Sugared,' Dry Coconut. When it is ground very fine; many brands will 'melt' when added to liquid.
- 1 tablespoon Vanilla Powder. **Optional:** one teaspoon of Vanilla Extract. **Optional:** one teaspoon Cocoa Powder, a dash of Chocolate Extract or a teaspoon of Coconut Powder.

Directions:

1. Combine the instant milk powder, sugar(s), and any other ingredient in a bowl or blender and mix on low speed.
2. Slowly, pour the mixture, into a sealable container; and store in a cool, dark place.
3. Serve when ready; one teaspoon (or to taste) in coffee or teas.

One special note, this works well in other recipes needing a 'flavored creamer;' such as with cakes or muffins!

For added flavors, like hazelnut or butter-pecan extracts; Be sure to use a good, 'pure flavor' extract. My favorite is 'J.R. Watkins®' brand – commonly, available through the internet or at state or county fairs. It might be best to check your local area for representatives. Other store brands – such as McCormick/Schilling™ – are good too! Even 'powdered flavorings' are acceptable for making coffee creamers; as are, powdered or granulated honey rather than regular or 'Raw' sugar.

BASIC FLAVORED, LIQUID COFFEE CREAMER

Ingredients:

- 14-ounces of Sweetened, Condensed Milk.
- 1 1/3 cups of 1%, 2%, Whole Milk, Raw Milk, or Cream (depending upon how 'rich' one might wish their creamer to be). However, Soy, Almond, Hemp, Goat, 'Non-dairy' Mocha Mix, or other Milk Substitute may be used.
- 1-ounce Chocolate Extract (**Optional**: Chocolate Syrup – 3 or more regular or 'Sugar-Free' teaspoons, or to taste).
- **Optional**: 2 teaspoons 'Dark or White' Vanilla Extract.
- **Optional**: Use one square of Natural Milk Chocolate, Dark Chocolate or Carob; melted, and added to the mixture.
- **Optional**: If using a blender, various Candy Bars, Cookies, or Chocolate Covered Malt Balls can be used for flavoring.

Directions:

1. One might wish to double or triple this recipe; to have creamer for a few days. This is the basic recipe for all Coffee Creamers. For a 'plain' creamer, mix milk and sweetened condensed milk. For a 'French Vanilla' flavor, add vanilla extract; and forget the chocolate extract. For 'Almond Creamer,' add Almond extract or flavorings. For 'Coconut,' add Coconut extract and so on. Any flavor can be added or substituted.

I often asked a lot about "*Salted Caramel, Coffee Creamer*;" which is, currently, a 'fad' where I live. There is not any secret to it, so it does not call for its own recipe; add ¼ - ½ teaspoon of 'Sea Salt' (or to taste) to 2 or 3 tablespoons of 'Caramel Ice Cream Topping.' Just follow the 'Basic Creamer' recipe.

2. Pour milk and sweetened condensed milk into a bowl – **Optional**: add a can of evaporated milk for 'richness.'
3. Add chocolate, or any other extract or syrup, to the milk; and mix/stir well.
4. Serve when needed.

Optional: Again, combine any powder, instant milk, sweetener, or extracts to make a 'Creamer!' I enjoy mixing in 'Boxed' milk – as shown earlier in this book. It makes the mixture taste more like what one would find in a store. However, again, as I have said often in this book, "*Drink your coffee how you enjoy it best*," as, there is no 'right or wrong way' to use a 'flavored' Coffee Creamer!

BONUS: COFFEE SPOON RECIPE

One 'flavoring' that 'Coffee Snobs' might enjoy – either professionally made, or 'homemade' by themselves – are 'Coffee Spoons' (spoons, which are coated/filled with chocolate or other ingredients). My son and I make some every few years to give as Christmas gifts to family and friends; or, to use as 'Stocking Stuffers!' They are both delicious and fun for kids to make – especially when done as a 'family' activity. The 'spoons' can be used in cups of coffee, cocoa, tea, or milk (or, just eaten as a snack). Here is how to do it:

Ingredients:

- 6 or more ounces (more or less) of Chocolate Chips or Semi-Sweet Chocolate, baking pieces.
- 4-ounces (more or less) White Chocolate pieces (**Optional**: or Milk Chocolate, Mint, or other Chocolate pieces – such as Peanut Butter or Butterscotch, for example.)
- **Optional**: Flavorings/Extracts of ones' choice; such as Brandy, Rum, Almond, Coconut, Mint, Coffee, Cinnamon, et cetera.
- Twenty or more plastic (or, metal) spoons. (**Optional**: for smaller cups, use 'Baby' spoons).
- Wax or Parchment Paper.
- **Optional**: Clear of Colored Cellophane for wrapping.

- **Optional**: Colored or Flavored Sugars or Cookie Sprinkles.
- **Optional**: Tia Maria™, Kahlúa™, or any Coffee Liqueur.

Directions:

'Chocolate Spoons' make a great gift – and can be made with 'simple plastic' spoons, or something 'fancier;' for example, one year, I purchased three Sterling Silver, 'mini-spoons' – the type of which, my sons 'adopted Grandmother' liked to collect – and coated each with 'Chocolate;' to give to her at Christmas! **Special Note:** Thrift Stores are great places to look for 'Silver' or 'Decorative' Spoons.

1. Place a piece of waxed or parchment paper on a tray; large enough to hold 20 or more spoons – of any sort.
2. Place 'Semi-Sweet' chocolate pieces in a saucepan, or better yet, a 'Double Boiler,' over low heat – a 'Double Boiler' can be made just by placing a pan or bowl over the top of another, slightly smaller, pan/kettle – with boiling water in it. **Optional:** Melt Chocolate Chips in a 'Drip' Coffee Maker – as previously, written! Stir, continually, until the chocolate has melted. Be sure not to <u>burn</u> the chocolate with too much heat – therefore a 'double boiler' comes in handy, as there is a 'water barrier' between kettles.
3. At this point, a 'flavored extract' may be added; or, some people might put a touch of a commercial brand, of Tia Maria, Baileys Irish Cream, Rum, or Kahlúa, into the mixture. **<u>WARNING</u>**: using too much Tia Maria or other ingredients can turn the melted chocolate into a 'watery' consistency; and, it will not 'set' unless frozen and removed just before use. Moreover, one might not want children dealing with any 'alcohol!'
4. Remove the chocolate from heat when smooth and melted.
5. Dip the spoons into the melted chocolate. Make sure the spoons are not 'dripping' chocolate when removing. Tapping the handle of the spoon against the side of the pan works well to remove excess chocolate. They may be 'half-dipped' or fully dipped – or, even at an angle! Place on the wax or parchment paper to dry/set.
6. **Optional**: 'Sprinkle' each spoon, before the chocolate has 'set,' with 'Colored or Flavored Sugars' or 'Cookie Sprinkles;' for decoration. Lightly press down 'Sprinkles' with one finger, if necessary, to 'adhere' to the chocolate. **Optional**: dip each spoon in 'Sprinkles' – then, slightly press to adhere to the chocolate.

7. When 'plate or tray' is full, refrigerate the spoons until the chocolate turns firm/solid.

8. **Optional**: While the dipped, 'Chocolate Spoons' are cooling, place 'White Chocolate' – or, other flavored chocolates of ones' choice – in a heavy saucepan or 'Double Boiler,' over low heat – just as was done with the first chocolate. Stir until melted.

9. Add in 'Flavored Extracts' if using.

10. Remove from heat and pour into a 'Pastry Bag;' or, 'dip' another spoon or stick into the mixture; to enable a 'drizzle,' so to speak, over the 'set' spoons. Again, the 'Chocolate Spoons' may be 'half' dipped, or 'dipped at an angle,' for decoration!

11. At this point, again, more 'flavored Sugars' or Sprinkles can be sprinkled over the top of the spoons – remember, 'Flavored Sprinkles' will only stick to the 'wet' chocolate.

12. Refrigerate, again, until set.

13. Wrap each spoon separately in clear or colored plastic wrap; or, add a ribbon to each spoon to decorate.

In the past, I have made, something, of a 'bouquet' of spoons; 'bunching' them all together and placing a ribbon around them to hold together. Sometimes, I have placed the 'Bouquet of Spoons' into a new coffee mug, to make a nice gift.

The spoons are, now, ready to use or give as gifts. They may be consumed as a 'treat' (as my wife enjoys); or inserted into a cup of Coffee, Tea or Hot Chocolate – which she, also, enjoys!

<u>Bonus</u>: Sugar or Chocolate Sprinkles/Shreds

Surprisingly, many people have asked me, "*What are, 'Sprinkles'* (as I have mentioned using in the previous paragraphs)?" Even more have asked, "*Can I make my own?*" Surprisingly, there are still some people who ask, "*What is the difference between 'Sprinkles or Shredded Chocolate, or 'Colored/Flavored' Sugars?*" I would have to presume; these people have not done a lot of 'cookie' or 'cake' baking; or, have shopped for those who do! But they are easy enough to make (or, easier to purchase at the store)!

However, 'Sprinkles, Shreds, or Flavored/Colored Sugars,' are just decorations; usually flavored, which can be 'sprinkled' (hence the name) on top of desserts or coffees… typically, over whipped cream, frosting or foam!

Although, not difficult to make, it is easier (not necessarily, better tasting) to purchase a bottle of 'Sprinkles or Flavored/Colored Sugars' at the grocery store!

'Sprinkles' can be prepared by taking a piece of 'Bakers' Chocolate,' a 'hard' candy bar, or chocolate chips, and 'chopping, crushing, or pulverizing' them into tiny pieces. Often, this can be done by using a 'Spice Grater/Grinder' (such as for nutmeg), a 'Cheese Grater,' or a 'Food Processor' to chop the chocolate pieces into small pieces. These pieces are then 'sprinkled' on top of many different beverages – or can used for an ice cream topping; to decorate frostings, or just about anything. They can be fun to make; and one does find 'satisfaction' in making their own. When I want a few 'Sprinkles,' however, I will use a bottle of them that I have purchased at the grocery store – such as this brand!

If one is looking for 'Shredded' chocolate, however, one can take a 'Cheese Grater' or 'Potato Peeler' to make 'Chocolate Ribbons' or 'Swirls' with the chocolate. Of course, if money is of no object, there are mechanical devices called 'Chocolate Mills;' which will perform the same function for you, automatically! Frankly, unless one is in a business to use many 'shavings,' a 'Chocolate Mill' is an <u>unnecessary</u> expense – that is, unless one wishes to own one for fun or 'Snobby' purposes!

I once had a student ask, "*Why not just use your Coffee Grinder?*" It is a good question; but the first answer is, the chocolate pieces would have to be <u>frozen</u>; as not to melt in the grinder… 'gumming up' the device. Of course, most grinders will 'create heat' as well; and thus, 'melting' the chocolate. A 'Food Processor' could be pressed into service; but again, it will be difficult to clean; and 'pieces' of the chocolate will not be in 'swirls' or 'long' pieces. It can be 'pulverized,' however! Again, starting 'frozen' is the best way to begin.

'Rainbow Sprinkles,' although difficult to see in this black and white photograph, can be made at home if one is ambitious enough; but otherwise, the easiest way to use is to purchase a bottle, again, at the grocery store; usually, in the 'Baking' department. Frankly, I have never even attempted to 'make' a

'Rainbow' Sprinkle; so, I am not going to go into any detail here as to 'how' to do it! I have, however, taken colored 'Candy Canes;' and placed into my food processor – and pulverized to small chunks.

'Color Sugars' can be made very quickly; with just some 'Sugar' in a plastic, sandwich bag or a bowl; along with a drop or two of 'Food Coloring;' and shaking or stirring until evenly 'colored!' Use additional drops of Food Coloring to make the sugar as 'dark' as needed.

However (and this is a big 'however'), unless one truly enjoys 'Do It Yourself' projects, bottles of 'Colored Sugar' can be purchased at any grocery or 'party' store; often, in 'Multiple Color' option bottles! I prefer these, myself; as the 'Colored Sugar' comes in large, crystal form; and *"Looks*  *'prettier' on the deserts or beverages,"* according to my wife, that is!

LIQUEUR ADDITIVE RECIPES

Many coffee drinkers enjoy a little 'alcohol' (from time to time, and type to type) in their coffee. For me, for example, when I was single (and in Winter), I would often take girlfriends to a favorite, 'Little Dive' in 'Old Sacramento, along the river, for an 'end of evening, nightcap' (usually, an Irish Coffee). Also, in the Winter, while on skiing trips, I would make a Thermos bottle full of coffee or hot chocolate; with a bit of Whiskey, Kahlua™, or Amaretto in it! I still do! Of course, one can purchase a bottle of anything (my Norwegian uncle enjoyed Aquavit – Potato Vodka – in his) to put in their coffee.

However, for fun (and economics) one can make their own 'flavored alcohols' or 'liqueurs!' For example, I enjoy Kahlua in my coffee; unfortunately, Kahlua has become very expensive – at least, here in California. When I lived in Tucson Arizona, and frequently traveled down to Mexico on weekends, I could purchase a large, 'Kahlua' (or similar brand) very inexpensively – usually, under $10.00 a bottle. But, now, (as a 1.75 LTR bottle costs upwards of $60.00 or more) I, generally, make my own version of Kahlua or Tia Maria (coffee liqueur); especially, during the 'holiday season,' when people, like my son, enjoy 'Peppermint' or 'Mudslide' Kahlua in their coffee. We, in my family, enjoy the 'homemade' liqueurs just as well as we do the name brands… perhaps, even more!

HOMEMADE KAHLÚA™ (Coffee Liqueur) or TIA MARIA™

Again, this makes a great gift; and remember, it can be 'flavored' numerous ways… just like a 'Kahlua brand' product!

Ingredients:

- 4 cups of Pure Water.
- 1½ cups Instant Coffee Powder or Crystals.
- 4½ cups 100 proof Vodka or Everclear (pure grain alcohol).
- 8 cups White Sugar (**Optional**: substitute Dark Brown Sugar for two of the cups to make it more like Tia Maria™.
- 2 Vanilla beans – seeds removed (**Optional**: 4 to 6 tablespoons real Vanilla Extract).
- **Optional**: Rum or Brandy; either added or substituted, for 2 cups of the Vodka to make Tia Maria. **Optional**: use a 'Spiced' Rum for a different taste; or, I prefer a bit of '151 Rum.' Of course, additional spices may be added to any Rum.
- **Optional**: Mint/Peppermint Extract, to taste; for a holiday, 'Candy Cane,' Kahlúa (my 28-year-old son loves it). Also, for a 'non-alcoholic' version, simply use a flavored Extract instead of alcohol!

Directions:

1. Mix and heat water, sugar, and coffee crystals, in a large saucepan, over medium heat, until dissolved – stirring, continually.
2. Allow cooling to room temperature.
3. Add vodka, whiskey, other alcohol to saucepan. Stir to combine.
4. Pour the mixture into 'sealable' bottles (I re-use the empty liquor or coffee syrup/creamer bottles; with the labels removed).
5. Cut each vanilla bean into thirds and drop into each bottle (seeds and all); or add in the vanilla or other flavored extracts.

After 2 - 3 weeks, remove beans and seeds by pouring through a sieve, strainer, or filter; and 'rebottle.' Allow the mixture to further 'age.' However, I have used this mixture immediately upon bottling – especially if using 'Extracts.' The Kahúla is best bottled in a 'brown' bottle; so, I either purchase 'Half-Gallon' bottles from my local Restaurant Supply or 'Craft Beer' store; or 'Liter-sized' beer bottles to store in; then, make a 'custom label' to go onto the bottle for gift giving.

HOMEMADE AMARETTO LIQUEUR

Again, this recipe can be 'augmented' as the preparer sees fit!

Ingredients:

- 1 cup Pure Water.
- 1 cup White Sugar (**Optional**: Sugar Substitute).
- ½ cup Brown Sugar (**Optional**: Brown Sugar Substitute).
- 2 cups Vodka or Everclear ™.
- 1 – 3 tablespoons Almond Extract (or to taste).
- 2 teaspoons Vanilla Extract (or to taste).

Directions:

1. Combine water and sugars in a saucepan over medium heat. Some 'Coffee Snobs' claim that the only way to make this is to use a 'wooden' spoon; however, I have used metal, plastic, and wood; and frankly, I cannot taste any difference!
2. Heat the mixture to boiling; stirring continually, until both sugars have dissolved.
3. Remove the pan from the heat; and allow the mixture cool for ten or more minutes.
4. Providing the mixture is cool, stir in vodka, almond and vanilla extracts.
5. Pour into a sealable bottle. (I use the empty, vodka bottle; with the label removed). **Optional**: Use a 'decorative' bottle, in which to store the liquid. Often, 'decorative bottles,' of assorted sizes, can be found in 'Dollar' stores. If not there, then, many 'Craft' or hardware stores carry them.
6. As most people have computers and printers at home, make an attractive label (blank labels can be purchased in most 'Office Supply' stores or Walmart) to place on each bottle; possibly, with the 'customized' names of the friends or family members on it… such as, "*Made especially for* (friends name).
7. With a ribbon wrapped around the neck, it makes a beautiful gift!

In years past, I have made bottles of assorted flavors of Liqueurs; to 'box' and present to family and friends as holiday gifts!

COFFEE SYRUP – AS IN, ACTUAL SYRUP!

To make approximately one cup of Syrup.

This 'Coffee Lovers' recipe, can be made many different ways; either with 'Coffee and Pure Maple (or some other) Syrup' with 'Coffee Extract,' Corn Syrup, Sugar Beet Sugar, Blue Agave Nectar, or anything sweet! Even, a combination of 'some or all of the above' tends to come out good! I suggest one try several options to see which one might 'taste better' on Pancakes, French Toast, Waffles... alternatively, used in some baking recipe. Oddly enough, I do know two 'Coffee Snobs' who make 'Coffee Syrup' to use as a 'sweetener' in their coffees – although, due to its content, it is not much different than merely using sugar!

Ingredients:

- ½ cup Extra Dark Coffee.
- ½ cup thick, Pure Maple Syrup.
- **Optional**: Finely ground Turkish Coffee.

Alternatively,

- Slightly less than one cup of Maple or Corn Syrup (other types of Syrup may be used depending upon taste).
- 1 teaspoon (or more, to taste) of Coffee Extract.

Alternatively,

- Slightly less than 1 cup of Maple Syrup.
- Coffee Powder or Crystals.

Alternatively,

- Add favorite alcohol – such as Whiskey, Brandy, Rum, or Coffee Liqueur to Corn Syrup.
- **Optional**: Any of the above combinations!

Alternatively,

- A combination of syrups and 1 tablespoon of 'extra-fine,' Espresso grounds!

[323]

Alternatively,

- Any 'sweet' powder or liquid.

Directions:

1. Using any of the above combinations, mix coffee, or grounds, with maple (or other) syrup – to taste. This syrup will be a touch thin; so, 'optional' sugar, nectar, or corn syrup may be added to 'thicken' the mixture. Of course, the ingredients can often be 'cooked down' over medium heat on the stove, until the desired 'thickness' has been achieved.

    Alternatively, working backward, start with slightly less than a cup of maple (or other syrup). Add one or more teaspoons of coffee extract or instant coffee crystals (or to taste). Some people enjoy using a 'Turkish' or 'extra-fine' grind of coffee grounds in place of 'instant coffee' or extracts.

    Optional: again, heat the mixture; and reduce to taste and thickness, over medium heat.

The easiest way (but, not as delicious in my opinion) is to take slightly less than a cup of any type syrup – even sugar-free – and add anywhere from 1 teaspoon to 1 tablespoon off 'Instant Coffee Powder/Crystals' to it. Again, add as much or little as you might wish, depending upon taste. The 'Crystals' will dissolve slowly; so, some stirring may be necessary. However, I do know one person who enjoys 'undissolved' crystals in his syrup; so, he pours syrup over his waffles or pancakes, then sprinkles on Coffee Crystals. I would not care for it; but this is how 'he' enjoys his waffles and syrup – especially, if he is eating 'Chicken and Waffles' (with a 'rub' of coffee on the chicken!

Serve over whatever one would, usually, put 'Flavored Syrup' on; i.e., Waffles, Pancakes, French Toast, et cetera… or pour in coffee!

Optional: Other ingredients, such as Caramel topping or Chocolate Syrup may be added to any mixture as well for different tastes; the same with distinct types of Coffee; French Roast, Espresso, High-Grade Instant, or et cetera.

Another Option: Syrup can be to add to the 'Base Creamer' (or some other creamer) for a slight, 'coffee and sweet taste!'

CHOCOLATE SYRUP

Ingredients:

- ½ cup, packed, Cocoa Powder.
- 1 cup Whole Milk or Half and Half.
- 2 cups Raw Sugar (**Optional:** Sugar-Free Substitute.)
- ⅛ teaspoon Sea Salt.
- ¼ teaspoon Pure, Vanilla Extract (**Optional**: Chocolate Extract).
- **Optional**: 2 ounces of 'Irish' Whiskey.

Directions:

1. Mix cocoa powder and milk, in a large saucepan, over medium to medium/high heat. Stir until cocoa has fully dissolved.
2. Add the sugar; and, again, stir to dissolve fully. Bring to a boil for 3 minutes; stirring, continuously.
3. Remove from heat, allow to cool for ten minutes, then 'stir in' the sea salt and vanilla extract.
4. Allow to cool, completely.
5. Skim off any 'skin' which may have formed on the top of the mixture.
6. Pour into a clean, 'sealable' jar or bottle; and, store in the refrigerator until serving.

ALTERNATE CHOCOLATE OR OTHER FLAVORED SYRUP

Ingredients:

- 1 bottle Corn Syrup or Blue Agave Nectar.
- Pure, Chocolate Extract (artificial, does not taste too good) to taste.

Directions:

1. To a bottle of corn syrup or nectar, add several drops of pure, chocolate extract. Mix a little at a time and taste. Add more extract, if needed. Depending upon the bottle of corn syrup or nectar, a small amount may have to be removed to allow 'mixing space' for the chocolate extract.
2. Store in the refrigerator; and use as any other syrup.

3. **Optional**: Any other flavored extract may be added to the chocolate – such as caramel or raspberry; or, different flavors of syrup can be made. One of my favorite syrups is made with 'Watermelon' (difficult to find) extract.

4. **Optional**: Boil down fresh fruit, with a little water, and pour into the corn syrup. Remember, any combination of flavored extracts may be mixed and added to the corn syrup for a 'Custom' taste!

5. **Optional**: Pour some of the Chocolate Syrup into a 'Base Creamer;' to 'flavor' the creamer.

HOMEMADE, SALTED CARAMEL SYRUP

Ingredients:

- 1 cup Sugar (**Optional**: substitute ½ cup of Corn Syrup. Or Sugar Substitute).
- 2 tablespoons unsalted Butter.
- 1 cup Brown Sugar.
- ¾ cup of Pure Water.
- 3 teaspoons Corn Syrup – omit if using Corn Syrup instead of Sugar.
- 2 teaspoons Pure Vanilla Extract.
- ½ teaspoon Pure Caramel Extract.
- 1 Pinch of Sea Salt.
- **Optional**: 2 tablespoons Salted, Melted Butter – for 'creamy and salty.'
- **Optional**: ½ cup Soft Caramel Candies.

Directions:

1. Melt and 'brown' the butter over medium heat in a large saucepan. Brown, but do not <u>burn,</u> the butter.
2. Combine sugar, ½ cup water, the corn syrup, and any soft caramel candies in a large saucepan. Stir over medium/low heat until all are dissolved. Bring to a boil – stirring constantly.
3. Cover the saucepan; and, allow to boil for 3 minutes. Remove the cover and stir, vigorously, until the mixture is an amber color.
4. Remove the saucepan from heat and allow to cool for ten minutes; after which time, 'stir in' the pure vanilla extract and sea salt.
5. Add the remaining water and stir well. Allow to fully cool.

6. Carefully, pour the syrup into a sealable bottle or jar; and refrigerate until use. Flavor with it to taste.

    Special Note: due to the mixture 'thickness,' it is sometimes easier to pour into bottles while the mixture is still a bit warm.

All the recipes are very 'forgiving' when it comes to substituting Corn Syrup for Sugar.

HOMEMADE BAILEYS IRISH CREAM

Another one of my favorites; and, it even goes good on Ice Cream!

Ingredients:

- 2 cups, Irish Whiskey.
- 1 cup Heavy Cream or Half & Half. **Optional**: 1 cup of melted, French Vanilla Ice Cream.
- ½ cup Corn Syrup.
- 1 (14-ounce) can Sweetened Condensed Milk. **Optional**: if needed to cut down on Sugar, use 'Sugar-Free' products or substitute Evaporated Milk for the Sweetened Condensed Milk. The mixture will end up being less sweet, but still very good!
- 2 tablespoons Chocolate Syrup.
- 2 teaspoons Pure Vanilla Extract (**Optional**: 1 teaspoon Pure Almond Extract and 1 teaspoon Pure Vanilla Extract).
- 1 teaspoon (or to taste) Instant Coffee or a dash of Coffee Extract.

Directions:

1. Combine all ingredients in a blender and mix on high speed for 30 seconds.
2. Transfer the mixture into an airtight container or glass bottle with a tight-fitting lid; and, store in the refrigerator. It should stay 'stable/fresh' for up to 1 month.
3. Shake well before use.

It would be very easy to add additional recipes in this section; but the whole purpose of them, was to give the reader an 'idea' of what can be 'done at home,' rather than having to purchase in a store – and thus, have a 'better product;' which, hopefully, will be less expensive as well!

I realize, that most 'Coffee Snobs' will not be making their own 'Creamers and Syrups;' but for those of us who enjoy cooking and trying new things, 'homemade' products can be very rewarding!

Let's look at a few more things:

"Coffee should not be drunk in a hurry. It is the sister of time, and should be sipped slowly, slowly. Coffee is the sound of taste, a sound for the aroma. It is a meditation and a plunge into memories and the soul."

~ (Attributed to) Mahmoud Darwish, Palestinian Author and Poet

OTHER ALTERNATIVES – AND A FEW RECIPES

Sometimes, an 'Additive' turns into an actual recipe – and, every country in the world has its own 'specialized' form of 'Coffee Drinks' by 'adding something' to the brewed coffee! For example, some Europeans (and, people high in the Himalayas) enjoy putting a teaspoon or two of unsalted, farm-fresh 'Ghee' (clarified butter) into their cup; as do the, so-called, 'over-aged Hippies' I know… who put Marijuana/Cannabis (Cannabutter) Ghee in theirs!

Other people, throughout the world, may add a tablespoon of 'natural, cooking oil,' to their cup or mug. It was only natural that early, immigrant farmers would do the same after migrating to this country. Years later, some bright person started doing research and combined the two; learning, that there may be specific 'health aspects' from mixing 'certain' oils – such as Coconut – and grass-fed, 'Unsalted Butter' or 'Ghee' to one's coffee.

Soon, it becomes a recipe for a 'Coffee Fad;' something, now, called: 'Bulletproof Coffee' (I suggest all readers search the internet for recipes; regarding, the 'best ways' to make this); but, here are some 'basic' facts and recipe for it.

Bulletproof Coffee: (A form of the company name – Bulletproof 360, Inc. and Bulletproof Nutrition, Inc.) has achieved something of 'Cult Status' at this writing – and is considered by some to be, not only a diet aid, but a "*Mind or energy booster.*" It was initially developed to help 'complement' the 'Keto' diet. In fact, many people concerned with 'health' drink it! The 'Family Fitness' center my family and I attend, even serves a version of this coffee!

Developed from a recipe researched in 1993 by Dave Asprey, an American Entrepreneur, 'Bulletproof' Coffee, apparently, is supposed to have, "*Two teaspoons full of Grass-Fed* (Irish, usually), *Unsalted Butter* (or GHEE) *in it; along with a dash of Coconut, MCT, XCT ('Superfood Oils'), or other 'Designer-type' Oils*" (generally available in most grocery stores – at least in my area). This mixture is said to "*Elevate fat-burning, brain-fueling, energy, 'ketones' in one's body.*" Some people dieting, may even substitute a cup of this coffee for an actual meal!

I have tried it, and it is not too bad… considering! My wife went on a diet, and I prepared her coffee this way; she did not care for it, however.

[329]

Butter and Oil are placed into a cup of coffee, or first 'mixed in a blender' to emulsify it, before pouring into a cup or mug – sometimes, with the coffee itself. In other words, some people 'blend' <u>with</u> the coffee. When just the Butter and Oil are blended, it is not only to 'mix,' but 'pre-blend' in order to 'froth' it; as with a 'Milk Frother'! In this photograph, however, I 'floated' my Butter, and just 'poured in' a spoon of Coconut Oil… it <u>still</u> tasted good; and still served the same purpose of "*Enhancing Ketones*!"

Some 'Coffee Snobs' really like this recipe; as it is 'fashionable;' especially when using a 'Brain Octane, MCT or XCT' oil! However, for those enjoying their coffee 'sweet,' then, it is acceptable to use an 'artificial sweetener' (for some reason) – but <u>not</u> 'natural' Raw Sugar, Organic Honey, Blue Agave Nectar, or another sweetener… as, that would be, according to some experts… "*Un-natural and unhealthy*!" This is, especially true when someone is dieting; and substitutes the coffee for one or more actual meals! Yes, one may 'lose weight' this way; but they still lack essential vitamins, minerals, enzymes, and other nutrients – such as complex proteins – found in 'real' food!

I take exception to this last part; as I find 'Raw Sugar, Organic Honey,' and especially, 'Blue Agave Nectar,' <u>all</u> to be '<u>natural</u>;' and 'artificially sweetened' substances, <u>not</u> to be! The truth of the matter is, Coconut Oil has <u>1/3</u> more saturated fat than butter, and <u>80 times</u> that of lard; and, despite being considered a 'healthy alternative,' Coconut Oil <u>raises</u> 'unhealthy' LDL Cholesterol levels.

I suggest readers interested in 'Bullet Proof Coffee' look up recipes on the internet for more details regarding its, so-called, 'Health' benefits.

However, as with 'Colloidal Silver' coffee, here in America, Scandinavia has one odd version of '<u>healthy</u>' coffee – although, I have yet to hear of any benefits, short of 'dilating the blood vessels' – and that is: 'Karsk' (coffee with pennies and alcohol). Karsk, has 'moonshine,' vodka, or pure grain alcohol in it.

Scandinavian Karsk: (Made a few different ways in Scandinavia) Karsk is, sometimes made like 'Bulletproof' coffee – with a spoon of Butter, Goat Ghee and Oil. However, Karsk is more of a Norwegian, 'hot cocktail,' rather than a coffee drink!

Known by <u>many</u> Norse names, Karsk is made by placing one or more 'Copper Coins' (preferably washed/clean), in the bottom of a <u>large</u> coffee mug. Then, enough fresh, 'hot' coffee is poured over it until the coins can no longer be seen through the liquid. This works out to approximately '½ cup' in most cases! The mug is 'topped off' with 'Pure Grain Alcohol'… in other words, 'Moonshine!' Enough 'Moonshine' is added, until the Pennies can, once again, be 'seen' through the liquid. Most people would find this mixture, 'very strong' – and, may wish to 'sweeten' the mixture with a little sugar.

Again, depending upon the Scandinavian region, people say the coffee must be, either *"Strong enough to 'float' a coin on,"* or, *"Extra Thin,"* to be more like a weak tea. My family, always, preferred 'strong and bold' coffee!

In theory, the coffee is supposed to 'extract' a certain amount of 'Copper' from the 'Pennies;' and thus, help arthritis and other maladies! It is, also, supposed to *"Be good for the blood,"* according to many Norwegians. The fact is, copper is an essential mineral which helps to make new 'Red Blood Cells.' It should, also, help to 'maintain' nerve cells; by reducing 'aging' of the skin, and 'boosting' the immune system.

In actuality, the 'Pennies' in the bottom of the cup or mug, are just a 'visual aid' and novelty (realistically, if one wants to ingest copper, the best way is to get it in one's food; such as, with 'organ meats, oysters or lobster, shiitake mushrooms, seeds and nuts or leafy greens! But in coffee, the best way would be to add a shot of 'Colloidal Copper' to the coffee; or drink out of a 'Copper' mug for 'trace' amounts of copper!

One will need to experiment with 'strong or weak' coffee to determine the 'strength' of the brew made; and 'mixture' with the alcohol! Just remember the old Norse 'rule of thumb:' *"The 'stronger' the coffee, the larger the cup or mug"* – as it will take more alcohol before the pennies can be seen.

If the alcohol content is 'too strong,' then one has a few options; either add more coffee to dilute, split the mixture with another cup, or take a 'lit match;' and 'burn off' some of the alcohol (my 'Norwegian family' way) from the cup. The coffee will have to be at least 60% alcohol, however, before it burns! Some claim *"Burning off excess alcohol vastly improves the taste of the Karsk!"*

Russian Coffee: Is the same as Karsk; but minus the pennies… except, it is topped with whipped cream – and, uses Vodka <u>exclusively</u>! In the same sense, some alternatives go back to some 'old-time' methods of coffee brewing; such as, adding <u>salt</u> to remove bitterness. Only, in this case, some people add, not only substantial 'Sea Salt' to the coffee but, sometimes, add fresh fruit as well – such as pieces of Watermelon or Pineapple – to make more of an 'evening' or 'dessert' drink. In some cases, a 'flavored' Vodka might be used as well; although, the use of 'regular Vodka' is the traditional way to make Russian Coffee. Often, some people serve this coffee with 'Beluga' Caviar!

Scandinavian Egg Coffee: Eggs or Eggshells… 'Eggpresso?' As I have said earlier, many coffee drinkers (many in my own family) feel that 'Eggs, or Eggshells,' can <u>remove</u> <u>a</u> <u>lot</u> of 'bitterness' from their brewed coffee – similar, to what salt does. My thought on the subject is, why not make one's coffee correctly, from the start? That way, no eggs or salt is required!

Frankly, if it were not for the 'excellent taste' of the coffee, I would doubt anyone would ever use this method – as it is rather revolting to look at! In any event, eggshells (dripping with 'egg whites') are placed into the 'hopper/basket' of a Drip Coffee Maker; or, into a 'Pour-Over' Cone; along with the ground coffee. Hot water is added. As the coffee brews, 'bitterness' is 'absorbed' by the shells! Alternatively, what my family used – primarily when making 'Cowboy Coffee' – was 'whole eggs' dropped into the 'hopper/basket' of a Percolator; or dropped directly into the pot to make a 'clearer,' less bitter, brew. This was, and still is, the favorite way to make 'Campfire' coffee; for many 'outdoors' people. However, many people will 'scramble' the eggs along with the grounds, first (to make something of a paste), before adding it to the pot – as shown in the photograph on the next page.

My advice is to make two pots; both 'with and without' the eggs; to taste and 'see' the difference between the two brews.

The uncomplicated, Norwegian way – that my family used to use, and what I previously mentioned – is to use a kettle or pot on the stove, and, 'heat' the water to boiling.

In another, small, measuring cup or bowl, lightly stir/whisk one or two eggs (including the 'whites') with four or more tablespoons of coffee grounds (depending upon the size and type of the brewer used) – any coffee can be used – but an inexpensive 'canned' coffee works well with this method! When slightly mixed, add a quarter of a cup of hot water to the mixture, and stir some more; before adding the entire contents to the pot. This action helps to 'prepare' the grounds for 'better' extraction – much, in the same way as 'Blooming!'

There is one more way to prepare 'Norwegian Egg Coffee;' and that is to separate the 'egg yolks' from the 'whites…' and use 'either/or' with the grounds! 'Whites,' tend to 'smooth' the body of the coffee more than yolks, alone, however.

In any event, allow the coffee to 'brew' to the desired color and strength.' Turn off the heat at that point – and allow the coffee mixture to 'rest' (stirring occasionally) for three or four minutes. Add ½ cup of cold water. This will help the grounds and egg mixture to 'sink' (as shown here) to the bottom of the pot… hopefully. The coffee can, then, be poured immediately into a cup; or 'streamed' through a small, hand sieve or filter of some sort, for additional clarity – which is what I prefer doing!

If not using a sieve or filter, when the pot is devoid of coffee liquid, throw away the 'Egg and Ground' mixture.

When I was a kid, my family <u>never</u> filtered anything; if the pot had 'eggs or grounds' in it… "*so be it!*" With the coffee shown above, I did try pouring a cup first; then one poured through a filter. The first cup looked fine – perhaps, with what looked like a bit of coffee oil floating on top; but when compared to the filtered cup, it was easy to see 'pinpoint specks' of 'egg' floating in the oil slick. The 'filtered cup' was clean and pure – and did not have that 'oil sheen' floating on top!

Cuban Coffee: Short, simple, and to the point, there are two ways to make Cuban Coffee; the first way is to take a 'double shot' of Espresso; and pour it into an 8-ounce glass of ice; and then, add one teaspoon of Raw Sugar to it. Then, fill the rest of the glass with 'Fresh Cream' or 'Evaporated Milk' and stir.

Another other way, is to 'measure out' 16 ounces of Espresso Grounds; and place them into an Espresso Machines 'Portafilter.' Add a teaspoon of Raw Sugar to the Portafilter as well, tamper and install. Make two shots of Espresso – then add to an 8-ounce glass filled with ice. Fill with cream or milk, stir, and serve!

Swedish Coffee: Very much like 'Scandinavian Egg Coffee;' in the fact that the way to brew 'Swedish Coffee' is to 'make a paste' of a scrambled egg and coffee grounds! However, instead of putting the mixture into a pot of 'boiling' coffee, the paste is poured into a 'French Press.' It is, then, filled  with <u>only</u> 212°F water (I have no idea why <u>only</u> that temperature should be used).

After three minutes, the top is placed on, and the plunger depressed. Most of the 'egg and grounds will remain at the bottom of the Press. If there is any question about 'clarity or oils,' again, pour through a paper filter into ones' cup – but, most people skip this step! An optional step, however, it to 'add' a pinch of salt to the coffee before depressing the plunger!

Oddly enough, both 'Norwegian' and 'Swedish Egg Coffees' should just be called 'The Scandinavian Way' – as most of the Scandinavian countries make their 'egg coffee,' roughly, the same ways! An egg is used to 'clear' the coffee and remove bitterness while brewing; then, discard… once it 'catches' all the grounds floating in the coffee!

Danish Egg Coffee: Danish Coffee is, again, like Cowboy Coffee… as is, 'Finnish and Icelandic' coffee too. As previously stated, all five of the Scandinavian countries make their coffee, almost, the same way – 'medium-roast' grounds; and then brought to a boil over high heat. Only, some brewing times and 'boiling methods' might make the difference; as in most cases, the coffee is 'overly boiled' to classify as 'Danish' coffee! The coffee can be brewed in a 'pot' or a 'Percolator' – if only using one, small egg.

The whole idea of 'Scandinavian' coffee, as said before, is to "*Use eggs to clarify the Coffee*;" creating a complete separation between the grounds and the water. Again, in theory, the 'grounds and eggs' are supposed to 'sink' to the bottom of the pot – especially, when a small amount of cold water is added. However, I have not found this to, always, be the case – as my 'Danish Coffee' photograph, on the previous page, shows!

However, the 'Danes' (like the Russians) may add a touch of salt to their brew at the same time – and, the 'American Lutheran Church' goers, might do the same – at least, I can speak for the ones in my family. I can still remember my family members in the kitchen at church; making a large 'Urn' of coffee and adding salt and eggs to it. Although I never tasted it, the result was a beautiful, golden-amber colored, coffee; free of cloudiness, bitterness, and sediment – as apparently, the 'cold water' technique after brewing, '*Always worked with the Urns*;" or, so my Norwegian Grandmother said!

However, because of the extreme 'high heat' – and, constant agitation from the 'rolling boil' that many 'American Churches' or the 'Danes' might use today (let alone, at the churches I attended as a kid) – the coffee tends to taste acrid, burnt, or over-extracted... when compared by most 'Coffee Snob' standards (church standard, appear to be different than 'Snob' standards)!

Surprisingly, 'Eggs in the Coffee' does not just stop with the Scandinavians! Many cultures and individuals enjoy having 'egg' left within their beverage; such as the Vietnamese people, for example.

Indonesian Egg Coffee/Kopi Telur (a.k.a. 'Egg and Poop'):
Often served as a dessert or treat, this coffee is 'traditionally brewed' with what is considered, the most 'expensive' coffee in the world – Kopi Luwak. Kopi Luwak is a strong, black, 'unfiltered' coffee... picked, and partially digested, by the Indonesian Civet Cat. The cats' feces are collected by the 'locals,' or by the coffee companies; whom, often, have 'caged' cats. The 'undigested' beans are extracted from the feces, cleaned, processed, then roasted, ground, brewed, and served!

I have tried it; and it has a delicious, slight chocolate flavor!

[335]

While the coffee is brewing by any type of brewing method (but with 195°F to 205°F water), 'one or two' egg yolks are quickly stirred (sometimes in a blender to be 'foamed,') and added to honey, vanilla extract, and evaporated/condensed milk; all 'layered' in a tall glass, by use of 'pouring' over the back of a spoon, on top of the poured coffee. Sometimes, however, the ingredients are all mixed before pouring over the coffee.

One variation uses 'Coconut Cream' instead of the evaporative, condensed milk!

The 'egg mixture' is, then, eaten with a spoon; and the coffee drunk.

I am afraid that I have only met a few 'Coffee Snobs' willing to try it – high price, or not!

Phin Vietnamese Coffee Filter/Cà Phê Trung (a.k.a. Weasel Vomit Coffee): Another 'Egg' coffee - like 'Kopi Luwak' Coffee – in the fact that is 'sounds,' somewhat, disquieting – 'Weasel Vomit (rather than poop) and Egg!'

Coffee is excellent in flavor and aroma – and, like Kopi Luwak, very expensive! It tastes very similar to 'Scandinavian' coffee. However, what is the difference between 'Scandinavian' and 'Vietnamese 'Egg' Coffee?' Well, besides the obvious, Scandinavians will use regular, 'fresh' coffee; rather than 'regurgitated,' processed coffee (I was brave enough to try it; and, I must admit, it <u>was</u> excellent). The egg still goes into the coffee; only, the Vietnamese people do not use the 'egg whites' – preferring, to only use the Yolks.

To make the 'Vietnamese Egg Coffee,' however, additional steps must be taken. While the coffee is 'dripping' through the 'Metal' filter, two (room temperature) eggs are separated; with the 'whites,' discarded or used in another recipe. The 'Yolks' are placed in a small, bowl or measuring cup; and two teaspoons of sweetened condensed milk are added, instead of going into a coffee cup or mug. They are 'whisked/mixed' together until 'light and fluffy.' For those wanting even more 'fluff,' a blender can be used!

When the brewing process is complete, the brewer is removed from the coffee cup; and the 'egg mixture' is, carefully, poured over the coffee… again, by pouring it over the back of a spoon, and 'floating' the mixture on top. The egg mixture is, somewhat, 'cooked' from underneath.

Sometimes, one teaspoon of vanilla sugar, a sugar cube, or a spoon of regular, evaporated or sweetened condensed milk, may be added to the cup as well, before pouring in the 'Egg Mixture.' The coffee is drunk, and the egg is eaten with a spoon! Breakfast or dessert? It is the 'drinkers' choice!

Optional: Depending upon the shape of the cup or mug, evaporated milk can, sometimes, be carefully poured into the cup; down the side or through the 'Egg Foam.' A spoon (often a 'baby' spoon) can, carefully, be inserted to the bottom of the mug or cup and stirred up – being careful not to disturb the egg on top; should other additives be poured into the cup. I once had the opportunity to try both methods, and I preferred the coffee with the 'evaporated milk' stirred in.

To me, sweetened, 'Vietnamese Egg Coffee' was more like a dessert than a 'breakfast food;' and it did, follow a traditional, Vietnamese dinner! Of course, any 'Raw Egg' concoction (even yolks alone) come with a 'warning' these days – however, these eggs are at least, somewhat, 'cooked' by the hot coffee; and 'denatured' by the sweetened condensed milk and 'frothing!' Of course, for safety, one can easily pasteurize ones' eggs before use.

This coffee reminds me of the 'Homemade Eggnog Coffee' my Norwegian grandmother used to make; of which, even as a kid, I would drink, when I would not 'touch' regular coffee – as it was more of a 'sweet, holiday dessert,' than coffee! It was nothing more than a small cup of coffee, with 'Homemade Eggnog,' carefully, poured on top – as not to mix. The eggnog would, somewhat, cook from the bottom; and thicken on the top. To this day (during the Christmas season), I will use 'commercial,' eggnog to 'float' on top of my coffee... alternatively, used as a creamer and stirred! When 'unstirred,' each 'sip' of hot coffee is mixed with a 'sip' of cold eggnog (at least to start). It is fun! Of course, being Norwegian, I put a touch of nutmeg on top too!

There are a few other 'egg' recipes to look up and try; in fact, most countries have a version of this type of coffee; and they are as varied as the methods of brewing! Here are a few more:

Primal Egg Coffee: Something of another 'Bulletproof' coffee (due to 'Emulsified Eggs').

There are many recipes one can find on the internet for this one – involving, several different ingredients. However, primarily, 2 ounces of

'Coconut Milk or Water' (or, to taste) is poured into a mixing container – such as a tall, 'sipper/shaker' cup – or a blender. To that, one to two tablespoons of 'Honey' or 'Blue Agave Nectar' is added; along with a 'pinch' of salt. Two whole eggs, and one, extra egg yolk, is added to the mixture. 8-ounces of 'extra hot' coffee is added; and the mixture 'shook' or 'blended' – to froth the liquid.

Cinnamon may be added to the mixture before blending; or used as a topping. Pour the mixture into a large mug for drinking.

Optional: 'Grass-fed, unsalted irish butter' – as with 'Bulletproof Coffee' – or even coconut oil may be added too; along with one teaspoon of sugar or powdered sugar and a pinch of salt – mixed into the coffee before pouring in the egg. If mixing and pouring separately, the egg can 'float' on top; and can be 'eaten' right off the top of the cup.

Look it up on the internet, for other options!

Sri Lankan Egg/Brandy Coffee – Known for the belief of *"Boosting one's metabolism,"* 'Egg/Brandy Coffee' is strong, black, and sugared; with one, whole egg 'cracked' into a cup of 'extra hot' coffee… moreover, a shot of Brandy is poured over it. As with some other 'Egg' coffees, this drink is 'layered' in a glass or tall mug (preferably clear, for appearance); to give the egg time to cook from below and 'denature' (chemically cook) from the top from the Brandy. Some people might even 'heat the Brandy and glass,' before pouring – thus 'cooking' from the top and sides as well!

Optional: this recipe can be served hot, cold, or over ice – being, carefully, transferred; and can have assorted spices added to it!

Again, there are recipes, literally, from <u>every</u> country; for variations of the afore mentioned mixtures. There are no 'hard and fast' rules or ingredients for any method – except to make it safe, with 'Pasteurized Eggs!'

Let us, now, look at 'Pasteurizing' eggs for coffee drinks:

"I went out the kitchen to make coffee — yards of coffee. Rich, strong, bitter, boiling hot, ruthless, depraved. The life blood of tired men."

~ Raymond Chandler, The Long Goodbye

HOW TO PASTURIZE (make safe) EGGS FOR RECIPES

When using 'Raw Eggs' in ones' coffee (or anything else, for that matter), it is considered 'best' to use 'Pasteurized' eggs. This is to help 'prevent bacterial diseases;' such as Salmonella (food poisoning). Many people do not worry about this; however, I must admit, that I grew up consuming room temperature, freshly laid, raw eggs, daily… moreover, they were not near as 'safe' as today's,  cleaned, processed, and refrigerated, 'store purchased' eggs! My grandparents owned an egg farm, and, apparently, the thought of 'pasteurizing' their eggs never came up!

For myself, being a very 'underweight child,' my mother would put a 'farm fresh' eggs into, daily, 'milkshakes' to help 'fatten' me up; this was long before products like Ensure™ were invented! Moreover, my father made one of the best Caesar Salads (with 'raw eggs') around! Even the local Orange Julius® stand used to put 'raw eggs' into some of their beverages; as they made their drinks both delicious and nutritious!

Family and friends (still) all ate 'raw cookie dough, homemade ice cream, homemade eggnog, chocolate mousse, freshly made meringue on pies, tiramisu' and more – all made with 'raw' eggs – and no one ever thought or heard about anyone getting sick!

Today, 'store purchased' (or even farm fresh) eggs are safer and cleaner than ever; regardless of what one reads in the news, or with product warnings! However, if one listens to the, so-called, 'experts,' one would think it would be '<u>certain</u> <u>death</u>' to consume a <u>raw</u> egg! So, why do some cultures (with far less 'safe eggs' than the United States) want to put 'raw eggs' into their coffee? Because it is tasty, nutritious, and 'traditional!'

Other countries 'eggs' are still very much like my childhood family's home; being kept in a basket – straight from the chicken! There is no 'processing,' short of perhaps, 'washing' the eggs to remove any left-over 'Chicken Poop!' In my research, I have found that few people in other countries (and not just under-industrialized) refrigerate their eggs; and fewer more, 'pasteurize' them… or make a special effort to 'only' purchase,

'Pasteurized Eggs!' Whole eggs are, often, just dropped into coffee pots, or stirred into other coffee mixtures – often, without allowing enough time, to <u>fully</u> cook the eggs!

However, if someone would like to drink something like a 'Vietnamese Coffee with Egg,' and worries about the 'raw egg' issue, they can purchase pasteurized, sterilized, and cleaned, eggs at many stores – and, keep them in the refrigerator for added safety; and, of course, using them as 'quickly' as they can!

However, again, in researching this issue, many grocery stores told me, "*Eggs are safer than ever to consume*;" and, many, do not bother to sell Pasteurized Eggs – or, if they do, they are costly; and are sold in the 'Organic' section of the 'Dairy, Cold Case!' Even so, consumers have been 'shying away' from 'raw eggs' for years – due to the 'negative propaganda' which the, so-called, 'experts' have put out. I will not say it is <u>all</u> nonsense; as many people, over the years, have developed Salmonella... and 'raw eggs' may have been involved. However, as I write this, the news on TV is talking about a local 'Salmonella outbreak' involving 'Romaine Lettuce!' No mention was made if the lettuce was used in a Caesar Salad, involving 'raw eggs,' or perhaps, 'Mayonnaise, or Salad Dressing,' which had 'gone bad!' Perhaps, stories about Salmonella involving 'raw eggs' might have been a bit misleading!

Nonetheless, rather than never use, 'regular' eggs, many cooks or coffee drinkers (who, like me, wish to experience as many 'different types' of coffee as one can) will 'Pasteurize' the eggs themselves; as it is so simple!

What is a 'Pasteurized Egg?' It is a 'fresh egg' which is, briefly, 'semi/slightly' cooked, to an elevated temperature – not so much that the 'Egg Yolk' congeals (cooks), but enough to kill any pathogen, with 'semi-high' heat, for a brief period. The eggs are, then, quickly cooled and refrigerated until use. For all intents and purposes, the eggs appear to 'fresh and raw;' but can be 'cooked with,' or 'consumed,' safely!

This how to do it:

The 'Egg Yolk' must reach an internal temperature of 138°F – 141°F. Remember, at higher temperatures... eggs 'cook' quickly! So, one wants to 'raise' the eggs internal temperature enough to 'kill off' any bacteria or pathogens – this, also, kills any pathogens on the outside of the egg too – which is, often, the main source of bacteria! That is all there is to it! Why don't restaurants use 'Pasteurized Eggs' in their recipes or beverages? I do not know… it is beyond me – especially when the chef can purchase them directly from their suppliers at 'wholesale' prices; and, eggs are so commonly used, they will never 'sit around' in a restaurant and get old! Most likely, it is a 'time' issue… moreover, 'time is money!'

The easiest way 'Pasteurize' fresh, medium, or large eggs, is to, first, bring the eggs to room temperature. Next, place the eggs into a 'cooking basket' of some sort – such as <u>from</u> a deep fat fryer – and place the basket into a large saucepan or kettle. Then, 'cover the eggs' (fill the saucepan) with water. The 'square copper' pans, I show in the 'Water' section of this book, work well; and, they come with a 'cooking basket' with a handle! The water is then 'heated' to 138°F – 141°F. Be sure to use a good thermometer – which is not allowed to 'sit' on the bottom of the pan. Heating the water to no more than 140°F is, sometimes (especially, with an electric stove) more difficult that it sounds; so, a 'close watch' of the thermometer must be made.

There are other methods to 'pasteurize,' however. For example, if I need just one or two pasteurized eggs, I will sometimes just put them into my Bonavita, temperature adjustable, gooseneck kettle, and set the temperature for 140°F; that way, I know that I am not inadvertently, 'cooking' the eggs. When 140°F is reached, I will 'time' <u>2 - 2.5</u> <u>minutes</u> (allowing the eggs to 'pasteurize'); then, I will remove the kettle from its heat, and 'pour off' the water! With the lid of the kettle on, the eggs don't 'fall out!'

I, then, 'refill' the kettle with cold water from the sink – and drop in a 'handful' of ice cubes; to 'quickly' cool the eggs. I know that eggs should be brought up to temperature for '3 minutes;' but by the time I 'pour off' the 140°F water, and start replacing it with cold water and ice, at least one more minute goes by!

Some people like to add a 'shot' of 'Colloidal Silver' to the pot as well – to further 'discourage' pathogens on the shell! Of course, one needs to use a 'cooking thermometer' to achieve the proper temperature – unless, using an 'adjustable kettle' like mine; or, an adjustable, 'Induction Cooktop' – like I have shown under 'Fish Eye' water, elsewhere, in this book. Even heating water in an oven to the proper temperature can be used.

'Digital' thermometers work best; however, I use an old, 'Candy' one – which as a 'clip' for hooking over the edge of the pan if I cannot find my Digital. If 'pouring off' the pans water might be an issue, be sure to use a 'basket' of some sort which will fit into the pan; then, while the eggs are rising in temperature, 'half-fill' a large bowl, kettle, or sink with water and ice; but, remember to keep a close watch on the water temperature. When the temperature has been met, and the eggs have had three minutes in the water, remove the basket and place it into the pan or sink with the ice water. When the eggs are cool, they are ready to use!

Special Notes: 'Jumbo' eggs, tend to need a 'minute or two' more (four minutes) in 138°F – 141°F to safely 'pasteurize!'

Use all eggs right away; or store in the refrigerator.

Disclaimer: Even though I have consumed 'farm fresh, raw eggs' many times – which, were never refrigerated – I need to say a bit more about safety. **PLEASE** **NOTE**: there is no 'guarantee' that 'home pasteurizing' is 100% 'sure' to kill all Salmonella bacteria! However, the best 'home pasteurization' is going to do is to be <u>very</u> effective! Remember... nothing is 100% certain not to contain bacteria – not even the 'Pasteurized Eggs,' one may purchase at the grocery store! I still tell my friends and patients, to avoid 'Raw Eggs'... if worried about Salmonella or pregnant.

To reiterate, today's processed, and refrigerated, eggs are very safe; and, 'Pasteurized ones,' are even more so! However, if one is going to use them in any cooking or beverages, only use fresh, un-cracked eggs; as most Salmonella bacteria is found in the shells, rather than in the eggs themselves!

"The morning cup of coffee has an exhilaration about it which the cheering influence of the afternoon or evening cup of tea cannot be expected to reproduce."

~ (Attributed to) Oliver Wendell Holmes, Sr

OTHER 'ADD-ONS' FOR COFFEE – NOT FOR THE SQUEAMISH!

Just the thought of some 'Add-Ons' to coffee, might make one 'sick to their stomach – I know, just 'cream' did to my Dad! However, other 'additives' are not too bad! Here are some popular ones I have heard of:

Red Bull™ or other Energy Drinks, Dr. Pepper™, Coca Cola™, 7-UP™, or other 'Soda Pop' – Some people brew with 'Sodas' or 'Energy Drinks' rather than water; while other people might pour one or more tablespoons into their cups along with their coffee. I am afraid I would have to agree with most of the 'Coffee Snobs' on this one; why ruin <u>both</u> a good cup of coffee, and a good bottle of soda pop? If 'mixing' is, honestly, desired, most people prefer it 'half soda/half coffee;' preferably, over ice!

Sriracha Coffee – Be it 'Sriracha Sauce, Chili Sauce,' or some other 'hot or spicy' seasoning, 'Sriracha Coffee' is an acquired taste! However, at this writing, the local Starbucks has introduced a 'Sriracha Coffee' to their menu… so, it is not <u>that</u> obscure! Just a 'dash' (or up to ½ teaspoon) in each cup is all that is needed; however, some people put in a spoonful of 'mocha' or 'chocolate' powder (or 'syrup) in their coffee or espresso/latte too!

I do enjoy a good, 'Mexican Hot Chocolate;' which is 'spiced' with chili peppers; so, I was willing to try this one. I must admit, it <u>was</u> interesting… however, again, an 'acquired' taste! Personally, I prefer putting a bit of coffee into my 'Mexican Hot Chocolate;' which is an excellent choice to enjoy all three flavors!

'Snob' rating, recently told me… "*Only in the winter; or, only when traveling… alone!*"

Maple Syrup Coffee – In the same sense of 'Soda Pop Coffee,' why ruin <u>both</u> the Syrup and the Coffee? Now, adding coffee (or 'Coffee Extract') to the syrup – maple syrup, corn syrup, or any other kind of syrup… that is quite a different matter! Nevertheless, when putting a teaspoon or tablespoon full of syrup into ones' coffee or espresso, some people say, "*It makes the coffee taste like candy!*" 'Taste' is why, I listed a recipe for 'Maple Syrup,' in earlier pages.

My opinion is the same as many of the 'Snobs' I have mentioned this to – "*Just eat some candy or pancakes; and drink some <u>good</u> coffee to appreciate the 'Maple' taste!*"

Cardamom – More of a 'Middle Eastern' way to drink coffee – however, Norwegians are known for putting 'Cardamom' into their coffee; as well as in many desserts! Some people say, "*Cardamom will neutralize the effects of Caffeine.*"

Some 'Coffee Snobs' are willing to try this one… I did! It is… different; and, I will leave it at that. Perhaps, I would enjoy it more during the Christmas season – as many holiday recipes for cookies call for Cardamom.

Ice Cream – I must admit, that I do this one! It is refreshing and fun in the summertime! However, I have been known to take a 'scoop' of 'French Vanilla, Chocolate Swirl,' or 'Soft-Serve' ice cream and put it in my morning coffee when there is no milk or creamer available!

As a dessert, 'Coffee Snobs' will tend to drink this one… except for 'hardcore' Snobs, that is!

Oatmeal – This one goes right back to 'Cooking in a Brewer;' except, it is performed the opposite way! Coffee is 'brewed and poured;' then 'Instant Oatmeal' (to taste) is added to the cup and stirred! 'Chewy' Coffee… ugh!

Few 'Coffee Snobs' (nor I) will drink/eat it.

Colloidal Silver Coffee – When attempting to 'boost' ones' immune system, nothing is better than 'Colloidal Silver;' plus, it is a natural antibiotic. Rumors of it 'turning people blue,' are utter nonsense – especially, when made and used correctly.

Homemade, 'Silver Chloride' (when someone adds salt to the brewing Colloidal Silver) is, generally, when people need to worry about 'turning blue – not, Colloidal Silver!' My family and I, pets, and patients have drunk 'high doses' for 20 years. We, also, spray it on 'topically,' spray it into our eyes when we have infections, 'breath' it with a nebulizer, or 'spray' it into our sinuses for lung issues, colds or flu, 'rinse' some of our food with it, and even put it into our Hot Tub; and none of us have 'turned blue' yet! So, putting a small amount into our coffee, certainly, is safe to do!

When serving a large group of people, using Colloidal Silver, instead of water, in ones' coffee maker could become quite expensive – so, a lesser PPM (parts per million) should be used if doing so; or, just add a cup of it to the coffee maker, while brewing. However, there is another way to do this as well – and, how I drink 'Colloidal Silver Coffee,' and I have my patients do it; after an 'extra strong' cup of coffee is poured, simply add a few drops, a teaspoon, a 'dash,' or a 'shot,' of Colloidal Silver to it. This action will, help 'cool' the coffee, somewhat, and 'dilute' the 'extra strong' brew. Colloidal Silver (depending upon its 'PPM' strength) is colorless, odorless, and tasteless; so, it will not change flavor in any way… except to 'water down' the cup, somewhat, if using more than a teaspoon full.

What do the 'Coffee Snobs' say about this one? Some will say, "*No way;*" while others (often, Vegans I know) say, "*I love it!*"

Colloidal Copper Coffee – As with 'Colloidal Silver,' some people put 'Colloidal Copper' (or, other Colloids: Gold, Platinum, et cetera) into their coffee. As they are, relatively, 'flavor-free,' I would suppose, it does not hurt either the coffee or the person drinking it. Colloidal Copper does have a slight taste, however, in my opinion; and, sometimes, has an unappetizing, 'green tint' to it!

Overall 'Snob' appeal? Zero! My opinion? Drink Karsk (Norwegian, 'Penny' Coffee) if you want only 'trace elements' of copper in your coffee!

Tonic Water – Coffee with 'Tonic Water' can "*Be refreshing, when drunk cold,*" or, so, some say; but it is not very good when 'brewed.' However, 'Tonic Water' can, also, be placed in the cup along with hot coffee – although, I do not know too many people who like it.

Some 'Coffee Snobs' feel this is a good starting point for a 'Coffee Cocktail,' by adding Gin or Vodka to the cup as well; or, just adding a shot of Espresso to a tall glass of Tonic water! Brewing with it, however, will tend to make 'sour' coffee; due to its high CO_2 content. 'Coffee or Cocktail Snobs,' however, will not wish to 'ruin' either the coffee or the cocktail!

However, if mixed with other ingredients (preferably sweet), it can make a decent 'cocktail' of sorts; and, if one suffers from leg cramps… some feel it could, possibly, help – due to the 'Quinine' in the Tonic.

Coconut Water – 'Flavored' waters, especially, 'Coconut Water,' can be either put into a 'brewed cup;' or used as the 'brewing water.' For myself, I find it is an 'acquired' taste; but I can see how some people might 'acquire' a taste for it. 'Coconut Milk,' however, makes a pleasant, light creamer – and is, generally, preferred over 'Coconut Water' added to the coffee! It must be noted, however, some 'Coconut Waters' may 'gum up' a brewer; as they can be very sweet or may have a certain amount of residual fiber.

'Flavored' Extracts – 'Vanilla Extract, Rum Extract, Brandy Extract, Peanut Extract, Banana Extract, Butter Extract, Butterscotch Extract...' coffee can be 'flavored' in countless ways! I have one friend (something of a 'Coffee Snob'), who prefers a drop or two of 'Lemon or Orange' Extract in her coffee! Of course, a 'sweetener,' sometimes, is required as well! She carries a small, 'eye dropper' with her favorite extract in her purse – and pours in a bit of sugar in the coffee shop.

Peanut Butter – Be it 'Peanut, Almond, Soy, Cashew, or Hazelnut...' any type of 'Butter' can be put into a cup of coffee. However, 'Peanut Extract,' as listed in the previous paragraph, or even 'Peanut Butter Powder' can be used for a 'Peanut' taste! Moreover, there is something to be said for the 'health benefits' associated with some butters – such as 'Cashew Butters, fatty acids' affecting blood pressure and cholesterol levels in a 'positive' manner!

However, a 'Butter,' is an excellent way to create a 'rich, creamy' cup of coffee; with healthy fats, fiber, and potassium. Some people, (although, I do not care for it) prefer to add a touch of salt to the brew – if using an 'unsalted,' natural Peanut Butter!

Considering 'Bulletproof Coffee,' a real 'Coffee Snob' might try Peanut Butter, instead of 'Irish' Butter. Alternatively, along with the Peanut Butter, some may add a 'collagen supplement' to the coffee. This is, also, often the case with 'Bulletproof' coffee as well! However, a 'mixed nut' butter may have all the 'butter and oils' one needs, or wants, in their 'Bulletproof' coffee!

Candy Cane (Peppermint) Coffee – This recipe is surprisingly good; especially, when mixed with 'Chocolate Coffee,' using a 'Chocolate Creamer,' or in a 'Hot Chocolate' beverage (the keyword here, is 'Chocolate'). Having once owned a beverage company, I used to make a syrup called 'Chocolate Candy Cane.' This 'syrup' was made with 'Chocolate' and 'Peppermint' extracts; and, mixed with 'corn syrup!' It was delicious; plus, one does not have to wait until Christmas (or use old, stale Candy Canes) to make this mixture after the holidays! Either, use a 'Candy Cane' as a 'Coffee Stirrer,' or add a touch of 'Peppermint Extract' to ones' brew.

What I have, also, been known to do, however, is to take the small, (Halloween, 'reduced size') 'Chocolate/Peppermint Patties' and drop one or two into my or my guests' mug; then, stir it up; after giving the 'Patties' a few minutes to melt! 'Sugar-free' patties work very well too – and taste better in coffee than they do by themselves! In fact, I have served 'Sugar-free, Chocolate/Peppermint' coffee to family and guests; and they never noticed the difference from a syrup, 'filled' with sugar!

Another way is to take a 'sprig' of fresh Mint, and 'crush' it into a cup; then, add coffee to it! I know a few 'Snobs' which will, 'secretly,' do this when 'out and about' during the holidays! However, my son does something else altogether; he makes 'Peppermint Kahlua' to pour into his coffee; or, sometimes, adds a drop or two of 'Watkins brand, Chocolate and Peppermint Extracts,' along with milk, to his coffee cup. It is very delicious!

Heavy Cream – Few coffee drinkers would have access to cream, 'spooned off' a dairy 'Separator.' But that is what my family, often, did. Being on a farm, they would take fresh milk, put it into the Cream Separator, and 'spin' it. The thick and heavy cream would sit on top of the milk; where it needed to be 'spooned off.' It could, then, be made into butter or used some other way. However, my family, enjoyed taking spoons of it, and either use it as a 'dessert topping' (putting a spoonful on top of a piece of cake, for example) or putting a 'spoonful' into their coffee cups – where it would 'melt' very slowly! If one ever gets a chance to try this, I suggest they do so; however, one must remember, 'fresh and heavy cream' does not have any 'sweetener' added to it… so one might consider adding a spoonful of sugar as well! Again, what my family did, was to 'sprinkle' raw sugar over the cream on the cup; rather than 'mix' sugar into the coffee. That way it was something of a 'dessert' as well as a beverage; and still, sweetened the coffee!

I have only tried a few of the following 'Coffee Additives;' and, I am afraid I do not, personally, know any 'Coffee Snobs' who would be willing to try any of them! However, the internet says, "*These are popular*" with many coffee drinkers!

[347]

Mayonnaise Coffee – This is another way to make something of a 'Bulletproof' cup; after all, 'Mayonnaise' is just another 'spoon of oil,' placed into the coffee – however, I would have to call it something of an 'Egg Coffee' as well – as Mayonnaise is made with 'oil' and 'eggs!'

I <u>have</u> heard of people using a spoon of Mayonnaise when out of cream – although, I would doubt I would ever do this. I know, technically, this is not very different from other 'oil' methods… however, the idea does not appeal to me any more than it does to most 'Coffee Snobs.' However, if making 'homemade' Mayonnaise, remember to use only 'Pasteurized Eggs.'

Sour Cream Coffee – This is an 'acquired' taste; I have tried it, and frankly, it is not as bad as it sounds! Once again, just a 'spoonful' is needed in the coffee – or to taste! I did not find much difference between the 'low-fat' and 'regular' types of Sour Cream! Depending upon the 'quality' of the coffee, 'taste' can be very much like that of coffee with a spoonful of 'heavy cream' in it – especially, if sugar is added.

I, always, enjoy watching a 'Coffee Snobs' face, after learning 'Sour Cream' has been put into their coffee!

Pink Salt (or Sea Salt)/Yogurt Coffee – Well, I can understand either… alternatively, both. I know, that I might use 'Yogurt' instead of 'Sour Cream' in some recipes, or, on a baked potato; so, in coffee, I could see that it might be a 'substitute 'for cream. Personally (if I had to), I would use plain Yogurt in my coffee; but 'Organic, Greek, Raw,' or any 'Yogurt' – with or without fruit – can be used as well. The 'Pink Salt' will help to 'bring out' the flavor of the Yogurt; and, perhaps, remove some bitterness from the coffee.

Anywhere from a pinch of 'Pink' salt to a teaspoon full of sea salt is placed into a mug of, any kind or type, Coffee. Then, a teaspoon to a tablespoon of any type of Yogurt is stirred in. Most people do not enjoy this – as 'Pink Salt' is 'saltier' than sea, kosher, or table salt; however, this <u>does</u> appear to have some 'bragging rights' by some 'Snobs.' For myself, a teaspoon of any 'salt' in an <u>entire</u> <u>pot</u> (let alone, a cup) would ruin it!

Cream Cheese Coffee – Not really 'for the <u>squeamish</u>,' this beverage is very much like using 'yogurt or sour cream' in coffee. The only thing missing is added salt. However, many people drink this as an 'iced beverage;' with a few other ingredients (such as cherry syrup), to make a '<u>Cheesecake</u>

Beverage!' Some drinkers may run the 'Cream Cheese and Coffee' through a blender, first! Other people even pour the mixture over ice cream – making a 'float (my favorite way);' while still more, may, also, add 'alcohol' (brandy, rum, vodka, or whiskey) to the coffee!

I would think that even a 'Coffee Snob' would enjoy this drink!

Gjetost (pronounced 'Yet-oast') Coffee – Gjetost is a Norwegian, sweet, brown, Goat Cheese; I grew up eating it… although I never cared for it as much as my parents did! It has a strong, somewhat 'wild' taste to it – which, obviously, 'tastes' like it is made from 'Goat Milk!' Cut like a piece of 'fudge' (which as the same consistency as the Gjetost), the cheese (a small, thin slice) is 'dropped into' a large mug of coffee.

Some 'Cheese Snobs,' do not consider Gjetost to be a 'true cheese' because of how it is produced; and, not to mention, it comes from 'goat milk' – but, all the 'cheese makers,' I have ever met, consider it 'cheese!'

Gjetost, partially, melts in the coffee; and, allows the drinker to 'spoon out' small mouthfuls of sweet, caramel flavor – followed, by a 'sip' of coffee. Only the Scandinavian 'Coffee Snobs' I have known, would even consider this kind of coffee; and those who do… think it to be more of a dessert!

Ground Reindeer Antlers or Bone – I am not even going to go into this; nor, haggis, blood sausage, salmon, trout, blue cheese, or beer! Some people will brew, or put, anything unreasonable, into their coffee!

I only know of one 'Coffee Snob' who would even consider any of the above, and he is a 'Survivalist!'

Turmeric Coffee (Golden Latte) – Although promoting 'Turmeric' as the main ingredient, this 'double-shot' of Espresso, also, contains ginger, milk, and cinnamon. However, I have heard of many people merely putting a 'spoonful' of Turmeric into their, plain, coffee; along with some milk or cream.

Prune Juice Coffee – Saving the 'worst' for last, a nurse friend, initially, told me about this one! Many 'elderly' coffee drinkers, in 'assisted living' complexes (but, just as likely at home too), will put 'Prune Juice' in their morning coffee – or at least, drink it as a 'coffee chaser!' Personally, I do not see too much 'wrong' with that – as I, myself, might drink a glass of Orange Juice, along with my coffee, while having breakfast in a restaurant.

However, others (especially, in Nursing or Retirement Homes) take this beverage 'one step further;' and make a drink called "*__The Bomb;__*" which is equal amounts of 'Prune Juice and Milk of Magnesia®' mixed into the coffee.

Why would anyone do this? Coffee has a certain amount of 'laxative' properties to it; and some people use a cup or two of coffee in the morning, to 'effectively' send them to the bathroom. Other people, however, prefer drinking a glass of Prune Juice; for the same results as a laxative – that is, if coffee does not 'do the trick,' or if they do not drink coffee.

However, many people (and nurses or nutritionists in nursing homes… not all, but some), as a 'time saving' measure, enjoy <u>combining</u> the 'Prune Juice' <u>with</u> the coffee; however, those residents 'indeed in need,' often turn to 'Milk of Magnesia' as well; if just the 'Coffee and Prune Juice,' do not work. Unfortunately, some 'sedentary' individuals in Nursing Homes <u>still</u> need a bit more help when it comes to their 'morning abolitions.' This is where '**The Bomb**' comes in – a combination of all three methods/ingredients… 'Coffee, Prune Juice, and Milk of Magnesia!'

Probably, invented by some nurse somewhere, this beverage, in my opinion, would taste just as bad as it sounds; and, using 'Milk of Magnesia' as a creamer… well, it makes me shudder; and, I would never try it unless absolutely necessary! However, some people are looking for a 'guarantee,' when it comes to 'Bowel Movements;' and many of those people love '**The Bomb**' first thing in the morning… <u>every</u> morning! However, I would suspect they seldom drink more than one! <u>Any</u> of the ingredients should help to 'send someone to the bathroom' (at least, to a certain degree); but mixed … well, would certainly make for something of an 'explosive' combination – one to three hours later!

However, those looking forward to both a 'good cup of coffee' and a 'good, morning, bowel movement,' run the risk of achieving neither; as the coffee is ruined (according to most tastes), and if 'mobility' is an issue… well, let's just say, one should not be 'too far away' from a bathroom; as one may experience be a bit more '<u>movement</u>' than they expect!

To prepare this concoction, mix equal parts of hot coffee – of any kind or strength – with 'Prune Juice;' and if 'severely' constipated, add two tablespoons of 'Milk of Magnesia'… then, 'watch out!' **Optional**: add a 'sprinkling' of Epsom Salts – for those who like a bit of salt in their coffee! I have known many people to use 'Epsom Salts,' alone, as a laxative; but I feel that it is unnecessary as a coffee additive; as 'Milk of Magnesia' is being used in **The Bomb** (and using the wrong type of Epsom Salts can be dangerous)! Of course, the use of a 'sweetener' or 'creamer' is accepted – although, 'Prune Juice' can, already, be slightly 'sweet!'

One of my patients, who is 'lactose intolerant,' once told me, "*I like to put a 'quarter teaspoon' of Epsom Salt into my large mug of 'extra strong' coffee; then, add some 'half and half;' which, the lactose alone, will generally, send me to the bathroom. The 'Epsom Salts' guarantees I do not get any blockages!*" I thanked her for "*Sharing that with me!*" I told her about **The Bomb;** but she was not interested. "*Why ruin my coffee?*" she replied. But I would think that a 'quarter teaspoon' of Epsom Salt would 'ruin' any coffee I was drinking!

I would suppose, certain 'Coffee Snobs' might be interested in **The Bomb;** although, not too worried about taste or 'bragging rights!' After all, few people would wish to brag about something like this! I have had a few people in Nursing Homes mention it to me, however; and have proud of their, daily, achievements!

My advice is, why not just have the 'best of all <u>four</u> worlds;' starting, with a <u>good</u> cup to two of coffee… then, following it up with a glass of Prune Juice, and a 'high fiber' breakfast?

It 'that' does not send one to the bathroom within an hour or so, then, take two tablespoons of 'Milk of Magnesia' or a good laxative. Of course, 'Epsom Salts' can work too – but, I do caution my patients against using them, as not all 'Salts' can be safe to consume! If one is <u>absolutely</u> sure about the safety of their 'Epsom Salt' (and a good way to find out is to 'read' the instruction label – there should be a 'recommendation for use of the 'Salts' as a laxative); then, adding a 'touch' to one's coffee is appropriate. However, the same can be said about adding the 'Epsom Salts' to the Prune Juice (or other juice) as well!

"*Instant Human! Just add coffee!*"

~ (Attributed to) Unknown

[351]

SERVING TO A GROUP, AND COFFEE CONCENTRATES

As 'Coffee Palettes' are tremendously different, it becomes more challenging, every day, to satisfy everyone involved! Therefore, when I am serving to large groups, I will do one of a <u>few</u> different things. First, the effortless way, is to use a large, 'Party Urn' (which is nothing more than an oversized, Percolator – designed for large groups). These have been around forever, it would seem – and 'poor coffee' is the expected 'norm!' Even to this day, every church, probably, owns at least one of these 'Urns' (therefore, this type of brewing is often known as 'Church Basement Coffee' – at least, on the East Coast)! Unfortunately, as many people view this method of brewing 'Percolator Coffee,' they feel it is "*Unfit to drink*!" 'Urn coffee' brews the same way as any other 'Electric Percolator;' coffee grounds are placed into a basket – with or without a paper filter – and water is added. It is switched on, and the coffee 'brews;' and the 'better the grounds' used, the 'better the coffee' brewed!

However, as I, often, lecture to various groups, I need to play 'Coffee Snob' a bit more! This is where a 'Fancier Urn' comes in handy! Frankly, I have found, that when it comes to 'Coffee Snobs' – even the amateur ones – the 'fancier the urn,' the 'cheaper' the coffee one can serve; and, the more likely the 'Coffee Snobs' will, happily, accept it! That does not sound very nice… however, it is a fact! People, in general, are impressed by 'Glitz!' Fortunately, or unfortunately, 'Glitz' can be forgiven much easier than 'bad coffee!' Remember, I spoke of 'atmosphere' earlier in this book!

When I am <u>not</u> trying to impress my 'Snobby' friends or family, I will use 'Airpots,' which are very practical, to serve the coffee in; especially, if I am serving, multiple, brewing types or kinds of coffees during 'Coffee Classes.' I do the same when differentiating between 'regular' coffee and 'Decaf.' Depending upon the brand, Airpots can run from twenty dollars to several hundred! Moreover, if serving multiple types of coffee, there are 'professional brands,' such as Bunn, which sell various racks; which hold 3, 6, or more pots at a time, so 'coffee drinkers' can have multiple choices.

However, there are other things one can do besides have an 'uncomplicated' way to serve. First, tempting as it might be for a large group, <u>do not</u> use 'canned coffee' – even though, there are several fine 'canned' coffees out there! It is just far too easy to buy 'fresh beans' at a grocery store – and 'grind' the grounds to a 'custom' size!

In any event, one is only talking about 2.5 to 3 cups of grounds at a time! Just because one is serving a crowd does not mean that they should 'skimp' on quality; and the price difference will not be too much different. Follow the general 'rules' for making a good cup of coffee; and, one will ensure that their guests are drinking something that they will love… even if it comes from an Urn!

Choose a Coffee Brewing Method that Works for a Crowd:

While one may love 'Espresso' or 'AeroPress' coffee for their usual morning cup, if one is serving a large crowd, they will, probably, need a different option… unless, of course, one is a 'well-trained Barista;' and enjoys 'pulling shots' as guests mingle. Other than the, previously mentioned, 'large Urn,' multiple, large 'French Presses' are my personal, and favorite, choice for serving a crowd. While one may not wish to make a <u>full</u> 'French Press' for their own use, if they have a 'table full of people' for brunch… it is the 'perfect moment' to put a large 'Press' to complete use; especially, if used in conjunction with an insulated 'Airpot' or extra carafe.

When I have tastings, or a party, of some sort, I will fill one or two Airpots with 'French Press' coffee – labeled, of course, if different in some ways; but, keep one or two 'Presses' in front of me, to pour out demonstrated 'Press' techniques. New drinkers, watch and learn – and; those who enjoy the coffee are free to 'serve themselves,' as much as they desire, with the Airpots, or wait for a cup directly from the 'Press!'

If one is willing to go through the effort of multiple, 'Pour-Over' (rather than, say, a Chemex), using 'Airpots' are still an excellent choice; which, of course, gives one the <u>impressive</u> <u>effect</u> of making the coffee in front of the guests. Again, as a 'Chemex' is only going to serve about a half dozen people (depending upon its size), it would be best to have a few of them for brewing; or, fill an Airpot or Carafe just before serving.

Another option for large groups, is to make coffee from a commercial, 'Coffee Concentrate,' ahead of time! Just a few years ago, 'bottles of concentrate,' in multiple brands, were available everywhere! Unfortunately, it is beginning to become difficult to find 'Coffee Concentrates' at the Grocery store; and, many stores are replacing them with, new, 'Cold Brew' Concentrates. What is a 'Cold Brew Coffee Concentrate?' It is nothing more than an '<u>extra-strong</u>,' coffee – presumably, 'brewed cold.

[353]

Some people view it as something of an 'Instant' coffee – as all one needs to do, is add water to it, and serve! Do a 'Google search;' it is difficult to find product that is not considered, or promoted, as a 'Cold Brew' Concentrate – as 'Cold Brew' is something of a 'fad' right now.

 Often, 'Concentrated Coffee,' even come in packets of 'Dried Granules!' However, again, isn't this just a form of 'Instant Coffee?' Some products might, indeed, *"Taste Great"* as advertised; but, couldn't one achieve the same results with, say, a bottle of Folgers™® Instant – which is it 'mixed up' too strong to drink straight? Just dilute it, and bingo… the coffee has been prepared! I have to admit, when I have been 'out' of coffee – and only having some 'packets' which were used for demonstration, or which were given to me – I have placed a couple into my 'Pour-Over' or 'Drip' coffee brewer, and made 'hot' coffee with them. The taste cannot compare with using 'fresh' beans; but then, it is not too different from coffee prepared with 'canned' grounds!

Of course, one can always make their own 'Coffee Concentrate' the day before an event; and store it until use… then, make their 'Urn Coffee' the same way as they would a commercial concentrate. However, add or 'refresh,' the Urn with more Coffee Concentrate as needed. I know, this contradicts what I have, previously stated, but let's face it… people are going to do what is easy!

"Coffeeology: Espresso yourself. So many blends, so little time. Take life one sip at a time and stay grounded. Better 'latte' than never. Take time to smell the cover!"

~ (Attributed to) Anonymous

SUMMING THINGS UP

Since the 10th century, man has consumed coffee many ways; and, once the 'Snobs' got ahold of it, 'drinking restrictions' started to arise – probably, starting with Monks and then with Royalty!

The aristocracy was quick to follow; and only allowed coffee to be consumed by 'certain people,' in a 'certain way.' Luckily, this did not last too long; as 'common people' still picked the 'wild' cherries and brewed their coffee anyway! However, by then, 'Traders' started moving the coffee beans and cherries all over the world! However, just because everyone was eating, cooking with, or drinking coffee, did not mean that a 'certain few' were not going to figure out 'just the right way' for everyone to do it; and, if one does not 'do it their way,' well… one can guess the rest! Those 'kinds' of people still think the same way today – and we know them as 'Coffee Snobs;' and, while they may or may not not tell everyone else 'how' to drink their coffee, they indeed 'demonstrate it' by how they purchase, prepare, display, or serve their coffee… at least, when others are watching!

Coffee Bars capitalize on this; even though, probably, more 'average people' purchase coffee than the 'Snobs!' However, is it 'bad' to be a 'Snob?' No! As I have said before, we all have specific 'Snobby ways' when it comes to how we enjoy our coffee!

Is one a 'Snob' if they buy 'high end' tools (toys), like $200.00, 'Fancy Tampers, $2000.00 Grinders, or $5000.00 Coffee Makers?' Well, no… I might question their 'money priorities,' however. It is only when these people start telling others, "*They must do the same*" to enjoy a cup of coffee, that I have a problem with them!

However, as someone whose philosophy has always been: "*He with the best toys wins…*," sometimes, just owning something which is 'different' to show off to our friends, can be great fun! My family has always done it; with things like 'Sterling Engines' to place on top of our coffee cups during 'Coffee Club' meetings, 'Self-stirring' mugs, or owning many different 'Brewers.' 'Different Brewers' are fun; as they, not only, can be 'impressive' to those who are just learning about  coffee, but it can be fun to 'taste' the difference between brewers! Plus, 'experimenting' with different brewers is quite 'educational!' Plus, as my family has learned over the past year (of going through devastating fires and power outages) if one has 'enough' variations of a tool – in this case, a coffee maker – something is going to end up being 'pressed into service!' For example, during a recent (almost statewide), 1 – 3 day power outage (still a result from our devastating fire, some 9 months earlier), we were still able to make coffee (at least 2 mugs at a time) by heating water over a BBQ and pouring it into a 'Pour-Over Cone;' or, by using our small, 2 mug Percolators. It wasn't especially handy to make 'small amounts' of coffee; but with no power, water, or sewer, it was nice to be able to enjoy an occasional, mug of coffee! Not surprisingly, I have heard from some of my 'Coffee Snob' friends, that they *"Wished they would have had a way to get coffee too – as, the entire town was out of power, and both gas stations and coffee shops were closed!"* Sometimes, necessity dictates desire!

Again, does being able to make coffee (and enjoy it) during an emergency make us a 'Snob?' I suppose, to a certain degree; however, it is harmless fun, after a disaster, to 'brag' that we *"Still had our coffee while everyone was sitting in the dark for three days!"* And, after everyone's 'disaster,' it is enjoyable to 'take our minds of what troubles we had;' and learn about 'Specialty or Designer' coffee, its 'toys,' gadgets, functions, options, and all that goes along with it – especially, for the 'next time' there is a disaster!

So, it goes to say, that there is a certain amount of 'Coffee Snob' in all coffee drinkers – however, some people may 'take it to the extreme;' by insisting upon everyone else, drinking it *"Their way!"* My opinion, as I have stated all through this book, is *"Enjoy your coffee… but, drink it your way and have fun with it; and forget about what anyone else might say or think about it!"*

I will leave this book by making one statement; which, will upset every 'Expert and Coffee Snob… moreover, ask just last question myself:

"Without my morning coffee, I'm just like a dried-up piece of roast goat!"

~ (Attributed to) Johann Sebastian Bach

First, <u>most</u> of what most people have, previously, heard or learned about Coffee, <u>is</u> <u>nonsense</u>! Just look at 'YouTube' under 'any,' particular 'type' of brewing. There will be many 'the only way' methods to brew coffee using the same devices! True, there are indisputable facts about 'coffee beans, pure water, grind, and brewing methods;' but, 'what and how' people do or use to brew their coffee all 'boils down' to… *"What the brewer/drinker enjoys most!"* Plus, 'water type or temperature' does not matter; if the 'drinker' enjoys what they are using.

In the same sense, 'the kind or grind of beans,' does not matter; as long as the 'drinker' <u>enjoys</u> the flavor. Nor, does it matter if someone uses 'canned' coffee or 'freshly ground' coffee!

Moreover, probably, the most important thing to remember is, it <u>does</u> <u>not</u> <u>matter</u> 'what' one puts in their coffee – eggs, salt, sugar, cream, camels' milk, alcohol, processed creamer… **ANYTHING** can be used to brew or 'augment' coffee; again, as long as the brewer/drinker <u>enjoys</u> what they have! I would encourage coffee drinkers to 'experiment' with different types of coffee, brewers, and additives – as well as techniques and temperatures; to discover a 'whole, new world' of coffee… that they, maybe, had never imagined! One might be surprised by what they might enjoy!

As a starting point, follow the 'coffee brewing device' <u>recommendations</u> regarding 'brewing times' and 'techniques;' when using any 'generic' type bean or canned coffee. Brew one pot, and taste. If the coffee is too weak or too strong, 'augment' the amount of grounds accordingly. One may have to do this a few times to determine the 'best taste!' After determining the 'best tasting' brew, 'research' other 'tips and techniques,' such as what are in this book, to augment further. Augmentation may come in the form of a 'filter,' 'pre-wetting' the grounds, or different water temperatures.

If purchasing directly from a 'Roastery,' listen to what the proprietors have to say and recommend – such as, using a ''French Press or a 'Pour-over' brewer, rather than a standard, 'Drip' coffee maker. Then, using their 'recommendations,' prepare your first cup or pot! Once again, 'augment' the coffee; should it be too weak or too strong by brewing additional coffee. Once you have the 'best tasting' brew, try a few more 'tips and techniques' (troubleshooting). Keep good notes, so <u>you</u> can 'brew it again' the same way, next time!

Just remember, all 'recommendations,' are just that; someone's interpretation of what they think the coffee should taste like (and what they think you should enjoy)! Listen to the recommendations... but do not allow anyone to tell you 'what or how' to drink your coffee! Taste, and make your own decisions!

Having one's own 'personal preferences' does not make anyone a 'Coffee Snob;' but, does help the 'drinker' to distinguish 'good coffee from bad;' and, hopefully, will help broaden ones 'view' of coffee... not to mention, always receive 'what they want' to drink at home or in a coffee shop!

"Coffee is the common man's gold; and like gold, it brings to every person the feeling of luxury and nobility."

~ (Attributed to) Sheik-Abd-al-Kadir

One final question that I am often asked; but have never been able to answer adequately (even though the term, indicates the coffee being 'expressed' into a cup); so, I have left 'unanswered'... for the reader to figure out:

Question: *"Espresso sounds 'Fast – like an 'Express Train!' How can something that is called 'Espresso,' sometimes take 'so long' in coffee bars to prepare; and, something served 'so small' (in Demitasse cups), be so expensive to purchase?"*

Answer: Your guess is as good as mine!

"I once dreamt about the book, 'The five people you meet in Hell...' and whom, my '5 people' were; but the scary part was, there wasn't any coffee when I met them!

~ James D. Skaug

Additional 'Group Lecture Books' by James Skaug:

<u>Peripheral Neuropathy: Neuropathy Case Histories, Myths, and Treatments That Work</u>.

<u>Peripheral Neuropathies: How to Treat Yourself Successfully</u>.

<u>Barbeque, Grill, Smoke, & Dehydrate in Small Spaces</u>.

<u>Coffee for the Average 'Joe.'</u>

Coming soon:

<u>Around the World in a Cup of Coffee</u>!

Manufactured by Amazon.ca
Acheson, AB

13185210R00199